SPY GAMES
Inside the Murky World of Corporate Espionage

COLA FUGELERE
AND
STEVEN FOWLER

TWO LOONS PRESS

SPY GAMES

Inside the Murky World of Corporate Espionage

by Cola Fugelere and Steven Fowler

Second Edition

First Edition
2018

Second Edition
2019

Spy Games is a work of fiction. Many events described in this book are a product of the authors' imagination and should not be considered as real or a depiction of actual events. Some individuals described in this book, living and dead, are real. Others are not. Some character and location names are loosely based upon actual individuals and places, but are presented in a fictitious manner. Some names used in this book as character names belong to actual individuals known to one or both of the authors, but have no involvement in the espionage arena. In general, any resemblance to actual persons, living or dead, events, or locations is entirely coincidental.

Publisher
Two Loons Press

Imprint
Two Loons Publishing

From the Publisher

Trademark Notice
Corporate or product names appearing in this book may be either trademarks or registered as trademarks. The inclusion of that information on these pages is presented for identification purposes or to offer contextual information, without an intent to infringe on those entities.

Disclaimer
Neither the Publisher, nor the Authors, have control over or responsibility for third party websites, or any material related to this work that may appear on those websites.

Original Cover Design
Two Loons Press

Printed in the United States of America

637 pages cover to cover, 175,185 words, 1,025,301 characters, 89 images
11pt Georgia, primary spacing = single, written Google Docs, odt formatting
metadata tags: spy, espionage, intelligence, cia, international, biography

Editorial Disclaimer

An Editorial Message
from
Two Loons Press

Cola is a Spy. Not a writer. That's why Steve Fowler was brought in to actually write this book and bring Cola's story to life.

Cola found it necessary to protect the anonymity of many individuals and entities mentioned in this book. As a result, few people had access to this material prior to publication. We know it was a challenge for Steve, as we worked to avoid rendering a number of clients, targets, colleagues, and business entities identifiable. Steve acquiesced when Cola firmly insisted the project wouldn't involve the assistance of an editor.

As Cola revealed his life to Steve it became clear to Mr. Fowler why Mr. Fugelere was adamant about the editor issue. Steve prefers to work with editors, but understood. Anyone other than Steve Fowler, Cola Fugelere, and Ryan Shaughnessy involved with the project could have undermined Cola's desire to avoid unnecessary or accidental exposure.

Additionally, an editor may have disagreed with Cola's decision to write this book in the first person, as well as his occasional departure from the first person. On occasion, writing this book involved the Cola's desire to refer to himself in the third person. He does it in real life, so on those occasions when he referred to himself as "Cola," it was natural and typical for him. That said, it would have given more than a few editors heartburn.

Cola has lived a life outside the structure of normalcy. Writing and formatting this book has been no different. He insisted on discarding certain established literary conventions relating to organization, layout, formatting, and more. In some cases, he fought conventions and prevailed. However, on other occasions Ryan, Steve and this publisher ganged up on him, and Cola lost.

Although Cola didn't use the services of a professional editor, we at Two Loons Press believe Steve Fowler's excellent efforts on Cola's behalf are well reflected in these pages. With very few exceptions, an editor wasn't missed. *Thank you Steve!*

The Adventures of Ryan Tate

I believe you will find "Spy Games" informative, interesting, and entertaining. My work on "Spy Games" is finished. I've moved on to a different project. I'm discovering fun in another book, and hope to present it to readers in 2019.

The central character in the forthcoming novel is Ryan Tate. Tate's adventures, history, knowledge, athleticism, skills, intelligence, wisdom, energies, personality, and wit will draw readers into his world, and beyond. I eagerly anticipate presenting Ryan's adventures; detailing how his life will impact, and be impacted by, world events.

All the Best!

Steve Fowler

Invasion by Proxy

A Ryan Tate Novel

Coming 2019

An Excerpt...

It was bad enough to have lost so much, but to endure the discomfort and indignity of the bug-infested swamp was the final straw. Santiago was a man of culture, status, and wealth. A man to be admired and feared, respected and honored.

How could this be happening? Something had gone terribly wrong. After all, he owned politicians, the police, judges, government officials, generals, and the press. His payments for their cooperation and silence should have guaranteed the security of his operations and protected him from this DEA sponsored raid. The Drug Enforcement Administration had gone too far this time. Santiago vowed somebody would die and the filthy Americans would pay dearly for their actions.

As insects ravaged his pampered brown skin, he swore vengeance upon America. His hate rose like bile in the throat. He would get even. Nobody, but nobody, did this to Santiago Monterra. As the morning mist began to rise from his watery hiding place, a vague plan began to form.

Corporate Orders

Quantity ordering options for printed editions are available. Discounts for promotional purposes or corporate/association use is possible. Send detailed request and contact information to:

contact@twoloonspress.com
Include “Spy Games Orders” in the Subject Line

Bookstore and Wholesale Orders

Send detailed request and contact information to:

contact@twoloonspress.com
Include “Spy Games Orders” in the Subject Line

Feedback

Send Feedback to:

contact@twoloonspress.com
Include “Spy Games Feedback” in the Subject Line

Cola's Contents

From the Authors

General Disclaimer
Please consider this a work of fiction; and any resemblance to actual persons, places, entities, and events is, and shall be deemed, unintentional and coincidental.

Autobiographical Novel
This book, written with an autobiographical novelistic approach, was inspired by real-life events, and is brought to the reader in a collection of short stories. Within these pages are many names, organizations, places, and events. We've done our level best to present forms of accuracy and detail, from Cola's memory, while blurring specific information to protect the privacy of many persons and organizations appearing in these pages. In that, specific identifying information, characteristics, particular events, and a number of details have been fictionalized. We employed pseudonyms and other methods of obfuscation to protect confidentiality needs associated with this material.

In some cases, we received permission to use actual names of individuals and businesses, as well as images. We wish to acknowledge the efforts of Two Loons Press in obtaining those permissions. Moreover, the authors genuinely appreciate those persons and business entities who granted us the opportunity to disclose their names and related information in this book.

Enjoy!

DEDICATION

THIS BOOK IS DEDICATED TO MY WIFE AND PARENTS

You have given me love, lifted me with encouragement, and honored me with your trust. Your faith in me has been a red carpet on my path through life. I credit you for my friends, siblings, children, and grandchildren. You continually favor me with opportunity and purpose. You laugh at my silliness, make me smile by just being you, and fill my life with mirth, peace, and joy. You've endowed me with tools for building valuable relationships; in doing so you've showered me with genuinely wonderful life experiences. You have blessed me with happiness, wisdom, intestinal fortitude, resolve, the ability to forgive, fond memories, and the importance of conducting my affairs with respect and care for others. I credit you for those blessings, those gifts.

Thank you. My life is yours. You have my unwavering gratitude and appreciation; as well as my undying love and devotion.

I Love You!
Cola

ACKNOWLEDGMENT

WORDS OF ACKNOWLEDGMENT FROM STEVEN FOWLER

I'd like to take a few moments and acknowledge some exceptional individuals and businesses who made this book possible. Without them, this book would not exist.

Two Loons Press, our Publisher, and Cola provided this author with time, information, liberty, resources, reasoned advice, and the motivational encouragement necessary to complete this work. TLP also deserves credit for creating an excellent cover design for this book. Each time I see the book, I recall one particular operation Cola recounted in detail, involving a large factory, next to a railroad track, on a moonless night. An image of that OP in my mind's eye came to life as my "Baseball Buddies" hit it out of the park; collaborating in a fantastic way, as they designed the perfect cover for this book. *Thank you so much!*

Although Cola is responsible for a majority of the photos in this book, it is important to share appreciation and offer acknowledgment for the photos, as well as other helpful contributions and encouragement offered by some very special people. Gene and Kathleen, Tracey, Sissy, Ty, John and Brenda, Kelly and Joan, Mike and Tanya, Milfy, Freddy and SJ, Ox, Mo, Peggy, my Writer's Bloc peers, the United States Government, John Phelps and Gretchen Mack. *Thank you!*

I'd like to take this opportunity to tip my hat to two special individuals who've been a tremendous encouragement to me in my role as a writer. Mark and Pam O'Brien probably have little idea of the significant role they play whenever I'm involved in a major writing project. More than twenty years ago Mark impacted me more than he could ever know when he encouraged me as a writer; after sharing his personal thoughts about a piece I'd recently authored. His bride, Pam, has always been a positive encourager when I put pen to paper and "Miss Pam" becomes a consumer of my words. Her faithful feedback is always welcome, constructive, informative, and educational. Whenever I'm involved in a big writing project, their words and encouragement consistently come to mind and provide the helpful medicine I need so I can successfully complete my work. Thank you both so very much!

My wife, parents, children, and grandchildren spent more hours than I can count, waiting for me as I wrote and edited this manuscript. Today's plethora of digital tools made it possible for me to work on this book daily; just about anywhere in the world. It was too easy to work too much on this manuscript. In doing so, I left others waiting for me. That was wrong.

I used three different laptop computers with three different operating systems (Chrome, Mac, and Windows), an iPad, two iPhones, iCloud, Google Docs, Email, Siri, text messaging, and various text to voice narration systems. At least 90 percent of this book was written on an iPhone using dictation or a typed into a Chromebook.

Dad and my wife endured untold hours in cars with a missing Steve Fowler, while his ears contained wireless AirPods and my brain was in far away places detailing the life of Cola Fugelere. I believe they suffered many hundreds of hours waiting for me, as Apple's Male Siri's most excellent voice narrated every word in this book, over and over and over; as we ate, rode in the car, walked, shopped, and relaxed. My grandchildren and others have waited patiently as I ducked out randomly, on many occasions, to commit thoughts to digital paper. On other occasions they sacrified as this author listened to countless hours of recordings I made of Cola's recollections. *My apologies and grateful appreciation to all of you.*

Apple and Google's tools have been indispensable. I wanted to remain within one ecosystem. However, each had software and devices necessary for Cola to make this book possible. I probably wouldn't have completed this manuscript without both of those companies. *Thank you.*

I've become close to Cola, Ryan, and Treena since this project began. I appreciate them very much. This author was blessed as I enjoyed two wonderful summers at the Fugelere home in The Hamptons, and a special working winter retreat at their home on Maui. We set the stage for this book in the summer of 2017 and finalized the project for publication during a summer getaway at Cola's Long Island home in 2018.

Finally, I'd like to acknowledge and thank everyone who has, is, or will be reading this material. Your interest in Cola's life suggests the sacrifices of those close to me wasn't in vain as I chronicled the life of Stefano "Cola" Fugelere.

Steve Fowler appreciates everyone who helped me bring Cola Fugelere to readers everywhere!

Preface

An Invitation to Skim or Skip

Please consider this an offer to skim over or skip this section. Reading the following information isn't necessary to enjoy Spy Games. However, we believe readers reviewing this material will be better prepared to understand Cola, the world of Corporate Espionage, and the stories in this book. At the very least, we recommend a cursory review of this section.

Short Stories

We've decided to introduce readers to Cola's life and career by sharing a collection of short stories. Most of the chapters in this book do just that. This section, however, does not.

Understanding this Book

Espionage has its own language. Certain words and phrases are decipherable; some are not. Some locutions are universal within espionage circles, whether used in corporate or state-sponsored espionage. In Cola's world, he used acronyms, phrases, and words that may be more confusing and less understandable to those outside his sphere. In some instances that is by design to protect Cola, his colleagues, his clients, and his operations.

We'll try to assist readers by mainly avoiding the use of unusual words where we can. However, to retain the flavor of this work, specific idioms will be used, as appropriate. The glossary at the end of this book may provide helpful information for readers.

Caps

You will see many words, such as "Colleague" and "Readers" capitalized. We used capitalization purposely. We'll explain our reasoning shortly.

Ryan Shaughnessy

Like Cola, Ryan Shaughnessy is not a professional writer. Ryan is a longtime espionage associate. We use the term "Colleague" often in this book. On many occasions, when you see references to a "Colleague," that person is Cola's dear friend and protégé, Ryan Shaughnessy. Spy Games was authored by Cola Fugelere and Steven Fowler, with the very able, and much appreciated, assistance of Ryan Shaughnessy.

Ryan's role was to fill in missing details and assist the authors with anonymizing information as necessary. Ryan was also an informed cautious proofreader of the manuscript. On Cola's Team for many years, his young Colleague is currently working with him to protect businesses from espionage-related losses. Ryan and other Cola Team members invest their time and efforts to harden and insulate companies from espionage activities.

The very nature of Corporate Espionage, as well as any activities Cola has had in that arena, requires us to withhold specific detailed information, facts, and disclosures that could prove harmful to particular individuals and business entities. Regardless, instructive material remains and is cautiously, if not always authentically, presented in this book. As you read through this material, be assured, foundation exists for individuals, entities, events, locations, and situations presented. Names, places, and precise details have been modified, where necessary, to insulate those involved. *Cola's a Spy. What did you expect?*

We've also engaged the services of Cutouts (unaffiliated individuals and entities) to produce and distribute this material.

Cutouts were necessary to protect the safety and security of those involved with Cola; past, present, and future. We believe readers will find sufficient information has been presented to provide a helpful understanding of the Corporate Espionage environment; without the need for a fully transparent exposé. Nevertheless, we believe readers will find this work an exciting journey into Cola's world, with revelations never before seen in printed form or otherwise available to the general public.

Sufficient time has elapsed relating to qualifying statutes for the presentation of this material (statutory time limitations required for the initiation of legal actions). Cola, with Ryan's assistance, reviewed the completed manuscript, page by page, chapter by chapter. Using a system the two developed together, Cola and Ryan independently reviewed and scored this material. After that exercise, they answered the following questions.

An Assessment of this Book

How do Ryan and Cola describe this book?

1. Fact
2. Fiction
3. Fiction Based on Fact

Ryan's Response: Number 3
Cola's Response: Number 3

What percentage of this book is factual?

Ryan's Response: 85%
Cola's Response: 88%

What percentage of this book could currently expose Ryan or Cola to arrest or prosecution, given the passage of time beyond the statutes of limitations?

Ryan's Response: 0%
Cola's Response: 0%

Does this book faithfully depict the world of Corporate Espionage?

Ryan's Response: Absolutely

Cola's Response: Certainly

These questions, as well as the answers provided by two former professional corporate spies, reveal the value of this work, as it allows for a peek behind the curtain of their world. It should also assist readers to accept that relationship needs, as well as contractual obligations, requires the withholding of full candor in some areas. After all, this is a work of fiction. *Right?*

What's in a Name?

We use the phrase "Corporate Espionage" freely and often in this book; and need to clear something up right away. For our discussion here, Industrial Espionage, Economic Espionage, Business Espionage, and Corporate Espionage are synonymous with one another. Political Espionage is a related activity and performed by many corporate spies; including Cola. Our use of the catch-all phrase "Corporate Espionage" involves each area mentioned above; and also references activities involving sole proprietors, partnerships, non-profits, and other non-corporate entities.

> ***An aside...***
> There is also the space commonly referred to as Opposition Research (OPR). Contrary to that commonly used, phony, and euphemistically nice phrase, there are two distinct differences between the term "Opposition Research" and fact. First, OPR is in fact, Political Espionage. Moreover, there is much more than *research* involved in the process. There is action. We perform research, then engage in acts to destroy the candidacy of others.
>
> Additionally, when others think of OPR, they think strictly in terms of candidates for office. Legislation, political alliances, ballot measures, and everyday political maneuvers are also often victims of of OPR.

> In OPR, spies like Cola engage in dirty tricks, media manipulation, bribery, information dumps, and more. Information dumps will often contain 90% fact and 10% fiction. That fiction is often picked up by desperate media types. Spies are users and we use OPR information dumps to dupe others into doing their dirty work.
>
> The political arena is a filthy environment filled with lying charlatans. Politics is a 365 day affair and, unfortunately, John Q. Public a 365 day victim of OPR.
>
> Why, Cola, are you so negative? Why are you so cynical?
>
> Cola's answer: *Cola is a cynical realist.*
>
> Politics is a nasty environment, filled with money and power. Where there's money and power, there are spies, nasty agendas, corruption, and sick narcissistic individuals; both in your face and behind the scenes. Anyone who thinks otherwise is a fool. An idiot.

Back to Corporate Espionage...
This book is not about State-sponsored espionage, and the authors will reasonably avoid discussions related to James Bond and Jason Bourne. State-sponsored espionage activities are often considered separate and distinct from Corporate Espionage. Traditionally, that is true. However, governments are increasingly involved with Corporate Espionage. The lines are blurring, but for this book, we'll attempt to limit references to 007. Regardless, many of the tactics, tools, and methods used by government-sponsored spies are and have been, utilized in the Corporate Espionage arena.

Spying is Natural - The Real Deal
It is certainly real. It happens daily. Disney, Google, Facebook, the NSA, marketing companies, and others are allegedly (and figuratively) peeking over the shoulders of people everywhere, on a daily basis. Fishermen will use binoculars to see what bait nearby fishermen are using with success and schoolchildren will

sneak peeks onto neighboring desktops to cull test answers. Office workers listen to gossip in adjoining cubicles.

Don't look now, but Gladys Kravitz is alive and well.

The Game

Although many espionage insiders refer to Corporate Espionage as "The Game," it is not a game. It is a serious problem, costing companies thousands, even millions, of dollars and market share. Espionage can result in damaged reputations, lost fortunes, and business failure. Corporate Espionage is theft of intellectual property and other assets; to include personnel. Spies who collect confidential, proprietary, and secret information, as well as other corporate assets, do so without the permission of the rightful owner(s). Tactics employed are unethical and often illegal. Espionage activities frequently involve extortion, deceit, shakedowns, and scams. That which they seek is often extremely valuable. The clandestine collection process is usually the work of either an individual or an organized group commonly referred to as a Spy Ring.

While this book follows the path of Cola's career, he frequently engaged the services of accomplices that possessed knowledge, skills, or talents he lacked. At other times Team Members served as force multipliers. There were occasions when Cola needed to be in multiple places, carrying out different tasks at the same time, he'd bring in others. All of them were members of his Team. The Cola Team.

HUMINT

Professionals with the Mossad, CIA, MI6, DGSE, FSB, SVR and other well-known highly regarded state-sponsored intelligence agencies will agree technology is critically important. However, Human Intelligence (HUMINT) is the bread and butter of their business. HUMINT involves human-to-human espionage activities. Cola fully embraces their HUMINT philosophy.

Signals Intelligence (SIGINT), Imagery Intelligence (IMINT), and other methods of gathering information, although helpful, relevant, and often necessary, are of less value and importance than HUMINT. Collectively, SIGINT, IMINT, and other "INT's" fall into a category I refer to as TECHINT, Technology Driven Intelligence.

In Cola's experience, the most significant assets, successes, and priorities in Corporate Espionage fall squarely into the sphere of Human Intelligence. Therefore, Cola finds it curious that so many focus their espionage attention on technology and high tech tools. You can find a plethora of books about hacking and technology in Corporate Espionage, but Cola believes the sheer numbers of written works about gadgets, hacking, and other technologies overstate their value in his world. In short, using TECHINT to conduct Corporate Espionage Operations takes a back seat to sitting in a Starbucks with a Tall Flat White or Iced Green Tea, while recruiting or debriefing an Asset or Agent.

> ***An aside...***
> An Asset is a person, system, or item, generally associated with our Target that holds value to an Operation.
>
> An Agent, on the other hand, is strictly a human being who is either associated with the Target or is an outsider working against our Target, which holds value to theOperation.

Back to HUMINT...
Spy cameras, listening devices, drones, hacks, and GPS trackers are great tools for professional spies. However, the book "How to Win Friends and Influence People" by Dale Carnegie is probably the single best investment any Spy could make. Yes, the book is an excellent tool. However, a few talented individuals are born practicing Carnegie's methods.

They make the best spies. They're naturals. That is why Cola works hard to recruit naturally personable, affable, intelligent individuals for the Cola Team. Cola believes people are born to succeed in his world and garner HUMINT wherever and whenever possible to prosecute a successful Operation.

Ones and Zeros
Hacking and related digital thievery efforts are highly specialized forms of Corporate Espionage and are the subject of many books. They are the genesis for a myriad of companies and service offerings. That is not Cola's specialty, even though he has a good understanding of that space and can comfortably guide Clients with security enhancements (occasionally engaging outside specialists). Regardless, we will generally avoid digital thievery in this book and leave that subject matter to those better suited to share with interested readers.

An Aside?
“Asides” are used in Spy Games. This manuscript contains approximately one hundred seventy indented sections beginning with, “***An aside...***”

We use asides as digressions, designed to assist Readers by providing context, offering clarification, delivering historical perspective, making introductions, or other information intended to enhance the narrative. We believe you'll find these digressions interesting, helpful, relevant, and worth reading.

Quotes
As you read this book, you'll notice we'll generally enclose the first reference to one of Cola's idiomatic terms in quotes. Afterward, we will use the idiom without the quotes.

Capitalization
Clients and Targets make it possible for Cola to pay his bills and enjoy life. In that, they deserve his respect. Therefore, whenever we refer (in writing) to Clients, Targets (Marks), and Colleagues (e.g., OneSeven), we try to routinely capitalize those references. We'll capitalize some words in lieu of revealing actual names. For example, instead of referring to someone as Bruce, we might call him “Playboy.” We will also attempt to consistently capitalize words that are especially valuable to Cola because they reflect something of great importance to him; having a tremendous impact on his life.

An aside...
What is a OneSeven?
Cola has always enjoyed great movies involving stings, scams, and espionage. His favorites include "Three Days of the Condor," the Danny Ocean movies, the Jason Bourne and James Bond franchises. Most Readers know grumbling "Q" of the 007 films. Although his total career screen time was minimal, his impact was considerable. He provided Bond with a wide variety of high tech devices and tools that 007 would eventually need to save the day.

Cola, too, required tools, technical skills, and inventiveness far beyond his ability to personally manage or create. Unlike Bond's single "Q," over the years he's enjoyed dozens of Q's to assist him with his needs. Electronic technicians, forgers, audio and video experts, pickpockets, carpenters, plumbers, electricians, chemists, microbiologists, fingerprint analysts, linguists, firearms experts, metallurgists, and others.

In most conversations, Cola uses the generic "OneSeven" when discussing any of his technical suppliers. OneSeven is a play on Q, given Q's position as the 17th letter of the English alphabet. Time has revealed that Cola's practice of referring to all of his various technical support people as OneSeven has kept them all safe.

A How-To Manual?

We have removed more than 90% of the operational details initially included in this manuscript. There is no valid reason to provide Readers with a "How To Manual" for conducting Corporate Espionage Operations. Any remaining operational information is provided solely to offer context and explanatory information.

The simple presentation of raw facts in a book of this type may hold value for a tiny percentage of book purchasers. However, we believe the majority of Readers will enjoy reading about Cola's life, presented with storytelling techniques. We trust you'll enjoy this book.

This Book is...

- NOT intended to be an instruction manual.
- NOT a "How To Become A Corporate Spy" book.
- NOT filled with operational information unavailable elsewhere.
- NOT meant to encourage anyone to engage in Corporate Espionage.

Contact
Readers are invited to contact the authors, through our publisher. Don't expect an immediate reply. If we do choose to engage with you, please understand we may want to take time and discover a little about you. You can assist in our decision making by providing:

1. Good contact information, and
2. Detailed information regarding your reason for reaching out

Persons reaching out to us will serve themselves well by providing as much detailed information for 1 and 2 above. If Cola smells a trap, ruse, game, question your motives or believe it would be a waste of time, we will immediately discard your communication.

Do Not Include Attachments
We will immediately discard any email containing attachments, without reviewing those emails.

If you're serious about contacting Cola or Steve with a serious matter, please reach out to us through our publisher, Two Loons Press, at the email address below. Please write "COLA CONTACT" in the Subject Line. All such communications will be forwarded to either or both of us by our publisher.

contact@TwoLoonsPress.com

INTRODUCTION

AN INTRODUCTION BY COLA FUGELERE

My Co-Author

First, I'd like to thank Steve Fowler for his efforts on my behalf. Finding an author to write my biography was extremely difficult. I needed to find someone trustworthy with excellent listening skills. Someone who would ask the right questions, perform discrete research, write my story, and edit the finished product; all in one person. This was necessary because of my background and the risks associated with the revelations detailed in this book.

A fine man discussed in this book, who I fondly refer to as "Diamond Dave," referred me to Steve. Dave said Steve is an excellent author for someone interested in writing a biography. Dave's referral was a perfect fit. *Thank you Dave Newman!*

Steve repeatedly asked me to allow him to use a book editing professional for the final edit of the manuscript. I firmly and consistently refused. Although he had little interest in carrying the burden of editing the book himself and claims he's an author, not an editor, I believe Steve Fowler did a remarkable job preparing the final manuscript for publication.

Although Steve is referred to as my co-author, every word in this book was committed to paper through Steve's efforts. I spoke. Steve wrote.

Steve spent hundreds of hours interviewing Ryan and me in preparation for this book. I kept him filled with hot coffee as Steve peppered me with questions and delved into every facet of my life. If not for Steve's prodding, details about my family life wouldn't exist in this book. I also credit him for insisting we use as many photographs as we did in the final book.

A gesture of my appreciation for him, as well as a bonus for his successful efforts in producing my biography, I donated many of my well-used spy tools and devices to Steve. It was fun watching his face as I detailed dozens of Cola operations and showed him many of the tools we used in those Ops (a number of those tools are described in this book).

We'd sit on my deck in The Hamptons, overlooking the Atlantic Ocean to the south, for many of Steve's interviews. I'd watch in amusement as Steve's fascination with my spy tools was played out as he handled and marveled over many of those devices. Now some of those tools are part of Steve's personal spy museum.

Thank you Steve!

The Dark Side

After years of playing in the increasingly crowded espionage space, it became clear my risk-taking days as a Corporate Spy would eventually land me in serious legal jeopardy. Moreover, I realized my considerable experience as a Corporate Spy could serve others well by assisting them in countering espionage activities that may affect their companies. I took an extended break from active espionage, in a cautious quest to methodically transition away from the Dark Side. I now assist others in thwarting spurious efforts designed to rob them of competitive opportunities, market share, and profitability. My activities primarily involve proactive Corporate Counterintelligence activities. In short, I plug holes before anything can get through those holes.

While my activities are generally focused on proactive defensive measures to assist Clients before they become victims, my skills occasionally drift into other related areas. From time to time I'll have my Team help Clients with Counterespionage measures; as well as the occasional uncategorized espionage-related job (See the "Bistro d'OC" section in the Memorable Locations chapter, as well as the "Taylor Chantay" Operation in the Chance Phelps chapter.).

I'm serious about the dangers of the Dark Side. My maturity and experience will often reveal the very dark motives driving those procuring the services of espionage operatives. The corrupting influences of money and power will occasionally lead those seeking information about their competitors into dangerously dark designs. Some individuals become obsessed with the pseudo-narcotic effects resulting from espionage activities. That addiction occasionally leads business leaders into felonious areas better suited for Hollywood fiction, than real life.

Corporate Espionage is more than familiar. It is my legacy. Corporate Espionage has been my life, and now I'm entirely dedicated to seeking penance by thwarting those who are traveling the path of the Dark Side; and leaving broken relationships, dreams, and damaged businesses in their wake.

> ***An aside...***
> My favorite movie is "Three Days of the Condor" starring Robert Redford. *Surprised?*

I trust you'll enjoy SPY GAMES!

SPY GAMES
Inside the Murky World of Corporate Espionage

COLA FUGELERE
AND
STEVEN FOWLER

About Me

Cola Fugelere

Photo of a Charcoal Original

Stefano Gino "Cola" Fugelere
My story and this book can be summed up in two words: Spy Games. I've spent my entire adult life actively working inside the murky world of Corporate Espionage. I AM Cola the Spy.

Stefano Gino "Cola" Fugelere is my nom de guerre. I've misappropriated, kept, protected, and traded in secrets for a living. Most of that time I was actively living the life of a Spy. Years of accumulated wisdom eventually changed me. I've crossed over into another facet of espionage. I now dedicate my time to Counterintelligence and Counterespionage efforts. My bailiwick is working with businesses to mitigate their espionage-related losses.

> ***An aside...***
> Change is inevitable. If you had told me when I was younger that one day I'd switch from the Dark Side, my response would have been, "The transition would be impossible. I'll never change." *Famous last words.*
>
> Armstrong's walk on the moon reminded me anything is possible. An inflection point in my life changed Cola's "I'll never change" attitude. A hearing aid, cell phone, and a Starbucks latte was the catalyst that reinforced my understanding that change is inevitable, natural, and possible.
>
> My father spent a lifetime saying he'd never wear a hearing aid. For a time he pooh-poohed cell phones, and I thought he'd never use one. He loved black coffee and thought Starbucks drinks were prissy. One day he stopped by my home with a Starbucks' latte in his hand. As he sat at my kitchen counter consuming the milky drink, his cell phone rang. Answering his phone, "Papa" turned his torso a little, revealing his hearing aid. At that moment it all came together. Papa morphed into someone I never expected him to become. If Papa could change, so could Cola.

Back to Me...
Cola the Spy is an actor, an enigma, investigator, a tactician, a psychologist, a chameleon, a confidant, and more. As an actor, I've played so many roles I cannot recall them all. The chameleon in me lifted my acting abilities to an entirely new level.

Late actor Antonio Rodolfo Oaxaca Quinn, better known as Anthony Quinn, was also a chameleon. His Mexican and Irish heritage resulted in a physical appearance often confused for something it wasn't. A visual assessment of Mr. Quinn, to determine his heritage, was very difficult. He could pass for many different ethnicities without makeup. The assistance of makeup artists expanded his options and opened a wide variety of ethnic roles to Mr. Quinn. He's been cast as a Mexican, an American, an Arab, a Hawaiian, Panamanian, an Englishman, a Frenchman, an Irishman, and a Greek. He also played a Hun, a Hebrew, and an Italian; as well as a person from the Basque region of Spain, a Portuguese, a Native American, a Mongol, a Spaniard, and a Ukrainian. His roles surprisingly included Chinese, Japanese, Eskimo, Filipino, and East Indian characters. Although some of his parts were less than believable, his acting skills and appearance worked for most of his characters.

STEFANO AND RAMUNNU "NONNO" FUGELERE

Cola and His Grandfather

Cola the Chameleon

I, too, have a rich history adopting a wide range of personas. My ethnic mix has given me chameleon-like gifts, not unlike Quinn's. According to my late grandfather, his father was born and grew up in the Sicilian mountains about 25 miles southwest of Messina, Sicily. I've not been able to find the exact location.

COLA'S GREAT GRANDPARENTS

Bisnonna and Bisnonno Fugelere

I believe they lived in a village very near Savoca. Savoca, Sicily was one of the filming locations for "The Godfather;" voted the Motion Picture Academy Best Picture in 1972. Michael Corleone, his new bride, and their wedding party exited a small Savocan church and traveled on foot down a narrow winding road.

The old man told me his grandfather (my great great grandfather) was an immigrant from England who initially settled in Messina. His wife was believed to be the illegitimate Black Dutch daughter of an American plantation owner and one of his slaves. We're not sure how she ended up in England and became the wife of an Englishman. Sometime after settling in Messina, the Englishman moved to the nearby mountains to grow sweet onions (Cipolla Dolce) and other crops. Many years ago I traveled to the area and discovered a patch of wonderful Cipolla's, adjacent to the small road traveled by The Godfather's bride and groom.

Backgrounds of the Sicilian people in that area included Italian, Norman, and Arabic ancestors. My great great grandfather was English. My great grandfather studied in Rome and married a woman whose father was Turkish Greek and mother Italian. As a result, I'm all mixed up and can readily blend into societies across Europe, North Africa, the Middle East, and the Americas.

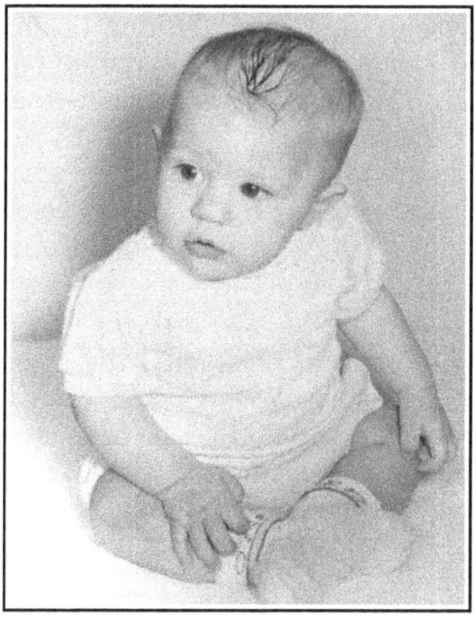

BABY COLA

My nickname is "Cola" because of my skin tone. Cola is an Anglo-Saxon Old English nickname that means "charcoal" and, when used, is usually given to dark-skinned individuals. When I was a little boy growing up in Texas, I spent a lot of time outdoors, without a shirt. Our priest nicknamed me Cola because of my tan. Although my natural skin pigmentation is only slightly darker than the average Englishman, when exposed to the sun I become very dark. If I know of a pending job and need to be a white guy, I stay out of the sun. Conversely, I've adopted Arabic roles that required me to spend a week or two on the beach, or at the pool, to enhance my coloring to a gradient more consistent with a Middle Eastern or Mediterranean skin tone.

> ***An aside...***
> I once ran an extended Operation that required my skin to be as light as possible. After completing the job, my wife and I joined friends on a red-eye flight for a nice vacation in Puerto Vallarta, Mexico. I didn't sleep a wink on the plane.
>
> We arrived early in the morning. Our rooms wouldn't be available for hours. The sun was about to rise, and I

wanted to witness the event. Putting on my swimming trunks in the restroom, I stationed myself on the beach. I sat on a lounge chair with my back to the water, so I could watch the sun ascend at a nearly imperceptible pace and rise above the horizon; into the morning sky. As it rose, I remember thinking the warm celestial ball felt good after flying all night in an air conditioned aluminum tube.

I drifted off. Waking much later, I discovered Cola was cooked. Burnt to a crisp. I realized even Cola's easily darkened skin was susceptible to a severe sunburn. I looked as though I was wearing a red shirt. In terrible pain for about ten days, I was neither brown nor white. Cola looked more like a wordless stop sign than a dashing corporate 007.

My friends occasionally remind me that a few days later, wearing a white tee shirt, I walked into the Pacific Ocean's cool refreshing salt water. I'd stand in the pain-relieving liquid for hours, submerged to my lower lip. A huge sombrero offered excellent shade. The ocean cooled my scorched body and felt good. When I emerged from the salty waters, my friends began laughing at me. I was so red under the wet white shirt, it appeared as though I was wearing a pink tee shirt. *Ugh! Not fun.*

Back to a Brown Cola...
I have dark wavy hair. Dark brown, not entirely black. I'm an even six feet tall and of medium build. My frame is well suited for everything from expensive Italian suits to a set of mechanic's coveralls. I have an everyday kind of face and body that's reasonably neutral and forgettable. Unremarkable. I don't stand out in people's minds. Cola is often overlooked when someone describes people recently seen in a room. Not a bad thing for someone consistently engaged in clandestine activities.

There is one aspect of my physique that is particularly worth noting, and described by an old nickname, "Plastic Man." Although "Rubber Man" would probably be more accurate, the moniker reasonably describes one of my natural talents that was very helpful at times in avoiding apprehension by the authorities. I can modify my body shape and mannerisms into many different personas. No, I'm not a shapeshifter like you'll see in science fiction movies. I merely alter my gait, frame, and mannerisms with ease and believability. With little effort, I can shrink into myself and look like a much older man.

In acting classes I've attended, we practiced something referred to as "Sliding Down The Pole." The intent was to project an aged appearance. As we age, gravity exerts a downward force on our bodies, and Sliding Down The Pole is reflective of that process. Most people think it is better to bend over forward to appear elderly. Not so. A hunched appearance appears less elderly, and more physically challenged. In life, we naturally collapse downward with the gravitationally enhanced aging process. It is as if you're sliding down an imaginary pole positioned within your body.

Conversely, in my youth and early adulthood, I could stand sufficiently tall and erect in a manner to give myself the appearance of an even younger person approaching 6'2". On the other hand, I could shrink into the comfortable 5'9" frame of someone a little older. I can tuck my jaw in such a way that I appear to have an overbite; thus changing my facial features. These physical adjustments have been a tremendous asset for me.

My "Plastic Man" talents, generic features, and ability to adjust my gait quickly and convincingly allowed me to avoid discovery by law enforcement officials and others with regularity. It served to fool witnesses who'd seen me previously. I was hard to recognize after the fact, especially if a few days had passed and I'd successfully avoided making eye contact with others.

I'm an English speaking American, born in Brooklyn and raised in New York, The UK, Texas, Wisconsin, Indiana, Colorado, Arizona, Nevada, California, and Alaska. I am comfortably fluent with every U.S. regional accent, except those from the New England states. I'm told I'm just fine. However, it doesn't feel natural or believable when I try to imitate someone from Vermont or Boston. I speak Italian and Spanish fluently. My

Sicilian is not entirely fluent, some French, and I am more than passable as a Londoner with an Estuary English accent.

Telephonic communications extend my speaking capabilities, by masking my appearance. That permits opportunities beyond the accents mentioned above. I can alter my vocal tone and convincingly sound like a woman, a teenage girl, or a child.

- Is that a man, woman, or child on the phone?
- Is he Chinese, Korean, or Japanese?
- Is she a young Vietnamese or Filipino girl?
- Ah ha! That's an adolescent Native American boy!

My verbal skill sets in the arena of radio and telephone communications are wide-ranging and have created many opportunities. I've procured volumes of helpful information by creating convincing illusions as to my identity, by merely changing my voice.

> ***An aside...***
> On a few occasions, I've taken unreasonable risks by pretending I'm different people at the same time, during the same call, speaking with the same person. To my knowledge, I've never been nailed. However, I'm sure more than a few suspicions entered the minds of those on the other end of the call.

Back to Cola's Chameleon-like Gifts...
I have blue-gray eyes that aren't overly memorable, but they were often covered with tinted contact lenses when I was working covertly as a Spy. In addition to masking my eyes with contact lenses, I employed some facial additions contributing to my anonymity, including various spectacle designs, dental devices, oral cheek enhancements; as well as fake mustaches, goatees, and beards. Clothing was no different. I'd carefully plan layering patterns for my clothing that assisted me in modifying my apparent weight. To this day, I never dress without wearing two or more custom crafted shirts, each with different colors or patterns presented, if turned inside out. Wearing just two carefully chosen reversible shirts offered me the opportunity to

reveal four distinctly different appearances. When possible, I tried to have reversible jackets available for immediate use. I always carried two nicely foldable baseball hats. One subdued and one was either bright in color or bore universally recognizable logos (e.g., Yankees, Green Bay, or Apple).

In a flash, the tall young brown-eyed man wearing the plain red shirt and a Packers green and yellow hat, became an older slimmer bespectacled gray-eyed man, somewhat shorter; wearing a plain tan hat and a light blue shirt with a surfboard pattern.

Anything is Possible

An espionage operator once asked me to explain my success in conducting Operations most spies would never consider attempting. My response to him was written years earlier as I planned my first Espionage Operation. Recalling those words I said, "Identify your goal, from simple and reasonable, all the way to the periphery of what is possible. Think outside the box. Plan well and work hard. Adapt as necessary. All the while, keeping your focus on the goal. In the end, you'll succeed in reaching your goal, or you will fail. No matter the outcome, you'll know you did your level best. Conduct yourself accordingly, and success will follow you like a loyal companion."

That precept was demonstrated to me on July 20, 1969, as I stood before a black and white television located in my parents living room, watching Neil Armstrong walk on the moon. As I watched the first human being step onto the surface of another celestial body, I was alternately looking from our TV to the waxing crescent moon. The fuzzy video of Armstrong was before me as I stood with my left shoulder at the opening of an open sliding glass door. From that vantage point, I could easily see the moon and the television with a little pivot of my head. Back and forth, back and forth. I marveled at the goal outlined by President Kennedy and realized just about anything within imaginative reason is possible.

An aside...
Fallible humans are essentially the same. As it is often said, "We all put our pants on one leg at a time." Although that is a rather simplistic way to say no person is better than another, it might help Readers understand me better. Over the course of Cola's life, I've brushed shoulders with notable leaders in politics, government, entertainment, business, pop culture, the military, and the media. I like to call them "Bubble People."

Unlike the rest of us, they live in bubbles. Insulated from real life, real joys, real experiences, and the many real problems experienced by 99% of the population. Although some people choose to drool over notable individuals, Cola does not. I have no interest in meeting most of them. My many points of contact with "Bubble People" leaves me thirsting for real people. Authentic people.

I don't believe I'm alone. I've enjoyed more than a few interviews spotlighting Mike Rowe. Mike is best known for the Dirty Jobs television program. He's out there pressing the flesh with real people. Mike gets it. So do most real people.

That said, there is one man I've always said I'd love to have met. I wish I could have enjoyed a handshake with him. A man who experienced something unique. Something special. That man was Neil Armstrong. Armstrong's unique place in history, as having been the first human being to step on another world, is special to Cola and others who actually watched that event as it unfolded. Relatively few people in human history past, present, and future were witnesses to Armstrong's actions that day. I am blessed to have been one of Armstrong's witnesses. I'd like to have met Mr. Neil Armstrong.

Cola's Non-Negotiable Rules

Although my chosen profession often resulted in conduct outside the law, I remained faithful to certain non-negotiables; for myself and others in my working sphere. Those non-negotiables included:

- No guns.
- No drugs.
- No pornography.
- No physical harm.
- No unpatriotic activities.
- Never impersonate a Judge.
- No activities that involve children.
- I don't discuss myself with Clients.
- No activities that might harm animals.
- My family is NEVER a topic for discussion.
- Respect and honor law enforcement officials.
- Never impersonate a law enforcement professional.
- All Operations and meetings are orchestrated by me.
- Never reveal methods and sources to Clients or other parties.
- No espionage activities involving private contractors working on behalf of the U.S. Government.
- Cola will never knowingly engage in espionage for foreign governments or foreign-owned businesses.
- Clients are not permitted to enlist others for the same services I offer, while I'm under contract with them.
- Cola, a Patriotic American, will never knowingly interfere with the activities of others working on behalf of the defense of our nation.
- No association with convicted felons, fugitives from the law, organized criminal enterprises (organized crime), smugglers, pedophiles, drug dealers, or persons I suspect to have been involved in kidnapping, rape, murder, or other similarly heinous crimes.

- Clients are to leave me alone. No surveilling or investigating me. I'm the Spy, not them. I will not abide by Clients who choose to ignore this rule. Those Client relationships will be terminated immediately and with prejudice.

Rules Are Important

I understand many Readers may have problems with my career path. I understand. I could, however, counter with an argument that we are a nation of laws or we are not. As I'm writing these words, I'm driving down the highway and dictating my words into a hands free recording device. I am traveling at the speed limit, which is something I generally do. Hundreds of cars have passed me today, driving much faster than the speed limit. They are risking the lives of others by ignoring the posted speed limit. In fact, I'm probably in more danger because I'm obeying the law, while tons of steel fly by at excessive speeds. It makes sense that a number of those speeding beyond me would condemn Cola for his chosen career. I call that a double standard.

> ***An aside...***
> I've argued with my father, wife, kids, and others about this subject. I place my debate points directly onto solid mathematics. If someone is traveling five miles and averages seven miles-per-hour over the posted limit, on a sixty-mile-per-hour roadway, the speeding party will arrive a whopping forty seconds earlier than the poor slob who believes in maintaining the posted speed. I ask my family members, "Are those measly forty seconds worth the cost of a life? Are they worth a ticket?"
>
> They bark at me, and the oft recycled conversation ceases.

Back to Double Standards...

My wife tells me I'm the dangerous one because I refuse to drive with traffic? Why drive fifteen to twenty miles an hour above the posted limit? Why do some condemn me for following the law in this area, when they don't? Why do some condemn me for espionage, when I'm only engaged in activities involving dollars, not lives? Why are pejoratives associated with espionage directed at me, when others engage in dangerous activities that often maim and kill?

I trade information for money. What I won't do is trade safe passage for the risks associated with arriving at a destination three minutes earlier, after a thirty-mile drive. After all, I'm Cola the Spy, not Cola the Speeder.

About Me

It was necessary for me to start this book off with a chapter, "About Me." However, this single chapter cannot begin to tell you about the real Cola Fugelere.

About Me? You'll get to know About Me in the following pages. You're going to learn my likes and dislikes, my passions and my ethics, my life and my stories, and much much more. Enjoy, as you read through the pages reflecting the life of Stefano "Cola" Fugelere.

IN THE BEGINNING

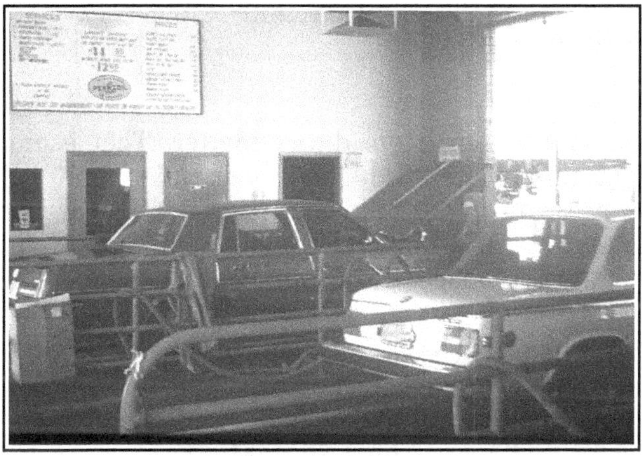

COLA'S DEBUT

The First Photo from My First Espionage Operation

The Quick Lube Job

It all began in the late 1970's with a peculiar call from my Uncle Frank. He was living in a distant state and owned a healthy robust construction company. To the best of my knowledge, his business was thriving, professional, and enjoyed a good reputation. Uncle Frank had seen a couple of franchised quick lube operations open in his community and wanted to know if the college town I lived in had any similar businesses. I said I'd check.

I reported back a few days later with the news that the same franchise he'd seen in his community had just opened a new store in my town. His initial call was, as I said, peculiar. The second call was downright bizarre.

Uncle Frank told me he was interested in learning as much as possible about the business in my town. He wanted me to provide him with service rates, customer counts, facility layout, detailed measurements, advertising expenditures, vendor information, revenues, expenses, projections, employee training, marketing strategies, and other detailed proprietary information. Uncle Frank didn't care how I garnered the information. He merely suggested I should be cautious. It was a tall order, but the fee he promised for my services would more than cover tuition for the next two semesters.

> ***An aside...***
> The next two semesters didn't matter. That espionage project immediately addicted me, and I quit college halfway through the following semester. I was hooked and almost immediately transitioned into full-time Corporate Espionage. It was initially very tough.
>
> It didn't help that I was an underfunded youngster with little experience and zero contacts. Without considering the consequences, I took Uncle Frank's payment and parlayed that into a blue 1975 Monte Carlo, complete with a sunroof, a built-in eight-track tape system (*wow!*), a white landau top, and white leather seats. It was an awesome ride. I still had a few bucks remaining and decided to fly to Europe for a youthful adventure. Then I was a broke Spy, needing work. *I digress...*

Back to Uncle Frank...
I agreed to do as Uncle Frank asked. It took several days to develop plans for my first engagement in Corporate Espionage and nearly three weeks before my dossier on the quick lube

establishment was complete. The process captured my undivided attention and put my adrenal glands into overdrive.

I was exhausted for a few days after completing the job, then had a strong desire for more of the same. It had been an exhilarating challenge, and I needed another fix.

◊ ◊ ◊

Those who knew me as a young person would readily understand my need for an adrenaline rush. I was a kid who performed risky underwater acts, did tricks on motorcycles, and jumped from perfectly good airplanes; all for the enormous rushes they offered. I'm sure part of it was for attention, but a large measure of my need was associated with a lust for adrenaline coursing through my veins.

While in college I jumped from perfectly good airplanes until a fellow jump school student's chute failed to open. He bounced, and I quit parachuting.

COLA THE STREAKER

Standing Next To "The Diving Bell" Swimming Pool

During those days a few of my fraternity brothers and I had a party that required a beer keg and a large galvanized tub to set it in. The next day I got the bright idea to turn the galvanized tub into a diving bell. Removing the loose weights from my barbell, I tied them to the tub's handles and lowered it into the deep end of a swimming pool. It was about six feet from the surface. Then my buddies and I would weigh ourselves down and sit on the bottom of the pool. Two and three at a time, we'd stick our heads into the tub and chat. Our discussions involved girls, whether or not we'd get the bends, and how often we should remove the carbon dioxide laden air and replenish it topside with fresh air. Yes, I know. Silliness. Although, I must admit very little adrenaline was involved in that one. We were just seeking a low octane thrill.

A few years earlier, naked public running became a flash-in-the-pan fad. My high school buddies and I watched with juvenile awe as 1974 Academy Awards presenter David Niven was interrupted by Robert Opel. Opel was naked and streaked across the stage, directly behind and very near to Niven.

> ***An aside...***
> Streaking has been around for hundreds of years. However, during the latter part of 1973 and into mid-1974, streaking became in nationwide fad in the United States. Colleges and universities were hot spots for the nutty phenomenon. Ray Stevens sold five million copies of his song, "The Streak," which became a #1 hit in June 1974. Group streaking became all the rage that spring. The largest recorded group from that streaking era involved more than fifteen hundred simultaneously streaking students at the University of Georgia in March 1974. Can you imagine how high the numbers would be today if social media drove spontaneous "Flash Mob" streakfests?

Back to Cola, the Adrenaline Junkie...
I was in high school during the streaking fad. Teo, one of my buddies wanted to get in on the action. He convinced Cola and another friend, Buddy, that we shouldn't miss out on the fun. One evening three of us drove to a large area park. We knew the park well and recognized the twelve side-by-side tennis courts would be a perfect place to streak. We could streak down one side of the tennis courts and, in mere seconds, traverse all twelve

courts by running in a straight line. The courts were usually fully booked for evening use, and we knew we'd have an audience.

"Use Gas Wisely"

The 1973 Arab Oil Embargo

> ***An aside...***
> Teo was always the one who came up with great ideas. Ideas that usually morphed into great memories. Teo deserves credit for being a memory maker, instigator, and an all-around good guy; adored by everyone. Whether it was co-opting great ideas for a carnival event from the campus of UCLA or spraying removable foam signage on neighborhood cars, urging drivers to "Save Gas" and "Use Gas Wisely" during the Arab Oil Embargo of 1973, Teo made things happen.

Back to The Streak...
Teo, Buddy, and I decided to, literally, take a run at it. On a dark Friday night, Buddy quietly drove his car into one end of the park. As the vehicle crept forward, Teo and I stripped to our birthday suits. Approaching the area closest to the tennis courts, Buddy killed his lights and quietly rolled the old sedan to a stop at the edge of the parking lot. We could see the bright lights of the tennis courts and all the players. Every court was occupied. Great! We had about a hundred yards to cover on the cool flat grass in the dark, before our inaugural performance under the lights, with an unsuspecting audience. Buddy let the two of us out of the car.

My heart was pounding, and the adrenaline rush was incredible. We were both running full tilt the moment our feet hit the ground. Just as the asphalt fell away and was replaced by grass, a crocodile bit my legs. Well, not really. However, it sure felt like it.

Teo lived a couple of blocks from the park. My home was a few miles away. He spent more time there and remembered what I didn't. The asphalt parking area was separated from the grass with evenly spaced vertical 8 x 8 railroad ties, sticking up about two feet and spaced about ten feet apart. A heavy chain was anchored to and slung between each 8 x 8 to create a barrier to cars and streakers, so they wouldn't leave the parking lot and go onto the grass.

I hit the chain hard and tore open the meager meat cushion barely present at the front of human shin bones. Rolling in agony on the ground, I was sure I'd broken both my legs. I recall looking back right away, hoping Buddy noticed my accident and was available to medivac me from the scene. No dice. He was well on his way to the other side of the park. *Uh oh!*

> ***An aside...***
> As I look back through the years, I wonder how Buddy avoided running with the bulls. I believe he drove us on two different streaks, and I certainly don't recall ever seeing his little white butt running like the wind.

Back to The Streak...
After a minute or two I realized I would live and my legs were sufficiently intact to proceed with our streak. Thanks to the adrenaline rush, we ran flat out through all twelve courts. We heard shrieks, laughter, and had more than a few tennis balls served in our direction.

As we shot out into the dark abyss on the far side of the courts, we took a hard right turn and had to run about 300 yards to rendezvous with our getaway driver. That should have taken us the better part of a minute. So much for expectations. It took nearly five minutes.

Departing the bright lights of the tennis courts we pivoted toward our getaway car. Something instantly captured my attention. I instinctively looked up when a police helicopter turned on his floodlight. It lit up the far side of the park, not far from Buddy, and began a methodical search pattern across the park. *Yikes!* Teo and I both found shelter behind a couple of fifty-five-gallon drums used as garbage cans. We pressed our naked bodies against the sides of the cans until the helicopter completed his sweep. Then we sprinted to the car, laughing and relishing the success of our adventure.

That week at school was fantastic. We were heroes. Everyone wanted to see my shins. They wanted every detail. We were like rock stars.

By the end of the week, We planned another streak. We were a tight-knit group of trusted friends. We kept the whole thing low key. After all, it wouldn't be near as much fun if someone sabotaged our streak. We had no desire to get caught with our pants down.

We set the second streak for the following Saturday night. We met at Teo's house for a pre-streak conference. I recall lifting my bell-bottom pants and reminding everyone to jog to the chain, step over it, then run like the wind.

Twelve of us mounted our steeds. I believe Buddy was, again, a driver. I don't recall who drove the second car. We pulled into the parking lot, and ten nudists jumped out of the vehicles. Everyone cleared the chain just fine, and we paused a minute or two, until our getaway drivers were well on the way to our far side extraction point. I've never seen such a frank display of nervousness as I witnessed in that small group of naked pimple-faced teens.

Out of the blue Teo hollered, "Let's Rally!" Man did those boys fly. Adrenaline is a potent drug. I sure wish Coach Preston could have seen us run.

One of the streakers, Bud, was a star linebacker from our high school varsity football team. Not to be confused with Buddy, Bud was a football player. Buddy's gifts were basketball and successfully getting out of streaking. *Smart guy!*

Bud didn't react as quickly as everyone else and was the last to take off. I was right in front of Bud, and he could have run faster than me, but he's always looked out for me and probably remained in the rear as a way to offer me a measure of protection. It turned out Bud needed the protection more than me. My penultimate position in the line of streakers kept my backside safe from the onslaught that was about to impact Bud.

As I watched the eight naked butts in front of me enter the first tennis court, I realized there was a little girl, probably eight to ten years old, on the first court and on the same side we were entering. She was playing tennis with a man we believed to be her father. He was a Mad Daddy. *Not good!*

I'm sure all the tennis players on the court that evening were shocked. After all, the instant introduction of ten hairy naked teenage male bodies into a public venue, with parts swinging freely, was probably new to everyone playing tennis. Except for the little girl, everyone on the court was a teenager or grownup.

I recognize the little girl may have been very unsettled by the entire event. In that, I'm sorry. To a person, all of us were, and are, decent moral people. If we'd known a child was on the tennis courts, we wouldn't have made the trek. We were kids then and didn't think things through. *Teenagers!*

Mad Daddy ran toward, and around, the net to come to his daughter's defense. Mad Daddy arrived on our side of the net just as Bud entered the court. I recall hearing a "Whack" followed by an "Ow!" Repeatedly. In fact, all the way down the dozen courts.

Whack! Ow!
Whack! Ow!
Whack! Ow!

Mad Daddy was wise enough not to follow us into the darkness, although it wouldn't have been a problem. We were just harmless kids engaging in silly kid stuff.

> ***An aside...***
> My wife and I recently enjoyed an excellent coffee at an outdoor Starbucks with Bud, his wife, and two adult daughters. We hadn't been together since the girls were preschool age. Great family. They all listened politely as Bud and I shared stories of our youthful exploits. When we came to the story of the second streak, our memories diverged. Bud's recollection of the unhappy father on the first court was markedly different from mine.
>
> According to Bud, the man just ran up to the net and calmly said, "Are you proud of exposing yourselves to a little girl?"
>
> First, I really don't recall it that way. In fact, I recall us inspecting his butt after the streak. I remember laughing with my fellow streakers when we saw the little square welts on Bud's butt. Second, I'm sure every Reader would agree, my version is a lot more fun than Bud's. *This is my book, and I'm sticking to my story.* Sorry Bud. You might be the smartest guy I've ever known, but here we are more than forty years beyond that night, and my story is the one that first made it into print.

Back to The Second Streak...
We made it to our getaway cars just fine, reveled in the fun of the event, and turned to other adrenaline generating events. I never streaked again.

◇ ◇ ◇

That darned police helicopter! A few months later he caught us. Yes, we were in a state of undress. However, we were neither naked, nor streaking. It was, indeed, nighttime once more. If memory serves me correctly, this time Buddy was part of the action.

The local state university campus had an incredible diving facility. It boasted an excellent ten-meter platform. At thirty-three feet above the pool, it towered over the 7.5 and 5-meter platforms. A very high red brick wall surrounded the facility, and we wanted to go diving.

We drove about eight to ten miles from our homes in two cars, driven by Sam and Hughes. We parked several blocks from the school on a quiet neighborhood street. It was about one o'clock in the morning. We all stripped to our tighty whities and boxers. Then we put our shoes back on to protect our feet. No socks.

According to one of our peers, jumping into water thirty-three feet below might hurt our feet. I don't know if that's true or not, but heck, we had to run down several neighborhood streets and cross a main thoroughfare to get to the pool. With that in mind, the shoe idea made sense.

I don't recall how we scaled the diving facility's ginormous wall, but I do know I was the first dummy up the ladder to the ten-meter platform. As my uncle "Cash" used to say, "It's darker than the inside of a cow's belly." It was, indeed, dark.

When I arrived at the top of the ladder and stood up on the platform, I could see neither the platform nor the pool. What to do?

My mother's cousin, Jackie, was blind and deaf. In her younger years, she was an acquaintance of Helen Keller. Jackie would tell me, to "Helen Keller" with my hands until I found the cookies in the cupboard.

There I was, "Helen Kellering" my way to the leading edge of the platform, feeling my way with my feet. I finally arrived at the edge and bellowed, "Geronimo!" Then I stepped out into the inky blackness.

Yikes! The moment I stepped off the concrete platform a terrible thought crossed my mind. *Is there water in the pool?*

Nope. Not a single one of us thought to check and make sure there was water in the diving pool. Geez! Twelve geniuses! Although we thought of ourselves as masterminds, we were idiots playing with fire. I now call such idiotic, misguided, stunts, "Young People Planning." A dozen teenage boys, pulsing with adrenaline and testosterone, don't plan, think, or consider. They act. In this case, we acted - foolishly.

Pools get drained all the time for maintenance and repairs. I thank the good Lord the pool had water that night. I plummeted downward in sheer terror, probably screaming all the way. When I collided with the hard surface of that wonderfully deep water, I was ecstatic. I jumped out of the water and scampered back up the ladder for another turn.

I'm shocked we didn't land on one another in the darkness. Fortunately, we weren't there long enough to have too many chances for such a collision. We were saved by The Bell.

Saved by The Bell? Yep. A Bell helicopter. I'm guessing someone heard my blood-curdling scream as I was rushing toward, what I believed to be, the dry plaster bottom of a deep swimming pool nearly fifty feet below. Whether they called the police or not, we'll never know. The only thing we knew is all of a sudden the night turned into day. I could see the water in the pool!

> ***An aside...***
> Chances were pretty good it was the same Bell helicopter that interrupted our inaugural tennis court streak; forcing Teo and Cola behind filthy 55 gallon drum trash receptacles.

Back to Getting Busted by The Bell...
Yep, the police helicopter lit us up and called in reinforcements. Twelve, nearly naked, teenage trespassers scattered. We somehow escaped the walled diving pool facility and ran back into the surrounding neighborhood. I recall hiding in a bush, next to someone's carport. A cruiser came by and shined his spotlight onto the vegetation. I didn't dare move. I froze like a terrified rabbit. It paid off. The Officer moved on.

> ***An aside...***
> My father loved to hunt. He taught me animals were difficult to see if they didn't move. Natural elements of camouflage built into their bodies protect animals. Rabbits and deer in bushes can be hard to see, but if they run, all bets are off. Humans and animals see and react to movement. I knew remaining stationary was my best option, tighty whities notwithstanding.

Back to The Chase...
Another of my buddies knew to remain still. He, too, escaped police questioning. Nine others darted when the spotlights hit, or were easily apprehended while running down the road. One guy pulled a Forrest Gump. He just kept running and was never caught.

Once the police were gone, we all piled in the cars, sans the Forrest Gump guy. We didn't know what happened to him. We drove around for a long time looking for Forrest and eventually went home. He showed up the next morning, after covering about 8 miles in the middle of the city, in the middle of the night, in a state of undress. The entire event was a hoot and certainly gave this author a huge adrenaline rush.

◇ ◇ ◇

My Uncle Frank's espionage job wasn't unlike streaking and jumping from planes. It offered powerful rushes of anxiety and exhilaration, and that was the attraction for me. In some ways, it was more exciting than my teenage adventures.

Yes, the money was good. However, nothing I'd ever engaged in compelled me so profoundly. That little job provided me with unexpected opportunities to think on my feet, think outside the box, and wear many different hats. I was an actor and a detective. A photographer, journalist, business analyst, statistician, an accountant and more.

My first self-imposed task was to get a good overview of the business. To see it up close and personal. The quick lube concept was new, and store owners wanted attention. My plan would leverage their desires and play into that weakness.

I placed a small order for business cards and letterhead. Using the letterhead and an IBM Selectric II typewriter, I wrote a Letter of Introduction. The letter introduced me as a journalist with the University's student newspaper. I approached the franchisee early one morning, armed with a leather-bound reporter's notebook, a gold plated Cross pen, the Letter of Introduction, business cards, a Polaroid camera, and a measuring tape.

During the process of verbally introducing myself to the franchisee, I handed over the Letter of Introduction. I told him I was writing a series of articles about how college students could save time and money. I informed the franchisee I believed his business would be a perfect fit for our Readers and how useful such an article could be at reaching more than ten thousand students with his story - at no cost to his business. The look on his face told me I had him.

I added a sweetener to the deal by telling him my cousin was a news producer with a local television affiliate. I promised I could get my cousin to run a human interest story on the quick lube store, but only if the franchisee could assure me he wouldn't speak to anyone in the print, TV, radio, or advertising business about my upcoming article until published in the college paper. The franchisee's face and eyes lit up. The look on his face reminded me of a three cherry jackpot on a slot machine. It was as if both eyes landed cherries. He was beaming. Glowing. I had him before, but now I owned him.

I explained that I'd like to take photos, interview staff and customers, and hang out for a day or two. He introduced me to the store manager, who was told to bend over backward to accommodate my every need. Then the franchisee left to attend to his other business. I never saw him again.

Over the following couple of days I measured the entire facility, photographed every inch of the place, spent time in the pit shooting photos and interviewing the service guys, counting inventory (filters, belts, etc...), asking customers about their needs and expectations, and generally learning as much as possible about quick lube operations. Then the real work began.

My uncle's directive also included knowledge about vendors, budgets, monthly revenues and expenses, marketing plans, and payroll. Little of the data I needed was onsite, but I wasn't through with the quick lube store yet. I needed to engage in some after-hours sleuthing.

Sleuthing? That's a nice word for dumpster diving. Although I believe they only had old metal garbage cans - no dumpsters. Over the course of a week, I went through their trash. It was a treasure trove of grease, oil, and credit card carbon copies.

Cash and credit cards were both common forms of payment in the 1970's. The real gold for me were the black carbons discarded after the clerk ran the manual imprinter across the customer's Master Charge or BankAmericard (I believe the name BankAmericard changed to "Visa" shortly before my first espionage adventure). Known as "Knuckle Busters," those old-fashioned imprinters made it possible for me to know how much each credit card customer paid for the services performed on their vehicles. I spent a generous portion of the week counting cars being serviced and estimating credit card payment percentages. I then extrapolated an estimate for cash transactions.

Once those efforts ran their course, I turned my sights on the franchisee's business office. I spent the next two weeks visiting the alley behind the franchisee's offices digging through the cans there. I used a Polaroid camera to photograph the contents at the top of each garbage can and placed the visible items in small numbered boxes. I then relocated the remaining contents into large boxes in the back of my old Volkswagen van and drove to a nearby truck stop, where I parked and sorted through the garbage. Once I collected all the information I needed, I'd return to the business office and replace the trash in the cans. I used the Polaroid photos and marked boxes to guide me in carefully replacing the garbage, in the same manner, as when I initially found it. If anyone looked into the cans the next day, everything would appear exactly as it did the day before.

My last evening in the truck stop parking lot turned into an unexpected adventure. While sitting in the back of my van, sifting through the last of the garbage on my final "dumpster diving" night, I heard a loud double bang on the back door; followed by three loud words, "Police! Open up!" *Yikes!* Prison bars passed across my mind.

An aside...
My only trip to jail occurred many years ago on Thanksgiving Day. I was driving from Indianapolis to a western Chicago suburb to spend the holiday with a friend and his family.

As I entered a small town south of Chicago, the speed limit dropped about 20 miles-per-hour. I was traveling the speed limit, as I tend to do, but didn't slow down fast enough. A police car was hiding behind a ground level billboard and the Officer pulled me over.

He saw I had an out-of-state driver's license. The Officer told me I needed to pay an $80 fine, in cash, for the ticket. I asked if I could mail it in. He said, "No."

I was from another state. The Officer said there was no way to guarantee I'd pay the fine if he let me depart without paying. I asked if he'd take a check. He said, "No."

I asked if he'd take a credit card. He said, "No."

I asked if we could go to a Western Union. He said, "No. They aren't open today."

Then "Officer No" told me to follow him. I asked where we were going. Officer No said I was going to jail. I did and received my one call. I used a long distance calling card and contacted my buddy. He drove two hours to bail me out. His family held Thanksgiving Dinner for me. His "Archie Bunker" father wasn't happy with me.

> Oh, well. At least I wasn't in the tiny cell long enough to have to use that goofy-looking sink/toilet combination unit.

Back to "Police! Open Up!"...
I obediently opened the door and faced a young Police Officer; although I couldn't see his face at the time. His flashlight blinded me as he demanded an explanation for my activities. Without thinking, I told him I was a university engineering student and was working on an environmental studies paper for one of my classes. The project was intended to determine ways to improve designs and processes for garbage disposal systems.

I had no idea where that line of bull came from, but that night I realized I was a guy who could think on his feet - quickly and with a full measure of confidence and competence. Although the scenario was unplanned, it didn't hurt that I was sitting next to an old discarded manual typewriter covered with the remains of someone's tossed salad. Whoever had been eating the salad had a penchant for sardines. It smelled to high heaven.

That unexpected event taught me a valuable lesson that became finely honed over the years. It told me I needed to have a backstop story and, if possible, props appropriate to reinforce my statements. I was awkwardly caught in high-risk situations more than a few times. Smart planning saved my bacon more than once when consumers of my backstopped stories believed me.

> ***An aside...***
> A Backstop is, for me, a Plan B (or one of several backup plans). It can also be stories, props, actions, reactions, etcetera; containing reasonably valid reasons for my activities. Emergency moves, last resorts, precautionary steps, and reinforcement actions. An absolute last resort Backstop is a Cola Trap Door.
>
> A Trap Door in my world is an Operational Escape and Evasion Plan. A trap door in a building might lead to a tunnel to an adjacent building, providing a secret way out. Sometimes Cola needs a way out. If Backstopping doesn't work, Cola always has a few Trap Doors up his

sleeve. I'll leave an Op behind if necessary. I don't like it when it happens, but sometimes Forrest just needs to run. *Run Forrest! Run!*

On the other hand, sometimes Forrest cannot run. Let me share a quick story about my brother's son, Eman. The little guy was a toddler when My Brother spent a weekend morning working on his laptop, while Eman was climbing in one of those two-story playgrounds you can find in many kid friendly fast food establishments. You know the kind. They have pipes and slides, and such.

Anyway, My Brother looked up from his work at one point and watched Eman crawl through a short section of clear pipe at the top of the tall structure. My Brother said he was shocked at what he saw. Little Eman was missing his pants and diaper.

Shortly after the little guy scurried through the clear section and was out of sight, My Brother heard an older kid scream at the top of his lungs. "*Eww! Poop!*"

Apparently Little Eman soiled his diaper and decided to rid himself of the evidence. My Brother had the unenviable task of crawling through the pipes like a little kid, looking for his son's missing attire. It's been almost 30 years since My Brother first shared that story with me, and I'm still laughing.

You just never know when things will go wrong. Moreover, you cannot have a backstop plan for every situation. The Spy Game requires the skills necessary to react appropriately to whatever you're presented with; just like a surprised parent. There's no choice. You just do it. You step up and get the job done. Period.

If you can't, you're not cut out for The Spy Game.

Back to The Police Officer...
The Officer dropped the beam of his flashlight to the nasty typewriter, took a long look at the scene, sniffed the air a few

times, made a terrible face, and said, "Have fun college boy!" He turned and walked away, apparently satisfied with my story.

Digging through garbage was neither fun, nor easy, but it provided me with helpful data. Vendor proposals, advertising methods and budgets, payroll, and even detailed information relating to their financing and construction costs for the quick lube store. Then there were the adding machine tapes, ledgers, and cash invoices.

Those items answered most of my questions. However, my list of needs included a few things I was unable to acquire in the store or the trash. I needed to get inside the offices and pull a few files.

I went by the offices one evening with a flashlight, a pen, a notebook, and my trusty Polaroid camera. A former cottage style residence housed the offices. The front door was impressive and a little overdone for the building. So was the fancy lock. Moving to the back of the house, I discovered an older cheaper lock. Side windows revealed no interior bolting or hardware securing the door, other than the inexpensive lock and standard non-security hinges. *Great!*

I wrote down a description of the knob, inside and out. Unfortunately, my Polaroid wasn't able to photograph the inside mechanism. Too far away and the light levels were inadequate. The exterior photographs turned out well.

The next day I went to a locksmith. I told the old guy in the apron that I was renting a room over a garage belonging to my father's boss, and I locked my key inside the tiny apartment. I needed to get to school, and my homework was inside. Dad's boss, a single guy, living alone had already gone to work. I didn't want to break a window, so I went into the garage and requisitioned a large pipe wrench. I used it to turn the knob. I destroyed the knob but managed to open the door. I needed a new knob, but it had to look like the old knob.

He asked to look at the old knob. I quickly responded by dropping my head and saying, "I'm an idiot."

"How so?" he asked.

I told the locksmith I'd thrown away the old knob, but remembered the color and shape. I asked if he had some old knobs I could see. He laughed loudly and pointed to a Maytag washing machine box in the corner. "Enjoy. Let me know if you find a matching knob."

Peering into the box, I could see it was half-filled with doorknobs of various colors and shapes. I glanced over to the locksmith. Hunched over a workbench, I could see he was using a pair of tweezers to place little brass pins into a lock. He was hacking and coughing in between puffs on his filterless Camel cigarettes. Disgusting.

I quickly pulled the Polaroid photo of the exterior side of the Quick Lube's kitchen lock and familiarized myself with the knob. I put the picture away and began digging. After ten or fifteen minutes I found its twin. *Yay!*

While paying for the lock, I told the old man I'd return the following day to have him key the lock. I informed the locksmith that I was running late for class and darted out.

Needing some of Dad's tools, I drove to my parent's home and ducked into Dad's shop. Opening his toolbox, I found what I was seeking. A set of feeler gauges. Feeler gauges are made from flat Popsicle-stick shaped metals, of varying thicknesses. Papa used them to set the gaps on spark plugs.

Heading over to Dad's bench grinder and working from memory, I ground several of the gauges into crude lockpicks. I found a small Allen wrench and ground it down into a homemade tension wrench. I was pretty pleased with my new "burglary tools."

> ***An aside...***
> My apartment manager was nowhere to be found on a previous occasion when I needed him so I could go home. I had locked myself out of my apartment. I called a locksmith and watched him pick the lock, remove the knob, go to his van, and return with a set of keys. Pretty

> cool. I have good graphical memory and vividly recalled the approximate size and shape of his picks. He also used a tension wrench.

Back to The Lock Picks...
Ducking out, I couldn't wait to get back to my apartment. I spent the next two days learning how to pick that lock. After a while, I was pretty darn good. At first, it took me about fifteen minutes to manipulate the lock. By the morning of the second day, I could regularly open the lock in ten to fifteen seconds. Game time!

That night I returned to the Quick Lube office and picked my way into the kitchen. It took about a minute. I guess my homework paid off.

Inside for less than an hour, I managed to acquire every single piece of remaining information I'd been seeking. To the best of my knowledge, I did so; without leaving any evidence of my presence.

The trick was to use the Polaroid before touching anything and making sure it looked the same afterward. Each time I took a photo, I used a marker to number the picture. I had a master list and added each photo into the inventory while it was processing/developing (the 60 second film development time). Each time I moved on to a different filing cabinet or desk, I checked my photos against the master list. I didn't want to leave any of them behind to prove someone was there.

Once I departed, I went home and revisited each photo to make sure I didn't overlook anything. Then I burned the pictures and the master list. After that, I completed the dossier on the Quick Lube Operation.

◇ ◇ ◇

The Operation took hours of analysis, offering me a few eye-opening surprises. For example, I was successful in discovering the franchisee was cooking the books; thereby robbing the franchisor of royalties - not to mention the IRS. He was sneaky, albeit sloppy. His system had some glaring flaws that a little trash collecting uncovered very quickly.

The franchisee was purchasing about 20% of his fluids and filters with cash, and I don't believe those expenditures ever hit his books. I determined about 20% of his paid-in-cash invoices were voided and placed in the trash. I'm confident he was manipulating his numbers and disappointed in Cola for not keeping that information to myself.

Several years after my inaugural Espionage Operation I teamed up with an individual for a short time. His ethical standards were shallow - even for a Corporate Spy. One evening while we were staking out a Mark from a parked vehicle, I regrettably mentioned my first foray into Corporate Espionage, and even disclosed the location of the quick lube business. Two years later I heard of his arrest through The Spy Game grapevine. He was charged with attempting to extort money from the franchisee, using coercion (blackmail). Apparently, he approached the quick lube owner and demanded several thousand dollars to keep his mouth shut. Big mistake. The original franchisee had a gambling problem and sold the business six months after I finished spying on his business. The new owner knew nothing about cooked books and went directly to the authorities.

> ***An aside...***
> Mark, Target, and Subject are words that describe the focal point of our espionage efforts. The person, place, or thing we target for espionage activities; to misappropriate information and/or items necessary for our mission.

Back to The Blackmail Scheme...
I ran into my blackmailing non-buddy about a dozen years later. During the trial, my non-buddy discovered The Mark was not the same owner I disclosed to him. His mistake was huge, and it cost him dearly.

My mistake in that situation became a lesson learned and a personal promise it won't happen again. I never disclose enough information about any of my past activities to make it possible for anyone to join the who, what, where, when, why and how with sufficient clarity to understand my actual activities. It's a personal security measure. I've been steadfast in maintaining that personal standard. That self-imposed promise was ever-present as Steve and I planned and began working on this book. To be sure, my consistent faithfulness for historical opaqueness has been very helpful in problem avoidance for myself and others. In that, I will not deviate from that decades-old promise to myself.

Even spies need to have standards.

◇ ◇ ◇

COLA'S UNCLE FRANK

circa 1975

Thank You Uncle Frank!

You greased the wheels and gave me direction for a nascent career move. I've had a fantastic ride. Who could imagine? It all began with a phony news article and oily rags; ending in a hugely successful Operation and a rewarding career path.

Uncle Frank is long gone. He never really knew the impact he had on my life. If he were alive to read the stories in this book, he'd shake his head in amazement. Even I, Cola the Spy, remain in awe and cannot believe what grew out of a greasy lube pit so many years ago.

That Stinking Spy

Stinking Spies Are Well Paid

Cola Bought a New Car After The Sewer Job
Photo courtesy of Skookum Jim

Cola was hired on one occasion to purloin some valuable internal documents and a small circuit board from within a high-security environment. After studying my options, I decided to use the sewer system to transport the materials and circuit board from the building. I directed an Inside Man to sneak multiple sealable lunch bags into the facility daily, containing his actual lunch. He was instructed to save every bag. After a couple of weeks, we decided it was time to launch the Op.

The Inside Man had fifteen pages of sensitive information I needed to pass along to My Client. He was told to fold each sheet to the approximate size of a book of matches. Then paperclip the document and place it inside a sandwich bag, add a quarter, a nickel, and two pennies to the bag. After squeezing all the air out of the bag, he was instructed to zip it shut, then wrap it with a measured piece of duct tape. Using a thick black marker, he would write the bag number on the tape. Then using a second bag, instructions were given to follow steps similar to those for the prior plastic bag. After packaging each paper into fifteen separate bags, it was time to do the same thing with the matchbook-sized circuit board. That small device was triple wrapped.

> ***An aside...***
> It's been a few years, and my memory might be off a few cents. A few cents? Yes. Before the Operation, I instructed the Inside Man to find out the brand and any other specifics available for the copy paper used in his office. One we were informed of the brand and type of thermal copy paper used in that facility, a Colleague and I went to work. We practiced flushing single folded sheets of thermal copy paper, bound with one large paperclip, down the toilet. Too buoyant, we began adding coins to the bags. Coins were small, dense, and easily cleared security. Using pieces of duct tape, cut to precise lengths, and adding coins, we came up with the exact formula for negative buoyancy. Those ingredients offered reasonably good odds for a trouble-free transition down the sewer lines.

Back to The Sewer...
Cola's operational post was inside something called a lift station. Lift stations are positioned at lower points within sewer systems and provide for the reestablishment of gravity flow. One or more incoming pipes fill those giant vessels with sewage. Sludge pumps then lift the bacteria-laden fluids up and out of the lift station to a higher level. At that point, gravity flow continues.

The lift station we used for the Operation had dozens of pipes coming into a massive circular underground vault. The vault, a mostly empty circular concrete room, was about twenty feet in diameter and perhaps forty feet high. The lift station was meant to fill up with sewage. Once that filthy germ-laden fluid reached a certain level, the effluent would be pumped to a much higher level and into a large pipe. Once in the larger sewer line, it would be carried away to a sewage treatment facility using the system's gravity flow design.

I had borrowed a new pair of coveralls from a college friend, Willy O', who had an apartment in that community. He was a bachelor and invited me to stay with him while I was in the area. I told Willy O' I was working for a contractor, who'd won a bid to review the airport's facilities for asbestos contamination. He asked if asbestos would be a problem with his coveralls and I said no. Willy O' said, "No Problem. I hope they keep your business attire clean."

He had no idea his coveralls would be going into a sewer.

My bad. I should have told my friend I'd be using his clothing inside a live filthy sewer.

◇ ◇ ◇

Rally Time

I went into a pump room and fired up the sump pumps. That would keep the water level in the vault manageable. Putting on a pair of chest waders, a raincoat, and a rubber hat I descended through a manhole cover and lowered myself down about forty feet of metal ladder rungs built into the concrete wall. A Colleague, using a winch, lowered a container several times with tools I needed. He also winched down a tall extension ladder. He'd filled the basket with different sized plugs, designed to seal off the pipes above where I needed to retrieve the sandwich bags. I didn't want water coming out of those pipes. The thought of turds and other nasty items raining down on Cola's clean body and my buddy's freshly laundered coveralls wasn't pleasant. The piping was, for the most part, six and eight inches in diameter.

I put in about a dozen plugs and twisted a tee handle to tighten them and stop the flow of water. If you can call that nasty liquid, "water."

We knew which pipe it was because several weeks earlier he flushed dye capsules down the same toilet he would use for flushing the documents. The dye caps were meant to dissolve quickly, freeing a red dye into the water. It worked well. It left a red mess in the pipes, but not inside the toilet bowl. We certainly didn't want to stain the toilet and raise questions.

The water ran red into the lift station, and I marked the pipe it was coming from, so I would know later which pipe would transport the stolen materials. Ideally positioned for the Operation, the ductile iron tubing was about knee high; making it comfortable for me when capturing the unauthorized materials as they flowed from the sewer line.

The Inside Man was told to begin flushing items down the toilet at 5:30 PM sharp. If nobody else was in the bathroom, he was instructed to send as much water down the pipes as possible, but only after he flushed the final item. I told him to open the hot and cold faucets in every sink. While water was running in the sinks, he needed to flush every toilet and urinal at least twice, running as fast as possible from one to another. We needed to make sure the plastic bags flowed, without issue, to my location.

> ***An aside...***
> This Operation underscores the reason for synchronizing watches. Espionage Operations and Military actions rely heavily upon coordination by those involved. If the Inside Man flushed too soon and I wasn't ready, I might miss some of the documents; they'd end up at the bottom of the sludge-filled cesspool. If he sent them down the pipes too late, the plugs installed to halt the sewage raining down into the lift station, may end up with too much volume-related hydraulic pressure behind them and begin blowing out.

Back to The Operation...
Waiting until the last possible minute, I began climbing the ladder and inserting plugs into the pipes above the pipe coming from the secure facility. Once the "rain" stopped, I moved back to the marked six-inch pipe and positioned a fishing net under the foul discharge.

Checking my watch after a few minutes, I realized there must be a problem. The plastic bags weren't coming out yet, and it was 12:06 PM. Pressure was building behind the plugs, and I was going to have a serious problem if he didn't hurry. Then the first document came out.

I counted fifteen bags with white paper inside. Followed by the unexpected appearance of a tampon. Only the circuit board remained. It was now 12:12 PM. I was getting worried about the plugs losing their purchase and gallons of diarrhea soaked water pouring down on me. Thankfully, I was completely covered with rubber garments. Then the circuit board arrived. I placed the circuit board into a rubber pouch I had around my neck and sealed it in, along with all the documents.

Great!

> ***An aside...***
> I don't know how it happened, but the bags didn't all come out in order. I distinctly recall they arrived in a strange sequence. The Inside Man later swore he flushed them in order. I don't remember them all, but the first few came out eight, followed by one, then three, then five, six, two, four. Why eight came first, I'll never know.

Back to Cola, The Sewer Rat...
Yep, I was thinking "great" when a plug blew. It was directly in front of me and slammed into my chest, knocking me backward and into the knee-high sewage. I tried to scramble up but was met with an onslaught of water, smelling like fish, that ripped open the front of my raincoat. I was knocked down into the sewage once more. I discovered later that a fish processing facility was in the area. *Ugh!*

When I had fallen backward that second time, fish guts and other indescribable items went down the front of my shirt. I climbed back out of the water as other plugs began to blow. It was like being in a war zone with vile watery ammunition filling the air.

I scrambled for the ladder rungs built into the wall, leaving the extension ladder and plugs behind. I had no choice. Just as I was about to exit the circular vault, I retrieved a waterproof lantern we'd affixed to the top of the lift station. I took one last look of that giant Petri dish and watched the last plug blow.

Crawling out, I told My Colleague I was glad to be out of there. He took one look and whiff of me and immediately threw up. Another Colleague was waiting to transport the waterproof pouch to a safe house. I removed it from my neck and placed it into a similar, more substantial bag. He sealed it and quickly departed.

My Colleague and I replaced the manhole cover. He wheeled out a contraption we made for the Op that housed the winch we used to lower items down into the sewer. I placed the lift station pump back into "Auto" mode. Then I closed the door to the pump house and replaced the padlock on the door. We hopped into our van, adorned with magnetic "U.S.A. Plumbing" signage, and quickly left the scene.

Once in the van, I removed the hat, torn raincoat, and hip boots. Instructing My Colleague to throw them away, I tried to wipe the mess out of my hair, off my face, and off my clothes. My Colleague kept saying, "Geez Cola, you really stink."

◇ ◇ ◇

He dropped me three blocks from Willy O's apartment, and I darted to the building running an SDR in the process. I ran up two flights of stairs and knocked on the door and opened it about halfway. I heard him in the kitchen. Willy O' was cooking something that smelled great. He said, "Who's there?"

"It's me, Cola."

"Well come in you silly. You know you don't have to knock."

"I need to know what to do with your coveralls."

"Just toss them on the couch, Cola."

"I shouldn't. They're pretty dirty."

"Then take them down the hall and put them in the washing machine."

"I dunno. I really think you ought to take a look at them."

He muttered something about Cola always making things difficult. As Willy O' rounded the corner and stopped directly in front of me, I watched his face melt into something horrible as he stared at my right shoulder. I glanced over and saw what appeared to be poop and toilet paper smashed into the shoulder of his newly oleaginous coveralls. Then the smell hit him and he gagged.

Bending over and moving away from me as fast as possible Willy O' yelled, "Get out. Get out. Throw those things away. Throw everything away. Don't come back unless you plan on being totally naked, dry, and your destination is the shower. Now get out!"

I backed up as he slammed the door, red-faced and gagging.

I broke out laughing and decided to follow Willy O's instructions to the letter. I darted downstairs to the ground level and went straight to the dumpster. Everything I was wearing went directly into the trash. I'd been operational and only had identity free pocket litter on my person. I a few short seconds I was my birthday suit. My naked body was dry, so I immediately ran back up to my buddy's apartment. The door was locked.

He didn't lock it on purpose. Things happen.

As I stood there banging on the door a little old lady next door peeked out to see what was going on. I turned when I heard her gasp at the sight of a naked man in the hallway. Then her eyes went down, and she got a look on her face that reminded me of the waitress at the beginning of "Terminator 2" when a naked Arnold Schwarzenegger stepped into the busy redneck bar.

Willy O' and I still laugh about that night. It was on that night that I finally revealed to that trusted friend what I did for a living. However, I didn't tell him anything about the Op. I said I just needed to drop down into a sewer before returning to his apartment for reasons I couldn't divulge. I wonder what he thought I was up to that night. Regardless, he ended up with three new pairs of coveralls and a plane ticket to Hawaii for his troubles. I'm sure any thoughts he might have had previously regarding the glamorous lifestyles enjoyed by spies quickly dissipated upon seeing his coveralls covered with feces and fish.

◇ ◇ ◇

That was a massive score for the young Cola. After I calculated all my expenses, the Cola net on that disgusting job was $35,000, in 1970's dollars.

For the Record...
That was the last time I set foot into a live functioning sewer. I got very sick within a day or two of that job and credit the illness to that horrible job site. *Yuck!*

INVISIBLE PEOPLE

Most people, when asked what superpowers they'd like to have, would likely select either the ability to fly or to become invisible. Invisible? Really? Why invisibility?

Many people are already invisible; and an unhealthy percentage of corporate executives, politicians, media types, highly educated professionals, self-styled intellectuals, and the affluent make them that way. Without question, an unspoken "caste system," not unlike that found in Hindu society, exists in America, and "untouchables" are rendered invisible by those in the upper "varnas" of societal culture. Similar attitudes exist in Europe as well.

It's not unusual for wealthy, privileged, and successful people to render others invisible, especially the working class. Restaurant, hotel, office, and janitorial staff members are often invisible to the very people they serve. The elite and entitled classes ignore and diminish those for whom they harbor indifference and disdain; and belittle through their actions. Spoiled egocentrics often believe themselves better and treat others as lessors financially, mentally, spiritually, socially, and in other ways.

Espionage professionals realize attitudes, promulgated by self-indulgent individuals, are revealed through actions. We launch preliminary investigative techniques designed to expose behavioral indicators. Once confirmed as EWA's (Entitled With Attitudes), these individuals usually become operational Targets. They are considered weak. Weakness in others is currency in my world. We invest in those currencies and, more often than not, reap the benefits.

Espionage efforts are often positively influenced by arrogant individuals with self-centered vices. EWA's are consumed with self and looking inward, and they don't often see the costs associated with their behaviors until it's too late. Character flaws become my strength in garnering information and culling opportunity.

There are many valid reasons the CIA, FBI, Defense Department, and other U.S. agencies employ behavioral psychologists. The ability to coerce, deceive, manipulate, and control individuals, groups, and situations can be a powerful tool for law enforcement officials and others charged with gleaning information to help them in their missions. Likewise, we in the Corporate Espionage space have learned to understand the psychology of behaviors we observe, to assist in mission-critical planning.

In the United States, various locations like Silicon Valley, Wall Street, the corridors of political power, and Hollywood are examples of great target areas for uncovering and preying upon EWA's. Of course, our contracts don't always take us to those lush gardens populated by the self-indulgent. Fortunately for us, conceit and ego aren't exclusive to those areas. Self-centered individuals litter society. Those with that personality type believe they are uniquely special and most others are unworthy and of less value.

In my world, many people exist that are invisible to those who become Targets for my espionage activities. People whose "superpower" of invisibility can be fertile sources of information are not invisible to me. They are valued Assets which, when I'm involved with them, have far more power than they or my Targets generally realize.

The Cola Superhero List

Who are they?
The superheroes in my universe are:

- Airport Lounge Attendants
- Appliance Repairmen
- Aquarium Maintenance Workers
- Bank Clerks
- Baristas
- Bartenders
- Blackjack and Poker Dealers
- Bodyguards
- Cable Company Technicians
- Car Wash Employees
- Caterers
- Children (small young people confused for children)
- Cleaning Crews
- Copy Machine Repairmen
- Couriers
- Cruise Ship Employees
- Dog Walkers
- Electricians
- Flight Attendants
- Flooring Installers
- Florists
- Foreigners feigning poor English skills
- Gardeners and Groundskeepers
- Hairdressers
- Handicapped and Infirm
- Home Decorators
- Home Healthcare Professionals

- Home Remodelers
- Household Movers
- Housekeepers
- Interns
- Indoor Plant Service Staffers
- IT Staffers
- Janitors and other Custodial Staff
- Landscapers
- Livery drivers
- Masseuses
- Mechanics
- Miscellaneous Maintenance Staff
- Nail Technicians
- Nannies
- Nurses
- Package Delivery Personnel
- Painters
- Personal Assistants
- Personal Chefs
- Personal Shoppers
- Personal Trainers
- Pest Control Exterminators
- Physical Therapists
- Pizza Delivery Guys
- Plumbers
- Postal Employees
- Prostitutes
- Security System Installers
- Senior Citizens
- Receptionists
- Retail Store Staffers

- Secretarial Staff
- Security Guards
- Shoeshine People
- Strangers in an adjacent airline seat
- Swimming Pool Service Technicians
- Table Bussers
- Telephone Repair Personnel
- Waitstaff
- Window Covering Installers
- and many others

The elderly and handicapped are phenomenally invisible; especially in airliners and on subways. Even if not treated as invisible, they're generally not considered threatening when proprietary information is discussed or displayed. I've never seen more concentrated rudeness and indifference anywhere as I've witnessed toward the infirm in First Class airline seating. Do elitists think they are better than those people? Do they believe such a fate could never befall them because of their loftiness? Are they afraid they'll catch some kind of infirmity if they demonstrate an interest in, or compassion for, an infirm fellow traveler? Have they no empathy?

The infirm are ignored and tuned out. It's as if that seat is empty, and that makes it a golden opportunity for espionage work. The only issue is getting seated next to our Targets. Depending on the Target, our expense budget and other considerations, we might book multiple seats and bring on additional operators to garner the informational crumbs we hope the Target will drop. One trick used is to reserve multiple seats and have a second operator try to get a glance at the Target's boarding pass, to confirm his or her seat assignment. We then have our primary operator take the adjoining seat.

> ***An aside...***
> Such activities are becoming increasingly difficult, due to cultural techno-changes in contemporary America. More

> and more travelers are traveling with digital boarding passes loaded onto their smartphones.

Back to First Class Seating...
You'd be surprised how much information we glean during phone calls made on taxiways. We also collect information seen on their computer devices. Documents laying on tray tables are often gold mines of information. Legal pads filled up or reviewed while in flight can make the trip very worthwhile. Marks will often fly with associates. In those cases, we generally capture a cornucopia of data from in-flight conversations. Airtight aircraft are essentially public places offering little privacy. Executives often drop their guard in that setting; especially when the audience is invisible.

Some elitists fall under a spell of their own design when they overlook someone who has little or no grasp of their language. Others, whom they assume are unable to appreciate their language, wording, or terminology, are deemed "safe" and incapable of information gathering. My associates and I have feigned mental and physical issues on flights to give Targets the impression that we weren't smart, sophisticated, knowledgeable, or threatening. We will also dumb down our language skills to further enhance invisibility. We had one Hispanic fellow with a round flat smiling "chato" face who was inordinately useful in feigning an inability to speak or understand the English language. He grinned in mock understanding and Marks usually swallowed his act; hook, line, and sinker.

EVA, MAE, AND ELIZABETH

Cola's Favorite Senior OneSevens

I've employed more than a few extremely competent little old men and women with energy, excellent hearing, and reliable recall. They are especially helpful with the additional time available on extended flights across the continental U.S. or on overseas trips. However, on long flights I prefer using them as carriers of hidden recording devices, rather than trying to remember minor details. Women are better suited for carrying such tools because they can openly clutch an eavesdropping equipped purse close enough to a Target to overcome ambient aircraft noises. Those recordings can be very helpful because nuances in delivery are not often captured and retained by those who are trying very hard to memorize critical details. Spoken nuances, if recorded, can assist us in understanding context and intent.

There are also different levels of invisibility. Invisibility varies depending on the viewer. It depends on who the viewer is and the nature of the situation. You might think electricians are somewhat more visible than plumbers. Heck, the guy with a screwdriver working on an electrical outlet is, for many people, remarkably invisible.

Believe it or not, I've found that plumbers remain too visible to be of much investigative value. We all know the caricature of a plumber bending over with a wrench, showing the fault line between his bums. We laugh about it but don't want to see it. Then there are the germs... People generally notice and don't want to be in the same room with plumbers. In some situations that can hold value, but in most cases, I try to avoid using plumbers in situations where invisibility is essential.

> ***An aside...***
> I once knew a plumber, Rick Pepworthy. He was a new construction plumber and didn't deal with old plumbing, with germs, or crawl under cabinets filled with cleaning products. Moreover, he didn't ordinarily frequent plumbing stores used by plumbing repair professionals. His supplier sold toilets, piping, and fittings in bulk.
>
> Many years ago Rick told me a great story, and I've never forgotten his sage advice.

> One morning Rick urgently needed a plumbing part, before a building inspector arrived at the site for a final inspection. Rick ran to the nearest plumbing supply store. There were some repair plumbers in line. Off to one side was a table with donuts and coffee. As Rick stood in line waiting his turn, the plumber in front of him ducked out of line briefly to get a donut. There were many flavors; some topped with colored sprinkles. The plumber reached into the donut box with his dirty meaty hands. He picked up and put down several donuts before finding the one he wanted.
>
> When called to the counter the plumber told the clerk he needed to replace a toilet's grease ring. He said the toilet had been leaking from the bottom. He complained that the "weird old purple grease ring" was a "bugger" to pull out. Then he popped the last of the donut into his mouth with his filthy hand, then reached into his pocket. He withdrew a dirty, greasy, purple lump about the size of his thumb and asked the clerk, "Have you ever seen a grease ring that looked purple like this?"
>
> *Yikes!*
>
> Rick finished telling me the donut and grease ring story with a wise admonition, "Don't eat donuts at plumbing supply stores."
>
> That was excellent practical advice. Thanks Rick!

Back to Electricians and Plumbers...
Average people better understand the previous paragraph. Affluent and other snooty self-indulgent individuals will often harbor disdain and an arrogant indifference for both electricians and plumbers. However, in the context of Corporate Espionage, electricians have more value. Electricians are, indeed, more invisible.

Plumbing tends to appear in specific, distinct, and expected areas, while electricity is necessary and generally located throughout homes, warehouses, commercial office space, and factories. The relative omnipresence of electrical devices, wires, and appliances creates an expectation that an electrician's presence is unremarkable, if not authorized, just about anywhere. Staff members encountering an electrician in a storeroom or an executive's office would accept their presence far easier, than if they discovered a plumber in the same setting.

◇ ◇ ◇

My first real experience in understanding the manifestation of invisibility was taught to me by the wife of the Governor of a very large state. I was relatively young and spying on behalf of a local politician. The gig required my participation at a fundraiser as a guest. The Governor and his wife had just entered an enormous ballroom. I was, at that moment, working a well-known political insider on the Governor's staff. The staff member noticed them enter the room and introduced me to the Governor, followed by an introduction to the Governor's wife.

It was painfully obvious which one was the politician. The Governor looked deep into my eyes, into my very soul, and greeted me warmly. At that moment it felt as if he and I were the only people in the world. I was warmly introduced to the Governor's bride after the chief of state moved on. I immediately conferred her with the unspoken nickname, "Ice Woman." She neither directed her eyes toward me, nor did she say a word. She did put on a very plastic smile while she held out her hand, and scanned for others in the room she actually wanted to see. I certainly wasn't someone she was interested in meeting. Then without hesitation, Ice Woman moved on. She acted like royalty. Her behavior was appalling.

I briefly wondered if I should have bowed down and kissed her outstretched hand. After that fleeting thought, I realized I had a superpower. I was invisible. I wasn't an elite, a known name, or special. Cola Fugelere was merely an invisible commoner. That phony graciousness provided me with an understanding of the potential power held by people deemed subservient and classless by those in influential positions.

Others have treated me similarly, from City Council members, Mayors, State Representatives, State Senators, Governors, Members of the U.S. House, U.S. Senators, Presidential Candidates, media insiders and other power brokers. However, there have been some notable exceptions. I'm not a political person and don't really care about party politics. I do take note when a member of the political elite fails to act in a manner consistent with behavioral expectations.

The most notable exception I've ever personally witnessed was in the person of Elizabeth Dole. Dole, a former U.S. Senator, U.S. Presidential Candidate, Secretary of Labor and Secretary of Transportation under different presidents, she was also President of the American Red Cross for most of the 1990's. A person many people might consider a political elite. An insider. Mrs. Dole was a person I found congenial, authentic, deferential, sincere, and a real lady possessing manners and poise.

◇ ◇ ◇

Invisibility Tour

I can think of more than a few Venture Capitalists (VC's) in the Sand Hill area of Menlo Park, California whose "invisible people" behaviors cost them millions. My ability to consistently poach valuable information was made possible by appearing invisible and working with invisible people. My costs were meager, but the income I generated over two decades involving several VC's was phenomenal.

None of the information I'm referring to here was gathered by penetrating their inner circles, bugging their homes or phones, document thievery, or by breaking any laws. They lost millions of dollars in valuations simply because they spoke in public places, openly and without reservation.

My first Menlo Park "Invisibility Tour" was set up after I performed a cursory investigation to determine how to best collect proprietary information, about a specific startup company, from an investing Venture Capitalist. My initial and continuing impression of the VC is that he's a low key pompous ass, a braggart, and a narcissist. He didn't protect his VC jewels (insider information) and spoke openly with associates, while in restaurant settings, without measuring his words or showing concern for his audience. He fell short in his efforts to project a reserved aura when in public.

A typical meeting over a meal with this VC usually involved one to three colleagues. This VC would discuss business challenges for startups he'd invested in, their business plans, proprietary data points, revenue and expense information, staffing and scalability strategies, vendor issues, financial projections, and more. Whether he was waiting for a table, surrounded by strangers and hostesses, or seated at a table with strangers or bussers nearby, this guy spilled the beans on the companies with whom he'd invested funds. He feigned a reserved elite tone, but remained too talkative, braggadocio, and at decibels comfortably sufficient for eavesdropping.

We successfully positioned a young college-aged operative on the staff of a well known Sand Hill area restaurant, popular with tech sector movers and shakers since the 1980's. The young man had phenomenal recall and could usually recount conversations word for word. He was hired as a busboy and earned the respect of restaurant management. He worked very hard and performed well most of the time. Management usually overlooked his occasional slowness. His reputation assisted him well, during eavesdropping assignments. He seldom endured chastisement. While listening in on conversations, he would linger at adjoining tables doing menial tasks such as refilling salt and pepper shakers. He conveyed a daydreaming body language and would often stare at nothing in particular with a blank unfocused gaze. He'd become invisible to our various Targets; while earning six figures annually for his espionage efforts, over multiple years. I'm confident he understood and appreciated his superpower of invisibility. I certainly did.

◇ ◇ ◇

Over the past few decades I've mentored a couple of great operators, new to Corporate Espionage. One neophyte Spy presented me with a paper he'd written after we successfully infiltrated a large corporate gathering. In the run-up to the event, we spent a few weeks planning our approach. He based his paper upon notes taken during the investigative phase. In that paper he wrote:

"When going in hot, overdress slightly and act like you belong. It creates an advantage. Provide the impression that you belong in that particular environment. Act confident, act comfortable, act a little bored, and reek [sic] with familiarity. Unless you want to be totally invisible... In that case go in as a janitor or some other person on the Cola Superhero List. Be someone that most shirt and tie types will choose to ignore."

◇ ◇ ◇

A Uniform Approach

Corporate Espionage Tradecraft can enhance invisibility. One example is using a variety of authentic uniforms as part of competent Tradecraft. While I was still an active Spy, my personal collection included but wasn't limited to, uniforms for the following: DHL, UPS, FedEx, AT&T, WestTec Security, U.S.A. Plumbing and Heating, Fourwire Cable, Uniform Security, American Airlines, Southwest Airlines (yes, I have the shorts too), a Chef, pool service companies, moving companies, and Sparky's Electric. I also owned a nondescript white panel van. Upon which I could affix a magnetic sign appropriate to my needs. I actually possess magnetic signs for more than 100 different companies. That signage assisted me with inconspicuous access to business parks, warehouse districts, and residential neighborhoods on many occasions.

My favorite surreptitious invisibility tool, for "flying under the radar," is to assume the persona of a gas company representative. My tool chest includes a fully functional gas sniffing device, just like those used by gas company employees. The detection device often gave me carte blanche access to various properties.

My health inspector gear and accessories provided me with great opportunities in restaurants and other areas. Yes, people noticed me and paid attention to my comings and goings. However, my access into various areas was, generally, unrestricted. Not really invisible, but near unlimited access provided many opportunities to plant listening devices in places, and at times, usually unavailable to espionage operators. My successes in the health inspector persona was occasionally enhanced when I'd dispense a homemade sulfur-based aerosol that smelled much like raw sewage. People are less likely to hang around when their noses are in full rebellion.

A young man, "LCC," recently told a gathering at my home that companies are now selling products online that smell much like our aerosol. Those companies, however, don't suffer the risk exposure we did. For us, the aerosol was a serious tool. The online product currently available is a novelty item sold for practical jokes and gag gifts.

As you can see, invisibility is a useful tool. Human nature makes it possible. Personal vices and prejudices are enormous factors potentially impacting the effectiveness of invisibility. Camouflage, misdirection, fear, discomfort, and expectations also give spies tremendous leverage and create opportunities in our quest to collect information and assets that benefit our Clients.

THE CANE MUTINY

We began a remarkably successful invisibility tour in the 1980's using a plant service company as our invisible operator. The setting was Manhattan, and the Client was a wealthy technology investor.

The Mark?
Sorry, you'll have to read between the lines for any clues about the Mark.

I playfully refer to this Operation as "The Cane Mutiny" because of the perennial herbaceous plant we used to secrete our listening devices, and My Client's short-lived decision to mutiny. The plant, formally called Dieffenbachia, is more commonly known as Dumb Cane. It's a hardy indoor plant that thrives well in the shade. Manhattan's skyline offers little direct sunlight into many windowed offices, and Dieffenbachia do well in such settings. It is not uncommon to see a 5' tall Dumb Cane in an office environment. However, New York City per square foot real estate costs make 3' diameter plants an inefficient, costly, use of Manhattan office space.

Our Target company's owner was enamored with the enormous white and green leaves and had the wherewithal to ignore costs associated with floor plan squandering. The operational setting for our Target, a technology vendor, was within a shiny steel and glass skyscraper in midtown Manhattan. His 5,000 square foot office environment had more than two dozen Dieffenbachias placed throughout the facility. Those several dozen plants occupied nearly 5% of the office's floor space. Fortunately, the company enjoyed huge profits and the costs for plants, floor space, and maintenance didn't appear to burden the bottom line. The plants were maintained, under contract, by a company I jokingly refer to as the Novocaine Company. You'll see, shortly, why I dubbed it the Novocaine Company.

During our pregame investigation, I posed as a building maintenance man reviewing the work of window washers who, the day before, cleaned the windows of the targeted offices. That permitted my easy access to three high-value corner offices belonging to C Level staffers; as well as the Executive Conference Room and a few non-corner offices occupied by additional senior executives. I walked into the executive suite wearing coveralls with a "Supervisor" tag on my chest and a squeegee hanging from my belt. I nodded at the receptionist as I confidently strolled past her desk. Not a single soul paid attention to me as I ventured into each room inspecting the windows.

> ***An aside...***
> During the Cold War, the Soviet Union continually played a dangerous game as they tested the North American Defense Early Warning Line (DEW Line), as well as other U.S. and Canadian defenses. TU-95 Bear bombers continually poked, prodded, and tested our defense capabilities and response times.
>
> In fact, Russia has reinstated those practices. It is 2019, and those dangerous games continue. In 2014, during a brief ten-day window, Russian strategic nuclear bombers crossed into U.S. airspace on 16 occasions, testing our reactive capabilities.
>
> Likewise, spies find value testing the defenses and reactions of their Targets. My time in the Executive Suites that day was intended for that purpose, as well as

collecting any other information that could prove valuable.

Back to The Executive Suite...
As I entered the darkened conference room, I noticed three men viewing slides on a projection screen. The screen was affixed to the ceiling, positioned slightly forward of a whiteboard flip-chart ensemble. The men were discussing revolutionary research developments at a well-known semiconductor company. Our Mark was a vendor supporting many notable technology companies. My primary purpose for opening the closed conference room door was to evaluate their internal security protocols. I quickly realized window washing supervisor Cola Fugelere was, for all practical purposes, The Invisible Man. They scarcely glanced at me and carried on without breaking a stride. I, in turn, marched over to the window like I owned it and made some notes on a clipboard.

If they even noticed, they probably thought I was documenting the shortcomings of invisible window washers. I was, in fact, taking "TwoStep" notes regarding their discussion, as well as transcribing the revealing information projected on the screen and easily visible to me. I also noticed an empty office suite one floor up in the adjoining skyscraper.

An aside...
TwoStep is a code system I devised that was easy to teach and use, but also simplistic and easy to crack by rookie cryptologists. I came up with it as I prepared for note keeping during my college-era Espionage Operation. One of the service bay guys in the quick lube store, during that first Operation, asked about the code. I told him it was "reporter shorthand." You'll recall me telling you, on that same job while I was reviewing the Target's accounting information, a Police Officer asked me what I was doing. I was comforted with the knowledge that my legal pad contained TwoStep encrypted notes, likely undecipherable by the policeman. I was prepared to tell him they were engineering notes.

> On other occasions, I've told people I was writing computer code for a vendor who wanted projections on hot dog and soft drink sales during different types of weather at football games. I actually wrote programming for those projections while in college, except the language was Fortran, not TwoStep.
>
> More secure communications between Cola and Colleagues, before smartphones, involved something we called, "CryptoCola." It was a collaborative approach to cryptic communications designed by Skookum Jim. A Printing OneSeven, Roy, manufactured customized cards for me (see the chapter "The Arch and The Needle" to learn more about Roy).
>
> CryptoCola involved the use of a card jacket having rectangular cutouts with the ABC's on the face. Inside the jacket a sliding card was used to change up the alphabet. I used a different set of sliding cards for each Colleague. Using something called "Master Numbers" that appeared along the top of the card, we'd be able to decipher each other's coded messages. It was slow and cumbersome, but worked well in maintaining a margin of security in our communications.
>
> *Note: CryptoCola and TwoStep are detailed in the Glossary at the back of this book.*

Back to The Conference Room...
I left the building armed with three crucial data points. The research data they were discussing, an empty office with a clear view of the conference room projection screen, and the realization that every office I needed to bug had a huge Dieffenbachia in one corner. The conference room had two. Good enough. I had what I needed.

◇ ◇ ◇

When I arrived at My Client's offices to offer an update to my investigation, I presented him with the original estimate. That document provided for short-term bugging of three C-Level offices and the conference room. During our data-driven pregame recap, I handed him an entirely new proposal. It was significantly more expensive and included long-term residual income for me. The new proposal included costs for six bugged offices and two listening devices positioned in the conference room (although he wasn't made aware of those operational details). It also contained a promise for regular reporting of high-value internal information; far beyond My Client's original expectations. To that end, I provided him with a taste of what I might present going forward.

> ***An aside...***
> Visual graphical recall has always been a strong suit for me. Not only is my visual recall solid, but I also possess an ability only available to 4% of adults. As a younger person, I underwent a battery of military tests to evaluate my spatial abilities. I scored a nine, on a one to nine scale. My "spatial intelligence" was far beyond the norm.
>
> Spatial abilities are characterized by the subject's success in visualizing stationary objects from differing perspectives. The test subject observes two and three-dimensional objects. The assessment includes success in rotating, modifying, and creating images in the mind. It's similar to having a computer complete a photograph of someone's face, when large portions are missing or if seen from a profile. Visual data is extrapolated and configured to generate a hypothesis of an image from a new unseen perspective. Those spatial skills permitted me a reasonably accurate analysis of sight lines into the conference room and several other potentially important offices.

Back to The Cane Mutiny...
My spatial intelligence, combined with an excellent graphical memory, made it easy to provide the Client with reproduced slide data from my moments in the conference room and the promise that similarly valuable data would be available in the coming months. I believed I could assure him with confidence that I'd be successful in providing considerably more quality data, if a new

arrangement was acceptable to him. I thought it would be a slam dunk. It wasn't.

The Client was a portly little man who had his own way most of his silver-spooned life. Mr. Portly wanted to know how I acquired the proprietary information I presented to him, and how I could assure him that I'd have continued access to internal data. I didn't answer his questions.

One of my Cola Non-Negotiables is to never reveal methods and sources to Clients or other parties. That rule had been made abundantly clear to him from the get-go. Mr. Portly reminded me who was paying the bill. Without saying a word, I leapt to my feet with deliberate haste, gathered my belongings, departed his office, and headed for the elevator.

> ***An aside...***
> My arrival at his office was unscheduled and involved SDR's, Cola Team surveillance, and exhaustive egress planning. I was wearing a frame altering, wide shouldered, "Fat Suit" created by a OneSeven. I also used several facial appliances designed to modify my appearance. Cola's gait was slightly altered, using a one inch insert inside one of my black lace up boots. Mr. Portly didn't know I'd anticipated his demand and would only be traveling down a single floor, where I'd get off and a Cutout would get on and take the elevator to the ground floor and an awaiting vehicle. The Colleague's manner of dress, gait (same boots), and face looked similar to mine.
>
> My exit would occur through a mezzanine-level kitchen back door, down a short stairway to the alley below. A Colleague was in a vehicle nearby and ready to transport an egressing Cola a few blocks to the subway. My appearance would be much different when I exited the car and ducked into the subway station. Dental appliances would no longer inhabit my mouth and three Fat Suit inserts (shoulders and belly) would have been removed. While in the station, another Colleague and I would execute a brush pass, where I'd pass off the large

white down filled coat I'd just donned in the car. Mr. Portly remained an unknown in many ways. Caution was the watchword that afternoon.

Back to My Exit from Mr. Portly's Office...
A man's dress shoe suddenly appeared between the elevator's closing doors. They were nearly closed when the shiny black Florsheim shoe appeared at the last second, stopping the closure. As they slowly reopened, I observed my red-faced Client gasping for air. Mr. Portly quickly apologized and asked me to return to his office. I theatrically paused and stared through his eyes for a long 5 or 6 seconds, shook my head, and told him I'd prefer to work with others who appreciated my need for independence and clandestinity.

I knew all was not lost. The data I provided was a treasure trove of information Mr. Portly received for free, only a couple of days after I agreed to investigate. I wet his beak within an unbelievably short timeline. He knew if I could continue to provide additional bounty of that quality, he'd be a fool to maintain his silly demands.

Mr. Portly jumped into the elevator and hit the stop button. The alarm clanged belligerently as he pleaded with me. I agreed to give him a temporary audience if he'd shut off the noise and take me back to his office. Once in his office, I made it clear I was the alpha male, and I'd only consider working for him if he agreed to my rules and accept a new pricing model. I demanded a pen and made modifications to my proposed fee schedule.

An aside...
Some of us in the espionage arena protect ourselves with what I call "Court-Free Documentation." Court-Free Documentation includes contracts, proposals, arrangements, and agreements.

In my Dark Side universe, documents outlining my efforts on a Client's behalf are dangerous and possess the seeds of my destruction. Therefore, I intentionally left such documents extraordinarily vague and without language that might land me in either civil or criminal courtrooms. They do, however, contain provisions relating to Specific Performance. Courts commonly order Specific Performance in matters associated with confidential information. However, there are no courts involved in a Cola contract. All orders for remedies are Cola driven and outlined in Client contracts. Client's know there's neither wriggle room nor acceptable breaches under Cola contracts.

Only My Clients sign the documents, not me. I keep the only copy and never give Clients an opportunity to duplicate contracts. The docs outline schedules of payments for "Consulting" services. Venturing into that level of documentation provides me with an opportunity to "remind" Clients how much they owe me and when; as well as stated actions and expectations, and other necessary minutia. I firmly advise Clients upfront that failure to hold up their end of our arrangements would, without exception, result in costly damage to their businesses beyond anything they could imagine. The method of presentation and an overt firmness in my delivery has been nearly 100% successful in problem avoidance.

Now that I'm no longer on the Dark Side, I handle Cola contracts much differently and consistent with contractual norms.

Back to Mr. Portly...
Doubling the figures, I informed Mr. Portly there would be no negotiating. I paused and remained in character, while letting the drama play out. He neither moved, nor spoke. I realized he was waiting for me to accede to his highness and figuratively genuflect. Mr. Portly was accustomed to wielding his money and power to earn deference from others. Sorry pal. That's not Cola. After five or ten seconds I stood up abruptly. He blanched and agreed without further hesitation. At that moment it became clear I would be well-positioned to handle his vanity. Mr. Portly's unabashed priority was to obtain non-public purloined information and make investments based upon that data. His receipt of ongoing intelligence of significant value was

paramount to the sums I demanded. It was on that day I dubbed The Dumb Cane Operation "The Cane Mutiny."

One of my young protégés secured a part-time position with the Novocaine Company after convincing the proprietor he was a Dieffenbachia expert. He was given our Target's account and told by the owner of the plant maintenance company it was a critical job, and the plants needed regular care. *We were in!*

> ***An aside...***
> My expertise with Dumb Cane was limited to a real understanding of the toxicity of the plant. While I was attending college, I discovered Dieffenbachia's poisonous nature could be rather painful. One evening while visiting my parent's home with a few fraternity brothers, I used young man logic and deduced that Novocaine and Dumb Cane were probably related plant species, because the names had similarities. Using that convoluted logic, I decided to test Dumb Cane to see if it would numb my mouth if chewed. *Yes, you're correct. Dumb idea.*
>
> Novocaine is a common dental anesthetic, also known as procaine hydrochloride, it is not plant derived. Procaine is artificially synthesized and not related to the plant we call Dumb Cane. The only real relationship in this matter involved a dumb idea; and a dummy who made a dumb decision to eat Dumb Cane. I didn't stop to consider the possibility that Dieffenbachia might be dangerous to ingest.
>
> So... This young college-age intellectual took the plunge. As I began to chew the Dumb Cane leaf, I noticed a tingling in my mouth. I incorrectly believed the tingling was the initial cessation of feeling at my nerve endings. It was the beginning of the numbing process. The feeling I had began to grow and become stronger. Then even stronger, followed by intense pain. I recall telling those in the room that it felt like 1000 sewing machine needles were attacking my tongue and throat.

It was about then when my mother entered the room and saw my distress. She asked what was happening and my friends told her what I had done. She picked up the phone and called the hospital emergency room. "Mama" Fugelere told a doctor that her son had eaten a Dumb Cane leaf and she wanted to know if she should bring him in. The doctor asked, "How old is your little boy?" Mama started laughing and informed the doctor that her son was a college student. The doctor said as long as my throat wasn't closing up and restricting my breathing, it wouldn't be necessary for her to take her little boy to the hospital. He told her to keep an eye on her little boy until the symptoms dissipated.

We all got a huge laugh out of it, and I learned another in a lifelong string of valuable lessons. The laughter hasn't subsided. Family and friends continually remind me about that silly situation.

Back to The Cane Mutiny...
My electronics expert went to work. "OneSeven" spent a week in her workshop designing listening devices. We successfully deployed them in the six offices and conference room. OneSeven used well-hidden electrodynamic microphones (EDM's). EDM's were used because of their directional abilities. That particular microphone type, commonly used before modern shotgun microphones, also met mission requirements for a self-contained power source. The transmitter and power source were housed in an artificial two-part waterproof "root-ball" and hidden under the soil in the Dieffenbachia pots. The root-ball had two primary sections. We called them the "hairy testicles." The larger of the two balls was a camouflaged power source. The smaller was a voice actuated transmitter. The transmitter communicated with a receiver in the adjoining skyscraper. I'd rented the vacant office space discovered during my window washer supervisor act in the occupied conference room.

The power source could be unplugged quickly and replaced in short order. Our invisible Dieffenbachia technician periodically replaced the power source and kept working on My Client's behalf for nearly five years. As the calendar approached the fifth anniversary of the first hairy testicle installation, Mr. Portly passed away. I planned on sending my protégé in for one last trip, to remove all evidence of our clandestine activities. Changing my mind at the last minute, I came up with a better plan. A profitable plan.

I continued to mine the Target's offices for salable proprietary data over the next seven years. I'd launder and aggregate the information, making it an untraceable commodity. Over that seven-year span, five different Clients happily paid enormous sums for the info. The "Cane Mutiny" was a phenomenal score, and it all began with invisibility.

THE MONEY

The risk-reward calculus for those engaged in any endeavor should be quantified; and choices made based on what makes sense to each of us, individually. Combat jet jockeys, kickboxers, crab fishermen, Police Officers, and others pursuing high-risk careers balance their needs and desires against the hazards of their occupations. Those of us who've worked full-time in Corporate Espionage know the dangers of risking our freedom, health, and personal relationships in this arena.

Here's a perspective to assist you in understanding why espionage occurs in big business. I'll use pharmaceutical manufacturers and pharmaceutical distribution channel companies that occupy the Fortune 500 as examples. In 2016 there were eleven manufacturers and seven drug channel companies on the list. Average revenues for the manufacturers exceeded $26 billion. Average 2016 revenues for the distribution channel companies reached $115 billion. Total revenues for Fortune 500 companies who manufactured and distributed pharmaceuticals in 2016 exceeded one trillion dollars ($1,093,200,000,000.00).

Fortune magazine reported the world's 500 largest companies generated a whopping $27.6 trillion in revenues and $1.5 trillion in profits in 2015. With these kinds of numbers involved, you can understand why greed, graft, and corruption occur at the highest levels. At the core of the matter, Corporate Espionage is driven by dollars; guided by people willing to spend tremendous sums to garner power, advantage, and financial opportunity.

I'm sure the sums involved assist you in understanding the attraction for talented, resourceful, individuals into the murky world of Corporate Espionage. Others are drawn in for vengeance. There are various reasons, but none as compelling as money.

On the other hand, I've known more than a few who are not unlike daredevils. They were adrenaline junkies who merely spied for the rush. Most, however, are purely mercenary. While I don't care for the term mercenary because of the negatives associated with the word, it very well conveys the fact that my espionage activities were money-centric. Yes, the exciting rush of my Uncle Frank's original quick lube project led me to my next job. Over time my penchant for living comfortably dominated any need to experience adrenaline rushes.

◇ ◇ ◇

You Have No Idea

Few individuals fully appreciate the scale and seriousness of Corporate Espionage. Some companies have more exposure than others and work hard to mitigate costs associated with the loss of their intellectual property and other assets. However, most companies fail to recognize the breadth and depth of their exposure and fall short in protecting their interests.

Apple, Inc., formerly Apple Computer, is perhaps the best-known example of continual targeting by spies intent on garnering every available tidbit of information to assist in revealing product and service development efforts, product availability data, and corporate strategies. Initiate a Google search for iPhone + "release date" (in quotes), and you'll discover the phenomenal interest in Apple's plans. The results will bury you with more than seventy million links relating to leaked data, product features, designs, and vendor issues, presented in the context of product release dates. Apple operates under extremely competent security protocols, but wolves remain at the door seeking every informational tidbit, especially unreleased product information, as well as smuggled parts associated with forthcoming product launches. The wolves continually, and often openly, solicit staffers who may be willing to disclose proprietary information.

Corporate Espionage is big business and most businesses, large and small, are not adequately equipped to combat the problem. When business leaders finally get around to protecting their proprietary intellectual property, they are generally engaged in reactive problem solving, rather than taking proactive measures to avoid falling prey to Corporate Espionage. Unfortunately, in most cases, companies that have fallen victim to corporate spying have no idea they've been victimized and, therefore, have trouble understanding and quantifying costs associated with such thefts.

◇ ◇ ◇

Apple's Gordian Knot

Apple's proprietary information represents dollars and other opportunities for those benefiting from such disclosures; to include journalists, websites, bloggers, analysts, competitors, vendors, and investors. Closely held information, once released, can generate generous profits for those in the know. Many resources, involving an untold number of corporate spies, are fully invested in uncovering as much about Apple's plans and products as possible.

Severe ongoing espionage efforts have become a continual Gordian challenge for Apple as corporate leaders work diligently to protect company assets, secrets, and future. Apple's unfortunate experiences in this area have assisted them in learning and iterating improvements to their internal systems. Apple's success in discovering leakers hasn't kept others from leaking. Apple's internal intelligence experts catch most leakers. Not expecting discovery, leakers often profess surprise when cornered. Arrogance and denial are traits one can associate with Apple's leakers.

Apple is a great company working hard to protect her intellectual property from a hoard of parasites. Given my experience from the Dark Side of Corporate Espionage, I can honestly say that Apple deserves tremendous kudos for their efforts to counter espionage-related attacks on the company.

Apple is not alone. Spies are everywhere and often remain undiscovered. Corporate spying is a worldwide problem.

◇ ◇ ◇

Spies are often staff members engaged in internal espionage activities working against their employers. Corporate Espionage is also driven externally by individuals, groups, and companies who gather reams of data without co-opting company employees. On the other hand, working with allies within corporations is generally the most damaging and pervasive method for achieving espionage goals. *Remember HUMINT?*

Corporate Espionage can appear to be benign. Occasionally intensively destructive and noticeable, it is most often nuanced and subtle. Its apparent benign nature results in the costs being difficult, if not impossible, to measure. Spying creates unnecessary and unexplained expenses for businesses everywhere. Few managers recognize espionage for what it is and the dangers it harbors. Espionage influences revenues and profitability, and will occasionally bring an enterprise to its financial knees. Leaders who understand the risks and costs are better prepared to address and combat Corporate Espionage. If not adequately contained, a company's productivity, research programs, market advantage, staff, share value, and corporate viability will diminish or disappear altogether.

The events reflected in this book served me very well. They underscore the potential profitability for those engaged in Corporate Espionage.

THE STING

In this particular instance, my risks were minimal, but the upside payday has been phenomenal. I continue to receive an annual income several decades after this particular engagement. Therefore, I must tread very carefully to avoid compromising my benefactor or my residual income from that job. I'm sure you understand.

I was contacted by an erstwhile Client, Tom Minsky, to secure the rights to a commercially viable household product developed by a retired chemistry professor in the retiree's kitchen. Five years earlier at Tom's direction, I successfully documented and publicly exposed the character flaws of a microbiologist who held a sensitive position at a large international pharmaceutical company. My efforts revealed illegal acts he'd been secretly conducting on company time. The goal was to have the microbiologist terminated and rendered untouchable within his industry. The details aren't necessary for this story, but suffice it to say the microbiologist became so unemployable My Client's small product development company was the man's only real option for short-term employment. Tom treated him well, and the man remained on Tom's staff for several decades.

My prior success on Tom's behalf made him a believer in my services. When he decided he must have The Professor's product,

Tom called on me. I was between jobs and quickly responded to Tom's call for assistance.

Tom's company was small and marginally profitable. He'd seen a demonstration of the household product created by the elderly Professor. Tom wanted the rights badly and believed the potential profits would be astronomical. The formula remained without a patent, because of the costs and time involved in securing patent protections. The Professor knew his remaining life was too short to consider personally patenting the product. He decided instead to show it to My Client. He only wanted My Client's advice on how to approach a local company that might have interest in the formula. It was one of the largest chemical and consumer product companies in the free world. Tom advised him, with all due honesty, that securing an appointment could be very difficult.

Tom reached out to the big corporation's Product Development Manager and said The Professor was seeking an audience with the CEO to demonstrate the product. The Product Development Manager granted The Professor an appointment with him and the CEO for the following month.

In the meantime, Tom realized the potential profits for the product was worth him taking some financial risks. He approached The Professor and offered to buy it himself. The elderly gentleman's heart was set on keeping the appointment and selling the product to the larger company. If the big company wouldn't agree to The Professor's terms and conditions, the retired educator promised Tom he could purchase full rights to the formula; at the same price points he'd reveal to the big company at the scheduled presentation.

Tom believed the large company would not hesitate to pay handsomely for The Professor's invention. He realized his only opportunity to purchase the product would require my involvement. Fortunately for Tom, I was available, and the challenge fit my style and interests.

After Tom shared the details of the problem, I went to work. First I looked into the viability of the product and, I too, realized Tom was going to become wealthy beyond his dreams if I successfully pulled off the assignment. I then considered how I'd solve the matter and calculated my costs.

Armed with the knowledge that this deal could mean a lot to me, I negotiated a handsome "consulting" agreement with Tom. The actual espionage work wouldn't cost Tom a dime. My only charges would be an annual annuity if Tom began selling the product. The numbers would scale with his revenues and, if the product sold well, I'd receive a very healthy annual income. Starting in year eleven, Tom's yearly payment to me would be an average of year's eight, nine, and ten. That particular part of the contract was a boon for me. During year seven, Tom sold the rights to the same big company The Professor initially targeted. Tom's sales agreement included language for residual payments to a shell company I control, for "consulting fees." Annual payments to both Tom and me would continue for a few more decades. Tom protected Cola well in the sale of the product rights.

The new owner aggressively marketed the product over the next three years, resulting in a very impressive three-year average. My annualized income from the consulting agreement remained frozen at that annual average. It has remained substantial and consistent for many years. When it was all said and done, Tom and I did exceptionally well; thanks to The Professor and some tremendous acting by a couple of unwitting thespians.

◊ ◊ ◊

My investigation revealed the big company's CEO was a no-nonsense manager. His team was fully expected to be 100% professional and never waste his time. The company's Product Development Manager reputedly screwed up royally just before I began my management review. The Product Development Manager was on thin ice with the CEO and feared for his job. It was apparent his fears could work to my advantage.

I also discovered the old Professor had an identical twin brother, Edward. Ed was an alcoholic and needed money badly. A background check on Ed revealed he had a long history performing on stage, mostly in dinner theater settings. That gave me an idea. It turned out to be a most valuable confluence of events and persons.

   No Nonsense Managers
+ A Scheduled Product Acquisition Review Meeting
+ The Hungry Twin Brother of a Retired Professor
= Opportunity for Cola.

◇ ◇ ◇

We quickly recruited Ed to destroy his brother's chances with the big company, although Ed did not know that part of the scheme. We told Ed a substantial Hollywood opportunity existed if he successfully passed a field audition. Ed understood his job was to convince a woman he was off his rocker. We told Ed the woman was a psychiatrist who professed she was 100% successful in spotting swindlers that wanted others to believe they were nuts when they weren't. His job was to see if his acting abilities were sufficient to outwit the woman we referred to as "Kate." We wanted Ed to be focused and entirely believable.

The woman was a London-based actress, Grace, I recruited to "pretend to believe an old lonely man" who had just won the "Date with Kate" contest. She was promised a huge bonus if she remained in character throughout her act and to return to London immediately after the performance on a flight I booked for her. Grace was told to eat up everything the old man said and never once show any disagreement or question the veracity of his statements.

We drafted a script and told Ed to follow it to the letter if he wanted the chance to be in the film for which he was auditioning. He was directed to be in character from the moment the car service arrived at his residence, until after he was back home. We reminded Ed he was being tested for his acting skills, as well as his ability to follow instructions.

The setting was a small quiet restaurant that was, at one time, a residence. It was quaint and unassuming. The decor was "down home," and the house specialty was fried chicken, sweet corn, mashed potatoes, and gravy. The dining room was tiny and only seated about 20 people in two and four-toppers. The big company's Product Development Manager, a single man, reportedly dined there alone every Wednesday evening after church. His usual arrival time was 7:30 PM. We also discovered Wednesday's were languid evenings for the restaurant. Perfect. We wanted the small room to be as quiet as possible so our "dinner theater" performance would be overheard and witnessed by everyone in the room; especially The Product Development Manager.

I arrived about 7:20 and took a seat along the wall in a two-topper. On queue, The Product Development Manager appeared at 7:30 on the dot. He was seated directly across the room from me. He wasn't alone. Another man was joining him for dinner. That was a problem. What if they were engaged in conversation and failed to overhear our actors at work? We discovered several days later that the second man was his subordinate at the big company. Fortunately for Tom and me, their conversation was light and intermittent. Terrific! They overheard more than I expected.

Neither man knew what The Professor looked like, but it didn't matter. They only needed to see the twin brother and witness his act. The twins were very tall and lean. Their appearance was unusual, unflattering, and very memorable. The Professor's colleagues described him as an Ichabod Crane look-alike. His nickname, behind his back, was Professor Icky. The Product Development Manager and his associate would meet the real Professor the following week at the product acquisition appointment. They would believe the man in the down-home restaurant, and The Professor who arrived at the scheduled meeting were one in the same. It would be an evening they'd probably never forget.

The car service picked up actor Ed as scheduled, followed by Grace at her upscale hotel. They arrived at the restaurant on time, precisely 5 minutes after the product development management team entered the cramped dining room. Ed and Grace were seated in the center of the small room at a table for four; just five feet from The Product Development Manager. *Perfect!* From my vantage point, I could easily see Ed and Grace, as well as the two employees of the big company. All the players were visible to me, in the same view, at precisely the same time. Positioned in a line across the room, I was beyond satisfied.

Ed and Grace were face to face and at a profile to me. Directly between them, I could see The Product Development Manager and the back of his dinner companion. His view was directed toward me and between the two actors.

◊ ◊ ◊

GAME ON

Lights Camera Action
Ed and Grace began with the usual pleasantries. Ed had been directed to get "Kate" to tell a little about herself before launching into his script. At the same moment the conversation turned to Ed, fried chicken dinners arrived at the table of the two managers.

Hunched over the red and white checkered tablecloth, Icky's twin brother knew a successful audition totally depended on his performance over the next half hour. During his final pre-performance session he was told that one or more patrons in the restaurant would be assessing his acting skills; and "Kate" would report his success, or lack thereof, in convincing her of his insanity.

Ed began telling Grace about his job as a cryptozoologist. He explained that cryptozoology is the study of any species for which there is no conclusive evidence of their existence. He informed Grace his career included excitement and adventures spanning every continent. Grace asked him to share notable highlights of his life's work. Believing Grace to be engaged in a psychiatric assessment, Ed gave a very believable performance, telling unbelievable stories. He followed the script to the letter.

◊ ◊ ◊

The first adventure he shared with Grace was a tale of his departure from the Anchorage International Airport in the late 1960's, bound for Prudhoe Bay on the oil-rich north slope of Alaska. He said the venerable propeller-driven Douglas DC-3 departed Anchorage and flew a northerly route toward the Arctic Ocean. Not long after they'd crossed the Arctic Circle and were flying above the Brooks Range, the sturdy DC-3 entered a region of severe turbulence. It fought its way through rough weather as the clouds closed in. Ed told Grace he was terrified and feared a wing would come off the plane as it bounced violently through the frigid Alaskan sky.

His fears about a wing coming off were designed to capture The Product Development Manager's attention. It worked perfectly.

The Product Development Manager stopped chewing his fried chicken and looked directly at Ed. The reference to a wing coming off hit pretty close to home. The Product Development Manager had recently witnessed an actual aircraft accident involving the loss of a wing; that's precisely why we included a reference to an aircraft losing its wing in Ed's script. We wanted The Product Development Manager's undivided attention, and now we had it.

◇ ◇ ◇

The Product Development Manager had been driving from Lockerbie Square in downtown Indianapolis to the Bent's Camp Resort, located on the Cisco Chain of Lakes near Land O' Lakes, Wisconsin. He was traveling to Wisconsin's Northwoods to enjoy a 4th of July fishing trip getaway. He told friends a dark and gloomy shadow descended onto his soul after he witnessed an aircraft lose its wing and plummet to the ground in New Berlin, Wisconsin. A family of five died in the accident.

An aside...
By coincidence, I ran a quick Op near Land O' Lakes a few years later. Bent's Camp Resort, was the setting for multiple Cola Team meals while running that Operation. Resting on the shores of the Cisco Chain of Lakes, that restaurant's kitchen dishes up some of the best-prepared

> Walleye meals I've ever tasted. The saloon and dining rooms, populated by equally awesome staff and customers, are extremely pleasant. Great meals, in a great setting, with a great view, and a grand history. After that Op, I returned on multiple occasions to vacation in and around Land O' Lakes. Winter and summer. Snowmobiling and fishing. Centered around Bent's Camp Resort, it couldn't have been a better vacation spot.
>
> Consider this rare Cola recommendation. If you're ever in the area, the Cola Team and I highly recommend Bent's, a remarkable Northwoods gem.

Back to The Professor...
In retrospect I believe it was an excellent decision to sprinkle an actual event involving The Product Development Manager into the script. I personally witnessed the power it held in garnering his interest. The devastating accident a year earlier appeared to haunt The Product Development Manager. Ed's story was utterly implausible, but I believed the wing angle was critically necessary for The Sting's success. It made the story both interesting and personal for The Product Development Manager.

Ed described his feelings as the aircraft jerked violently, and careened up and down, above the one hundred fifty mile wide mountain range. Then, without warning, the turbulence dissipated. The clouds parted above the DC-3, revealing a bright blue sky. Looking down, Ed saw a lush tropical rain forest filled with lush green vegetation and enormous dinosaurs.

At that point, I was surprised to see The Product Development Manager blow a mouthful of corn and mashed potatoes across the table. His face turned red and his eyes teared up, as he fought to suppress laughter. I heard later that his reaction was not about the dinosaur comment, but at the unmitigated acceptance of the story by Grace.

Ed told Grace they flew around the beautiful valley until fuel became an issue, then departed for their destination. He said they refueled and returned, but were unsuccessful in their efforts to locate the previously discovered hole in the storm clouds. He said his greatest disappointment was forgetting to pack his camera.

Then, without pause, Ed began telling Grace about a day hike to a mountaintop he and a colleague took in southeast Alaska the following year. The two men were hiking on a high ridge line when they encountered a one-eyed Sasquatch. A Bigfoot. Ed had a rifle for bear protection, but no camera. Ed told Grace he almost shot the one-eyed beast, but his friend implored him to hold off. The friend told Ed to look at the furry animal closely. "It looks almost human, Ed. If you kill it, you could be charged with murder."

Ed disagreed. He believed it was an animal and looked like an animal. According to Ed, he realized he had another dilemma. If it was an animal, Ed didn't have a hunting license and killing it would have been against the law. The charges? Hunting and taking big game without a proper permit or license. They decided to run down the mountain to their camp and return with a camera. When they returned to photograph the elusive animal, it was gone.

I looked at The Product Development Manager. He appeared to be choking on his dinner. He wasn't. The poor guy was just trying very hard to maintain a straight face and keep from bursting out laughing. I turned my attention to the actress. She remained very much in character; composed with a seriously interested demeanor. She appeared to be believing Ed and showed nothing to the contrary.

Ed's next story was about an unusual encounter he had on the banks of the Amazon River. He was resting on the river's edge and eating lunch. All of a sudden a giant sea creature emerged from the water and landed on the shore next to him. It took Ed a moment to recognize the beast. It was a living mermaid. Tail and all. Ed shared that his initial shock was replaced by astonishment when the mermaid introduced herself to him.

At that point, The Product Development Manager was shaking like a massive bowl of jello. His face was cherry red, and water was pouring out of his eyes, down his face, and dripping onto his fried chicken. At that point I, too, was doing everything possible to avoid bursting out laughing. The Product Development Manager glanced my way, saw my dilemma, and lost it. He was laughing out loud and uncontrollably. To my surprise, neither Ed nor Grace appeared to notice the spectacle unfolding around them. The other man had turned around. His face was frozen. He was eyeing Grace's stoic face with total incredulity. The Product Development Manager's companion appeared to be in shock. His mouth was agape and frozen in place. Nonplussed, Ed continued spinning his yarn without missing a beat.

Speaking English, the mermaid told Ed her family lived in the Amazon. She said she wasn't permitted to engage with humans, but she'd been watching him and found him to be both interesting and non-threatening. She enjoyed one of Ed's cookies, then told him she needed to return to the water. Her skin and scales were drying out.

Reaching for his camera, Ed realized he'd left it back at his tent. He wanted a photo with the mermaid and needed her to come again after he'd collected his photographic equipment.

Ed then asked the mermaid if she'd be able to return for another visit. She indicated she'd like that and hoped to do so the following day. She returned to the river and waved goodbye. Then she was gone.

Ed returned the following day, and each day for eight consecutive days. The mermaid never returned, and Ed was unable to secure photographic evidence of her existence.

There was a final story told by Ed that escapes me. As Ed began telling the story, I pretended to "accidentally" knock my coffee cup to the floor. That was Grace's cue to feign a migraine headache and asked to go home to her hotel. The couple departed a few minutes later.

I'd planned on departing immediately after Ed and Grace left. However, before I could sneak out, The Product Development Manager came over and yucked it up with me. While at my table, he gave me the opportunity to plant an important seed.

The manager asked me, "By any chance, do you know that guy?"

I told him I was a representative for a chemical vendor serving the University of *** and knew the man from there before he retired. I said I recalled fellow staff members referring to him as Professor Icky or Professor Yucky, or something similar. I then glanced at my watch and exclaimed, "Oh no. Sorry, I didn't realize the time. I must go." I hustled out of there quickly; disappointed I became part of the conversation that night, but happy to have planted a seed.

◇ ◇ ◇

The Appointment

Not comfortable going to meet with the corporate guys alone, The Professor invited Tom to join him for the appointment. They arrived shortly before the appointed time. An aide to The Product Development Manager escorted them to a glass-walled conference room. They enjoyed complimentary coffee while awaiting the CEO's arrival.

The Product Development Manager entered the room for the planned meeting and froze in his tracks. Sitting before him was the nut who spoke with mermaids, saw dinosaurs, and ran into a Sasquatch. Tom said The Product Development Manager was stunned. He blanched. According to Tom the man no longer had the face of the man I witnessed laughing and spitting food across a restaurant table only a few days earlier. His eyes were wide and staring straight at The Professor.

At the same time a man in a white shirt, tie, and plastic pocket protector ventured by the glass-walled conference room and glanced in as he passed. Stopping abruptly, the passerby turned and entered the room. He exclaimed, "Professor Icky! It's so good to see you. How's retirement?" The two men exchanged a few pleasantries. Moments later the man departed the room.

The Product Development Manager regained his composure. Tom said he appeared to be engaged in deductive reasoning, calculating his options. According to Tom, all of a sudden the man's face changed. He seemed to have made up his mind about something. A look of determination spread across his face, and he quickly excused himself. Tom watched him dash down the hall and stop the CEO, as the big company's leader entered the corridor. Tom said The Product Development Manager's animated body language reflected fear and anxiety. Perfect. We knew he was in the CEO's doghouse and would be fearing for his job if the CEO realized The Product Development Manager scheduled a meeting for him with a nutty Professor. Tom was acquainted with the CEO and appeared relieved when the executive turned about and disappeared into the office from whence he came.

The Professor turned to Tom and complained about the young man who entered the conference room and called him Professor Icky. The Professor told Tom the man was a former student. However, The Professor couldn't remember him. He said students and staff referred to him as Ichabod Crane and Professor Icky behind his back and on occasion, a new student would slip and call him Professor Icky to his face. The Professor told Tom he detested the nickname but decided it was better to ignore the sleight, rather than give it an audience.

The Product Development Manager reentered the room and directed his attention to The Professor. He said something came up and the CEO wouldn't be attending the meeting. He also apologized and said he'd only be available to give The Professor a brief three minutes to describe the product.

Taken aback, The Professor stammered. He'd been prepared to take 20 to 30 minutes for the presentation. He lost his composure and, according to Tom, was pitiful in his attempt to woo The Product Development Manager with information about the benefits of his formula. The meeting ended. Then The Product Development Manager shocked both Tom and The Professor with a curt, "We're not interested in your concoction. Please don't bother us again."

Tom was victorious. So much so, the product has always enjoyed association with Tom and his company. The Professor was never part of the public narrative involving the product. Sad in a way, but Tom made up for his duplicitous actions by paying The Professor ten percent more for the product's rights than the old guy wanted from the big company.

Unfortunately, The Professor's life was cut short about five years after that meeting when he suffered a major stroke. Tom's payments to the old man did, however, offer him the opportunity to travel in style and see the world before his death. The retired Professor was fond of cruises. According to others close to The Professor, cruising the seas of the world became his passion and joy.

◇ ◇ ◇

Little Touches

Readers might wonder if the hilarious scripted events at the tiny restaurant encompassed the entire scheme. It didn't. There were many small moves conceived to provide cover and insurance for our efforts. One move involved the former student that entered the conference room and said hello to "Professor Icky." That man was never a pupil of The Professor. He attended chemistry classes at the university shortly after The Professor retired. He was coached to drop in while The Product Development Manager was in the room, and say hello to The Professor. The man, a husband and father, gladly agreed to the strange request after an associate of mine presented two photos to him. One picture showed the man with a wrinkled marijuana cigarette between his fingers and kissing a young man; while sitting on a beach, bathed in the amber light of the setting sun. It appeared the other photograph represented a vantage from outside, into the man's home. In that picture, the man was nearly naked; wearing only a red bra, black pantyhose, and red high heeled shoes. *The poor soul didn't know we would never use the photos against him. Not our style.*

We had several other options in play that ultimately proved too dull for this manuscript or proved unnecessary to carry out the job successfully. For example, I cannot believe Readers care how we managed to convince The Professor to invite Tom to join him for the appointment. Most successful espionage jobs and cons require a full complement of simultaneous moves, alternatives and backup plans. This was play no different. It would be neither prudent nor interesting, to cover the many little touches necessary for successful espionage activities.

Finally, the events as I've described them took place after Richard Nixon was president and before Bill Clinton left office. Security needs compel me to avoid nailing it down any closer than that. I can, however, say the product continues to sell well and often maintains a valued eye-level position in most grocery store environments. Tom sold the product rights many years ago but continues to reap financial benefit from that sale. I, too, receive an annual stipend; as well as a yearly "Thank You!" card from a grateful Tom.

WALLY

Neophytes Err

The success of my initial foray into Corporate Espionage notwithstanding, espionage is fraught with incredible hurdles, phenomenal risk, and countless failures; especially for clueless abecedarian spies having little understanding of, or experience in, The Spy Game.

Let me introduce feckless Wally. His short-lived venture into my cloak and dagger world was both pitiful and comical. Wally's bumbling was on par with Lou Costello's, but unlike Abbott and Costello, Wally's career never really developed. His espionage skills were more closely related to Maxwell Smart's or Inspector Clouseau's, rather than Jason Bourne's or James Bond's.

Wally was an intelligent, geeky, introvert who over-analyzed every situation and executed his activities with little personality, wit, or common sense. Wally was a short, scrawny, balding, bespectacled man who would never be confused for the stereotypical Spy. At 5'1" and 88 pounds dripping wet, Wally also sported a very long greasy comb-over beginning with a part at the top of his right ear. Wally's dome looked like a picket fence that had blown over. The top of his head was very unattractive and extremely noticeable. Don Rickles' hairdo looked normal by comparison. Memorable Wally stood out in a crowd. Not useful in the espionage field.

Longevity in the espionage arena requires a practical, level-headed, ability to think on your feet quickly, blend into the environment, pivot and discard all prior planning with little notice or expectation, and act instinctively to salvage deteriorating situations. Wally was inept in all those areas, and that's where the fun began.

◇ ◇ ◇

In 1975 the Securities and Exchange Commission (SEC) established rules abolishing fixed commissions. A new era of trading began at that point because some firms started allowing their customers to trade stocks at discounted commission rates. That rule change was the genesis for "Day Traders."

Paul, Wally's best friend and fellow computer nerd, inherited a few hundred thousand when his parents passed away in an aircraft accident. He invested his inheritance in the market and was frustrated by uncontrollable market forces and disillusioned with his portfolio's performance. According to my source, Paul and Wally hatched a scheme to leverage Paul's investments by focusing on a single company and, effectively, trade stocks with insider knowledge. They aligned themselves with two men who had reputations in political circles for engaging in dirty tricks.

◇ ◇ ◇

Here's the story I heard years later, from someone closely associated with Wally's interviews with law enforcement.

Wally and his nerdy friend Paul researched companies that appeared well-positioned for acquisition by larger entities. Once a target company was deemed likely to be acquired in the short term, for significant dollars, the conspirators began efforts to uncover which companies might be expected to acquire the subordinate entity. They narrowed the list to three companies.

The dirty tricksters were responsible for disrupting operations at two of the three companies. I know little about their activities, but understand they focused on hurting cash flow, revenues, and the reputations of the two larger companies. Those entities were much more substantial and financially stronger than the third. The goal was to make an acquisition less likely for either of the larger companies. The plan was to cause many problems. If timed correctly, it would be so late in the game, few individuals outside those companies would know the big companies were out of the running. Moreover, the two larger companies would have sufficient time for proper damage control.

Paul and Wally believed the valuation of those two entities would be less likely to surge as high as the third, their "Target" company, during a potential corporate acquisition. They briefly considered selling the two companies short on the stock market, but weren't comfortable taking the financial risks; since the two dirty tricksters were managing that side of the operation.

Wally managed the acquisition of inside information from the Target company. Geeky Paul would focus on research, watch the markets, oversee the disruption efforts, keep an eye on the company about to be acquired, and provide support for Wally during his insider play. Paul would also control the timeline for his planned investments in both the acquiring company and the entity about to be acquired.

The conspirators believed the blueprint for their success hinged upon gaining access to acquisition-related documents from the target company's CEO. I'll refer to him as "Philip." That was believed by them to be the best way to confirm if and when an acquisition would likely occur.

The entire scheme was half-baked from its inception. They failed to adequately consider the impact of their efforts on market forces and stock valuations. They also underestimated their visibility as investors. Worse yet, Wally was an utterly clueless operator. Inept and comical, Wally would ruin any chance the conspirators had for success.

Investor insiders engaged in intense speculation about which company would make the acquisition. Smart investors, not knowing the conspirators' plans, speculated the winning company would be one of the two companies about to be hammered by the dirty tricksters. Market insiders were paying little attention to the company that Wally's team believed would eventually make the acquisition - with a little help from Paul and his buddies. That company was all but invisible in the pre-announcement hullabaloo. The CEO's of the two larger companies were being courted for information by business reporters and investors. The third CEO, Philip, was engaged in a series of unannounced trips across the continental United States before the highly anticipated acquisition announcement. Philip was largely ignored by the media.

◊ ◊ ◊

Wally subverted Philip's travel company with a series of bribes. He successfully garnered information relating to Philip's upcoming flight schedules, accommodations, car services, and restaurant reservations. Wally keyed on Philip's proclivity for securing the largest hotel suite in every hotel where he'd be staying during his pre-announcement travels. Wally also received what he believed would be a very helpful tidbit.

The travel agent told Wally about Philip's disdain for flying, in what the CEO described as, "Flying Petri Dishes;" a reference to the medium used for growing bacteria in laboratories. The agent also shared that Philip traveled in sweats and slip-on deck shoes. That ensemble offered Philip easy transit through security and a comfortable flight. Philip told the agent he couldn't wait to get from an airport to his hotel to "clean up." The CEO referred to his soiled sweats as "Petri Pajamas." He shared that his first action each time he entered a hotel room, after a flight, was to remove his clothing and shoes; then place them into a plastic bag. Philip's second act was to get into the shower and wash away "airline germs."

◊ ◊ ◊

Game Time

On game day, Wally arrived at Philip's hotel 14 hours before the CEO's flight was scheduled to touch down. Wally knew where the largest suite was located and casually walked down the hall every 15 minutes until he discovered the maid servicing the room. Wally then continued up and down the hallway until the maid completed most of her tasks. She had finished working in the bathroom and moved across the suite to adjust the thermostat. Her back was to the door. Wally quickly entered the room. He ducked into the bathroom and hid behind the shower curtain.

Wally planned to hide in the bathtub until the maid departed. Then he was going to disassemble the lock on the door, rig the mechanism so he could quickly open the door from the exterior, and reassemble the device. He then intended to leave the room until shortly after the CEO checked into the room. Once the CEO was in the shower, Wally planned on entering the room very quickly to steal the man's briefcase and laptop computer.

Unbeknownst to Wally, the maid depleted her shampoo inventory before making up the suite. She walked to the end of the hall for additional containers of shampoo and conditioner. Once she resupplied her stock, she positioned the service cart in front of the adjoining suite. Picking up bottles of shampoo and conditioner, she returned to the room in which Wally was hiding. She had only been gone about 2 minutes. She reentered the suite, went into the large bathroom, and walked to the shower area.

When she pulled back the shower curtain, the housekeeper screamed at the top of her lungs. She was shocked at the sight of the little man crouching in the bathtub. Wally is said to have screamed as well. The maid claimed he yelled, "You're done here. Why are you back? You weren't supposed to find me!"

Wally bolted from the room, took a left turn, and ran squarely into the housekeeping cart. The impact sent tiny bars of soap, the little bottles of shampoo, linens, and cleaning equipment all over the hallway. Wally's eyeglasses went flying as well. The maid ran down the hall in the opposite direction. Witnesses said she screamed all the way down the hall. Those witnesses said Wally was sprawled out on the floor and appeared unconscious. Then he slowly got to his feet, shook his head, and collected his spectacles. Once Wally had his wits about him, the little man sprinted down the corridor to the emergency exit door. Wally later told investigators that he was skipping two or three stairs at a time as he descended the dark stairwell. Wally departed the hotel in a frenzy. His mad dash to escape was successful.

◇ ◇ ◇

Wally didn't give up. The conspirators needed the laptop and briefcase for their plans to succeed. Wally knew Philip's next destination. He immediately secured a flight there for another attempt to get into a room ahead of Philip, and modify the lock mechanism for easy entry.

Wally repeated the room surveillance process and ducked in as the maid was finishing up the bathroom. Wally learned his lesson after being caught in the bathtub. He decided a closet was just as dangerous. As he surveilled the room, he noticed an oversized easy-chair positioned at the far side of the suite, angled into the corner.

As I indicated earlier, Wally wasn't a large man. His new plan was to dart into the room and hide behind the large chair. He told investigators the area on the backside of the chair was comfortably spacious. Wally knew it would provide excellent concealment.

As the maid was cleaning the toilet, Wally removed his shoes and quietly made his way into the room and over to the chair. His plan succeeded and the maid didn't discover him. However, hotel security thwarted his plans shortly after he stepped out of his hiding place.

You cannot plan for every contingency. However, in Wally's haste after the bathtub event, he failed to reconnoiter the hotel room. A trained eye would have quickly noticed the motion detector on the ceiling above the bed.

The hotel was an elegant southern property probably known to many of you. Two different employee problems resulted in management's decision to place motion detectors into each room. One prior employee was selling rooms, off the books, for discounted cash prices to customers, then showing the rooms as unavailable in the booking database. One of the guests didn't follow instructions and ordered room service. That guest also contacted the maintenance department to complain about a smell coming from the ventilation system. Those two calls unraveled the "off the books" bookings and led to an internal investigation. During the course of that investigation it was discovered a different employee had many trysts with fellow employees, and the occasional hotel guest, in unsold rooms. The outcome? Termination for both men.

The hotel's owner and management team decided to remove any opportunity for other staff members to engage in similar indiscretions. A security company was contacted to install motion detectors in every hotel room. The room booking database continually received data from the motion sensors. A computer automatically generated pager alerts for management whenever an unoccupied available room reported motion activity after the room had been cleaned and placed into an inactive, but available, status.

Poor Wally. The system's motion detector triggered an alert for management when Wally came out of his hiding place. Managers dispatched security personnel to the suite. Once again Wally darted from the room. However, this time the security team apprehended the little man. Held for a few hours, Wally was threatened with trespassing charges and released.

◊ ◊ ◊

Third Time's the Charm?

Wally wised up. He left town and caught a flight to the CEO's scheduled destination three days hence. On the day before Philip's planned arrival, Wally paid for a full night in the same suite where Philip would check into the following day. Unfortunately for Wally, unlike the two previous rooms that had keyed mechanical locks, this hotel was equipped with an electronic model.

Wally didn’t have the proper tools to handle the job, but the little guy was an intelligent geek who believed he could “MacGyver” the problem. He fiddled with the electronic mechanism throughout the night and eventually created a triggering system that would permit him to unlock the door from the hallway, without the customary magnetic stripe card necessary for customer and staff entry.

Wally checked out of that hotel room the following morning. Housekeepers serviced the suite shortly thereafter. Later that afternoon, the CEO checked into the same room. Wally had successfully checked into a smaller suite directly across the hall from Philip's room a little earlier. Watching through the peephole, Wally witnessed Philip’s entry into the room. After Philip closed the door, Wally stepped into the hallway and listened carefully with his ear on the door. He heard the shower start and waited one minute. Wally opened the door and stepped in. Required fire code hinges quietly closed the door behind him. The locking mechanism engaged. Wally spied Philip's briefcase and laptop sitting on the desk across the room. He darted over to the desk and picked up both items, then turned as he heard the bathroom door opening.

Wally didn't know Philip habitually hung a clean shirt somewhere in the bathroom when he first entered his hotel room. Before removing his germ-laden sweats and placing them in a plastic bag, Philip would steam up the room to remove the shirt’s suitcase wrinkles. The CEO’s habit was to have the shower running from the time he began the dewrinkling process until he had returned to the bathroom for his shower. Philip had just finished hanging his shirt and was leaving the steamy bathroom to remove and bag up his “Petri Pajamas.” Wally was about to learn the hard way that Murphy’s Law could sabotage a budding career.

Caught off guard when Philip exited the bathroom, Wally reportedly stammered, “How can this be? You’re supposed to be in the shower!”

Philip, a former collegiate football star walked over and grabbed Wally by the shoulders. Wally kicked Philip in the crotch. Big mistake. Acting on instinct, Philip released Wally and took a step backward to protect himself.

Wally was 16" shorter than Philip and about 150 pounds lighter. Too short to plant a firm kick into Philip's groin, Wally's shoe barely made contact with his adversary's privates. Thinking he'd bought some time, Wally tried to flee. However, his MacGyver activities on the lock backfired. Unknown to Wally, he damaged the locking mechanism when he unlocked the door and entered the suite. At the moment Wally most needed the door to open, the interior latch failed to release the bolt. He found himself locked inside the suite, with a very upset former linebacker bearing down on him.

Philip was distressed someone entered his room without permission and was in possession of his laptop bag and briefcase. The big athlete was also offended by Wally's failed attempt to neutralize him with a kick to his private parts.

As Wally was desperately yanking on the unmoving door, Philip quickly darted over to the little thief. The big guy peeled Wally off the door handle. Philip picked up the smaller man, pinned him to the wall, and delivered a headbutt to Wally's nose. Wally passed out and dropped to the floor like a wet towel.

◇ ◇ ◇

Philip informed investigators the attaché case contained a précis of his company's negotiations with an interested party. Near the start of Wally's interrogation, police questioned him about Philip's assertions. The little man began sobbing. He knew it was all over. Wally spilled the beans on Paul, the dirty tricksters, his activities at the other hotels, and the overall plan.

Wally's full confession, immediately after his arrest, gave investigators everything they needed for the prosecution. Charged with a series of federal and state crimes, Wally, Paul, and their two associates were facing stiff sentences. The two dirty tricksters, having full knowledge of the entire scheme, negotiated a plea deal to avoid prison time. They testified against both Wally and Paul at their respective trials. Although I never heard how much time they had to serve, I do know they received years in prison, rather than a few months.

◊ ◊ ◊

I met Wally a few years after his parole. A friend of mine was a retired police investigator who operated a small detective agency. He was present during Wally's interviews and subsequent confession. Over beers one afternoon, he told Cola the story of Wally's misadventures in Corporate Espionage. It was hilarious. After we'd stopped laughing, the man offered to introduce me to Wally.

Wally survived by assisting several dozen companies with their computer-related needs. My detective friend was one of Wally's clients. In fact, Wally was scheduled to install a new computer at the detective agency that very evening. I quickly accepted the invitation to meet a real-life Maxwell Smart.

As you might imagine, prison life was very difficult for the little man. It appeared to be a well-learned lesson for Wally. Upon meeting Wally, I tested his civic obedience. I told Wally I had a laptop computer and wanted to know if he'd be willing to sell and install an inexpensive bootlegged copy of Microsoft Word onto my device. Not a candidate for the diplomatic corps, Wally invited me to go have sex with myself. He said he'd made one mistake with the law and he'd never again engage in criminal activity. At least he learned from his mistakes.

THE ONESEVEN CLUB

My career path would have been radically different, and far less successful, if not for The OneSeven Club. OneSeven is a name I've affectionately bestowed upon a group of individuals with highly specialized skills. They are not known to one another, and it's not actually a club. OneSeven's include a collection of insightful masters of design and problem-solving, as well as expertise in fields critical to carrying out Espionage Operations. Some possess abilities uncommon in the general population, but vital to my needs. I refer to many of them as "techno-geeks." Most are creative, clever, and costly. They have improved my ability to produce favorable outcomes on behalf of My Clients. As indicated earlier in "The Language of Cola," the OneSeven's are contractors who've made my business life much more manageable and positioned for success.

> ***An aside...***
> My collegiate Greek system fraternity history continues to sneak into Cola's lexicon. Although it isn't necessary for inclusion elsewhere in this book (including the Glossary) I occasionally refer to OneSeven's as Rho's. Rho is the 17th letter in the Greek alphabet. *Enough said.*

Back to The OneSeven Club...
I've always enjoyed great movies involving stings, scams, and espionage. My favorites include "Three Days of the Condor," the

Danny Ocean movies, Jason Bourne, and the James Bond franchise. Most Readers know grumbling "Q" of the 007 films. Although his total career screen time was minimal, his impact was considerable. He provided Bond with a wide variety of high tech devices and tools that 007 would eventually need to save the day.

When actively engaged on the Dark Side of espionage I required tools, technical skills, capabilities, and inventiveness far beyond my ability to personally create or manage. Even today, in my Counterintelligence and Counterespionage roles, their expertise is often required to achieve positive outcomes. Over the years I've been successful in surrounding myself with a phenomenal group of trustworthy professionals.

Unlike Bond, I have dozens of Q's. I fondly refer to them, collectively, as OneSevens or Rhos. Electronic technicians, forgers, audio and video experts, pickpockets, carpenters, plumbers, electricians, chemists, microbiologists, fingerprint analysts, linguists, firearms experts, metallurgists, and others.

I decided to offer you a glimpse into their sub rosa world and introduce a few of these helpful individuals.

◇ ◇ ◇

WOOLLY MAMMOTH "TROJAN HORSE" RUSH JOB
A Cola OneSeven Carved this in a Single Day
10" Wide x 12" Long x 15" High
Contains a Recording System Created by Jo

Jo-Anne

Jo-Anne, whom I usually refer to as "Jo," has been my most versatile continually available OneSeven. Jo has a single client in espionage - Cola the Spy. She is a solo shop and has never reached outside her family to assist me in creating items and methods necessary for my efforts.

On occasion, she relies on members of her immediate family to assist me with my needs. Their combined expertise and intelligence is phenomenal. They are all well-educated, creative, insightful, productive, and are all Mensa qualified.

Jo married her high school baseball star boyfriend, James. After graduating, they attended the same prestigious college. James walked away with his Masters in Chemistry. Jo's Masters was in Electrical Engineering. Their son Hank became a physicist and possesses remarkable computer skills. Although I'm a serious student of the game and can hold my own against solidly competent chess players, Hank blows me away. I don't stand a chance when Hank and I face off in a game of chess. Daughter Katherine, whom we call "Kat," is both a metallurgist and a practicing pediatrician. Her husband, Gary, is a psychologist. Gary's professional pursuit is consumer marketing. He's a marketing genius and understands the human psyche. An impressive family!

Although their kids have only known me in my Corporate Counterintelligence role, James and Jo have known me since my college days. I only work with Jo, but accept that James and the kids offer advice, direction, and expertise when Jo is wrestling with technical problems. They are a quiet, cerebral, family and I've never had reason to believe they would compromise my safety and security.

Jo worked for a brief time using her degree before becoming a mother. She's not been a regular employee of any company since. A contractor, yes. An employee, no. She has worked under contract for me, and only me, in the decades since her children were born. It started out slow but became an unexpected near full-time avocation for Jo.

An avid fan of the This Old House television program, Jo convinced James they needed to buy a fixer-upper home on a lake. Although Jo is a good negotiator, those skills weren't necessary. Getting James to agree with the plan was easy. Jo knew James wanted to own and live in a secluded lake house. James enjoyed fishing. He also loved the tranquility offered by lakeside homes. James knew Jo was leveraging his heart's desire when she presented her plan to him. She needed him to agree to the considerable investment necessary to purchase the property. She didn't have to try very hard. It worked. He agreed.

Perfect for her needs, the house was an excellent specimen that would require years of Jo's efforts to make it their dream home. Her carpentry, plumbing, electrical, sheetrock, painting, and other remodeling skills were self-taught. A perfectionist to the core, Jo became well-skilled in addressing nearly every need within the home.

One of her first projects after purchasing the home was to build a large multidisciplinary workshop adjacent to the residence. Over the years she's added on to the enormous building. It's filled with lathes, hoists, welders, drill presses, high tech diagnostic equipment, a professional film development lab, compressors, a paint bay, kilns, a high powered microscope, and more. Powered by three-phase electricity, the building is a remarkable testament to her skills, ingenuity, and detailed planning abilities.

The building is also a giant Faraday Cage. While her physicist son was still in high school, she and Hank reengineered the structure to reduce RF and other electromagnetic signals emanating from the building. They also worked to restrict incoming signals as well.

One particular room centered within the primary structure, and not near any exterior walls, goes beyond restricting signals, it actually stops signal transfer altogether. It is constructed above the floor on four shock absorbing pedestals. A heavy copper mesh covers interior and exterior walls. An additional layer of sheeting, I believe to be lead, appears to offer further shielding.

The inside of the room has very strange walls and an odd ceiling. It's the quietest place I've ever been. At times, because it is so quiet, I'm sure I can hear blood pumping through my head and the sound of my own blinking. Jo told me it is an acoustic anechoic chamber. It's a strange and wonderful place for holding espionage-related conversations.

Hank once told me the room is nearly impenetrable to all eavesdropping efforts. The first door leading into that room has a curious sign posted above the door. The sign is about a foot square. There is a single character on the sign. It appears to be the mirror image of an inverted lowercase "y" constructed from a fine copper mesh. On one occasion I queried Jo about the sign. She merely smiled like a Cheshire Cat and shrugged her shoulders; reminiscent of Michael Byrne in Clancy's, "The Sum of All Fears."

> ***An aside...***
> Byrne's character in that movie, Anatoli Grushkov aka Spinnaker, shrugged and smiled at Ben Affleck. That scene occurred in front of the White House at the end of the film when Spinnaker was asked how he knew Affleck

was going to propose to his girlfriend on that day. Byrne's body language and smile were identical to Jo's reaction to me.

Back to Jo's Workshop...
Heating, cooling, roofing, and a few other needs required the involvement of outside professionals, but otherwise, every improvement, upgrade, and repair on their property was Jo's handiwork.

An aside...
I'm well aware that handymen, carpenters, plumbers, electricians, and others who work with their hands suffer callouses, staining, and torn dirty fingernails. How she does it, I don't know. Jo's hands look like she just jumped out of a television commercial for hand creme. Her hands are clean and dainty. Her fingernails are perfect. Amazing.

It's a testament to Jo's planning and careful execution. She has a myriad of specialty gloves at the ready. Rubber, cotton, nitrile, canvas, and wool. One unusual pair of Jo's gloves reminds me of chain mail armor, like that worn by ancient warriors on the battlefield. When asked about the gloves, Jo muttered something about butchers and shark lovers, but didn't clarify. She was in her Jo Zone.

The Jo Zone
When Jo is busy with a project or a deep thought, her focus can become so intense those around her often go unheard or unseen. At first, I found the behavior troublesome. Over time, I've learned that it's merely Jo focusing and tuning out extraneous stimuli, to include Cola. I call it The Jo Zone.

One evening I noticed Jo standing over the sink in her kitchen with a toothbrush, brushing her fingernails. I don't know what solution she was using, but it reminded me of shaving cream. I asked her about the white cream on her hands. No reply. She was in The Jo Zone. The next day I paid particular attention to her hands and noticed

> fresh, perfect, fingernail polish and perfectly clean hands. Amazing.

Back to OneSeven Jo...
The workshop facility is 100% hers to maintain. After completing the structure's major construction, the only persons believed to have entered the building are Jo, her family, and Cola the Spy. All HVAC systems, except for the ductwork, are positioned outside the main workshop structure; thereby keeping any repairmen on the exterior of the facility. It's a secure facility, state of the art, and would be the envy of any home hobbyist or professional craftsman.

> ***An aside...***
> An air conditioning maintenance man once asked Jo about "all the secrecy" and why he couldn't go inside to adjust the thermostat. I was there and watched with fascination as she smartly and politely shut him down.
>
> Jo told him she was an inventor working to perfect a silica chip manufacturing process. She alluded to inventive secrecy needs, as well as clean room protocols required under her contract with the manufacturer underwriting her work. The mundane business of silica chip design was sufficiently boring. The guy appeared to lose interest in her workshop rather quickly. He backed off with a yawn.

Back to Jo's Efforts on Cola's Behalf...
Early on I had Jo develop a few audio devices (bugs) that required her electrical engineering skills. Over time she taught herself to craft concealments for those devices. Jo eventually transitioned into manufacturing full-blown Trojan Horse creations for me. Her woodworking skills are incredible. I've never known anyone able to produce finished works with wood reflecting such precision and perfection. Jo can duplicate any piece of furniture, and turn that clone into a remarkably flawless concealment. Her detailed perfectionism is beyond belief. She even paints perfect wood grain where wood grain is non-existent. Heck, very often the underlying material isn't even wood - but sure looks like wood. She's learned to cast in bronze, sculpt

marble, and design furnishings with complicated wooden cipher locks. Jo has hit it out of the park for me many times. She's amazing.

Cola's Hollywood Caper

Here's an example of one particular Op that involved Jo's competence and ingenuity.

I was contacted by a high profile Hollywood Agent who came well recommended by an existing Client. The Hollywood Agent wanted my assistance in knowing the thinking of a movie mogul for a contract negotiation with his client. The Movie Mogul, who owned a movie production company, was a tough negotiator. The Hollywood Agent needed all the help he could get to meet his client's expectations.

After our initial meeting, I realized the job wouldn't be easy and would probably prove too expensive. A cost-benefit analysis demonstrated the type of OP, involving me and necessary for the job, wasn't justifiable. After noodling the matter a while, I began seeking ways to provide additional value to The Hollywood Agent. I decided to offer him an option with higher upfront costs, but offering more significant potential for The Hollywood Agent's long-term profitability. The plan involved placement of permanent bugs in The Movie Mogul's executive offices.

I submitted a "consulting" proposal requiring a hefty initial payment. The contract also contained a schedule for annual prepayments. I presented The Hollywood Agent with a vague outline of the Op to demonstrate the potential upside for him and his clients. There would be reasonable monthly monitoring and recording-systems maintenance fees as well, based upon my ongoing costs, plus a negotiated value for pilfered conversations I'd pass along to my new Hollywood Client. I based the charges for those conversations on the box office draw of the actors involved. If an actor's previous movie contract was below a certain threshold, there were no additional costs to The Hollywood Agent. There were three tiers beyond that, allowing me to earn greater income when larger fish, represented by My Client, found their way into my audio net.

I reminded The Hollywood Agent that his upfront costs would be significant. That investment would only inure to his benefit over time. He was, therefore, advised to judiciously wash and cautiously use any information I collected on his behalf. If The Movie Mogul realized a leak existed within his organization, it would jeopardize the Hollywood Agent's career and freedom; not to mention a decidedly wrong turn for the Operation. The Hollywood Agent agreed, and I went to work.

Before presenting a proposal to The Hollywood Agent, I discovered The Movie Mogul was about to remodel both his home office in Palm Springs and his Los Angeles business office. He intended on moving his massive walnut desk and a custom desk lamp from Palm Springs to his LA office. The lamp was designed to accommodate two telephones within its structure. Our HUMINT revealed The Movie Mogul maintained a red telephone, along with a typical black version, on the lamp's framework. He reportedly told a few close associates he believed the red phone made him look decisive and presidential.

The combination lamp and telephone stand was a large one-of-a-kind bronze and Cocobolo specimen. The desk was so massive, the lamp didn't appear oversized. Just ridiculously ostentatious. It looked like a large balance scale, not unlike that held by Lady Justice. The two telephone platforms were at the two outer edges of a long horizontal beam. They were specially designed as telephone stands and were part of the bronze section. Each tray contained a telephone jack. Just above the bronze beam, and centered atop what appeared to be a carved fulcrum, was a sumptuously adorned goblet-looking vessel; out of which sprang a beautiful Cocobolo carving.

Cocobolo is an exotic Guatemalan wood used for high-end chess pieces, woodwind instruments, grips and handles, pool cues, jewelry boxes and other expensive personal items. Cocobolo is a rare ingredient in more significant items, due to availability. Over-exploitation has rendered this wood rare and internationally protected. Raw pieces of Cocobolo, larger than a coffee cup, are seldom seen. Its irregular grain, glass-like finish, and coloring make the exotic wood extremely attractive. Cocobolo also possesses a property rarely seen in wood. Like

Ironwood and a few other kinds of wood, Cocobolo will sink in water. Cocobolo's specific gravity is such that buoyancy eludes this particular wood. The Movie Mogul's lamp was ornate, large, and expensive.

The Movie Mogul wanted his contractors to remove the furnishings from his Palm Springs office and place them into storage while his men fully remodeled that space. The project was scheduled to take about two weeks, while The Movie Mogul was away on a six-week Mediterranean holiday. A new office desk had been ordered and scheduled for delivery to the desert city after the project's completion.

After completing the remodeling project, the crew would transition to Los Angeles for the remodel there. That job was scheduled to take about three weeks. Once completed, movers would collect the desk and lamp from storage and transport them to the executive's newly remodeled LA office.

After ferreting as much information as I could about the various remodeling projects and The Movie Mogul's vacation plans, I made a weekend entry into his about-to-be-remodeled Palm Springs office. After reviewing the scene, I went to the nearby storage facility to study the desk and lamp. They were both sitting on the floor and covered by white sheets. I used a Polaroid camera to photograph placement of the covered desk and lamp, as well as the position and appearance of the two bed sheets covering those items.

After carefully removing the sheets, I took several hundred photos of the two key items. Using a 35mm camera and my trusty Minox, I photographed every angle, nook, and cranny possible. I removed the drawers and shot every side and surface. The inside and underside of the desk were also captured on film, as was the bottom of the curious lamp. The small Minox allowed me to reach into places the 35mm Nikon couldn't access. I sketched and recorded measurements, then carefully replaced everything when the photo session was complete. The sheets resumed their protective positions. Using the Polaroids, I made sure to return every wrinkle and fold to the protective linens.

When finished, the storage room looked no different than when I arrived.

Armed with my sketches and exposed film I flew out to see Jo. She processed the film and studied my drawings. After a full day analyzing the data, she keyed on the desk's relationship with the lamp. The Movie Mogul obviously had the desk designed to accommodate the lamp and telephone without the need for exposed wiring.

The lamp's base was concave. There was a short eight-inch electrical cord hidden within the lamp's melon-sized bottom cavity. There were also two RJ11 telephone jacks.

The left side of the desk had a round custom carved walnut protrusion, on top of which was a single electrical outlet and two telephone jacks. The surface of the raised round section was about a half inch above the desktop. It was dome-like. The top of the dome was flattened to accommodate the jacks and outlet. Jo concluded the receptacles were elevated to avoid liquid infiltration if a spill occurred on the desk.

She said the design permitted the lamp's placement directly above the three outlets. The lamp was very heavy and had a rubbery ring around the base of the bronze section.

Jo said the design served three purposes. The ring provided slide-resistant friction, intended to "grab" the desktop and help keep the heavy lamp securely centered on top of the raised walnut dome. The ring also provided a rubbery barrier designed to repel spilled liquids. Finally, it protected the desk from scratches by the metallic lamp base.

Jo noted the top left side backplate of the drawer stopped about 4" from the inside front wall of the desk, when in the closed position. Had the drawer been able to travel farther into the desk, the drawer's back would have stopped against a stapled 12-2 Romex cable. On the bottom end, the wire disappeared four inches above the base of the desk when it entered a small electrical box. A one-foot electric cord with a typical male plug hung from the box. The top end of the Romex weaved its way to the left underside of the top of the desk, directly below the raised walnut protrusion where the Cocobolo lamp appeared to sit. A similar wiring configuration, using a smaller wire, was present on the same side of the desk. That wiring was intended for use with The Movie Mogul's telephone system.

After carefully reviewing the electrical and telephone wiring systems, I told Jo I noticed, but at the time failed to consider, something critical to the desk. Two telephone ports and an electrical outlet were located on the floor of the Palm Springs office; positioned directly below the underside of the desk, on the left side of the desk's footprint. Jo told me she was pretty confident the remodel of the LA office would include placement of similar outlets in the floor there. I agreed.

Jo indicated she wanted to use something called an induction coil to power one of the three bugs she'd plant in the furnishings. That bug would go into the handle of the drawer, another bug would go into the lamp, and she engineered a final system connected to the telephone wiring. The use of the induction coil permitted Jo to design a charging system for the drawer handle bug that wouldn't require a direct connection between the bug's power system and the electric wiring.

I flew back to Palm Springs and broke into the storage facility. I collected the left side drawer and the lamp; and placed them into sizable wooden shipping containers with folded shipping blanket inserts. I drove non-stop from Palm Springs to the eastern United States so that Jo could perform her magic with the two items.

The drawer bug was installed, as promised, inside the handle. The microphone looked like a minuscule dark dot in the grain. Upon close inspection, it appeared to be a tiny wormhole. She did an unbelievable job hiding the wiring from the microphone to the back of the drawer. It was somehow buried inside the wooden faceplate, along the inside of the bottom board, and up again on the backplate of the drawer. Her newly manufactured and appropriately aged backplate looked identical to the old backplate, except it was about a half inch thicker. Jo also elongated the drawer. The new drawer was about three and a half inches longer than the original. She told me a charging induction coil, a rechargeable battery, and a tiny transmitter were all hidden within that backplate. *Unbelievable!*

Jo removed the Cocobolo wood from the bronze and installed several items inside the bronze base. I don't recall the entire configuration, but I do remember her saying the antenna, receiver, and transmitter needed to be inside the Cocobolo wood. She secured the rest within the bronze base.

The real work was the lamp. Jo installed a bug, a three signal receiver, a four signal transmitter, multiple devices for power management and VOX recordings, multiple rechargeable batteries, and an antenna. One receiver was intended to capture telephone calls, while the other two were for the bugs. She also included a system to monitor battery health in the drawer, as well as the batteries she placed within the Cocobolo lamp. Jo told me she was using electricity from the phone system to power a set of secondary, redundant, emergency backup bugs connected to a low power auxiliary transmitter. The induction coils used power from the lamp's electrical system to recharge the backup battery concealed within the drawer's backplate. If the backup batteries failed, our systems still had power from the lamp's electrical line. She also carved something into the lamp she referred to as a Venturi ventilation system, designed to draw off and dissipate excess heat from her components. It was a complicated project requiring more work and components than I expected. The primary system was so reliable, we never had to use the auxiliary transmitter. To Jo's credit, the lamp appeared unchanged when reassembled.

In the process of modifying the lamp for her components, Jo used a lathe and other tools to create several relatively large cavities in the Cocobolo carving. While engaged in that activity, she became very ill. Dr. Kat was home at the time. Kat told her mother she was having an allergic reaction to something. Her skin, eyes, and throat were involved. She began having trouble breathing and became sick to her stomach. I don't recall what treatment Kat gave Jo, but she recovered fully by the following morning. We discovered Cocobolo oil produces allergic reactions in most people. Working with Cocobolo can be dangerous and requires appropriate precautionary measures.

Jo learned a valuable lesson that day. She now researches the potential for toxicity involving any material with which she's working.

A final, onsite, installation would be required. Jo prepared something she referred to as a coil pigtail. I needed to open the electrical box on the underside of the desk's top. Once inside I was to connect a black and a white wire to the existing wiring. I'd made such connections in the field previously, but Jo had me practice on several different mockups she prepared. Once satisfied I could handle the job, she walked me through the placement of the power side of the induction coil so that it would be directly in line with its mate on the backplate of the desk drawer.

Once Jo completed her part of the alterations, I picked up a rental van and returned to Palm Springs. I replaced the desk and lamp, using the Polaroids I took to ensure proper positioning. Nobody was aware the items had been temporarily out-of-state.

Everything worked perfectly. The system Jo designed required the system to dial out on one of the Movie Mogul's phone lines at three o'clock each morning and trigger a receiver we had in a nearby office we'd rented. That call lasted less than ten seconds. Then the system would transmit the recorded conversations under low power, using an obscure frequency unlikely to be discovered. If the transmitter ever failed, the two phone lines acted as redundant transmission systems. We hoped it wouldn't come to that, because discovery of conversations held by the Movie Mogul could be heard by anyone picking up the correct phone on his desk.

Although the batteries failed after a few years, power was sufficiently consistent for uninterrupted eavesdropping. After more than 15 years, the desk was sold and shipped to Manhattan. We had an opportunity to manage the shipment. Having a bug in the Movie Mogul's office was useful. En route to New York the truck diverted to a secure warehouse, where I rendezvoused with

Jo to remove all traces of her eavesdropping equipment. She'd kept the original drawer, so that part of the project was relatively easy.

Removing the induction coil from the underside of the desk was a little more difficult. Jo had to retouch the walnut to cover staining caused by the plastic materials housing the induction coil.

> ***An aside...***
> I would have never anticipated a staining issue. During our pre-Op planning for removing the devices, Jo told me to expect to see discoloration under the induction coil. The kit she packed for the trip included paints and stains to address the issue. Once more, Jo's attention to detail and understanding of the chemistry involved reminded me that I was fortunate to have this wonderful OneSeven in my corner.

Back to The End of the Op
The items buried within the lamp were a little easier. Once removed, the lamp looked normal. The cavity Jo created in the Cocobolo, resulting in her allergic reaction fifteen years earlier, appeared constructed as designed. I'm guessing only the original craftsman would have paid any attention to the hollowed out section in the Cocobolo carving.

The Hollywood Agent's cautious use of the information I garnered over those 15 years resulted in him becoming one of the most successful Hollywood brokers, representing more than a few well-known A-list actors. He was carefully judicious with the information we collected on his behalf. The man successfully acquired a reputation for savvy negotiation skills. Insiders spoke of his prescience in knowing the best approaches and tactics when dealing with some of Hollywood's most influential executives. The Hollywood Agent's stable of successful actors enriched him and he, in turn, was able to ensure his clients received excellent service and good contracts. He parlayed those positive outcomes into other successes he developed without my involvement.

Although I played a role in the production of more than a few of Hollywood's most celebrated films, released near the end of the twentieth century, I believe the real credit goes to Jo and her insightful expertise. Thanks Jo!

◇ ◇ ◇

"Skookum" Jim

My dear friend "Skookum" Jim shares his nickname with the famous Skookum Jim Mason who, along with George Carmack, is credited with launching the 1896 Klondike Gold Rush near Dawson City in Canada's Yukon Territory. Skookum is a word used in that region to describe someone as strong and reliable. Like the Skookum Jim of the 1800's, my Skookum Jim is a large man with great physical strength. He loves to run. I once ran a 100+ mile relay race on a team with Jim and eight others. Seeing that huge strong man running at me to pass the baton was breathtaking.

Skookum Jim has proven himself extremely strong and reliable in Cola's world. His strengths in database creation and management are impressive. I decided to introduce Skookum Jim to offer Readers a glimpse into a type of OneSeven that assists me in my espionage-related efforts, but who does not participate in, or support, actual espionage activities. Although Jim is vaguely aware of the nature of my business, he's never had any knowledge of any real espionage-related actions involving me. I look at him as arm's length back end support. He helps me in what I do without really knowing my business. He is not unlike the sign company that makes magnetic vehicle signs at my request or the dentist I frequent who has created a cornucopia of dental appliances necessary to alter my appearance.

I became acquainted with Jim, a native American from the Arctic Circle region of North America, through a collegiate computer sciences class. I'd been struggling with a Fortran programming issue and met Jim when my 16" stack of keypunch cards fell out of the long narrow box I was using to carry them. Out of nowhere, a big dark-skinned fellow dropped to his knees. He helped me pick up my cards and return them to their proper order. Little did I know then, the man who introduced himself as Skookum Jim would become a valued friend.

Our chance encounter was serendipitous. If not for the gravitational pull on my box of cards and my clumsiness, I may not have ever met the big guy. Jim had been on his way out of the Computer Sciences Building.

Jim's stack of keypunch cards, sitting on a nearby table, filled three or four long boxes and involved many times the number of cards I was using. I asked him about his MIS project. He had been working on a big project for the fire department in his hometown. The programming needs were far beyond my understanding. As I recall, they were intended to validate fire hydrant water volume and pressure needs for the type of structure fires that could occur in his community.

Ugh! I was glad it was his project and not mine.

While picking up the cards, Jim said he had watched me scratch my head throughout the night. He asked about my problem. I told Jim I'd written a program, using historical sales and weather data, to estimate hot dog and soda sales at the college football stadium, during a future game; given certain weather conditions.

Jim told me that wasn't what he wanted to know. He actually wanted to know why I spent the entire night scratching my head, reworking my flowchart, going back downstairs to the keypunch machine to perforate new cards, and returning upstairs so I could feed them into the hopper for the mainframe computer. He said he'd observed me during my repeated hour long vigils in the "Penalty Box" waiting for the computer tech to hand me a printout.

Penalty Box? Yes, MIS (Management Information Systems) students at that time referred to the long waits for a printout as being in the Penalty Box. In the coming days, I would discover that it was Skookum Jim, an avid hockey player, who assigned the phrase "Penalty Box" as a way of describing our long waits for the printouts.

> ***An aside...***
> Skookum Jim had a knack with words. His inventiveness didn't cease with coining Penalty Box in the computer lab. He was the first person I ever heard utter the term "Computer Wrestling." Whenever someone was fighting with a computer problem, he referred to it as computer wrestling. He might say something like, "Cola spent the entire night computer wrestling." Heck, I still use Jim's phrase in 2019.

Back to The Computer Lab...
Jim had studied several programming languages, including Basic, Fortran, and COBOL. Although a student like me, he was a year ahead. I was about to discover his additional year, combined with his geeky smarts, made Jim light-years ahead of me with Fortran.

After helping me clean up my gravity related mess, Jim asked if he could review my work. I had a pile of printouts that began to accumulate nearly 24 hours earlier. He began his review by familiarizing himself with my programming flowchart. Then he turned to the stack of printouts. Jim started with the most recent product from my time in the Penalty Box and worked his way backward. Within 15 minutes Jim looked me in the eye and said, "You, sir, were snookered by a whoop-de-doo."

Huh? What the heck is a whoop-de-doo? Is it another word Skookum Jim coined for the computer realm? Yep.

Jim explained that a whoop-de-doo is his way of describing a comma. A comma? Yep, according to Jim, my first version of the program had a single errant comma in a formula (or a missing comma - I can't recall which).

That single issue, involving a single comma in an "IF, THEN..." statement, cost me a full night at the computer lab. According to Jim, every time I tried to correct the programming error and re-punch my cards I was making things worse. My all-night vigil in the Computer Center resulted in me moving farther and farther from running an error-free program. Skookum Jim solved the problem in mere minutes.

We went back and assembled my first stack of keypunch cards, changed out the offending whoop-de-doo card with a newly punched version, and placed my stack in the card reader's hopper. An hour later I received a printout clearly showing projected revenues, based on weather-related concession stand sales. *It worked!*

Jim was, and is, my hero! Over the coming days, we formed an incredible bond that continues to this day.

Thanks, brother! I am no Doubting Thomas when it comes to your intelligence and wisdom. I'm a believer in you and appreciate your involvement in my life. You're the best!

Nearly a decade after my Quick Lube espionage gig I realized I was in The Game for the long haul. I also recognized I needed to maintain a safe repository for contact and other data, free from prying eyes. I had been using 3 x 5 cards to record all of my activities and contacts. I had a couple thousand cards, and they were getting unwieldy. It took me forever to find what I needed when I pulled out those hard copy records.

One day I showed my system to Jim. He laughed at me. I reached out to grab the big guy. He pulled back to protect a wonderfully handcrafted crystal rose he picked up as a gift for his wife, Rose. Guarding the rose was instinct for Skookum Jim. When he jerked back to avoid my grasp, he knocked my carefully organized box of 3 x 5 cards off the counter. Now Jim and I were both laughing.

Fortunately, the beautiful rose was undamaged. It was clear I needed to address the problem of my 2' x 2' box of 2002 cards. The box and cards were a jumbled mess on the floor. That was the final straw. I needed a new system that didn't take so much time, was efficiently organized, took up less space, and was more secure.

Jim offered to solve my problem. Skookum Jim hooked me up with a Macintosh Plus, an external 20-megabyte hard drive, and a LaserWriter from Apple Computer. That hardware was necessary to run and print data from a flat file database program called FileMaker Plus.

An aside...
I laugh now thinking about that 20-megabyte hard drive. I thought I'd never fill it up. Heck, today I have thousands of individual files that are much larger than my original hard drive. More than a year later, when the drive was almost full, it took several hours to backup data from that hard drive, onto a stack of 3.5 floppy disks that could hold 1.44 MB each. One of the reasons it became so full, so fast, was Jim's pseudo encryption system.

Over time Jim would assist me with real data encryption, but in those early years, he helped me by creating something he referred to as Leprechaun Encryption. If you've never heard of "Leprechaun Encryption," that's because Jim made up the phrase. He explained he based his self-developed pseudo encryption system upon the actions of a Leprechaun in a story he once heard. Here's the story...

A farmer was walking through a forest and sat down at the base of a tree to eat a snack. While sitting there, he noticed a hole between two large roots at the bottom of the tree. In the hole was a pot of gold. The farmer jumped up and tried to lift the pail, but it was too heavy to move. As he was trying to figure out what to do, a Leprechaun appeared and told the farmer the gold belonged to him. The farmer knew the Leprechaun couldn't keep him from taking the gold. He also knew the Leprechaun couldn't break a promise. The farmer told the Leprechaun he was going home to fetch his horse and cart. He made the Leprechaun promise to leave the gold where it was. The farmer took off his red handkerchief and tied it around the trunk of the tree. He also made the Leprechaun promise to leave the handkerchief on the tree. The Leprechaun pledged to keep both promises. When the farmer returned to the forest he was dismayed to see every tree, thousands of them, had a red handkerchief, identical to his, tied to each tree in the same place on the trunk where the farmer left his handkerchief. The farmer never found the pot of gold.

> Jim's pseudo encryption system is similar to the Leprechaun's handkerchief system. In both systems, the prize is hiding in plain sight. Jim loaded so much data, in so many places, it was nearly impossible to find my info on the hard drive in those early days. Today, however, that tactic wouldn't stand a chance. Now you know about Skookum Jim's Leprechaun Encryption System.
>
> *Shhh, don't tell anyone.*
>
> It probably doesn't matter any longer. Jim and most spies are comfortably ensconced in the world of 128 bit and higher PGP encryption.

Back to Filemaker...
Produced by a company called Nashoba, FileMaker had a Graphical User Interface (GUI) that allowed me to work with, and print in, WYSIWYG (What You See Is What You Get). Of course, the WYSIWYG approach is standard in today's computer technologies and taken for granted. However, back then it was a radical departure from the standard DOS interface that's pretty much useless now, for day-to-day consumer needs.

FileMaker is still around. Today it's called FileMaker Pro. It's a successfully robust relational database application owned by Claris, a subsidiary of Apple, Inc. Businesses from Mom and Pops, all the way up to Fortune 500 companies have, like me, found FileMaker a highly valuable tool in meeting their needs.

When Skookum Jim set me up with my Mac Plus, I recall showing it to my CPA. He was visiting me in my home office. "CPA J" laughed and said, "I've heard about these things. It's not a real computer. It's a toy dreamed up by a couple of kids in California and built in a garage."

A few weeks later I was in CPA J's office. He told me to come around his desk and look at a "real computer." It was an IBM PC. Looking over his shoulder, I saw a screen showing a DOS command line interface. I recall having to stifle a laugh. No WYSIWYG interface. It was simply a 12" CRT (cathode ray tube) sitting atop a box with slots for two 5 ¼" floppy disks (no hard drive) and a separate keyboard. I believe there was also an external cassette recorder. The screen had green phosphorus characters and a blinking green cursor.

CPA J said, "My IBM PC runs circles around your cute little Mac. Your toy computer's gimmicky desktop, files, folders, arrow, and the trash can are all controlled with a rodent [the mouse]. Sorry pal, your Mac will be a flash in the pan. Face it, Cola. The Mac isn't a real computer."

More than ten years later I walked into his office on a Saturday afternoon. CPA J and his family were having lunch and getting ready to catch a flight for a fly-in fishing trip. They had just eaten lunch. His family was in the office to help CPA J set up a new computer on his desk.

As I entered the office, I saw his auburn-haired wife, LJ, laughing. She was watching CPA J, and their redheaded son Josh, doing the Michael Jackson moonwalk. CPA J stopped moonwalking as I entered the room. He looked at me beaming, like a new father. I asked CPA J why he appeared so proud, so happy. He told me he just booted up his new computer. At CPA J's invitation, I walked the same path around the desk that I took a decade earlier and, once again, looked over his shoulder. I broke out laughing.

CPA J asked what was so funny. I pointed to his desktop. I was looking at Windows 98. I recall wiping away tears and laughing out the following words, "Geez J, a toy computer! Lookee there! You have a new computer with a gimmicky desktop, files, folders, an arrow, and a trash can; all controlled by a little black rodent."

CPA J corrected me. He told me his computer had a recycle bin, not a trash can. I later discovered Apple computer filed suit against Microsoft for stealing Apple's Graphical User Interface for their Windows product. A Federal Court eventually decided in Microsoft's favor but did rule that Apple's "Trash" can was protected. That's why Windows has a "Recycle Bin" instead of a "Trash" can.

...and you thought Microsoft was just being earth-friendly by recycling electrons in a Recycle Bin.

That afternoon with moonwalking CPA J and his family, and engaging in wonderful laughter enjoyed at his new computer's expense, was the last time I would ever see those beautiful people. I mentioned they were about to embark on a fly-in fishing trip. En route to their fishing destination, the charter flight's pilot was guiding the aircraft through a narrow mountain pass outside the United States. Investigators believe there must have been low clouds in the valley, forcing the pilot to attempt a 180° turn and return to better airspace. The light plane completed about two-thirds of the maneuver. The valley was too narrow. The aircraft went belly first into the side of the mountain. All souls aboard were lost. The accident killed a deer on the ground, as well.

Buck? What are the chances the buck would be in that particular spot when the airplane pancaked into the mountain?

An official accident investigation report noted that the pilot, J, and Josh died upon impact. LJ survived the crash with severe survivable abdominal injuries. However, the poor grieving lady succumbed to hypothermia during the night. A terrible tragedy. I cannot imagine her pain, knowing she'd lost her husband and son.

Whenever I think about that little plane going down, in my mind's eye, I always see a young redheaded boy smiling and moonwalking with his delighted parents looking on.

My CPA's joking notwithstanding, that Mac Plus was a real gem. My "toy" Mac, when combined with an Apple LaserWriter and software programs like MacDraw, MacPaint, MacWrite, Excel, Ready Set Go, Pagemaker, and FileMaker Plus, became a beneficial tool for this particular Corporate Spy. Pagemaker, MacWrite, and Ready Set Go assisted me with document creation. MacDraw and Ready Set Go (and MacPaint to a lesser degree) helped me with floor plan creation and mapping for surreptitious entries, bug placement, and other inside building planning. Excel and FileMaker were excellent tools for record-keeping and data aggregation. I have Skookum Jim to thank for smartly directing me to go digital.

Over the years I've come to rely on FileMaker, going far beyond capabilities Apple, Claris, Jim, and I could have ever imagined. Although my decades-long relationship with FileMaker is no longer a part of my everyday computing life, it's been a faithful partner throughout. Jim and his lovely wife recently moved to the state where I reside, along with a grandson they're raising. He's retired now, but we both continue to rekindle old memories of how FileMaker helped us both in business for many years.

Jim tells a story about programming Filemaker for one of his clients who ran a very successful business that ticketed U.S. airline flights, back in the days before the terrorist attacks of September 11, 2001. The businessman used generic unisex passenger names for dummy frequent flyer accounts. He used the first names Terry, Kelly, Lee, Leslie, Stacy, Taylor, and Tracy. They all had the same last name as the businessman. That worked out well because the businessman had relatives with those names. If there was a problem, there were real people behind each of the names.

However, Jim told me his client did have an occasional hiccup. On one occasion two individuals, flying under the same name and same frequent flyer number, ended up scheduled for the same flight. It was neither the fault of Filemaker or the businessman. It was fate.

The problem occurred when Kelly #1's aircraft broke down. Kelly #1's flight diverted to another hub airport on a different plane. Once there Kelly #1 was supposed to board yet another flight. When Kelly #1 arrived at the gate, officials informed him the airline's computer indicated he was already on board. In fact, Kelly #2 was already on the same plane, with the same frequent flyer number. I don't recall how it ended up working out, but it did create some issues for Jim's client.

Selling discounted tickets under those names saved clients money and loaded his frequent flyer accounts. Men or women could travel under any of those names. Titles like "Mr." and

"Mrs." weren't required for ticketing in those days. The client told Jim if titles were ever required, he'd simply have every client travel as "Dr." He said if "Sex" was required, it would hurt his business.

Note: After 9/11 "Sex" became a requirement.

Skookum Jim's client then sold flights using miles. I'm not sure exactly how it all worked, but the guy supposedly did well. September 11th changed everything because people began having to present identification matching names printed on airline tickets. Filemaker was used to manage the client's flights, accounts, client lists, and more. That was just one of Jim's clients.

In short, I wanted to bring up Skookum Jim and FileMaker to underscore the sophistication that the computer age, and its various technologies, have brought to The Game. Although there are more than a few bumbling Wally's in the espionage arena, there are more and more tech-savvy individuals leveraging today's technologies to undermine the profitability and successes of good companies. Computers and spies are here to stay. Your profits enjoy no such guarantee. Teenage hackers, spammers, and scammers are, in many ways, the least of your worries.

While those clowns can screw up your computers and valuable data, corporate spies can rob you of your assets, intellectual property, clients, vendors, personnel, and more. Yes, you need safeguards against hackers and their ilk. Safeguarding your company from spies is critical as well. Remember, most of those hackers and scammers are aiming a scatter gun at you and many others simultaneously. They are often on the other side of the globe or sitting on their fat butts in their mother's basement two time zones away; eating chips and drinking sugary caffeinated beverages. They might damage thousands with the press of a single keystroke.

Corporate spies, on the other hand, are like snipers. They're often physically closer than you might realize. They are methodically putting single entities in their sights for a single

OP. When they strike, their methods are so surgical you might never know what hit you.

Heck, look at Professor Icky and The Hollywood Movie Mogul. They didn't see me coming and never knew they'd fallen prey to Cola the Spy.

◇ ◇ ◇

DAVE NEWMAN

A Prince Among Men

Note: Just as we were going to press with the first edition of this book, a Colleague informed me that "Diamond Dave" Newman passed away from a brief, unspecified, illness. Dave regularly appeared healthy and energetic. He was consistently personable, congenial, and warm. Diamond Dave always had a twinkle in his eye, an ever-present smile, and was both positive and kind. I didn't know Dave as well as I would have liked but recognize a real prince when I see one. Dave was unlike anyone I've ever met. In a different life, I would have enjoyed having Diamond Dave as a mentor and role model. May God Bless Diamond Dave Newman and his family.

Diamond Dave

OneSeven's in my playbook fit into three separate groups. Group One members are "Involved." Group Two members are "Not-Involved" but are aware of my occupation. The final OneSeven's are in Group Three, the Unwitting. Jo is Involved. Skookum Jim is Not-Involved, and Diamond Dave is an example of an Unwitting OneSeven.

Don't misunderstand. Diamond Dave is neither unintelligent nor without street smarts. Diamond Dave is smart, resourceful, scholarly, intuitive, keen, and more. I just haven't let him peek behind the curtain and know what I do for a living. I decided to dub him "Diamond Dave" after our first meeting. Let me explain.

I was staying in San Francisco for a time while conducting Operations in Silicon Valley. One afternoon I was killing time and drove into South San Francisco. I noticed a small pawnshop and ducked inside. I asked a middle-aged woman if they had any good deals on Rolex watches. She introduced me to her son, whom I've since discovered is an internationally known Rolex expert. He showed me a few pieces. As I said, I was killing time. After wasting about 15 minutes of his time, I excused myself and departed.

A few months later I was working an Op in Menlo Park and needed a high-end watch. I went back to the pawnshop in South San Francisco. I never saw the Rolex expert anymore but did meet his brother Diamond Dave. Diamond Dave showed me the Rolex's again, and a few other brands. I ended up buying one of the other brands. It fit me nicely. Diamond Dave said it's a much-desired watch. I didn't care. I'm not a jewelry guy. The timepiece was merely a prop, filling an operational need.

Two hours after completing the purchase, I was still in the store. Diamond Dave is a phenomenally interesting guy who loves sharing with others. He doesn't mind sharing good educational information. Diamond Dave taught me more than I thought possible about diamonds, moissanite, emeralds, rubies, and a wealth of information about his specialty - opals.

Over the years I've popped into his store and learned even more. I learned he is married to a schoolteacher. I also discovered his mother is a phenomenal people person and loved by their many generational customers. Diamond Dave is a handsome smiling man who wears a Jewish symbol on a neck chain, smokes small cigars, and sports an attractive ring on one pinky. His friendly outgoing nature is well-reflected in his consistent "Top of the Day" greeting. He's taught me about sarongs and pawnbroking. Diamond Dave knows volumes about Hawaii, Japan, Internet businesses, wine, and dogs; teaching me about them all at every opportunity. *Dogs?*

Diamond Dave is involved in search and rescue. He has raised and trained more than a few German shepherds. His dogs are beautiful. Without question, they are excellent guard dogs, but the kids that enter his store see them as cuddly friendly teddy bears.

One of his dogs is named Max. Max is huge. I love to jokingly tell Diamond Dave that dog is a mixed breed. Half German Shepard and half Black Bear. He is a sweet dog, but the hair on my neck always stands up when Max walks toward Cola.

A big Samoan guy came in while I was there on that first visit with Dave. He gave Diamond Dave a huge bear hug. They called each other "Brother" and were clearly fond of one another. Diamond Dave told me the Samoan, and his buddies, helped protect Diamond Dave and his assets after the 1989 Loma Prieta earthquake. It's unfortunate his Samoan buddies weren't around to protect him on a different occasion. I don't know the entire story, but somehow discovered Diamond Dave suffered a gunshot wound to the back, at the hands of a student immigrant.

I was traveling somewhere once (pre-9/11) and bumped into Diamond Dave in an airport restaurant. I noticed his briefcase and jokingly asked him if it contained diamonds. He chuckled and carefully lifted the case onto the table. I was impressed when he opened the case. No, not diamonds. You'll recall me saying Diamond Dave taught me about wines. The case contained a bottle of expensive wine, and two fine stemmed wine glasses, as well as a few accessories. The man travels in style.

Here's the fun part. Diamond Dave doesn't know me. Each time I visit his store I go in disguise. I wasn't in disguise when I saw him at the airport. I recall him working hard trying to place me.

Wanting to keep Diamond Dave out of my affairs, but needing his knowledge and merchandise on occasion, I decided to rely on Colleagues to visit him in his store. I still visit him, but not as often as My Colleagues. Colleagues and I also speak with Diamond Dave occasionally, on the phone. I have no reason to distrust Diamond Dave, but I conduct my business on a need to know basis. Although I don't pay him for information, we've made more than a few higher dollar purchases from Diamond Dave. We do so without asking for discounts, as a way of rewarding him for his assistance. Diamond Dave shares freely with others and is a great guy. I'm glad to have had his unofficial, unwitting, support with my espionage activities - both on the Dark Side and in my more recent role as a Corporate Counterintelligence professional.

Diamond Dave is just one of many Unwitting OneSevens I lean on from time to time for information, products, and services.

An aside...

A Special Note from Cola

Diamond Dave is credited with referring me to his friend, Steven Fowler. He only knew I was seeking someone of high character, an unbroken track record of honesty, excellent writing skills, and possessed the ability to maintain confidences. A man who could write my authorized biography. Dave didn't know my real occupation when he provided me with Steve's contact information. Regardless, at Dave's recommendation I contacted Steve. After conducting a thorough interview and background check I chose Steven Fowler as the trusted co-author my biography.

Thank you Dave!

◇ ◇ ◇

Cola's Best Friends

As I said a few paragraphs ago, Diamond Dave knows dogs. I've leaned on him more than once for helpful information with my Canine OneSevens.

LET ME INTRODUCE
COLA'S FOUR FAVORITE CANINE ONESEVENS

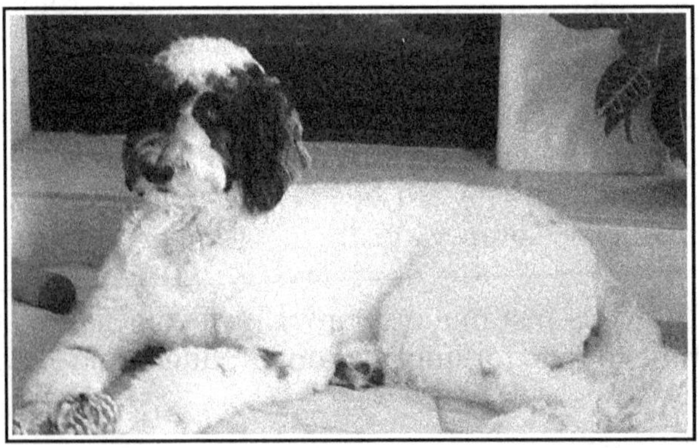

TRIXIE

The U.S. Military introduced Sheepadoodles into their ranks in the 1960's. They love people, water, possess a great sense of smell, and are easily trained. Part Sheep Dog and part Giant Poodle, they are large, fast, smart, and make great OneSevens.

We used Trixie in a few water situations, as well as sniffing out objects Agents tossed from cars for us. However, Trixie's greatest gift to the Cola Team were the many "Sticky Ears" she set for us over the years. "Trix" would dash across large fields and parking lots with tethered audio devices. A huge dog, she'd get on her back feet and, using her mouth, press temporary audio bugs onto windowpanes. We'd capture the audio we wanted and give a yank to the tethered device. It would pop off the window and we'd spool it back to us, leaving no trace we were there (except for an occasional round suction cup mark on window glass). No human prints were ever left behind in the immediate area of the windows. Just stray dog tracks.

Trixie recently retired and is living comfortably in Beverly Hills.

CANDYMAN

Candyman was my very first Canine OneSeven. He had an excellent nose and could run like the wind. Unfortunately, he was always running off. It seems he had a lot of girlfriend Beagles.

After we retired Candyman, a large German Shepard killed him in a fit of jealousy. Our old Beagle had no respect for other male dogs and wouldn't stay away from their girlfriends. *Big mistake little guy!*

BOBO

Bobo was our Small Space Canine OneSeven. A smart as a whip Yorkie, he pulled wires and carried objects into small crawlspaces, through drainage pipes, and across attics. Bobo was a nifty dog with a timid temperament. He loved to talk a lot! We had to fit Bobo with small slippers (actually socks), because he sounded like a tap dancer as he tiptoed across floors and above ceilings We lost Bobo long before his time. We believe a bobcat took our little guy from us.

LITTLE GIRL

We often joke about Little Girl's breed. She is a Havanese. I tell people she's a cross between a wild Arizona Javelina (pronounced “hah-vuh-lee-nuh”) and a Maltese. Havanese is a dog breed native to Cuba. They are quick and intelligent. Easily trainable, they are known throughout Europe as circus dogs.

We purchased Little Girl from a defunct circus company. Her roles are tailored to the needs. She's the most amazing little dog we've ever used for Cola Ops. One of her best tricks has never been used in espionage. She speaks English. She can say, "Hello" very well. She also sings along anytime someone strikes up "Happy Birthday."

◇ ◇ ◇

Vivian

Vivian is an interesting person. A professional artist and graphic designer by day, "Viv" is a phenomenal forger by night. I won't go into detail about Viv's work for me, let's just say my cover has never been blown because of Viv's work. They are always masterpieces.

I've given Viv some unbelievably complicated projects over the years. It's funny. I always know when a project has been especially tricky. Viv will look at me when I enter and say two words with great emphasis, "Mother Bear!" I've never been able to tell if I'm the Mother Bear or if Viv is saying the project was a Mother Bear. The point is, when I hear those two familiar words I know it's been a tough project. I also realize I probably need to pony up a few extra dollars when paying for Viv's services.

I met Viv in the late 1970's or early 1980's. Viv was an art student at the time. We met over a series of competitive backgammon games in a classy restaurant bar on St. Patrick's day. Viv waxed me that day and took a chunk out of my wallet. Chunk? Yep, they were high dollar games. I don't recall winning a single match and felt over-the-hill drained by the end of that day. However, all was not lost. In the succeeding years, Viv and I have both become winners through our business relationship. Thanks for everything Viv!

◇ ◇ ◇

Improvise and Repurpose

Repurposing is using something for a purpose different from its original intended purpose. It might be the modification of a device, tool, or something else. For example, if someone uses a computer monitor stand, as a stand to hold an office telephone system above the surface of a desk, that is repurposing.

A newly manufactured truck with a service bed is intended to carry parts and tools for an electrician. It is later sold and used by a camping enthusiast for pulling his camper. The external lockable compartments are for storing camp chairs, firewood, a generator, tools, and hiking gear. That is repurposing.

THE ONE-EYED MINKEY

Mrs. Cakes' "Baby"

I have a repurposing expert in my OneSeven Club. We call her Mrs. Cakes. She only has one eye, loves to drink Corona beer, and I once watched her smoke a cigar. She has a one-eyed dog to complement her own single eye. A very unusual person, Mrs. Cakes is an engineer, an outside-the-box thinker, and a superb brainstormer. She claims the secret to her success is brainstorming; nothing more and nothing less.

Brainstorming is an activity generally involving multiple individuals. They play off one another and come up with ideas out of the blue. Ideas are often the product of a process, based upon one or more thoughts originated by one or more individuals. Those thoughts are usually expressed earlier in the brainstorming session.

Mrs. Cakes is exceptionally gifted at brainstorming with herself. I've seen her muttering, arguing, and agreeing with herself. It's a great spectator sport. Her only rule for me, once she gets started, is to stay out of her way and keep my big Sicilian mouth shut. I'll only speak when she asks. That's when she needs me to clarify something or have me answer a question.

The overarching rule in brainstorming is to avoid dampening the spontaneity and creativity of the session. Nothing is off limits, and nobody is ever wrong. The idea is to throw every neuronic thought against a wall and see what sticks. The process is filled with creativity and should be devoid of criticism.

The way it works for Cola the Spy is to sit down with Mrs. Cakes and share a problem in general terms. An overview of the situation. Then I'll provide a sufficiently detailed description of my problem. I'll also present my opinion regarding opportunities and assets, while concurrently exposing what I see as immovable obstacles and dangers. I'll field questions from Mrs. Cakes then give her time to absorb, qualify, quantify, and prioritize. From there she's on her own.

It's pretty much a one-woman brainstorming session. It's as if Mrs. Cakes has multiple personalities, all battling with one another. Thinking on different levels, approaching problems from different perspectives, and each person seeing potential solutions differently than the others. Weird, but fascinating.

The venue is her in-home conference room. We'll sequester ourselves in there for as long as it takes. We'll break for meals, bathroom breaks, and a good night's sleep (if the session extends beyond that day). Our most extended brainstorming session lasted three and a half days. Once completed she has often reworked my planning, repurposed Colleagues and other assets, and reconfigured priorities, timetables, and benchmarks. Bringing order to my disorder. She's an excellent strategist and a phenomenal tactician.

I've always considered myself good. Mrs. Cakes reminds me I have many flaws.

Her repurposing and improvisational skills also appear in the kitchen. I was in her kitchen once after a brutal, albeit successful, brainstorming session. We just finished an operational planning session and Cola needed fuel. Mrs. Cakes, an excellent gourmet cook, offered to whip up something in the kitchen. I told her not to worry. I said she was too tired to perform her usual magic. I figured I'd rummage around in the fridge and pantry and whip something up for myself.

I couldn't find a single thing to eat. Yes, there were food items present, but nothing that looked even mildly appealing. I couldn't find enough ingredients to make a single thing that made sense.

Mrs. Cakes pushed me out of the kitchen and told me to turn on the television. I sat down and watched an episode of "Star Trek Voyager." I recall a couple Voyager crew members were stranded on a planet when their shuttle suffered a major problem. Like Angus "Mac" MacGyver and Mrs. Cakes, the crew repurposed some parts and successfully flew the shuttle back to Voyager, or fixed the radio and called for help, or something else that I cannot recall. I recall chuckling and thinking Mrs. Cakes would have been an excellent addition to Captain Janeway's crew.

When I got up from the couch and sauntered over to the kitchen, I stopped and stared at the elongated kitchen counter in shock. Frozen in awe. During that hour I wasted trying to help the Voyager crew get home, Mrs. Cakes prepared a gourmet meal. The colors, textures, smells, and overall presentation was a sight to behold. It was magnificent!

That's how she works. I look in a refrigerator and see a myriad of leftovers and disconnected items. Mrs. Cakes sees a collection of harmonious ingredients and food pairing opportunities. She sees order, where I see disorder. She sees opportunities, where I see dead ends. Mrs. Cakes innovates and improvises reasoned solutions, in situations where I'd just wing it. It's not unusual for her to forcefully say, "Improvise, Adapt and Overcome!" in her brainstorming sessions. She would have made an excellent Marine. She develops and implements quick solutions, while I'm still scratching my head. She is an off-the-charts creative genius, a problem-solving professional, an all-around awesome person, and a fantastic cook. Her improvisational skills and repurposing talents are beyond those I've ever seen in anyone - ever. Now you know why Mrs. Cakes is a valued member of the OneSeven Club.

◇ ◇ ◇

McOrner

"Mac" McOrner is an exceptionally great guy. I occasionally refer to him as McSeven. He is a personable prankster that would have been an excellent HUMINT Asset handler in the espionage space (corporate or state-sponsored). I smile thinking of the occasions where he and his brothers employed imagination, ingenuity, mirth and good-natured deviousness to create more than a few fond memories for those within their circles.

Mastering chemistry in college, Mac has a knack for creating unique drinks at parties. Many of us have encouraged him to become a professional mixologist. However, his true love is chemistry.

I employ Mac's skills in many ways. In fact, I am currently using Mac to assist a Client. The fertilizer in this current Op is less nasty and revolting than the raw sewage I encountered and shared with you in the Stinking Spy chapter. Mac has been enlisted to analyze soil samples, seeking evidence revealing the presence of synthetic fertilizers.

I was recently approached by an organic farmer for my Counterintelligence and Counterespionage skills to uncover a fraud perpetrated by a competing farmer. My new Client has reason to believe his competitor, who advertises his business as 100% organic, is using petroleum-based fertilizers.

Ryan Shaughnessy drove nearly halfway across the country on My Client's behalf. He took a short course on collecting soil samples. His class materials included a drawing showing an "S" pattern he needed to follow during the collection process, spanning 160 acres. Using a stainless steel soil auger and the cover of darkness, Ryan collected the soil samples needed from the "organic farm." Ryan delivered more than 300 sample bags to Mac for testing.

Mac's report just arrived, and I'm looking at it as I write this chapter. In short, My Client is correct. His competitor is cheating. Mac's analysis proves the "organic farmer" has been adding petroleum by-products to his soil (ammonium nitrates, ammonium phosphates, potassium sulfates, and a large quantity of superphosphates). A little sleuthing by Ryan revealed the man has been purchasing those chemicals from a facility several states distant.

Thanks Mac!

◇ ◇ ◇

Yowman

I refer to my audio expert as "Yowman," because every time I see him his customary greeting is, "Yow!" When I answer the phone, and he's on the other end, I instantly know it's Yowman because the moment I say "Hello" the immediate response is "Yow!"

I met Yowman in the early 1980's. He was employed by a large retail store in Las Vegas that specialized in appliances, electronics, and other cutting-edge items. At that time the store sold VHS and Betamax camera systems. Two boxes were necessary for the camera to collect and store video. One was a large battery pack and the second box was the recording device.

After purchasing more than a few of those video systems, I became well acquainted with the man I affectionately referred to as Yowman. His understanding of and appreciation for the multidimensional world of audio, audio electronics, audio mixing, and sound manipulation is second to none.

Yowman became one of my OneSevens when the substandard surveillance equipment I was using recorded stray RF interference from a nearby hospital. I was using items provided by a new unproven contact. The equipment was so low grade I never used that supplier again. The tape recorded terrible interference during a vital part of a lengthy conversation. The words spoken were rendered almost unintelligible.

I recalled a conversation I had with Yowman. He told me of a problem suffered by an event coordinator a few years earlier. The quality of the keynote address recording was terrible. It wasn't good enough to create a post-production written transcription of the event. The Event Coordinator contacted Yowman's boss, Richard, and asked if he knew anybody who could clean up the recorded sound. Richard recommended Yowman, who worked his magic and produced a cleaned up version of the keynote address. The result was an intelligible recording; offering a transcription service company the ability to generate a written version of the keynote in its entirety.

I ran a background check on Yowman. Result: "No Red Flags." I then sent in an attractive Colleague of mine to pose as the assistant for a potential competitor. Her assignment was to see if Yowman would disclose the status of Richard's business and provide some internal data points (marketing budget, revenues, vendor information, etc...). She implied she would provide sexual favors in exchange for his assistance. She said her boss would guarantee employment, a considerable increase in his salary, and a company car. All would be available to Yowman if he jumped ship and helped the new company compete with Richard.

Yowman refused to take the bait. In fact, he became very agitated and made it abundantly clear he wouldn't turn on his boss. Yowman was a married man and vowed things would get very ugly, very quickly, if she didn't knock off the sexual innuendo and promises for reciprocal sexual favors. He was beside himself.

After that, I reached out to Yowman. I was in disguise and came clean with him. I told him he'd passed a series of loyalty tests. I then explained I had a significant secret corporate recording needing addressed. The approach was entirely honest. I told Yowman I was under contract with a company wanting to know what a competitor's VP for Sales was promising conventioneers (potential clients) during conversations in his hotel suite.

Yowman was intrigued, and I spoke at length with him about loyalty, silence, discretion, and the dangers associated with unauthorized disclosures. I had a Colleague, who pretended to be a high power attorney, sit down with Yowman and lay out a series of legal threats and outline the ramifications if he failed to keep his mouth shut. He had Yowman execute an NDA (Non-Disclosure Agreement). He was so effective in scaring Yowman, I almost lost Yowman's cooperation. In the end, I managed to mitigate his fears and enlist his assistance with cleaning up the audio.

Yowman took the better part of a week to filter out the extraneous RF interference. He cleaned up the audio nicely and made it possible for me to provide My Client with an excellent recording. Yowman was paid handsomely for his efforts and begged me for future opportunities to work with Cola. Over the next few months, we conducted a series of low-key sophisticated tests to probe Yowman's willingness and ability to remain steadfast in his commitment to me. The probing paid off, and we were convinced. Yowman would not only keep his mouth shut but would also become a beneficial member of The OneSeven Club.

Yow!

MY DAD IS A CIA AGENT

In this chapter, I'm going to make an uncomfortable departure from one of Cola's Non-Negotiables. I've spent a lifetime remaining faithful to this particular Non-Negotiable. When assessing events in my life and screening potentially interesting information for inclusion in this book, I carefully evaluated the impact of espionage on my family life. After much reflection and all due consideration, I decided to offer Readers a glimpse behind the curtain of my personal life. I reluctantly decided to include this chapter to reveal how espionage has impacted my family.

To do that I'll be breaking the Cola Non-Negotiable that reads, "My family is NEVER a topic for discussion."

So much for capitalizing "NEVER."

The pathway to this decision has been difficult. It's an unfamiliar awkward departure from my standards. However, I believe cautiously including a few anecdotes from my personal life is essential in rounding out this book; and can be accomplished without revealing too much personally identifiable information.

My son, John, is a brilliant and curious young man. He, like many little boys, was always very inquisitive. "Dad, why you pack white socks and black socks for you trip?" "Dad, why you say you go to a covitchon in Cheecago? You tell man on phone you go Sanfrisco? Why you meow Dad?"

> ***An aside...***
> I have the ability to meow like a cat, but at decibels ranging from a near whisper to a loud yell. I use that gift personally and professionally. When my children were young and we'd be in a place like a mall, instead of calling for them, I'd simply meow at the top of my lungs; without moving my lips/mouth. People couldn't tell where that sound came from and I, like the rest of them, simply looked around in confusion. It worked though. In a few minutes my kids would show up. They knew if they heard Dad meow, they'd better find him right away.

> **Cola and the MCR**
> A Cola Meow heard during an Operation served as an alert to My Colleagues that the Op was either over or blown. If they heard a Cola Meow, the Op's pre-planned "Meow Contingency Response" was invoked. Everyone knew what to do.

Back to John's Questions...
As John grew older his inquisitions and snooping became worrisome. "Dad, why do you hide that little Minox camera in your shoe? Why is that shoe inside a bowling ball bag in the back of the closet?" "Dad, your passport says you were in Sweden two months ago. Why were you in Sweden? Does Mom know?"

Mom didn't know. John made it perfectly clear. I was getting sloppy. Until he mentioned my Swedish trip and asked about the Minox Spy Camera, I hadn't given sufficient thought to my personal security on the homefront. Although I know better, I should have been going the extra mile to insulate my family from my business activities. Sweden was a problem and held seeds capable of bringing harm to my relationship with my bride.

I've worked hard to be as honest as possible with my wife, whom I'll refer to as Treena. I have never done anything to hurt her intentionally and have always remained faithful. It's important to me that I never cause Treena to be either jealous or distrusting.

My carelessness on the homefront, as revealed by John, alerted me to take serious steps to correct my shortcomings.

Those early errors provided a foundation for John's belief that I'm a government-sponsored Spy. Over the years John's curiosity morphed from questioning into belief. He eventually convinced himself that I was a professional Spy, employed by the Central Intelligence Agency. Unfortunately, John was 50% correct. I am a professional Spy, but not affiliated with the CIA in any capacity. Fifty percent was too close for comfort.

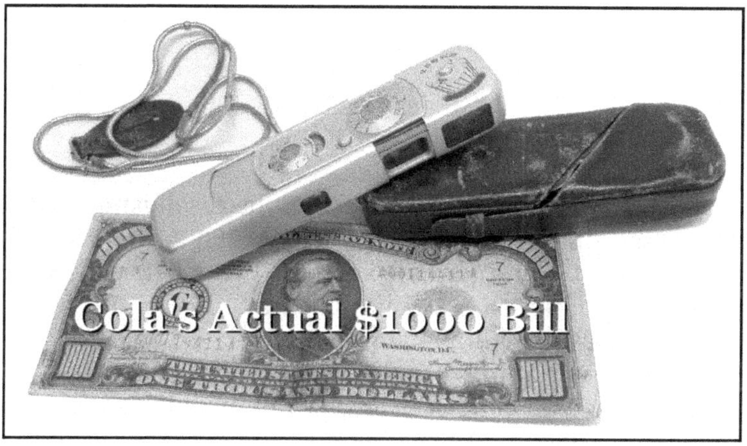

MY TRUSTY MINOX SPY CAMERA

This is the very camera John discovered in my closet
The $1000 Bill is discussed in the "Parting Thoughts" chapter

It didn't help that he somehow viewed an R-Rated movie called "The Falcon and the Snowman" when he was 7 or 8 years old. Timothy Hutton's character in that adult movie was a Spy. My little boy witnessed Hutton take a series of surreptitious photos of documents affixed to a wall. He also used his spy camera to shoot documents laying on a porcelain toilet. Hutton's tiny camera, known as a Minox, was used in actual Espionage Operations; including those conducted by me. That same weekend my son saw James Bond use a Minox as well, in the 007 movie, "On His Majesty's Secret Service."

I'd been away on a ten-day mission and was accused of being a Spy the moment I returned home. John and his friends had an entire weekend to hash out all of John's tales relating to my frequent travels, the Minox camera he discovered in my closet, and what John learned in the Timothy Hutton and James Bond movies. As I crossed the threshold into my home for the first time in days, he cornered me. John said, "Hi Dad! My friends think it is real neat that I have a real Dad who is a real Spy."

When I denied being a Spy John said, "I know Dad. I know. I know you are a Spy and I know you shouldn't tell me any secrets. But I won't say anything. Please Dad. Tell me what it's like to be a real 007. Please."

At first, I lightheartedly pooh-poohed his notions and thanked him for realizing I'm a "real" dad.

Over time I was increasingly forceful in disabusing his CIA-related assertions. A few years of trying that tactic proved my approach wasn't working. One method I've tried, with varying degrees of temporary success, has been to embrace John's belief that I'm a swashbuckling Langley insider. I'd even push the narrative with variations of agreement, conceding that I was a real secret agent. At times I'd verbally agree with his suspicions and semi-sarcastically support his theories. On other occasions, I would employ concessions and admissions, off-hand comments, and occasionally whisper spy terminology in his ear. I began to embrace John's questioning by responding with jokes. I made wisecracks about being the American 007 and spoke in whispering tones reflecting mystery and intrigue. My joking became so silly and ludicrous, for a short time, my son almost believed I was just a boring traveling salesman attempting to be funny. Reminiscent of the Arnold Schwarzenegger character in "True Lies."

In general, I find it useful to deal with problems head-on. For example, if someone said to me, "I know you're the guy who robbed the local bank yesterday!"

I might respond with "Yes" and brag with a conspiratorial tone, "The bank is lying when they say they only lost $40,000. I scored 2.3 million, but don't tell anyone."

I've discovered a carefully crafted mix of sarcasm and exaggeration will often send the curious away in awkward embarrassment. The idea isn't to embarrass anyone. It is to stop them in their tracks and make the problem of their chatter go away.

That said, the use of reverse psychology hasn't worked well with John. It has, however, evoked occasional laughter and the oft-repeated, "Ah Dad, quit joking around. I'm being serious." He is correct. John has been exceedingly serious about his CIA theories for nearly 30 years. He's always assessing me and seeking clues to the truth. He's patient, tenacious, and continually working the evidence. It is no surprise John grew up to become a law enforcement investigator. I fear it'll dawn on him one day that, although I'm a Spy, I'm not exactly the kind of good guy Spy he's always believed me to be.

I mentioned "True Lies" earlier. When that movie came out, John was beginning to doubt his theories about my secret professional life. Unfortunately for me, Arnold Schwarzenegger's character reignited John's fires and gave him resolve and a belief that's only faltered for brief periods since the mid-1990's. He continually reconsiders the reality of my CIA involvement, but that thinking doesn't last long. The lifestyle of the Schwarzenegger character, both at home and while on secret missions was entirely in line with John's long-standing beliefs about me; as well as my intimate knowledge of myself. The parallels were scary. Other than the CIA connection, everything else was perilously close to my lifestyle (except for the roses in the mouth dance moves, embassy Operations, and the silly action scenes).

Of course, Readers might surmise that the adrenaline seeking Cola Fugelere they know (the 10 meter platform jumping streaker) would probably send his horse from the top of LA's Bonaventure hotel into a swimming pool at an adjoining hotel. *Hasta La Vista, Arnold!*

To this day John often argues adamantly for my affiliation with the Central Intelligence Agency. Then he second guesses himself and starts thinking he must be wrong. Later John will again embrace the belief that I'm a Spy. Afterward, he'll predictably discount his thinking and tell himself he's being silly. Then, true to form, he's back to believing I'm a CIA Agent.

Of course, I'm not, but John isn't convinced. His suspicions have waxed and waned over the past three decades. More wax than wane. John seldom strays far from believing his father's life and travels are far more consistent with those of James Bond 007 than those professed by Stefano Gino Fugelere, the traveling salesman, consultant, and retail store operator.

John's thinking makes me dizzy. Around and around he goes; always arguing with himself and others. I'm sure those mental wrestling matches are far more difficult for poor John than those around him. He just cannot let it go. I sure wish I could come clean with my boy, but that kind of news wouldn't serve John well.

There was a time in John's young adulthood where he was going to be working hard to achieve something special involving the government. I wanted him to succeed. If he did, his achievement would enjoy well-deserved acknowledgment. To incentivize my son, I told him, "John, let me give you an extra measure of encouragement to help you focus on succeeding. If you pull this off, I'll permit a single question of any kind and will provide a fully honest succinct answer."

John was successful in his efforts and was acknowledged by those inside and outside of the government for his success. I was thrilled. He was ecstatic. Immediately after the announcement of his achievement, John asked me the following question:

"Dad, are you now or have you ever been involved with the FBI?" My one-word answer was simple, direct, succinct, and honest. "No." I quickly walked away.

I don't know how it happened, but John made a huge mistake. *Seriously? The FBI?* Where did that come from? I couldn't believe he gave me an out. A way for me to get off the hook for the incentive I offered.

Of course, in reality, John wanted to know about my affiliation with the CIA, not the FBI. A few minutes after asking the question he came running down the corridor of a government building waving his arms and shaking his head. "Dad, Dad, Please stop! I messed up! I just realized I said 'FBI.' I meant to say 'CIA.'"

I reminded John I'd offered him a single chance to ask a single question. I told him the answer was forthright and honest. John cried foul and is still unhappy with me. I was both relieved and saddened. I felt sorry for John.

At least he didn't ask me if I conducted Espionage Operations for a living.

Shortly after that fateful day, I explained to John that his question placed me in the unenviable position of not being believed. Because John so adamantly embraced his conclusion that I was a CIA Agent, my "No" would have always been doubted by him - even if he'd said CIA instead of FBI. I told John if my answer would have been 'Yes' to any question he asked, I had no intention of responding beyond giving that one-word answer.

I said, "Just so you know son if my answer would have been 'Yes' to either the FBI or CIA question, you wouldn't know if I was a vendor, a mailroom clerk, a consultant, a part-time custodian, or a bean counter. If I said 'Yes' to your FBI question, you wouldn't know if my answer in response to your acronym for FBI meant the Federal Bureau of Investigation or Fugelere and Boutell, Inc. Fugelere and Boutell was a real business my father and an English businessman opened in the 1950's. My first job was to sweep the floors for Papa's FBI. I would have been answering honestly. So any answer to your FBI question wouldn't have been helpful to you. If your acronym were CIA, that would have been equally troublesome, because I was once on the board of an association sharing those identical letters. You should have crafted your question with better care."

After John became an investigator, he thanked me for that lesson. He said it was a valuable teaching moment that's paid him huge dividends. As an investigator, John has to be very careful when crafting questions for interviews involving suspects, persons of interest, and witnesses. He's learned to avoid opportunities to offer wiggle room to those he's interrogating.

It's been a tricky path selling my fictional life while remaining a fully closeted Spy. As with any investment, it has taken hard work and involved some risks, but the payoff has rewarded my family with a healthy measure of safety and security.

Geez, Cola, we're beyond the statute of limitations. Why not be more transparent about your life and Dark Side adventures?

I'm sure some Readers are frustrated with me for not being more transparent in this book. My goal is to educate Readers about Corporate Espionage. This book is not intended to steer attention toward me. Some Readers may argue that we're beyond the statute of limitations for my Dark Side endeavors. My answer is that it's no longer about the law. It's about protecting people.

What About My Personal Life?

Why am I stubbornly recalcitrant about sharing more of my personal life? The short answer is John. Revelations about his father could derail John's career. No, he still doesn't know my activities in espionage are business-centric (good and bad); not government. He does know it's no longer helpful to ask questions. Regardless, John continues to embrace a belief that his father has ties to the CIA.

Also, you'll recall me sharing earlier in this book that I continue to enjoy annuity-like income from "consulting" work I did many years ago. There are also concerns relating to information coming to light involving Clients and Targets. Increased transparency would present too many pitfalls, for too many people.

Treena doesn't know about my espionage activities. It is possible on some level she might have some suspicions of her own. If she has, she's kept them to herself. I don't believe she suspects anything, even after listening to John's conspiracy theories for nearly 30 years. While I hope she doesn't discover what I currently do for a living, my overriding desire is to continue insulating Treena from the truth regarding my activities while on the Dark Side. She says she thinks of me as her white knight on a steed. It saddens me to know any revelation would likely tarnish our marriage. I'm afraid she'd say something like, "All these years, we've been living a lie!"

My sudden unexpected departures and trips to unusual destinations have been part of my marriage from the beginning. Immediately after we returned from our honeymoon, I left home on short notice to manage a five-week Operation involving the Tennessee Valley Authority (No, the TVA was neither the Client nor the Target. See the chapter, "THE NUCLEAR OPERATION" for more information.).

Although I'd like to cast off my continued habit of obfuscation and secrecy, I've successfully restrained myself. Refraining from sharing the truth with those I love has been painfully awkward. I'm sure you understand. The espionage dimension of my life is who I am. Hiding who I am from loved ones gnaws at me daily.

While an active Spy I maintained cover jobs and had ownership in many cover businesses, to protect the integrity of my actual workplace activities. Those businesses and cover employment offered opportunities for me to travel on short notice, and be out-of-pocket for varying periods of time. They also provided me with excuses to be away for defensible purposes. It was all about protecting my private life.

Back to Cola's Trip to Sweden and The Minox Camera...

I certainly didn't want Treena to think I had a woman, or a family, in Sweden. Heck, it was nothing. I flew all that way for a quick turn to photograph pharmaceutical research data taken home by an Inside Man. He had been planted within a Swedish pharmaceutical company by My Client and was on My Client's payroll. My time on the ground in Sweden was less than 12 hours. The entire trip was short. I flew out on a Sunday night red-eye and returned home Thursday morning, after delivering the photos to My Client.

> ***An aside...***
> An Inside Man is a person, male or female, closely associated with, and trusted by, the Target. An Inside Man is simultaneously valuable and a potential threat to an OP. An Inside Man is often seen as a potential Double Agent and is usually on the payroll of both the Target and the Client.

An Important Side Note From Cola

I'm neither young nor blown by the winds of cultural whims and political adaptations. Cola Fugelere is an experienced, pragmatic, man who speaks in an unabashed straightforward manner (except when operational and in character). Therefore, I've shrugged off suggestions that I modify wording in this manuscript to always embrace men AND women. Some have advised me this work would enjoy better reception if I use words like "womankind," and phrases like "Inside Men or Women."

This is not a work about political correctness. I'm no cultural meme and have no interest in playing PC games.

I Love Women! Without the women in my life, I'd be a lesser man. Women, for me, are necessary, appreciated, and welcome. I believe in chivalry, I love opportunities to treat women special, I eagerly open and hold doors for them, and don't for a moment consider women lesser than men.

Let me be entirely clear. Only an idiot would consider the sexes equal in all ways. Men and women are different. Neither is generally better than the other. Generally speaking though, women are better able to accomplish some things men cannot. Conversely, men are better equipped to succeed in ways women might find challenging.

It's about the sexes. The contemporary use of the word "gender" means little to me. Gender, for some, changes daily. Cultural norms seem to change monthly. The world has gone mad and everyday people are under consistent manipulation by others with nefarious agendas. Unlike young college students still fighting acne and living under collegiate bubbles constructed by tenured idiots, I'll keep my feet firmly planted on terra firma in the real world.

I'm a practical realist and, as such, will keep it Cola Simple. Men are born with specific plumbing parts. So are women. However, the English language has, for generations, used the masculine word to describe men and women. Mankind is an excellent example. Therefore, I'm not going to engage in a cultural game, or an agenda driven goal, that seeks to modify the language my fellow Americans have used for generations. That's where the buck stops for Cola.

Therefore, I instructed Steve to faithfully follow my desires in these areas as he prepared the SPY GAMES manuscript for publication.

Back to Sweden...
Upon my arrival in Stockholm, I cautiously executed a carefully planned SDR to make sure a tail didn't pick me up at the airport. When I decided I wasn't under surveillance, I made my way to the Inside Man's neighborhood. Once in the area of his home, I began running counter-surveillance tactics. After several hours, I decided all was well.

> ***An aside...***
> SDR's, aka Surveillance Detection Runs, are tactics used to ensure a Spy isn't under surveillance. SDR's are critical to maintaining anonymity and in preserving the integrity of a Spy's identity; and the sanctuary of his residence, hotel room, operational and non-operational relationships, travels, and so forth.

Back to Stockholm...
The Inside Man was expecting me to phone him at home, after work, with instructions regarding a meeting place. Little did he know, that approach wasn't in the cards. Instead, I planned on surprising my contact with a face-to-face in his apartment, thereby reducing opportunities for a set-up by the Inside Man. If things went awry and the Op blew up, it would be on my terms.

The apartment's location, near the rear of a large complex, offered several ingress options. I opted for a direct, crowd-parting, approach. My manner of dress was meant to plant three thoughts into the minds of potential witnesses. Unkempt, hairy, and physically challenged. Gruff humming and mannerisms were added to assist in repelling others. I was wearing Rubber Overshoes to protect and hide the Florsheim shoes I would reveal later.

> ***An aside...***
> Rubber Overshoes are also known by the following names: Rubbers, Shoe Condoms, Galoshes, Dickersons, and Gumshoes. Overshoes are, in essence, a form-fitting rubber shell designed to protect the footwear underneath.

Back to Mr. Gruff...
I approached his building dragging one leg slightly, as if moderately disabled, and humming with a gruff demeanor. I made my way upstairs to his floor and followed a long corridor to the back of the building. Once there I went about reconnoitering the layout, identifying all the ingress and egress points, planning my approach, and uncovering any potential threats. I calculated the number of steps he'd take from the elevator to his door. I performed the same calculation for the steps from the stairwell door to his residence. In that, I had an advantage. A Colleague working with me, who'd been on the ground tailing the Inside Man for the previous three days, told me the man was about 5'8" tall and of medium build. My Colleague was kind enough to collect an actual measurement of the Inside Man's stride as he was walking home from work one afternoon. His footprints in a light dusting of snow revealed the precise distance between his steps.

My Colleague also shared that the Inside Man's typical walking speed was leisurely and what I might expect from a man walking aimlessly down a sidewalk in a large park on a Sunday afternoon. He also provided me with timed step rhythms for the man. Armed with that information, I calculated the number of steps I expected him to take, and estimated the time of his walk from both the elevator and the stairwell door, to his apartment door. Then I went to his door and walked in the opposite direction until I noted a point in the hallway that should allow me to walk toward him, using an estimate of his speed and stride, and timed to coincide my arrival at his door shortly after him. I factored in a couple of adjustments that might have become necessary, depending on whether he entered the hallway via the elevator or stairway door. If he had groceries in his arms or if he didn't have a key in his hand, I had several different delays planned. A short delay might have required me to slow down somewhat to cough or act as if I'd stumbled. A longer delay might have been to drop something or even stoop to tie my shoe.

> ***An aside...***
> Although it's not possible to plan for every contingency, I attempt to do so. For example, if I know I might have to feign tying an untied shoe, I keep a shoelace available, identical to those laced in my shoes. I stuff half the shoelace down into the shoe, leaving the other half hanging loose on the floor, so it appears untied. I'd never purposely ignore an untied shoelace or tie the extra shoelace to my shoe. If a need arose that required me to run, I didn't want a loosened shoe falling off, or a dangling shoelace causing me to stumble and fall.

Back to The Inside Man's Hallway...
I recognized the Inside Man the moment he exited the elevator. The man entering the corridor looked exactly like the face in a photograph I carefully studied earlier that day, as the colossal jet arced across the Atlantic on the flight's great circle route. The hair, though, was different. The photo likeness showed a well-manicured hairstyle. The blonde man in the hallway had longer stringy, greasy, unkempt hair. Same guy, just different hair.

He strolled down the narrow hallway, walking precisely as expected. I looked up from a clipboard held in one hand. Then, leaning forward, picked up an oversized briefcase made of ripstop nylon and set off in his direction. I matched his cadence and stride. My carefully timed approach was working flawlessly. I was set to pass him in the corridor at the exact location of his apartment door, just as he turned the key and opened the door. Without altering my pace, I pivoted and created a CCM (a Candid Cola Moment). As he opened the door, I casually followed him into a tiny, filthy, studio apartment.

> ***An aside...***
> CCM is an acronym I use for a "Candid Cola Moment." In short, it means I surprised someone with my presence when they least expected it. Candid Camera was an American television series created and produced by the late Allen Funt. Funt's genius was behind the success of what may have been the first ever reality program on television. The program used hidden cameras to capture ordinary people involved in extraordinary situations that were often funny, and always caught The Subject fully off guard. Funt's tagline for the program was, "Don't be surprised if sometime, somewhere, someplace when you least expect it, someone steps up to you and says, "Smile, you're on Candid Camera."
>
> A "Subject" is an individual focused on at a particular time. Sometimes we are tailing a Subject, on other occasions we might be meeting with a Subject. At times a person who is the focus of our due diligence is considered a Subject. *You get the idea.*
>
> In my own lexicon, a Candid Cola Moment generally reflected the culmination of a clandestine Surveillance Detection Run, where I surprised The Subject of my surveillance; when they'd least expect my presence. The purpose for the contact was to force impromptu meetings when The Subject could have no foreknowledge that I'd be making an appearance; thereby creating a situation and an environment designed to insulate me from vulnerabilities. A self-preservation ritual, if you will, that

I'd use to gain the safest access possible to Clients, Agents, and other actors in the theater of my working life.

Although I refer to the meetings as impromptu, they are neither improvised, nor conducted without preparation. The impromptu nature of such meetings were from the perspective of The Subject, as the contact was made without expectation, preparation or foreknowledge by them. However, my efforts to prepare for such meetings were thorough and cautiously considered.

My favorite "attack point" for a CCM was when Subjects were on vacation, especially overseas. My Subjects were caught off guard 100% of the time and certainly didn't expect Cola to interrupt their detached bliss. Risk mitigation was the ultimate goal and serious purpose for the approach.

That said, however, overseas attack points did present entry and exit exposure when traveling to foreign countries. Those adventures could fill volumes, but they were mundane. Reader interest would be minimal, and those exploits aren't worthy of your time. Government agencies have never detained me outside the United States. The few close calls were short-lived and inconsequential.

Back to Sweden...

The startled man had just entered a small room that reeked of smoked salmon and dirty clothes. It looked like a tornado had passed through the space. The sink was running over with dirty dishes and garbage. The small kitchen's window panc and the larger studio picture window were hazy with old grease and grime. The apartment was an honest-to-goodness man dump.

Not a man cave. Calling that apartment-based landfill, a man cave, would be a disservice to most men. It was a filthy disgusting dump. A pigsty.

No dainty smells, no art, no lacy window coverings, no doilies, no candles, no photos. Nothing reflective of a woman's touch. I noticed several glass jars containing white portion snus (a smokeless tobacco common in Sweden) and more than a few empty containers that appeared to have once held pickled herring. There were a half-dozen bottles of low-grade brännvin (an inexpensive vodka) scattered about the apartment. Everywhere I looked empty raisin boxes were lying about. He was about as fastidious as a slovenly caveman.

As I was introducing myself, the startled man just stared at his unexpected bearded intruder. Before his eyes stood a total stranger with huge buck teeth and fuzzy eyebrows; wearing a white knit hat, and a tan and white plaid coat. He relaxed once he realized I was his contact; not corporate security demanding to know why he'd taken sensitive documents home from work.

I told him time was short and I needed to shoot the photos immediately. He was directed to make a flat space available for me about a half meter square. He looked around the pigsty and did the unthinkable. He took two steps and bent over at the waist. In one fluid motion, he slid everything off his overloaded coffee table, onto the raisin boxes and dust bunnies that littered the floor.

Books, cans, newspapers, magazines, empty herring jars, snus containers, raisin boxes, empty soda bottles, and other debris unceremoniously covered the cluttered floor. There was a sticky blue substance, probably the remains of many spilled beverages of some kind, encasing more than half the table. A copy of the Swedish tabloid Aftonbladet was firmly affixed to the table with the adhesive-like sugary substance caking the marginally visible surface. The headline appeared clearly through the translucent blue layer covering the tabloid. Raisins stuck to the curious blue material. They looked like ancient insects trapped in amber, except for the coloring. Although it was oddly attractive, Treena would have been appalled at the sight.

> ***An aside...***
> When my children were entering their teenage years, I was in transition from the Dark Side of espionage. At that

point I hadn't launched into my current role as a Corporate Counterintelligence consultant, helping businesses harden operations to assist them to avoid falling prey to corporate spies. That time of transition from the Dark Side gave me ample opportunity to travel with my family. The blue concoction covering his table reminded me of glacial ice. On one trip during my post-Dark Side transition, we journeyed north to Alaska. While there, we visited a tourist destination near Anchorage called Portage Glacier. We enjoyed the privilege of viewing a large iceberg up close. The color was beautiful and challenging to describe.

Glacial Ice from Alaska's Portage Glacier

The goofy Swede's table had a near perfect representation of the Alaskan iceberg we saw that had calved off the gigantic glacier. The flattened shape was wrong, but the color was dead-on identical. I should have asked Mr. Clean about the blue substance. I could have packaged the goo and sold it in an iceberg manufacturing kit for school science projects.

I had Mr. Clean scrape, chisel, mop, and dry the tabletop so I could use it for my photographic tasks. It had to have taken him at least ten minutes to clean up that disgusting table. It gave me the opportunity to advise the Inside Man to take better care of the "borrowed" documents if he didn't want security officers to discover his misdeeds.

The photo session required the use of 5 or 6 rolls of film in the Minox. I also took a backup set of photos with a 35mm Nikon and dropped the 35mm film into a purple Crown Royal bag. Careful with every action, I handled the photographic process methodically; following a well-planned set of procedures.

I didn't want to chance Mr. Clean phoning the authorities or other parties after my departure from his personal landfill. As I was packing my camera gear, I handed him the purple Crown Royal bag containing 35mm film.

He did not know the purple bag with the gold drawstring was not the same bag I dropped the exposed 35mm film into a few moments earlier. It was a second, identical bag, also containing film. Before departing the States for my trip over The Pond, I pulled the film out of each canister, fully exposing the media, then carefully rolled the film back into its housing.

I informed him he needed to follow me out of his apartment and take the elevator down to the second floor. After arriving, he was instructed to hold the elevator door open until the alarm sounded. That noise would be his cue to walk down the hallway to apartment 212 and wait outside that door for precisely 8 minutes. When the time was up, the slob was instructed to knock three times slowly, pause, followed by two quick knocks. The slovenly Swede asked why.

I ignored his question. I told him if an Asian man opened the door, he should hand him the purple bag. If there was no answer, or if the person answering wasn't Asian, he should return to his apartment. Once there he was directed to force the film canisters open and expose the film near a bright light in his apartment, then melt the film with a candle; and carry the debris to a trash receptacle behind a busy restaurant.

> ***An aside...***
> Spies will often use trash receptacles behind busy restaurants. Few individuals have interest in digging through the vile remains associated with cooking and half-eaten meals. In retrospect, it was a mistake to reveal that tactic to him.

Back to Business...
I departed the apartment less than an hour after surprising the Inside Man with my rude uninvited entry into his home. He went left, and I ducked right. I didn't care if someone opened the door in apartment 212 or not. I was buying time until I could create some distance between myself and the rubbish laden apartment.

As I descended the stairwell, I removed part of the beard from each side of my face, dislodged and removed the dental appliance, and peeled off the bushy eyebrows; leaving only a nicely trimmed goatee. Several floors down I abandoned the stairwell and walked back into a hallway; following it to the front of the building.

As I descended the next stairwell, I stopped on a large landing. I removed the 35mm film from the purple felt bag. I sealed the 35mm canisters within a tamper-evident container and dropped the purple bag to the floor. I put on a pair of horn-rimmed glasses and turned my coat inside out, revealing a dark woolen material. Removing the winter hat, I picked up the purple bag and placed it inside the hat. I wedged those items behind a fat vertical steam pipe in a dusty corner on the landing. A black woolen French beret took the place of the white winter hat. I removed the Rubber Overshoes and placed them behind the pipe, on top of the hat.

A casual observer would likely believe that an entirely different man appeared at a different emergency exit than entered by the hairy gruff stranger who was in the area earlier. The well-kept man, wearing shiny Florsheim shoes, exited the complex and casually walked toward a red Saab 9000 luxury car idling nearby.

Carrying myself with an air of sophistication, I strolled over to my waiting Colleague. Getting into the warm sedan, I handed My Colleague the container with the 35mm film. He pulled away from the curb.

My Colleague was responsible for safeguarding the film for a few days in country before taking a flight to the U.S. himself. As I recall, we routed him through Germany and Canada, with plans to meet me for an exchange. *The film for a handsome increase in his bank balance.* Although I didn't know it at the time, I really didn't need the 35mm film, but I'm a huge believer in redundancy.

If...

What if my Minox film was lost or seized? What if there was a problem developing the small media or if there was an exposure issue?

The next two hours with My Colleague were devoted to running a complicated SDR, designed to pick up any tails. Then off to the airport. The timing was perfect. He dropped me off. A few minutes later I walked into a Boeing aircraft only moments before the scheduled departure of my flight. My homebound itinerary took me to London. From London, I flew to Mexico City, then to Puerto Rico. From there I flew to Miami, then took several commuter flights along the eastern seaboard before flying to My Client's home city.

After passing the undeveloped treasures to My Client, I performed yet another SDR. Once I believed I wasn't under surveillance, I boarded a southbound Amtrak. A few stops later I disembarked and bought a Greyhound ticket at a nearby bus station, on a westbound bus. After an hour we stopped for a quick bathroom and snack break at a truck stop. I did not reboard. As with my Amtrak trip, I ceased my ticketed journey before reaching the printed destination.

Darting across the dark truck stop parking lot, I hopped onto the back of a lowboy hauling a monstrous D9G Caterpillar bulldozer, sans its colossal dirt pushing blade. An hour later a cold and uncomfortable Cola Fugelere jumped off the 40' trailer when the trucker stopped at a red light two blocks from where I staged my car a few days earlier. I would be home in another hour. *Ah, the life of a globetrotting Spy. Ugh!*

A long route, but well worth the zigzags. I journeyed home knowing $80,000 was awaiting me in a bank account I used strictly for wire transfers. *Did I say, "Ugh?" Shame on you Cola!*

Once in my car and believing I was going to make it home safely, I finally relaxed. Relaxation is a welcome physical and mental transition after a stressful overseas OP. Unfortunately, my relaxed state was only temporary. It lasted until John asked me about the trip to Sweden and my trusty Minox camera.

No, I didn't get to keep the entire $80,000. Just $40,000. My Colleague's portion, a referral fee, travel expenses, and other lesser expenses added up to nearly $40,000.

John's curiosity made it necessary for me to remove all incriminating evidence of my activities from my home. The solution was to position a small travel bag away from my residence and John's prying eyes. I filled the bag with items deemed essential whenever I was operational. My trusty Minox camera was in the bag. The kit also included miscellaneous Backstopping items to support my cover story. Those items included what we in The Game refer to as Pocket Litter. Pocket Litter is an innocuous assortment of business cards, claim checks, documents, receipts, and other seemingly inconsequential items designed to support and Backstop my cover. The bag also had several phone cards, a couple of pagers, and in later years, 2 cell phones and 4 sim cards. Of course, it contained an assortment of baseball hats, various colored contact lenses, a variety of identification documents, reversible shirts, a couple of light jackets, makeup, several spectacles, facial additions (e.g., mustaches and goatees), freelance photographer gear, oral appliances, sunglasses, and more.

A decade earlier I prepared similar bags and ensconced them at the ready in secure locations near hub airports and other popular flight destinations. Those locations included New York, Chicago, Miami, Charlotte, Atlanta, Dallas, St. Louis, Denver, Salt Lake City, Phoenix, Las Vegas, and Los Angeles. Each bag went into a box. A large plastic bag covered every box. Cosmoline encased everything with a moisture-proof barrier. Wrapped with plastic a second time, I further sealed everything within a second box.

> ***An aside...***
> Cosmoline is a petroleum-based rust inhibitor. I used the waxy substance, along with the plastic bag, as a moisture

barrier to hermetically seal the contents of the first box. My primary goal was to keep moist air from penetrating the box. By sealing out humidity and air, the contents would remain well-preserved for many years.

Back to Cola...

Everything in the bags supported my primary cover story (yes, I adopted other Backstopped personas as well). My standard traveling persona was that of a photographer. I presented myself as a freelance artistic photographer and an international photojournalist. In that role, I was a world traveler who sold his work to a number of publications and business entities. I threw in the "artistic" slant to justify the inclusion of the oral devices, mustaches, several spectacles of differing design and purpose, and makeup. The international freelance angle offered me many excuses to sleep, and not engage in conversation, on flights. It also allowed me to forget where I'd just been. Destinations were often described as, "where my spirit leads me." My photographer lifestyle made it possible not to have either a home or reason to be in any particular place, at any specific time.

It was a good cover and gave me many spur-of-the-moment opportunities to get out of situations and excuses to change travel plans. However, the photography cover didn't exist on the home front. I wanted a full separation between my traveling Backstop story and my personal life. Therein lies the reason I needed to move that gear out of my home.

When my children were young, and I was a little more cavalier with my personal security, I made a mistake that brought fear upon my head. The failure appeared to have made it possible for a Target to uncover my home address. In the short term, a quick fix was put into place until I could ensure my family's safety. When it came to my attention that I might have inadvertently exposed personal information to the Target, my reaction was instantaneous.

I was inside my home and received a late night coded telephone call from a Colleague. Within moments I was outside my house on a ladder with a handful of tools. The numbers above the garage door for my home address were 1001. I was at the end of a cul-de-sac, and vacant properties were on each side of me. I removed the last two numbers from the house, cleaned discoloration and grit from the siding, and reinstalled the numbers. My home address morphed from 1001 to 1010.

I didn't stop there. Our home was part of a subdivision recently developed in former farmland. It was so "farmy" I would drive the car into the city, park it, and return some hours later. I'd get into the car, only to find it smelled like a cow pen on a farm. The smell was so intense when we purchased our home, we were required to sign a document indicating our awareness of the unpleasant aroma. We had to accept full responsibility for any negatives associated with living with the odor.

Several hundred yards from our home and around the corner was a state highway flanked by farms for miles on each side. One farmer sold 400 acres to a developer. Just before turning into the entrance to our subdivision, residents could pull over and check their mail. The developer promised to construct a pedestal system with nicely appointed wooden mailboxes, covered by a pitched roofing system matching our homes. It never happened. He went belly up, and the temporary mailbox system remains to this day.

Our subdivision mailboxes were of various sizes and screwed into long horizontal 2 x 8's propped up with 4 x 4 posts. At one time there was a rash of incidents involving passing vehicles shooting at the mailboxes. Our boxes were perforated continuously in drive-by shootings and destroyed. We were also victimized by baseball bat toting vandals who would smash the mail receptacles, rendering them unusable. At one point I purchased a dozen mailboxes and a large black marker. Whenever our box bit the dust, I would yank it off the plank, affix a new box, and scrawl "1001" on the face of the box.

On that fateful night when I believed someone might have uncovered my home address, my second act was to add "1010" to the family of mailboxes. I found an open space on the rail and added a "1010" box. Then I went about aging the box by standing back and tossing farm dirt at the mailbox system. After a few minutes and brushing the debris off a few times it fit in nicely.

An aside...
A few weeks later (after we were once again residing in 1001) I went about changing my address with a few key entities, including the DMV. I used the 1010 address for mail, such as automobile registrations, that could connect me publicly to my home. There wasn't a 1010 address in our neighborhood, but who's checking?

Back to The Fugelere Family's Safety Needs...
Until I was able to discern my level of exposure, I needed to be absolutely certain of my family's safety. Fortunately, the problem arose only two days after Christmas. To my children's delight, I announced a sudden unexpected late Christmas present. Disney World! As usual, my bride was confused and surprised, but could only agree. On those critical occasions when we'd need to rally quickly, I would inform the kids before discussing it with my wife. I couldn't chance her saying, "No Cola, we're not going."

I'd already revealed to the kids that they were the recipients of a surprise 7-day trip to Disney World. Ugh! I hated doing that to my wife. They were on a plane to Orlando the following morning.

An aside...
It wasn't unusual for Treena and me to unexpectedly gather the kids and travel to places like Florida or California (Disney, Universal, etc...), Hawaii (the beach), New York (various attractions), Washington DC (the history), Boston (more history), Denver (ski vacations), and other such places that didn't often make sense for unplanned vacations. When I couldn't manufacture an excellent work-related cover story, I simply said, "Let's Rally!" My wife and kids knew that was Daddy's pack-n-go rallying cry. Treena would merely chalk it up to Dad's impulsive nature. The real purpose was espionage.

I knew "Let's rally" was a red flag for John. Each time the rallying cry echoed through our home, John would predictably say, "Cola Fugelere, your mission, should you decide to accept it...," then trot off to his bedroom to pack. They knew the drill and what to expect on our unplanned vacations. My entire family knew I'd go MIA for a time on our spur-of-the-moment vacations. Although there was no way he could really know, at some level John realized Dad was going operational.

Back to Dad Dropping His Guard...
However, I wouldn't be going on this particular trip. There was much to do. I had two tasks. The first was to determine my level of exposure. The second was to make relocation arrangements. I secured a Realtor and paid cash for a new residence.

Three days later I was relieved to find the Target did not have access to anything related to my personal life. I sighed a breath of relief and drove home to reverse the house numbers. I have no reason to believe the postman, my wife, or our neighbors noticed the temporary alteration of our home address. I held onto the newly purchased home for a dozen years. It remained vacant and available for my family's next quick getaway. Fortunately, I never needed to trigger an unexpected relocation. After more than a decade I sold the home. I realized a tidy profit, but I'm sure you understand, that wasn't my goal.

I learned a valuable lesson through that situation. I never again took shortcuts in my professional life, that might expose my family to danger. The information I received that resulted in the Disney trip was twofold. The first was word that the Target may have fingerprinted a hotel room I used during the Op against him. The second was that one of his goons tailed me to my home city and may have had the license plate number affixed to my personal car.

A little sleuthing revealed the room underwent dusting for fingerprints by local police detectives after a date rape was alleged to have occurred. The hotel room was across the hall from mine.

The Target did have someone tailed. Fortunately, the guy tailed was a vendor who had a legitimate association with the Target's company. Apparently meant for me, the tail keyed on the wrong guy when we stepped out of the elevator. I was asleep at the wheel and, in retrospect, realized I'd taken some dangerous SDR shortcuts on the trip home.

Why didn't I recognize a tail was at work? My counter-surveillance skills were above par. Those skills were, in fact, carefully honed and fully developed. I must have relaxed before the Op completed. A dangerous mistake. I'd clearly dropped my guard.

Never again. I would never again drop my guard when operational. No more SDR shortcuts.

In the end, it was a valuable lesson. I was never again cavalier when it came to personal and family security.

CIA Agent Dads never made such mistakes, right?

◇ ◇ ◇

I took many other steps to bring protective measures to my family after that particular episode. I won't go into everything I did, but I'll give you an example of one of my tactics. It has to do with automobiles.

First, let me set the stage by sharing my philosophy regarding cars. For Cola, a car is a chair with wheels that transports occupants to a destination. I don't fall in love with cars, name them, or allow them to become a fixture in my life. They are a tool. An appliance.

> ***An aside...***
> Yes, you're correct. I previously mentioned the 1975 Monte Carlo with the white leather seats. You've also seen a photo of young Cola Fugelere with a briefcase and a Cadillac Eldorado. Those two cars were my attempt to fall in love with cars. It didn't take. Nice rides, but they didn't give me a thrill Cola expected.
>
> I know part of the issue is my chosen career. I've never been comfortable standing out and being noticed. Nice cars have a way of pulling spies out of the shadows. Not a healthy path for someone in The Spy Game.

Back to Cola's Car Philosophy...
People continually laugh at me, saying I change cars too often. They don't believe I'm satisfied with cars or, for other reasons, seem to go through a lot of different vehicles. It's actually a defensive measure. I certainly don't want to be known for driving a particular car. Doing so makes it unnecessarily easy for those persons seeking to track me down. I've continually and pretty regularly changed vehicles throughout my adult life for precisely that reason.

◇ ◇ ◇

Let me share a story with you that underscores just how serious I am with personal family security. My wife, kids, and I were a little north of Albuquerque, New Mexico on a family vacation. I received news of a long-awaited trigger giving me a green light for an Op to commence forthwith. It was all about allowing me to score a large data dump on behalf of a Client. I told my wife something came up at work and I needed to duck out for two or three days. We kissed goodbye, and I caught a short flight to Denver. I knew my trip to New Mexico was well-sanitized, so my counter-surveillance needs were minimal, therefore the quick flight was low risk and of little concern.

> ***An aside...***
> In Cola's world, sanitize refers to the removal of all traces of espionage activity, to include travels to and from an Operation. I take it a step further and sanitize my six o'clock with traveling with my family.

Back to Colorado...
The job took a day and a half to complete. After the Op, I caught a flight from Denver's Stapleton airport to Chicago O'Hare. I hailed a taxi at O'Hare and traveled to an upscale hotel in the city. I ran a Surveillance Detection Run through the hotel and departed the back of the hotel through one of the kitchens. Walking briskly to a different hotel, I waved down another taxi. That second taxi ferried me to a low rent motel about a dozen miles away. From there I walked an SDR to a city bus stop a mile or two away. I caught a city bus to the Greyhound Bus Depot. The Greyhound took me to Indianapolis, and the familiar smell

someone told me originates from a manufacturing facility near downtown Indy.

I caught a cab from Greyhound to the Indianapolis airport; and jumped on the first flight to Atlanta. From there I flew to Dallas, then grabbed a different plane to El Paso. I rented a U-Haul in El Paso and drove to Las Cruces. I had my wife drive down and pick me up in Las Cruces about a mile from a U-Haul yard. I drove us back to our vacation spot north of Albuquerque. I had my eyes glued to the rear view mirror the entire drive.

Some might think my post-Denver SDR was a ridiculous waste of time and money. They might be correct, but I believe I was exercising reasonable caution and prudence. The Op in Denver had a dangerous side and high risk, even though it only involved a day and a half on the ground in Colorado.

The entire round trip cost me several thousand dollars. Short notice flights and ground transportation took me great distances out of the way and drove up costs. However, it was well worth the headaches, time, and expense.

The Denver job allowed me to go home with $27,412. My costs were high, but the Client understood my risks and paid me accordingly. Those were the pre-tax profits after my actual costs for the travel and my Denver area expenses.

Yes, even spies pay taxes on their "consulting" income.

Although the money was good, something made it even better. John was having so much fun in New Mexico, he didn't seem to notice I wasn't around for a chunk of the vacation. Regardless, John will probably always cling to the notion that his Dad is a CIA Agent Dad.

SURFER

I've enjoyed a fantastic Client portfolio. The cross-section of individuals and companies has been vast and offered me a most interesting career, filled with varied opportunities and experiences. Although a few scallywags wormed their way into my client list, most have been reasonably decent individuals. When actions and information come to me revealing substantial character flaws in a person, I summarily terminate Cola's association with the ne'er-do-well.

Granted, I haven't always conducted my affairs in ways generally acceptable and expected in a model citizen. However, I do have standards, morals, and ethical boundaries. Client's conducting themselves inconsistent with Cola's Non-Negotiables, and behaving in ways unacceptable to Cola, quickly become Former Clients.

On the other hand, I've had some great Clients. As I think back about the Clients I've had over the years, certain words come to mind. Exceptional, neurotic, competitive, fascinating, driven, focused, cautious, unique, and calculating are just a few. None of them are cut from the same cloth.

Idioms aside, one in particular Client stands out as exceptional and unique. "Surfer" is a fascinating man. I can neither understand his intellect, nor keep up with his continual brainstorming. I cannot offer any reasonable explanation for his energy, other than to tell you his coffee consumption is excessive. He's a pleasant distracted man with an IQ north of 165. He's a wise and decent problem-solving curiosity whose mind never seems to turn off or rest.

His business practices are always above board. Paradoxically, Readers will be surprised to know my involvement with him over the years, and the activities I've managed on his behalf, have remained consistent with high ethical standards and always 100% legal. I know, what I'm telling you is oxymoronic.

> ***An aside...***
> Surfer's brother-in-law, Louis Lopez, is a former law enforcement professional who became a contractor after retirement. L^2 uses his crime fighting experience, combined with his building skills, to construct props and other tools for various Cola Operations. He loves motorcycles and mortar. L^2 can do some amazing things with concrete and handguns.

Back to Surfer...
In the years I've known Surfer he's owned or had an interest in so many businesses, it boggles the mind. Surfer was a once and future consultant who has had his fingers in real estate, manufacturing, multiple Internet sales and services companies, radio and television, many brick and mortar retail operations, data and personnel management services, international mining concerns, and in U.S. politics (locally and nationally). Surfer conceived a 1990's era predecessor to YouTube. Surfer held a leadership position with an entity that gave eBay a run for their money during eBay's early days. He was a negotiator that held court in Priceline's corporate offices and an adviser to widely known personalities. His relationships reach or have reached, high into Wall Street, the U. S. Government, Silicon Valley, leaders in Medicine, sports, and the energy industry.

I'm proud of the Clients I've amassed over the decades, and Surfer is one of the most amazing individuals on that valued list.

Beautiful Santorini

Oía, Santorini, Greece

circa 2013

Santorini

My favorite meeting place in all the world is Greece. Specifically, a restaurant called Pelekanos, on the Greek isle of Santorini. The island is part of a volcanic caldera in the southern Aegean Sea. Santorini's small village of Oía, often recognized in panoramic photos of whitewashed buildings sporting beautiful blue domed cupolas, is an outstanding meeting place.

Pelekanos rests near the highest point in Oía. The food is excellent, reasonably priced, and the views are priceless. I discovered this location when planning a clandestine meeting involving a successful businesswoman on vacation. She was in a manufacturing business specializing in customized laser cut miniature brass poles, rods, and studs used in the development of cutting edge mechanical robotic metrology devices and drone technology.

I was engaged by the businesswoman to consider taking on an Espionage Operation targeting a smarmy competitor. The Op would be dicey. It appeared to harbor considerable risk, but with an attractive offsetting upside. The potential Client appeared to be both professional and decent, while the competitor's reputation is best described as sleazy.

I'll refer to the businesswoman as "Bren" for this story. She only knew me by reputation and a one-time nom de guerre I used so she'd recognize me, "The Maltese Falcon." I was recommended to her by a valued Client who passed along that particular code name at my request. Bren was under investigation by a specific government agency for activities seemingly unrelated to my involvement. I estimated it would be prudent to schedule approximately eight focused hours with her. I also believed my exposure was unacceptably high; given the ongoing investigation. My desire to handle the job was considerable, but securing the required sanitary Client time was a problem. Anything less than the estimated hours necessary would be insufficient for my personal security needs.

My pre-relationship investigation into the life of this potential Client revealed she had plans for a much-needed vacation. Bren had no idea I knew she was about to depart for a two-week Mediterranean cruise. Obtaining the itinerary from her travel agent was easy, and done without agency knowledge. The purloined travel information reflected more than the cruise itinerary, it also detailed flights, booked excursions, and other helpful information.

The ship's route through the Mediterranean Sea took the luxury liner from an Italian port, to the Greek isle of Santorini, to

Athens, across to Turkey and onward to North Africa, then northward to Spain; with some minor ports of call in between. I decided to make my appearance in Santorini and arrived there a week before her ship was scheduled to arrive. No vacation for me. The week was designed to enhance my safety while laying a foundation for a good Client meeting.

Bren had booked a day trip with the cruise company to visit the scenic Santorini village of Oía. Her hobby was photography, and Oía's enchanting Grecian scenery was a perfect setting for my photo hobbyist Client-to-be. Sorry, ma'am. You won't be taking many photos on this day trip. My week-long reconnaissance of the area revealed when and where the sightseeing Client would be getting off the tour bus for her Oía adventure.

I determined the path she'd likely take in her quest for the best photos. We located a restaurant for our "chance" encounter and secured accommodations for the unplanned evening stay. I also booked a charter flight to Athens for the next morning so that Bren could resume her vacation. Many contingency plans and alternative moves were drafted to ensure all went well (I won't bore you with the details). When the ship docked, everything was in place.

Accompanying me on the trip was a young protégé I'll call Jon Shaynor. For some odd reason, I consistently and alternately refer to the kid by his first and last names. Regardless, he was a perfect match for this particular job. Shaynor is a shutterbug, and we needed to provide as much cover for our prospective Client as possible. Since my plans with Bren wouldn't provide for a good photo record of her time in Oía, Shaynor was responsible for shooting some magnificent photos as cover for our meeting. He was instructed to make sure neither his shadow nor a reflection of his likeness appeared in any of the frames. Jon's additional duties included diverting the unwitting Bren to a meeting place of my choice. Shaynor provided external security, while Bren and I met during the day and later that evening.

◊ ◊ ◊

When Bren's bus arrived at the appointed time and location, Shaynor and I were in place. She didn't know either of us, so blending in with disembarking tourists was easy. Jon took the lead, anticipating Bren's path, based upon our week long research. I followed, conducting counter-surveillance measures. Shadowing Bren using a bookend tailing technique wasn't really necessary, but performed out of an abundance of caution.

Her occasional anticipated photo stops gave us additional opportunities to know if Bren was under surveillance by others. We determined all was well. She moved reasonably fast in the desired direction. At one point she reached a particular photogenic vista on Nikolaou Nomikou, a small pedestrian street in the shopping district. As expected, Bren stopped and set up a tripod for a photo of the magnificent view. That was my cue to switch places with Jon.

Jon took up the rear, by positioning himself in a small store to try on sunglasses, while keeping an eye on Bren. I had Shaynor spend twenty minutes trying on shades each day at that store, over the previous three days; always purchasing two pairs on each visit. The plan included the multiple purchases because we feared our favorite photographer might have to linger, and Jon didn't need anyone bothering him as he surveilled Bren. The shopkeeper recognized my protégé as a cash cow and was wise enough to leave him alone. While the shopkeeper kept his cash register at the ready, Shaynor performed his sunglasses routine. This day, however, he wouldn't be making a purchase. No sense in giving Bren an opportunity to disappear while Jon waited for his change. *Besides, Shaynor already had six pairs of new shades for his troubles.*

In the meantime, I darted ahead and ducked into our restaurant meeting location. I met the proprietor of Pelekanos shortly before Bren's bus was scheduled to arrive, and reserved a table for four. Securing the table with a crisp one hundred dollar bill as an advance gratuity, I told him I'd be returning within an hour or two. Like the sunglasses salesman who knew Shaynor as someone who fed his bank account, the money I splashed around the restaurant made my fresh face a favorite dining guest at Pelekanos. I'd eaten there the previous three days, with Shaynor, and always left an incredibly generous tip. I wasn't worried about the proprietor meeting my needs and keeping a table available.

Again, as anticipated, Bren's photography session at that stop only lasted about 5 minutes. By then I was seated at the table in Pelekanos, with a red rose dramatically resting on one ear. I'm sure restaurant staffers believed it was going to be a romantic encounter. They were accustomed to such behaviors. It was, for me, merely a calling card so Bren would know which table was intended for her.

As Bren began to move further along Nikolaou Nomikou, Jon, now in the rear, departed the small store and tightened the distance between them. As she approached Pelekanos, Jon was on her heels. He saddled up next to Bren and alerted her of my presence.

"Ma'am, if you please. The Maltese Falcon would appreciate your company at a midday meal in this lovely restaurant. He is anxiously awaiting your arrival at a table inside. Look for the red rose. In the meantime, I'll be happy to look after your camera equipment and keep it safe."

I was about to discover that Bren was good-natured and charming. She instantly grasped the nature of the situation, transferred her equipment to Jon, and darted into the restaurant. As Bren approached my table, she blurted out an altered version of the well-known phrase often uttered by "Candid Camera" producer Allen Funt. "I guess Santorini is a place where people spring surprises on you, when you least expect it. Are you going to say, 'Smile, you're on Candid Camera'?"

> ***An aside...***
> It's fair to say, Allen Funt was the originator of Reality TV. He brought laughter to millions. His message was positive, as opposed to the contemporary negatives found in today's so-called Reality Television. Funt's son Peter followed in his father's footsteps and retained the positive approach crafted by his father. I tip my hat to the Funt duo. *Well done!*

Back to Bren...

Ever since hearing those words I began referring to such meetings as "Candid Cola Moments." CCM's became an integral part of my Operations, and have remained in my bag of tricks since I transitioned over from the Dark Side of espionage. They are helpful on many levels, and never dull.

Bren and I became acquainted over lunch and she very much appreciated my discretion. We informed her that counter-surveillance measures were employed and that our meeting would be private. Bren was thrilled and looked around in both directions, then leaned across the table toward me. Affecting a conspiratorial whisper, Bren said, "This is so much fun! So cloak and dagger!" Then she giggled and sat back in her seat.

Staring straight into Bren's eyes with all due seriousness, I quickly placed my index finger to my lips and said, "Shhhh!" I looked both ways and told her "Careful, we're being watched. People on rooftops all around us are observing our meeting." She stiffened and straightened up in her seat. She jerked her head around quickly. We were seated very high on the island, and she suddenly realized nobody was watching us. I broke out laughing, followed shortly by Bren's tension-relieving laughter.

That action by me was intentional. Although Bren may not have realized it at the time, she was very keyed up. She was nervous. Of course, she should have been nervous. It's not every day you have a clandestine meeting, in a faraway land, with a Spy. There is ample evidence to prove that a good belly laugh relieves tension. After she calmed down from her bout of laughter, she relaxed and almost appeared to be a different person.

I regained my composure and explained that Jon would be taking photos in her stead during our extended lunch meeting. I also disclosed her evening accommodations were secured and I'd arranged transportation to fly Bren to Athens the following morning. I asked if she needed anything from the ship. She indicated she could purchase anything she required on Santorini. I asked if she'd let the bus driver know she planned on remaining on the island overnight, so she could capture the sunset and the morning sunrise. She agreed. I also explained it would be wise to write a note for the ship's staff explaining that she'd catch up with the ship in Athens, and give the document to the bus driver. She said she appreciated the cautionary operational security measures I'd taken to ensure a safe, secure, and productive meeting. Bren told me she was thrilled to have an opportunity to meet far from home and the annoying investigation.

We enjoyed a pleasant lunch, soaking in the unforgettable scenery. Later that afternoon, Bren purchased toiletries and other necessities. Afterward, we relocated our meeting to the island hotel where I'd previously secured individual rooms for Shaynor, Bren, and myself.

> ***An aside...***
> As of this writing, Bren has no idea Shaynor and I didn't stay at the hotel. As usual, we were engaging in self-protection measures. Jon and I would be ducking out ten minutes after we appeared to have retired for the evening. We'd tell Bren both goodnight and goodbye, followed by a carefully planned SDR. She wouldn't be seeing us again on Santorini. Our accommodations were miles away, in a home; and not a hotel. Such is the life of a Corporate Spy.

Back to Bren and Operational Planning...
The remainder of the day was spent outlining an Operation intended to corrupt a marketing plan she designed. A competing company misappropriated the detailed plan. She wanted the use of her plan to backfire on the competitor. She expressed a desire for retribution. I don't typically engage in retaliatory activities, but understood and, on some level, agreed with Bren that it was warranted. She pressed me and said she'd appreciate anything I could do to punish the offending company. I promised to take reasonable actions to meet her desires.

A departing marketing executive embezzled the plan. He'd taken it under the direction of Bren's competitor. Bren had two options. One was a costly legal route that could result in adverse publicity if the matter ever went to court. That process could take years, and Bren wasn't willing to let the legal timeline play out. The other option was to engage my services to irreparably harm the offending company, for stealing both her employee and her marketing plan. We agreed our primary goal would be for Bren to retain her competitive advantage.

◇ ◇ ◇

Bren is a lovely lady, a kind person, and a fantastic entertainer. She's a class act, and every bone in her body is reflective of an upscale business-driven socialite. We've remained in touch over the years, and the relationship has remained professional and pleasant. It's been an honor to know Miss Bren.

She was initially uncomfortable engaging the services of someone specializing in Corporate Espionage, but ultimately grew to respect my approach and ethical boundaries. Bren has shared with me that she appreciates my candor, sense of humor, cautious nature, and Cola's Non-Negotiables.

Yes, we brought the other company to its knees. However, we did it in a manner that permitted us to use their duplicitous actions against them, while keeping Bren and the theft of her marketing plan out of the equation. The other company had squirreled away so many skeletons in its various closets that our efforts were relatively easy and reasonably distanced from scrutiny.

The government agency investigating Bren's company ultimately dropped the matter. I, too, had a hand in that. While rummaging around in her competitor's skeleton-filled closets, I discovered they created and provided false documents to the authorities, in a manner prompting the initiation of investigatory actions against Bren's company.

That encouraged me to covertly deliver incriminating proof regarding the plot and plotters to the investigating agency. The information I made available to investigators fully revealed a cornucopia of illegal nefarious activities undertaken by Bren's competitor. The files from her competitor's figurative skeleton-filled closet left no doubt about their intentions and outlined their plans to the last detail. Their plans were designed to intentionally cause a government reaction, resulting in a costly investigation into her company's business practices involving alleged involvement with foreign entities that didn't actually exist.

In the end, Bren was thrilled with my involvement and rewarded me handsomely for my efforts on her behalf.

The Arch and The Needle

The St. Louis Gateway Arch

The St. Louis Arch Client Meeting

I once had a prospective Client, who I now refer to as "Archie 3X." I only knew him as Antonio, until after I rejected him as a Client. Antonio wanted a Cola meet to occur at the top of the famous Gateway Arch in St. Louis. I'd never been there before, but I knew it was a public place and didn't believe it would be a problem. My background check on him failed to turn up anything of either significant value or immediate concern. His need was compelling, and the referring party was someone who'd never created any issues for me.

Against my better judgment, I agreed to the Midwestern rendezvous and flew in a few days early. As is often the case, Archie 3X was a controlling alpha male. He insisted on setting the meeting place.

This was one of the few times I deviated from Cola's Non-Negotiables. I cannot fathom why I made an exception for him. My rule, "All Operations and meetings are orchestrated by me" is a self-protection device. My deviation almost cost me dearly, and I never again allowed others to dictate meeting places or times.

> ***An aside...***
> Not only do I set the meeting place, but I also dictate the date, time, and the manner of approach. When on the Dark Side, and in my current good guy Corporate Counterintelligence role, I usually incorporate diversions and last-minute deviations into my plan. Here's a simplistic example of a manner of approach deviation.
>
> I might ask a prospective Client to board a subway car and travel ten stops, get off and I'll approach them. Long before the subway reaches the anticipated meeting location, I rearrange the table. At stop three I might have an unaffiliated Cutout approach the prospective Client and utter a predefined bona fide into his ear. The Cutout will then instruct that person to immediately depart the subway car and get into the red VW Beetle waiting just outside the subway station at the curb. Then onward to an alternate meeting place.
>
> Certain additional steps are taken to thwart unacceptable actions others might take against my wishes. Our measures include surveillance detection, identification of GPS tracking, and spotting the placement of "cookie crumbs" by the person traveling to meet with me.
>
> Cookie Crumbs are physical or digital footprints indicating where someone has traveled.

> Such systems help me avoid getting set up to be surveilled or snatched.

Back to The Gateway Arch...
Although I agreed to his chosen location and day for the meet, Antonio allowed me the opportunity to set the time. Ceding the meeting time to me was curious, but not overly concerning. Probably just a concession to artificially remove any concerns I might have about him setting the venue and meeting day.

I asked Archie 3X to contact me the evening prior, and I'd provide the time. Several days before the meet I began surveilling the meeting area; consistent with my standard reconnoitering protocols. The difference on this occasion was the meeting place was chosen by, and known to, the prospective Client. *Not good.*

As I was familiarizing myself with the venue, I took the time to visit with someone from the Arch's custodial staff. The friendly fellow was busy emptying trash receptacles near the base of one leg of the arch. Peering over his shoulder and looking down, I could see a young couple descending a brick stairway leading underground. The stairway funneled them downward. They turned left and followed a wide ramp into a gaping chasm; swallowed by darkness leading them into the belly of the monument. That subterranean journey was necessary so they could travel to the top of the arch. I craned my chin up and looked skyward. I was looking far overhead at the shiny underside of the top of the 630-foot stainless steel arch. *Yikes!* It finally dawned on me that it was a closed loop system. Visitors entered the loop at the base of either leg and ascended to the observation area. Once they were back down, there were only two ways out. *Hello McCola? What had I been thinking? Why did I allow the prospective Client to set the meeting?*

The custodian informed me a tram system traveled inside the arch. It was designed to ferry passengers to the top of the stainless steel arch. He said it was small and pivoted on a series of fulcrums as it curved upward toward the apex of the great landmark. He said the tram's design included an attitude positioning system, similar to that found on Ferris wheels. As with a Ferris wheel, the system was designed to keep passengers level during the tram's ascent, and as it later descended the curved structure. Once on top, he said I'd find myself in a confined room with a low ceiling and small observation windows. He suggested people shouldn't go up if they were claustrophobic. I realized I'd made a mistake.

No, I'm not claustrophobic. I am, however, risk-averse when it comes to ingress and egress; especially when immediacy isn't part of the actionable equation and routing alternatives become limited. I am not fond of bottlenecks, limited options, or a particular smell. Particular smell? Yes.

I'm sure you've heard the song that goes something like, "The knee bone's connected to the thigh bone..." In Cola's world, the Olfactory Bone's connected to the Foot Bone. When my olfactory system smells a trap, Cola's foot bones go into action. My "Fast Jumpers," aka tennis shoes, figuratively kick into motion and transport Cola away from the Operation. It's performed without much deliberation and initiated rather quickly.

> ***An aside...***
> When I was a little boy, I began rating tennis shoes by how fast they allowed me to run and how high I could jump when wearing those shoes. Like other little boys, I selected my shoes based on a marketing campaign launched by B.F. Goodrich for PF Flyers. I vividly recall an advertisement that ran on Saturdays during the Johnny Quest cartoon with the slogan "Run faster, jump higher." Advertisements promoted PF Flyers as having a "magic wedge" that made better running and jumping possible.
>
> My mother would take me to the shoe store for new shoes. A natural skeptic, I tested PF Flyers against other shoes each time I outgrew my old shoes. I would run all over the store each time I tried on a pair of shoes. I'd jump over shiny Brannock Devices (the funny looking foot measuring instrument) and those short angled shoe fitting stools used by shoe salesmen. My goal was to determine which shoes were the fastest and helped me jump higher than the others. Although I eventually cast

off that system for validating good sneakers, I continue to refer to my tennis shoes as "Fast Jumpers."

Back to The Arch...
I carefully assessed the situation. Small tram system. Confined observation platform. Ingress and egress restricted. Funneled entrances and exits. Not a good meeting place. It felt like a trap. I discovered later that it was, indeed, a trap.

A subsequent investigation revealed Archie 3X wanted me to meet him at the top of the arch. He would feed me a detailed line of bull about a phony job he needed me to perform. He was setting me up. After detailing the fictitious Operation in the confined apex of the arch, we'd return to ground level. Once there, a Snatch Team would move in.

A Snatch Team? Sounds illegal, right? Smells like a kidnapping, right? That was the plan. These people were hardcore criminals, and I was their Target. *Their prey!*

Before the planned meet, Archie 3X informed me through a Cutout that he needed access to sealed bids relating to an eight-figure contract he wanted to win. The story sounded plausible. Moreover, the referral was solid. *Or so I thought.*

Archie 3X was running an interstate criminal enterprise operating in a space far outside the law. His successful use of ownership in several legitimate businesses stymied my original foray into his background. Those businesses served as fronts for his actual activities. I erred by not exercising better due diligence when performing my initial background checks on him. Clandestine Operations can suffer a multitude of catastrophic issues. As with aircraft accidents, it's generally not a single error or broken system that brings down an Op. It's often a series of compounding issues. Boy did I fall short when doing my homework on this one!

The more I learned about that iniquitous criminal, the more concerned I became. My fears were not misplaced. I'd stepped into a world filled with dangerous people.

Archie 3X believed I was responsible for an action against his business activities involving pornography. He'd suffered a considerable loss and wanted payback. During a conversation with someone about his loss, they informed Archie 3X it sounded like "a slick Cola Operation." I don't know who dropped the dime and fingered me for a repugnant Operation I would never handle. Many reasons could have been in play. Perhaps the dime dropper was very cruel. Maybe the dropping party didn't like me for some reason. Perhaps he or she wanted to get even with me for some unknown slight. It's possible someone mistakenly believed I was responsible for the caper. I am confident my ethics, character, and sense of decency wouldn't have permitted me to knowingly engage with a man of Archie 3X's reputation; and I'd never handle an Operation involving pornography.

> ***An aside...***
> "Dropping a Dime" on someone was a 20th-century phrase that originally meant someone turned someone else into the authorities, using a payphone to make an anonymous call to report a crime. The cost for payphone calls, for many years, was a dime. Over time, "Dropping a Dime" on someone transformed into a generic term meaning someone told on someone else.

Back to Dangerous People...
I wasn't able to find out how Archie 3X tracked me down and came into contact with the referring party; resulting in the planned Gateway Arch meeting. The referring party became persona non grata with me, as did the person who originally placed me in contact with the referring party. I hate losing good referral contacts. However, if someone burns Cola, he's done. I'll work hard to ensure I become unavailable to others with ill intent, and will quickly erase all identifiable paths leading to me.

I was not responsible for the action against his criminal enterprise. It involved a nexus between porn and illicit trade. There were truckloads of pornography associated with the job. XXX Porn. Now you know why I refer to him as Archie 3X. *Yikes!* That was NOT the kind of Operation with which I'd have involvement.

The St. Louis Gateway Arch meeting was one of those situations that could have ruined me. Perhaps it was just common sense leading me to turn down the meeting with Archie 3X. On the other hand, maybe my gut was remembering a learning experience involving the Seattle Space Needle when I was a much younger man and relatively new in The Game.

The Seattle Space Needle

A scheduled Space Needle meeting was the genesis for the Cola Non-Negotiable that reads, "All Operations and meetings are orchestrated by me." I expected to meet a potential OneSeven in Seattle early one evening. He suggested the meet be held in a busy public venue and specifically mentioned the Space Needle. I didn't see an issue, so I agreed to a meeting at that location. Although I'd been in Seattle a few days, I decided to wait and reconnoiter the area the day before my scheduled meet.

> ***An aside...***
> In my younger days, I was sloppy and too predictable. Over time I learned to modify my habit of reconnoitering meeting locations the day before. I began mixing it up. Three days before, then maybe 2 or 5 days prior, followed by 1 or 4 days.
>
> It wasn't long before I routinely reconnoitered planned meeting locations multiple times. I developed tactics that kept meeting places with prospective Clients shrouded in secrecy until last minute diversions took them there. It didn't matter to me that people I would be meeting with wouldn't have any idea where the meeting would occur. Out of an abundance of caution, I continue taking these and other elaborate protective measures before any meeting.
>
> However, I wasn't so fastidious as a neophyte Spy. My youthful Space Needle meet was sloppily planned and poorly executed. The standard "day prior" review of the meeting site was merely one of the dozens of ways I demonstrated ignorance and poor judgment while spreading my wings as a young Spy.

Back to The Space Needle...
Although I was a young and relatively green Corporate Spy, I was sufficiently competent to recognize that I needed to know how to get in and out of the area, quickly and safely. While planning the Space Needle meet, I thought back to my nocturnal garbage sorting duties during The Quick Lube Job for my Uncle Frank. I considered the unexpected visit by the young uniformed Officer who wanted to know what I was doing in the back of my van. That memory prompted me to review the Space Needle's law enforcement and security composition as part of the reconnoitering process.

Reconnoiter Day
I wandered around the grounds but didn't go up into the Needle itself, saving that activity for the meeting day. *Not smart.* Another mistake. I later learned to know every nook, cranny, and sight-line of a potential meeting location far in advance of the meeting day.

Dressed in someone's dirty baggy checkered chef pants and a white shirt, I attempted to make myself invisible by walking the grounds and pretending to smoke a cigarette. I borrowed those items from a kitchen in a nearby hotel. In my opinion, I did a reasonably fair job playing a cook on a lunch or cigarette break. My review for law enforcement Officers, uniformed or not, resulted in only one hit. It wasn't a cop, just an elderly security guard. Once I achieved a certain level of comfort with the area, and knew my way around, I departed.

Meeting Day
Meeting day arrived. It was a drizzly Seattle afternoon, and I was wearing a medium gray London Fog jacket I'd picked up in Loveland while doing a small job on Colorado's Front Range. Under the coat, I wore a nice three-piece suit, designed to reflect professionalism and competence. I probably should have prepared better for the meeting by wearing sweats and a good pair of Fast Jumpers.

As I approached Seattle's unique vertical landmark, I realized something felt different. My reconnoitering visit the day before occurred on Saturday. I thought the crowd on Sunday would feel the same. It didn't. It felt like something was wrong. What was bothering me? What was different? It was sunny and comfortable on Saturday. Sunday was cold and rainy. Was that it? No, I didn't think so.

> ***An aside...***
> Memory, attention, and change detection are all critical components in reconnoitering potential meeting places and, at a later date, executing those meetings. They are essential and can make or break those engaged in espionage. Good spies recognize their value in planning and in running Ops.
>
> Over the years I've worked hard to embrace what some refer to as "Pigeon Memory." I once read an article on Pigeon Memory written by a Safety and Security Professional. It was an excellent piece, and I received his permission to use some of his wording in this section (I'm a Spy, not a plagiarist). His thesis opened my eyes. I realized I, too, use Pigeon Memory. Like pigeons, I create mental maps and subconsciously refer to those established "images" to assist me in spotting changes.
>
> Pigeons, ducks, and other animals possess a natural ability to immediately see changes that could help or harm them. If a piece of bread suddenly appears in a courtyard, and a pigeon familiar with the area flies over, the bird will take note of the opportunity. If the object is a snake, the pigeon will also notice it quickly and avoid the danger. This explains why scarecrows and plastic owls lose effectiveness over time. Pigeons and other birds will, in due course, tune out the stationary, and only see new threats and opportunities.
>
> Good recall is an integral part of the equation. Like pigeons, humans tend to filter what is unchanged and expected. That's precisely why it is so important to form and retain a good mental map of the norm. When something is different, it should jump out at you like a lump of coal sitting on top of fresh snow. It is a

dangerous hollow approach for anyone in The Spy Game to ignore potential dangers. A Fool's Hollow.

Attention is a limited resource and very selective. When you walk into your home, your eyes will see walls, photos, electrical outlets, flooring, furniture, colors, window coverings, door knobs, hinges, ceilings, lights, etc. Your brain is likely to filter out most of those items. You won't consciously process the scene because doing so would result in overload; besides you see them every day, so why squander limited mental resources to inventory and assess each of those items? Now, take that example to an extreme and imagine processing everything as you walk through a busy mall or the state fair. Your mind would be reeling under massive sensory input.

If I spend sufficient time reconnoitering a meeting place before a meet, I become very familiar with the sights, sounds, smells, and the overall feeling of the area. Unlike the mall or state fair exercise noted in the previous paragraph, I don't need the distraction of massive sensory input. I need to focus. Therefore, I try to avoid meeting others in places that might result in sensory overload. Malls and busy fairgrounds have their upsides but possess too many sensory downsides to make them viable meeting places.

The reconnoiter process pays off handsomely for setting Pigeon Memory. When meeting day arrives, those expected norms are tuned out, allowing me to focus on what I need to recognize - the changes. I need to perceive and assess anything out of place, out of character, modified, or otherwise incongruous. The ability to detect changes has been for me, as with pigeons, necessary for my long-term survival in The Game.

Back to Seattle's Space Needle...
Looking around I noticed the crowd was slightly less dense, but something else looked and felt different. As I was about to go inside and make the trip up, I decided to see if the old security guard was on station. Sure enough, there he was. Sitting on a

chair, smoking a filterless cigarette. *Were their other guards in the area?*

Looking around, I noticed several men wearing suits standing alone; looking out of place, taking shelter from the incessant drizzle. They looked like cops wearing off-the-rack suits. None of them were wearing raincoats. They were soaked. They stood out from the crowd as they casually loitered alone, fighting to remain dry. At first blush, they appeared nearly identical. They were also wearing identical highly polished rubber sole dress shoes. Odd. They wouldn't fool anyone with even modest discernment capabilities. They acted as though they were wholly disinterested in anything in the area. Each of them adopted a similar nonchalant attitude, looking down whenever they thought someone was looking in his direction. The rain could have been responsible for their kindred postures. All the while, each man was covertly checking out everything and everyone. Their necks acted like slow-motion swivels or windshield washers. Back and forth, back and forth. Without question, these were cops; and not part of the Space Needle security team.

Then I noticed the same loitering uninterested swivel-headed behavior involving several men wearing windbreakers, blue jeans, and Fast Jumpers; as well as two men wearing overalls and the same dress shoes, pretending to look for something in their toolboxes. *Dress shoes and overalls? Idiots!* To a man, they all appeared to have the same haircut, and the cuts were very fresh. More cops.

I paid particular attention to the men in overalls. Although their faces fit the part of blue-collar repairmen, their hands and fingernails didn't. Their nails were clean. Their hands lacked the telltale signs of a man who works with his hands. As I passed by one of the overall-clad men I watched him scratch his right palm with the fingers of his left hand. The palm was fully visible and very clean. No calluses. Moreover, the tools looked like they just came from the hardware store. *C'mon fellas. You can do better than that!*

An aside...
I know a little about this subject. In preparation for Operations where we need to be in character, I'll have my Team look at the role they're about to play and make sure they fit the expectations of anyone in the area. For example, if one of my guys was pretending to be an overall wearing worker with a toolbox, I'll have him chew his fingernails to rough them up two days before the Op. Then he'll rotate all four tires on his car, using dirty tools. The day prior, I'll have him reverse the process AND change the oil in his car as well. Then, before washing, I'll have him use a combination of lotion and black printers ink on his hands. Once washed, the skin will have the appropriate coloring in the correct locations (e.g., black under the fingernails and around the nail bed). At that point, his hands are ready for prime time.

Back to Bad Surveillance Tactics...
A few days later I discovered a big cheese in their organization visited them several days before my Space Needle meet. I heard most staff members spiffed up for the visit. A supervisor issued an edict to his field agents, requiring them to get fresh haircuts, consistent with established regulations. That, too, explained the high polish on all their shoes.

I detected a slight bulge under the arm of a man in a too-tight suit. I realized his bulge wasn't the only one showing. All the loiterers wearing suits had bulges, but his was the most obvious. I expected better. It was a setup. A poorly executed setup.

The Game I'd been planning, was to ruin a day of bird hunting involving the Vice President of Sales for My Client's company and the owner of a competing enterprise. My Client was the CEO. He believed the competitor was the recipient of proprietary information, being fed to the competitor by his VP of Sales. The Client thought his VP was "spilling the beans" relating to his company's inaugural supply chain management system, sales and marketing plans, and other closely held information. My marching orders were to determine if the Client's suspicions were correct.

The two men were scheduled to rendezvous at the competitor's cabin early one morning and spend the day hunting birds. I needed them indoors. I wanted the two men in an environment that would encourage them to speak freely, and where my audio devices could record their conversations with clarity. The plan was to have them forget about bird hunting and get them inside the cabin. For that, I needed the involvement of a OneSeven.

The plan was to make the competitor's prized shotgun inoperable, without damaging it. It was his pride and joy. Fortunately for me, it was his only shotgun. I needed the assistance of a competent Gunsmith. If the competitor couldn't shoot birds, I believed he would retire to the log cabin and invite the VP to join him in his second favorite activity - drinking whiskey by his large stone fireplace. He was known to indulge morning, noon, and night. Perfect.

I spoke with a guy I knew, who knew a guy, who knew a guy, who knew a Gunsmith in the area. *Ugh!* Great in the movies, but not in real life. I wanted the Gunsmith to make the firing pin on the shotgun fail, so the two men would give up on bird hunting and loosen their lips with the competitor's expensive Scotch whiskey, Laphroaig, from the Scottish Isle of Islay. Laphroaig is great, although my preference is Lagavulin.

I didn't know the Gunsmith had a problem with a law enforcement agency. He needed to continually appease an Officer who held the Gunsmith's freedom in his hands. The Gunsmith was pressured to pass information to his law enforcement contact whenever anything suspicious and gun-related hit his radar. The Gunsmith, therefore, became a reluctant informant.

The Gunsmith assisted his law enforcement contact by reporting a meeting the Gunsmith scheduled with a guy (Cola), who wanted to do something suspicious involving firearms. The Gunsmith had no idea of my actual plans; and thought it might be more sinister than it was.

Men in suits. Men with matching haircuts. Men with bulges in places suggesting they were carrying concealed firearms. *Yikes! Should I have been worried?*

Indications of an obvious setup notwithstanding, I wasn't worried. There was no reason to believe anyone present could recognize me. So long as I didn't introduce myself to the Gunsmith, I'd be okay. I didn't have anything incriminating on my person, nor was there anything they had that connected me, in any manner, to the Gunsmith.

The meet with the Gunsmith was organized using a female Cutout. I had seen a photograph of the Gunsmith and would recognize his face. He knew nothing about my appearance. The Cutout gave him a temporary nom de guerre that was intended to serve as my bona fides. My Cutout told him to wait on the Space Needle Observation Deck, near a specific public telescope. Someone would approach him at 7 PM. The Gunsmith was instructed to have a folded New York Times from the Sunday prior wedged under his arms. He was directed to make sure the headline was clearly visible to others. The Cutout told The Gunsmith a man would approach him and introduce himself as Molinio. The Gunsmith's response to indicate it was, indeed, him and to assure me everything's okay was "It has come to my attention 'Richard John' and Molinio found a Bone within the Gates." If a single word or syllable changed in any manner, the planned meet wouldn't occur. The stage was set.

It was 6:15 PM and they would be expecting me in less than an hour. Wanting to arrive early to assess the situation better, I hopped into the elevator. As the car began to ascend the 60 story structure, I carefully evaluated the other occupants. Although the centerpiece of the 1962 World's Fair is just shy of half the height of the Empire State Building, the ride was reasonably quick. I needed to work fast. There were three others in the rising elevator car. A little girl of nine or ten, accompanied by a handsome couple probably a little north of thirty years old. The little girl was wearing a Minerva Brace.

I needed an opportunity to blend, and I knew enough about cervical braces to strike up a conversation. Four of our airline traveling Invisible People sometimes wore Minerva Braces. Dottie and her husband Raymond, as well as Mr. and Mrs. Pauleze, feigned physical issues and occasionally used their braces to assist in rendering themselves invisible.

I looked down at the little girl and said, “I’m impressed. Your cervical brace is designed to restrict spinal movement. That makes many activities difficult, if not impossible. It’s not everyone who can wear a Minerva Brace and travel to space inside a Space Needle.”

The man chuckled and said his little girl, “Savannah,” was a real trooper. A woman, whom I believed to be the mother was nodding her head and smiling at me. *Perfect.*

I looked down at the little girl and said, “Savannah is a beautiful name. I flew to Seattle from Savannah, Georgia yesterday. It is a beautiful southern community.”

> ***An aside...***
> Since the little girl's name was Savannah, I didn't mind mentioning to the family that I had just flown in from Savannah, Georgia, via Atlanta. The flight was a coincidence and part of an SDR, so I didn’t see a downside to the comment. Besides, I actually flew in a few days before, not the prior day. However, now that I'm a little older and wiser I would probably not say anything along those lines. The less information, the better.

Back to Cola's Elevator Ride...
As the elevator came to a stop near the top of the tall landmark, I said, “Do you mind my asking, was Savannah in an accident?”

We stepped out of the elevator and Mom muttered something about it being a long story. Dad looked me in the eye and told me they traveled to see the Space Needle after an afternoon appointment with a team of physicians at Children’s Hospital, on the campus of the University of Washington Medical School. He said they had nothing to do until the next day. The trip to the Space Needle was intended to fulfill a sightseeing request for Savannah, before heading back to their hotel for the evening.

I responded by telling him a two-day meeting I was scheduled to attend failed to materialize. The last-minute cancellation left me stranded in Seattle until my flight the next evening. I told Dad that I, too, was killing time. I mentioned I was considering a meal at the Space Needle's gourmet restaurant. Looking down at Savannah, I informed the small family that my niece, Faith, also wears a Minerva Brace.

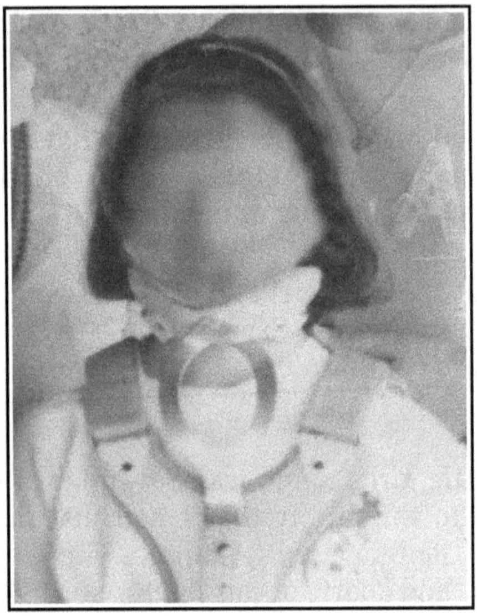

FAITH IN HER MINERVA BRACE

Savannah's face brightened. She said she'd like to hear more about Faith. Mimicking Savannah's mother, I said it's a long story. I asked if I could treat them to supper and I'd share Faith's story. Looking at the little girl, I said I was sure Faith would like to know about Savannah and her brace.

> ***An aside...***
> Relationships are essential in Corporate Espionage. Gaining the confidence of others is also key to successful Operations. After all, I needed to make sure none of the law enforcement "Watchers" keyed on me.
>
> Surveillance teams are often referred to by me as Watchers. When others and government agencies use

> Watchers, they may be a single individual or a group of people. I seldom use a single Watcher. A single Watcher provides too many opportunities for detection and/or visual loss of The Subject.
>
> This handsome young couple and their darling little girl offered me perfect cover. Savannah and her brace also provided our foursome with a certain amount of invisibility. Besides, I was sincerely interested in hearing Savannah's story.

Back to The Nice Family...
Mom and Dad looked each other in the eyes. I observed a brief silent conversation occur. Then they turned to me and said yes, but said they'd pay for their meal. I protested and begged them to allow me the treat. They partially relented. The husband informed me they'd only agree to the meal if they could pick up the gratuity. I agreed.

We sat down approximately 600 feet above the base of the structure for an exceptional dining experience at the "Top of the Needle" restaurant. I told them my name was Cola. Dad introduced his wife, Lily, and said his name was Roy.

Faith wasn't actually my niece. She was a OneSeven's nine-year-old child who'd suffered a terrible illness. She'd been a patient at the Cleveland Clinic; diagnosed with a bone-eating disease called Eosinophilic Granuloma. The condition had eaten a vertebra in her neck. She wore the Minerva Brace to protect her spine and hold everything stationary while bone from the vertebrae above and below grew and filled the void.

> ***An aside...***
> I didn't share with my dinner companions that Faith lived in continual pain. Her parents began to worry about Faith becoming addicted to the narcotics prescribed to dull the pain and opted to self-medicate her with blackberry brandy so she could sleep at night. On one occasion a few years later, they shared with me Faith often wet the bed during the night, as she was too intoxicated to get up and relieve herself. They laughed

> about her becoming a sassy drunk and scolding her parents for things only sensible to an intoxicated person. The situation wasn't funny, but her parents recognized the need to maintain sanity and find stress relief where possible. It appears they were successful in that quest.
>
> I'm glad to report to the Readers of this book, Faith grew up to be a lovely woman. That dreadful year in her life faded into a distant memory. After a full year away from school, Faith resumed her education and caught up with her peers. As of this writing, she's a mother of four beautiful kids, the bride of a very proud husband, and works with first responders in her community. Although Faith still suffers persistent neck pain, she endures it with a cheerful disposition.

Back to The Top of the Needle Restaurant...
After I finished sharing about Faith and why she had to wear a Minerva Brace, Lily told Savannah's story. Lily recently enrolled Savannah in a gymnastics class. On her first day there (a week before the Space Needle trip), she was tumbling and injured her neck. Everyone there just assumed the little girl strained her neck. Lily gave Savannah some Children's Tylenol when she got home and again at bedtime. She didn't complain about pain anymore that day. Her parents thought Savannah would be just fine.

The next morning Roy and his daughter hopped into the family minivan for the short trip to Savannah's school. As the van approached a stop sign, Roy realized the vehicle wasn't slowing down. It had been a cold evening, following a drizzly day. *Black ice!*

> ***An aside...***
> Black ice is a transparent layer of ice that is very difficult for drivers to see. Drivers look down and see the blackness of the street's asphalt, often failing to realize a layer of clear ice has formed on top the roadway. Black ice can be extremely slick, especially when the surface isn't completely frozen.

Back to Roy and Savannah...
Roy's van blew through the stop sign and broadsided a huge motor home. Savannah cried out in pain the instant the vehicles collided. The local Fire Department responded to the accident. Savannah told the Emergency Medical Technicians that her neck hurt. One EMT said the crash wasn't sufficiently severe to have caused her harm. He scolded her for trying to get out of school.

Roy wasn't happy about the EMT's attitude, but he refrained from commenting. Roy's van was fully operable, so he took it upon himself to transport his daughter to an emergency room. X-rays revealed Savannah suffered a broken neck, in two places. She underwent several additional tests. A neurologist examined Savannah and reviewed test results. According to that specialist, there was no damage to Savannah's spinal cord. Then an orthopod fitted the little girl with a Minerva Brace and referred her to the University of Washington's Children's Hospital.

This afternoon's visit was for an evaluation by a team of specialists. Tomorrow they'd know the course of treatment Savannah would need. The breaks were such that Savannah's prognosis was excellent. They told Roy and Lily she should heal just fine. No permanent damage.

At that point, our appetizers arrived. I kept our conversation going, wanting to disappear from any surveillance suspicions. I asked Roy what he did for a living. He said he owned a sizable full-service printing company. He excitedly told me about a new computer he purchased, along with something called a LaserWriter. I asked Roy if he acquired a Macintosh Plus. He nodded emphatically and told me it was an incredible machine.

> ***An aside...***
> Roy told me his printing jobs usually required prepress originals with high dpi's (dots per inch), before using his camera for creating printing plates. Although the dpi on the LaserWriter was 300, Roy managed to produce printing plates with 600 dpi or greater.
>
> Roy would output huge originals from the LaserWriter for his camera. For example, business card originals

would be many times larger than the final product. By photographing and downsizing the large originals, Roy managed high dpi's in his final printed product. It was an ingenious approach to save on typesetting costs.

I quickly realized Roy was a sharp cookie who thought outside the box. I tend to pay closer attention to those who have skill sets, not unlike my own. Little did I know, he was a risk taker who was about to center himself squarely within my radar screen.

Back to The Computer Conversation...
I shared that I, too, was the proud owner of a new Mac and a LaserWriter. We exchanged thoughts about the state of personal computing and the direction it appeared to be going. I laughed and shared about CPA J and his friendly condemnation of the little computer operated with files, folders, and the rodent. Roy thought that was hilarious.

Then, in jest, I asked if technology had progressed to a place that would spawn an increase in counterfeiting. The levity initiated by my question was contagious. Roy playfully tucked his neck down into his upper torso; then his eyes began darting to the left and right. He grinned and whispered, "Yes, but don't tell anyone. I didn't counterfeit any money. Honest. I printed some tickets that could have gotten me in hot water."

I instinctively glanced at Lily and Savannah. Both of them had mischievous grins on their faces. I looked directly at Lily and said, "Lily. What? Tell me."

Lily explained that she and Roy were in the printing company office one afternoon recently. A client dropped by and asked if he could speak with them privately. After closing the office door, the man pulled out a floppy disk-sized card and handed it to Roy. The card was a Department of Defense pass, authorizing access to an aircraft carrier that would arrive in a few days.

It was part of a U.S. Navy public relations campaign. The Navy distributed a limited number of passes for VIP tours of the vessel. Recipients of approximately three hundred passes included the offices of the two U.S. Senators and area Congressional representatives, the Governor's office, as well as the Mayor's office. Passes were then delivered to select supporters and others. Roy and Lily's client was the lucky recipient of one of those vaunted tickets.

He asked Roy and Lily if they could duplicate the ticket, so his wife could join him on the VIP tour. Lily said Roy thought about it, then told the man he'd see what he could do if the man didn't have a problem with Roy printing up a few extra so he, Lily, and Savannah could go as well. The client agreed.

Roy realized the printed card stock and ink were unusual. He called their paper supply salesman. The man was a nature loving guy from Michigan named Zyk, who eventually became an unwitting OneSeven. They call that networking.

Roy asked Zyk to stop by ASAP. He asked the salesman about the paper and ink. Roy said Zyk agreed to search for the paper and ink, but wanted two tickets for himself if he successfully secured acceptable stock and ink for the counterfeiting job. Zyk had gotten married the previous weekend, and there was no way the salesman would get involved if his wife couldn't join him.

> ***An aside…***
> A few months later, during a discussion with Roy (yes, as you've probably figured out by now, this wasn't our only encounter), he informed me that it wasn't unusual for concert tickets, and other sought-after tickets, to be printed on stock only available many states distant. For example, east coast concert promoters would often use paper supplies only available on the west coast; and vice versa. That mitigated counterfeiting activities associated with highly desirable tickets.
>
> Event access has become more difficult with the advent of smartphone apps and traditional printed tickets that contain barcodes. Contemporary tickets are often designed for scanning with cloud-connected mobile readers. Those readers verify the presented barcode, by comparing it with available inventories of unused

barcodes in a database far from the venue. Unless counterfeiters engage the use of a hacker, who can modify the database remotely and approve the barcode we present, phony printed tickets or app ticketing will likely fail; as well as placing the holder at risk.

It's more than just the data that needs addressing as part of the counterfeiting process. App screens need counterfeited, and the producers need to make sure fonts, sizes, and colors match expectations. Fonts, RGB'S, graphics, sizing considerations, and other details are as relevant today, as it was for us in matching stock colors, sizes, textures, and grain patterns in the old days.

Back to The Counterfeiting Project...
They went to work. Zyk used a Pantone color matching system and weight comparison cards to determine what he needed to tell his paper industry contacts. He located a few pieces of sample card stock closely matching the VIP ticket. That paper was no longer available, but a few samples remained. The samples were discovered in a warehouse over 1000 miles away. Zyk successfully located an ink closely matching the official VIP cards. That ink was more than 1200 miles away. Both products were flown in right away.

In the 1980's logistics differed from those we enjoy today. It was no small feat to quickly locate and fly in ingredients necessary for Roy to duplicate his client's VIP ticket. The quantities Roy received were just enough to pull off the job, but only if Roy made no mistakes. He didn't.

Roy printed the six counterfeit VIP tickets. It had only been three days since his client made the counterfeiting request.

Roy said his family joined the client and his wife, as well as the Zyk's, on the dock early the next morning; hoping to avoid arrest as they tried to gain access to the multi-billion dollar nuclear-powered vessel. They used the tickets without incident. Roy said he felt good that his work in creating those six forged tickets gave six regular people an opportunity to hang with the high and mighty for a day.

Roy said the tour was worth the risk. Savannah and Lily nodded in agreement. I looked at Roy quizzically. He knew. He knew I was wondering about his daughter's knowledge of his activities.

Savannah was a very sharp little girl. She knew too. The little girl looked at me and said, "My Daddy served on that ship and wanted me to see where he was on the day I was born." Savannah said it was okay because her Daddy was a hero and couldn't be there for his wife when Savannah was born.

> ***An aside...***
> In my line of work, a common thread exists in the lives of many Agents, Assets, Clients, Contacts, OneSevens, and others. That thread is justification. Gary, Kat's psychologist husband, once told me it is normal for humans to twist circumstances and situations to justify their actions.
>
> In my opinion, counterfeiting those tickets was harmless. However, letting Savannah in on the secret was unacceptable. I eventually shared as much with Roy.

Back to The Top of the Needle...
While dining with the young family, I noticed the Gunsmith walk through the restaurant a few times. I also identified two of his law enforcement chaperones. Their eyes never lingered on the four of us. I'm sure we looked like old friends enjoying a nice dinner. We chatted a while longer, had dessert, then went outside onto the observation deck.

Horizontal cabling enveloped the deck. It felt as if I were inside a spider's web. I felt trapped. *So much for a hasty suicidal departure from the edge of the observation deck.*

As the ladies walked around the perimeter, taking in the spectacular vistas, I visited with Roy. I asked if he had a calling card. I told him I needed printing services from time to time and would like to call on him, if that was okay. Of course, Roy was more than happy to entertain the possibility that I might become a new client.

While he dug into his pockets seeking a card, I recall placing my foot on an iron bar that served as a brace or step for the large iron telescope Roy was leaning against. The telescope permitted public viewing of the surrounding area, but also helped me by concealing my face, as one of the Gunsmith's law enforcement escorts approached our location on the observation deck. Just as the G Man passed behind Roy, he whispered into a large handheld radio "Stand down, let's go home and dry out."

That was my cue to get to work. I wanted to learn from the situation and intended on tailing the team to their vehicles. I wanted to know their force strength, the type of cars they were driving, and see what government plates might be on their vehicles.

As Roy was handing me his business card, the two ladies completed their circuit. I wished Savannah well and thanked the family for the delightful visit. Roy shook my hand and Lily gave me a gentle hug. When I bent down to Savannah, she squeezed my neck; asking me to give her hug to Faith. Nice kid.

I pivoted and headed inside for an elevator ride with two men. They were discussing their disappointment in not being able to present a set of "silver bracelets" to a guy named Molinio. One, who I believe was acting in a supervisory capacity, told the other he was sick of wasting time working with the man I now believe to have been the Gunsmith's "Handler." The supervisor was complaining about the man-hours involved with that Sunday's Operation and how it would impact the budget.

> ***An aside...***
> It came to my attention months later that law enforcement officials had been seeking me. Through a miscommunication, The Handler believed Cola was wanted in connection with the disappearance of a cocaine dealer, turned informant. That explained the very large force of Watchers at the Space Needle. The surveillance failure that day led to the discovery of their error. Valuable time and resources had been squandered. Higher ups were upset. Somebody needed to be held accountable. *The Handler? Yep!* He was transferred to a

little-appreciated outpost somewhere far away and very cold.

Back to The Elevator...
As the elevator began to descend, the undercover twins continued their conversation about the wasted day. The Cop I believe to be the subordinate complained about his ruined Sunday. He blamed "that idiot and his stupid snitch" for the wasted day. The supervisor continued and piggybacked his conversation with more thoughts about The Handler.

Then, without any apparent provocation, he suddenly stopped speaking in mid-sentence and looked directly at me. When he opened his mouth to speak, I recalled my dumpster diving evening and the cop's words, "Police, Open Up!" I thought I'd been nailed.

His words, however, were far less disconcerting. In fact, they were reassuringly tame. He said, "Sir, I couldn't help noticing you ordered Italian Gelato for dessert. How was it?"

Relieved, I said, "Thanks for asking. It was very tasty. Necessary too. I ate Sauteed Oysters for the main course and needed to flush out the fishy aftertaste."

Pleasantries ceased as the door opened. They were, thankfully, gone in a flash.

I followed from a discrete distance. The officials walked about four blocks to an area where four unmistakable government issued sedans were parked, along with two white panel vans. All had U.S. Government license plates. Ten men gathered on the sidewalk for a post-game conference. Their situational awareness was turned off. Four men were in suits. All four had the same shoes. Another four wore jeans, tee shirts, Fast Jumpers, and windbreakers. The two in overalls looked like they just came from taking a shower. Their overalls were clean, and their dress shoes looked new and out of place. All ten men appeared to frequent the same barber at the same time.

It was on that day I added the new Non-Negotiable to my growing list. "All Operations and meetings are orchestrated by me." That trip taught me the need to scout meeting locations for gatherings of men and vehicles consistent with what I'd just witnessed. It also reminded me to look at haircuts, shoes, and clothing designed to cover concealed firearms. The real takeaway for me, however, was the telltale look I've seen many times since in the evermoving eyes of Watchers with slowly swiveling heads.

The Space Needle setup taught me that I must set the meeting places. Moreover, I knew I needed to develop tactics that would allow me to smoothly redirect potential meeting attendees from whatever venue I initially disclose, to a location better suited for my safety and security. Planning misdirection and creating an atmosphere of spontaneity would serve me well over the coming years.

I also knew I needed to develop systems to ensure meeting attendees were well-screened when redirected to the actual venues. I needed to make sure communications with Watchers, Handlers, and Colleagues weren't possible. Tails and traps need identifying before I reveal my presence. The process of planning and carrying out those tasks differentiates professionals from wannabes.

> ***An aside...***
> In those days it was easier to spot concealed firearms on Officers wearing civilian clothing. Revolvers were the most common handgun carried by them. Revolver cylinders made concealment difficult, as opposed to the more easily concealed flattened pistols generally carried today.
>
> Also, a trained eye can spot shoulder holsters in the body language of the wearer; and on occasion, the appearance of the fabrics worn; offering telltale signs that a concealed weapon is in play.
>
> On the other hand, the same issues exist for those wearing firearms on their hips and in the small of the back. A concealed weapon on the ankle affects the

wearer's gait and produces a noticeable bulge to a trained eye when the wearer's leg is in certain positions.

Back to The Space Needle Meeting...
When all was said and done, I decided the Gunsmith was too hot to handle. I reached out to a wonderful gun expert I know. Jeff is a big guy of Polish descent, originally from Chicago. Jeff is not a gunsmith but knows more about firearms than any person I've ever met. Jeff is a trustworthy intelligent firearms expert with a phenomenal memory and a wonderful sense of humor. A good guy who is exceedingly decent.

I explained the firing pin need to Jeff and he offered a slightly different approach to rendering the shotgun temporarily useless, without causing damage of any kind. Jeff flew out on the next plane and I set him up in a low budget motel about 20 miles from the competitor's cabin. I picked the lock on the cabin one evening, disabled the alarm system, and removed the shotgun from its station above the stone fireplace. I wrapped it in a blanket, and placed it in a duffel bag; followed by a half hour drive to Jeff's motel.

Jeff's bona fides were interesting, and I'll never forget them. My task upon arrival was to knock on the door and say the following words, "A Master Collimator is not a Cordless Drill." Jeff's prepared response was supposed to be, "I'm no Morgan," followed by me handing Jeff a box of glazed donuts. Everything went as planned.

To be clear, Jeff and I are not strangers. The bona fides were intended to confirm to one another that all was well. If either of us deviated from the script, the Operation would cease. An occupational necessity.

Jeff performed his magic in less than 10 minutes. He inserted a dummy shotgun shell into the chamber. He cocked the gun and pulled the trigger. When Jeff removed the shell, the dummy primer was free of the expected firing pin depression. It worked! I paid Jeff $5000 for his brief work on the shotgun and returned it to the cabin.

Jeff returned to Chicago the next morning. Two days later the bird hunt quickly turned into a whiskey-driven conversation, proving My Client's suspicions were dead on correct.

> ***An aside...***
> Weeds can destroy beautiful landscaping very quickly, if not addressed when they first appear. I recommend you pull weeds when first noticing them to avoid propagation. The matter of the events uncovered by the fireplace in the whiskeyed atmosphere of the cabin underscores the value in following through with doubts. There's a good lesson here for business owners if they begin to suspect there's a problem. If suspicions exist, it could be suggestive of a potential problem that should be addressed sooner, rather than later.
>
> If a business owner doesn't have confidence in staff members, perhaps that business owner needs to replace those employees. Trusted team members are vital to operational success in any endeavor. If that business owner hasn't anyone he or she can trust, and if that owner doesn't trust anybody, perhaps it's a case of paranoia. Engaging the services of a Counterespionage professional is one method of determining if a problem actually exists. Maybe it's paranoia or a perception issue.

Back to My Client and the Outcome of The Operation...
My Client summarily terminated the VP for cause; thanks to a guy named Cola. A little research into the VP's background turned up information proving he lied on his resume. He claimed to have had a Masters, when in fact he'd never graduated from college.

During the VP's dismissal process, My Client reminded him he'd previously executed several legal documents requiring him to keep My Client's business activities confidential. He was threatened with exposure and public humiliation if he remained in that business space. He moved to Mexico and bought a tourist related business in Acapulco. The economy in Acapulco declined rapidly because of narco-terrorist activities, tourism waned, and ten years later the VP returned to the U.S. broke and destitute.

My Client wanted me to destroy the competitor's business. Six months later the competitor closed his doors and retired.

> ***An aside...***
> I mentioned that I set Jeff up in a low budget motel. Why a cheap motel, when Jeff's expertise and value warranted a $5000 payoff? Simple. The word motel is a contraction of the words "Motor" and "Hotel." Motels are generally designed to allow traveling motorists the ability to pull their vehicles up to the doors of rooms positioned at ground level.
>
> Carrying a shotgun through a hotel lobby presents several problems. The short distance from my rental car to the motel room door negated those problems. I backed up to within five feet of Jeff's door, in a dark parking lot. That made it easy to transport the long duffel bag into Jeff's room quickly and without suspicion.

Back to Roy...
That Sunday at the top of the Space Needle with the little girl and her parents resulted in the birth of a new OneSeven relationship. I kept Roy's business card and, over a three month period, performed many personality and background checks on him. I needed a good printing OneSeven and liked Roy's ballsy counterfeiting stunt that landed him on the deck of U.S. Government property. My assistants informally interviewed Roy and people who knew him. He didn't realize he was being checked out. I had Colleagues poke and pry in Roy's world, to learn as much about him as possible.

Roy's only dark side history we uncovered, besides the aircraft carrier counterfeiting job, was a business arrangement he previously had with a bookie; as well as some gambling-related matters involving Roy when he was a very young man. Over the course of several previous professional football seasons, Roy provided weekly printing services for a bookie in his community. The documents he printed listed every NFL game and included betting odds. The documents also contained something referred to as Overs and Unders. I'm not familiar with bookie jargon. Please forgive me for not providing more information about that.

I had no reason to believe Roy had any other involvement within the gambling world at that time. However, I did learn he was a poker, blackjack, and craps dealer before meeting Lily. Our research indicated that Roy isn't a gambler. The late-night after-hours alcohol and gambling scene wasn't for him. Once he and Lily met, it appears Lily successfully encouraged Roy to disassociate himself from that community.

Lily wasn't alone in her disdain for Roy's after-hours involvement. My legal OneSeven didn't really like what Roy was doing. However, he believed Roy's exposure and potential impact on me were minimal. I agreed. That was part of Roy's ancient history. It didn't appear any baggage was present to weigh him down or create any issues for me. Had Roy been a gambler, I would have had no use for his services. Taking a chance on someone who might become indebted to a bookie is dangerous.

I discussed these matters with Roy when I recruited him. I also made it clear that any involvement with those from his past gaming experience would, without exception, bring an end to any relationship with me. He was okay with my edict, and I didn't have any reason to believe it would ever become an issue, and it hasn't.

I did not like him having so many people in the loop when he counterfeited the VIP tickets. I was especially disappointed he didn't keep it secret from Savannah. Regardless, I knew Roy could become a valued Asset. Like a wild pony, he needed to be tamed and educated.

> ***An aside...***
> An Asset is a person, system, or item, generally associated with our Target that holds value to our Operation.

Back to OneSeven Roy...
Over the years I taught Roy well, and we're still working together after more than thirty years. He readily embraced the secrecy needs of life in the espionage arena. Roy did it so well even Lily is unaware of his clandestine work. Moreover, Lily and Savannah still don't know I'm a Spy.

I value the friendship I still enjoy with Roy, Lily, and Savannah. I see them often. To this day, none of them know the circumstances that led to our original encounter on that fateful drizzly day in the Space Needle elevator. Perhaps I'll give Roy a copy of this book with a wink and a nod. Then he'll know.

Back to The Gateway Arch...
A couple of months after my cancellation of the Gateway Arch meeting, Archie 3X was the recipient of information clearing me of any association with the heist of his porn. Good! I didn't want that baggage following me and endangering my safety and security. Little did I know, Archie 3X and I would cross paths again more than ten years later. Not to worry, you'll hear about that situation in a future chapter.

The failed Arch meeting was the best example I've had as a reminder that I must always set up meetings correctly, not allow others to dictate how I conduct my business, to consistently know the venue better than those with whom I'll be meeting, and never to telegraph the meeting location ahead of time. I was additionally reminded to conduct multiple reconnoitering reviews. Unlike my review of the Space Needle before the meeting when I dismissed the need to go up into the Needle and thoroughly review the restaurant, observation deck, and other areas, I would never skip such vital steps in the future.

Finally, the Arch situation was an excellent reminder that my very life could be jeopardized by me failing to follow my own rules. It reinforced the need to keep Cola's Non-Negotiables, NON-NEGOTIABLE!

FOOL'S GOLD

A BONANZA CREEK MINING OPERATION
circa 1986

Dawson City, Yukon Territory, Canada
There's a charming little town on the western border region of Canada, near the Arctic Circle. Nestled onto the banks of a slow sweeping bend in the Yukon River, a few miles from the Alaskan border, Dawson City in Canada's Yukon Territory was the setting for the 1896 Klondike Gold Rush. Tourists and gold miners trek

to this historic northern community each summer in search of history, photographic opportunities, and gold.

Few visitors travel to this region during the wintertime. Winter temperatures are unbelievably cold. I once conducted a Cola Operation in a community 330 miles due south of Dawson in the dead of winter. The town was Whitehorse and the high temperature on one particular day was -55°F. I spent that day, running inside and out, taking care of our Op. Our work took place outside in the cold weather at an area copper mine. We ran 45-minute surveillance shifts. We'd then go inside to warm up. After I'd been outdoors for more than fifteen or twenty minutes, my mustache began to grow long icicles on each side, as moisture from my nostrils accumulated and froze. By the time I returned indoors, Cola looked like a dark-skinned walrus, with long white tusks.

That winter, Dawson's temperature during one particular cold snap didn't enjoy official documentation, because the certified thermometer didn't register low enough. One of My Colleagues and I were in Dawson during that record-breaking cold snap, performing investigative work prior to launching the Whitehorse Operation. Townspeople, relying on unofficial thermometers said the temperature dropped to -80°F.

A MATSON CREEK MINER OUTSIDE THE ELDORADO HOTEL

We couldn't turn off the rental car, fearing it wouldn't start again. The power steering fluid froze up and My Colleague couldn't turn the steering wheel. Someone suggested we "plug in the car" and stick around a few days until the weather warmed up. We did.

> ***An aside...***
> Cars in Arctic regions often have "head bolt heaters" installed on the engine. An extension cord usually dangles from the front of the vehicle's grill. When plugged into electricity the heaters help keep engine coolant from freezing up and cracking the engine block. Some "head bolt" heating systems also circulate and warm the antifreeze, thereby keeping the entire system warm. When warm, cars start much easier in cold weather.

Back to The Klondike...
My Colleague and I were staying in the famous Dawson Eldorado Hotel. A superb Klondike property. The proprietor, Peter, was an excellent host. I believe, at the time we were in Dawson, he may have been the current Mayor of the small mining town. While visiting with Peter in the Eldo's dining room on one of our three trips to Dawson that year, he told us a story about a famous local drink, flavored with an amputated human toe. Peter directed us to the Downtown Hotel so we could see the toe with our own eyes. With nothing else to do on that particular day, we darted down the street to see the unique Dawson City attraction.

Tempted by the Toe, but This Guy said "No!"

After arriving at the Downtown Hotel, we witnessed an American woman lift a glass filled with whiskey. The drink included an amputated human toe, resting on the bottom of the tumbler. The

American Woman took a sip of the beverage. The bartender congratulated the woman, but said her lips must touch the blackened toe before her validation as having consumed Dawson City's infamous "Sour Toe Cocktail." The Woman tipped the glass a little more and drank more of the whiskey. The toe remained at the bottom of the vessel. The American took a final large gulp, and the nasty-looking appendage rolled into her mouth. She spit out the toe and sent it back into the whiskey glass, gagging all the while. The American Woman nearly composed herself, then suddenly seemed to go crazy. She began acting as if she'd just won the lottery. Silly girl. Nasty activity. *Where are my OneSeven Microbiologists when I need them?*

Ugh!

Later that year, during the summer months, I ventured back to Dawson City to assist a gold miner in the sale of his mining claims. I met the miner during that terrible cold snap and realized potential existed for a Cola relationship with him. He'd been sharing his frustrations with me, regarding a desire to boost the salable value of his gold claims. I found his needs interesting and decided to try something new and unknown to Cola. The job was far outside my wheelhouse. My comfort level was, at best, unsteady. After all, I'm Cola the Spy, not Cola the Swindler. Regardless, I decided to assist the miner.

A wealthy Canadian investor was interested in the Client's property and would be flying in to assess the feasibility of the purchase. Cola was brought in to make sure the Client, "Lubo," could successfully sell the claims for as much as possible.

A OneSeven Mining Engineer and I surveyed the claims for about a week. It didn't take long to determine there was little placer gold on the claims. The property was of no value for a mining operation. However, Cola performed his magic and the property sold for much more than Lubo expected.

Here's how it unfolded. After my OneSeven and I determined the property contained little gold, I put the OneSeven on a plane. He was headed home. I saw no value in keeping him on a barren mining claim.

The day before the Wealthy Investor was scheduled to arrive, I told Lubo I wanted to spend the day alone. Cola needed time to think. I considered options while I walked Dawson's gold fields, ending with a tour of Bonanza Creek's world famous gold dredge.

Bonanza Creek's Dredge No. 4

circa 1981

An aside...
Bonanza Creek's Dredge No. 4, constructed in 1912, was the largest wooden-hulled bucket dredge in the world. Nearly as long as a football field the dredge is almost eight stories tall. That behemoth was capable of processing more than 22,000 cubic yards of gold-laden gravel each day. It successfully mined placer gold until 1959, when it ceased operations and came to rest in its current location.

Dredge No. 4

circa Summer 1980

Back to The Tour...
I'm glad I decided to tour the dredge. I discovered Dredge No. 4 is a designated Canadian National Historic Site. An official with the Canadian government, Sue Murphy, gave an excellent enjoyable presentation. I spoke with the woman after the tour and found her a fascinating repository of Bonanza Creek's contemporary history. She said her family mined Bonanza Creek downstream from the dredge for many years. Sue and her husband Don, like a lot of other Canadian citizens, winter in Mexico and return to the gold fields each summer.

I told her I was fascinated by the history of the area. Sue suggested I crash a barbecue currently underway on a gold claim a few miles away. She said many miners would be attending the lower Bonanza Creek function. Sue promised I'd get my fill of stories, real and imagined, from the old timers in the crowd. I thanked Mrs. Murphy, took her advice, and crashed the party.

The barbecue was a great time! I recognized the proprietors of my lodging accommodations in the crowd. Former school teachers, John and Gail Hendley were the owners of the Bonanza Gold Motel. They seemed to know everyone. I met them at their motel when my OneSeven Mining Engineer and I checked in. I also played Hold 'em Poker with John one evening at Diamond Tooth Gerties Gambling Hall in Dawson City.

MURRAY AND VIOLET ORBANSKI

It's a Small World

The Hendley's weren't the only people known to me at the barbecue. While at the party, mingling with miners and other attendees, I turned and literally bumped into a couple I knew from thousands of miles away. Murray Orbanski and his wife, Violet. When I accidentally bounced off Murray, I knocked a tumbler containing vodka out of his hands. Bending down while apologizing, I had no idea these were people known to me. Moreover, they didn't have a chance to see my face before I bent over.

As I stood and looked Murray in the face, I recognized him immediately. In good Cola form, I didn't let on I knew him. He didn't seem to recognize me. However, Violet did and dished out some of her quick wit. Called "Vi" by her husband, she instantly recognized me. Without missing a beat, she exclaimed, "Well, look what you've gone and done Cola. That's a terrible waste of good vodka!" Then she laughed.

I'd been on a romantic cruise vacation with Treena. Our assigned dinner seating placed us at a table for six. It was a ten-day cruise, and I got to know two of our dinner companions, Murray and his wife, reasonably well. Murray was born Canadian with a Ukrainian lineage. We spoke at length about his ancestors. It interested me because I'd been to Ukraine on several occasions.

Cola loves deep sea fishing, and I vividly recall Murray's animated gestures and excited words as we sat at the ship's bar one afternoon. Murray was recounting a fishing adventure. While vacationing in Hawaii, he caught and successfully landed a 300 pound Blue Marlin (he may have said 310 pounds).

The other couple at the cruise ship table were from Alaska and traveling with the Orbanskis. I didn't recall their names but would know them shortly.

Violet recognized me right away. She asked what brought me to the Yukon. I lied and told her I was passing through on my way to Fairbanks. Grabbing me by the arm, she excitedly pulled me to a huge barbecue grill covered with flank steak. Standing there flipping the meat were our other cruise dinner companions. Vi excitedly said, "Look who I found!"

"JOKER THE MINER"

Oil Painting Cola Purchased in Dawson City

The couple showed signs of recognition as they turned their heads. Their faces also bore expressions of confusion. They recognized me but didn't know why. Violet picked up on their difficulty and said, "Joker. Cathy. This is Cola. You remember him. He was on the cruise with us."

They responded immediately with recognition. It was nice to see the foursome again. Seeing my cruise companions gave me an opportunity to tell Cathy I'd seen her on television. I'd been watching a show on TV about the Klondike Gold Rush. It was all black and white historical photographs. The only real video used in the program was a short clip showing a woman squirting a gravel bank with water from a fire nozzle. That video was in color, and the woman was undoubtedly Cathy. I believe it was a National Geographic documentary. Cathy and Joker said they'd seen the show. They were thrilled I'd seen it as well. Moreover, Cathy was shocked that I recognized her when watching the program. After all, formal cruise ship dinner attire and hairdos don't look anything like someone wearing rain gear and mud, actively using a "monitor" to shoot high-pressure water against the gold-bearing Bonanza Creek gravels.

After a catching up with one another, Joker offered to show me around his placer mining operation. It was a large scale operation. Pumps, generators, fuel tanks, parts trailers, excavators, loaders, bulldozers, and gravel shaking plants were everywhere. Nature was part of the landscape as well. While Joker and I were walking the claim, we watched a large moose enjoy respite from the long hot day in the sanctuary of a refreshing pond. The gigantic beast was kind enough to remain absolutely still while I snapped his photo.

A MOOSE ON JOKER'S MINING CLAIM
A Cola Fugelere Photo

Joker took me into a fifty-year-old mining tunnel; filled with beautiful ice crystals and boxes of dynamite. He told me the tunnel was mined by an old timer named Harry Leaman, then Don Murphy with KMA (Kiss My Ass) Mining worked it for a while. A few years after my visit with him during that afternoon barbecue, I heard Joker erased all evidence of the tunnel when he "monitored" and sluiced the hillside above, and down to, the old drift mine.

KMA's ICE CRYSTAL MINE

He then directed me to his office trailer and opened a huge safe. Joker allowed me to hold six, one hundred ounce gold bars. Holding them all at once was challenging. Solid gold, they were extremely heavy.

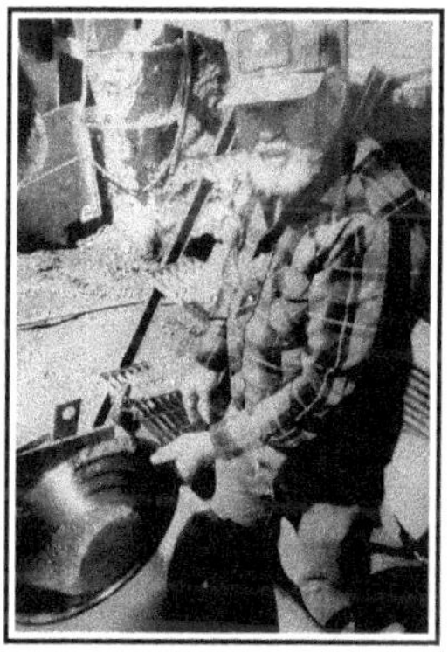

JOKER MONITORING AND PANNING FOR GOLD

While walking his property that afternoon, Joker pointed to the gravel face of a thirty-foot-high embankment. He told me one day he walked over to a section of bank similar to that one and decided to test it for gold. Joker removed a shovel-full of gravel and dropped it into a gold pan. He said he swirled and cleaned the gravels until the gold separated from the rocks and dirt. Gold flakes littered the black plastic gold pan. He quickly panned two more sections and discovered those areas had even more gold.

Moving his equipment into the area, Joker mined the cliff. On the first day of mining, he recovered more than $100,000 in gold. He mined that gravel deposit for two more months.

◇ ◇ ◇

That evening I was sitting in Lubo's cabin thinking about Joker testing the cliff. It was about eight at night, and the Arctic's "midnight sun" was still high in the sky. It wouldn't get dark tonight. It was June 21st, the longest day of the year. I was all alone on the Hunker Creek claim. Lubo made the trek into Dawson for a summer solstice celebration and left me alone with my thoughts.

I really didn't feel like sitting in the cabin doing nothing. I had pismires in my trousers (ants in my pants) and was frustrated. I had a problem needing solved. What to do? *hmmm...*

Joker's sampling was the only thing necessary to convince him to invest time, equipment, men, and fuel into mining that cliff. As I was considering Lubo's needs, as well as Joker's discovery, my eyes fell upon a double-barreled shotgun leaning up against the wall next to the fireplace. I quickly glanced around the room and saw a box of No. 00 Buckshot sitting in the middle of the kitchen table. Bingo, I had an idea.

I went over to the table with a paper plate and removed two "double-aught buck" shotgun shells from the box. Using my pocket knife, I carefully uncrimped the business end of one shell. As I tipped the shell toward the table, eight lead balls rolled out and dropped onto the paper plate. Careful not to disturb the powder wad, separating the lead shot from the gunpowder, I turned the shell upright and sat the brass and primer end on the table. I handled the second shell in the same manner.

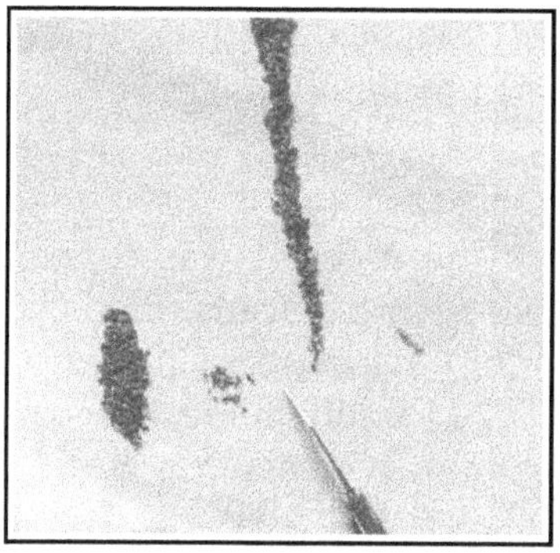

LUBO'S ACTUAL GOLD FLAKES

Lubo had shown me a bottle of gold flakes he kept hidden under the sink. I removed the bottle of gold from its hiding place. Using a folded piece of white paper, I carefully poured a line of the fine placer nuggets onto the paper. Lifting the paper, I carefully folded it into a makeshift funnel. Tilting my creation, I allowed the gold to slowly run down and into the shells. Once each shell was full, I re-crimped the shells closed.

I collected the shotgun. Using my right thumb, I pivoted the opening lever to release the break action and open the shotgun. I then removed the two bear loads from the breech end of the barrel and sat them on the table. Then I carefully inserted one gold-filled shotgun shell into each barrel and closed the breach. Keeping the barrel pointed up to make sure gold didn't spill, I exited the cabin and walked about a quarter mile to a huge gravel cliff.

Most of the cliff was inaccessible by foot because Hunker Creek ran up against the base of the cliff. However, a cleft had formed in one area about six feet wide and eight feet high, with plenty of room for standing and panning at the base of the cliff; and next to the creek.

Standing back from the cleft about twenty-five or thirty yards, I aimed about two feet up from the base and fired the first barrel. Raising the barrel to five feet above the water, I pulled the trigger and sent the second load of gold into the cliff. I walked over to the creek and waded through thigh-high water and inspected my handiwork. No gold was visible, and that was good. I believe most of the gold flakes probably burrowed up to an inch into the gravel face. Perfect!

Walking back across the creek, I was fortunate enough to find and collect both plastic powder wads. Placing them in my pocket, I smiled. There was no evidence of my effort to "salt" the cliff with the scattergun. If someone collected samples from that cliff and performed perfunctory tests for gold, they'd find a wide disbursement of gold flakes across the face of the gravel bank; suggesting the entire gravel structure was laden with valuable gold.

> ***An aside...***
> In mining terms, "salting" the cliff fraudulently suggested value by embedding the fine gold particles into the gravel.

Back to Cola, The Spy with The Midas Touch...
Once back in the cabin, I quickly cleaned and reloaded the shotgun; then placed it back against the wall. Snooping around the small cabin, I discovered another box of identical shotgun shells. Removing two rounds from that box, I refilled the box on the table.

When Lubo returned home, I detailed a plan that should result in the Wealthy Investor's desire to pan the gold on the face of the gravel cliff. I showed him where The Mark would find gold. I instructed Lubo to "Trust me." I also told him, "Do not sample the gravels on the face of the cliff."

He responded with, "I've already tested that spot. There's no gold there."

I looked Lubo straight in the eye and winked.

The next day The Mark arrived. I was already onsite and was posing as another potential buyer for the property. Lubo performed well. Consistent with our plans, we ended up at the base of the gravel wall. The Mark, without any prompting from us, asked Lubo if it was permissible for him to take a couple of samples from the cliff for testing. Lubo agreed.

The Mark went to his rented car and removed two five gallon buckets with locking lids from the trunk of the vehicle. He borrowed a shovel from Lubo and walked across the creek, soaking his slacks, shoes, and socks. The Mark opened the first bucket and made sure it was clean. He then placed the shovel into the creek and cleaned it thoroughly, until he washed away all the caked-on dirt. Satisfied the material collected from the bank wouldn't be contaminated, The Mark scraped gravel all around the face of the gravel wall, from creek level to about 3 feet up. Once the bucket was full, he replaced the lid and secured the lid latch with a braided wire-lock tamper-evident, serial numbered, security seal.

My, this guy was both anal and security conscious!

He took the second bucket and repeated the process; gathering material from three feet above the creek to about six feet up. I was delighted. He was digging in both my bull's-eyes. Lubo was a bundle of nerves. He didn't know what I'd done and couldn't understand how the samples could benefit him. I looked him in the eyes and calmly uttered five reassuring words in a soft voice. "Just relax, it'll be okay."

As the Wealthy Investor was collecting the salted material, Lubo and I began negotiating loudly, consistent with the script I developed that morning. We were, in effect, driving up the price.

The Wealthy Investor told Lubo he'd get back to him in a few days. The Mark then returned to his car with the two heavy buckets and drove away.

Lubo demanded to know what to expect and what I did, if anything, to the gravel bank. I reminded him that our agreement included the Cola Non-Negotiable that I, "Never reveal methods and sources to Clients or other parties." His demands ceased, and he nervously waited out the week, hoping for good news from The Mark.

A few days later Lubo and I were enjoying an excellent breakfast in the Eldorado Hotel dining room when he received a message to contact the Wealthy Investor. He went to a pay phone and spent the next fifteen minutes on a call with The Mark. After hanging up the phone, he just stood there shaking his head in wonderment, then staggered back to the table.

He looked drunk but wasn't. Lubo was concurrently in a state of shock and amazed to his core. He whispered to me that he'd just agreed to sell his claims for two million dollars. Looking at me, he said, "Cola, I don't know how you did it. You're amazing and worth every penny. Thank you! You're the best!"

My contract was for $20,000 or 10%, whichever was greater. The agreement stipulated that a sale must be $200,000.00 or greater. He'd just sold his property for ten times his expectations. The Mark just blew a fortune on barren ground. I'm sure he wasn't happy when he discovered the claim was worthless.

Cola grossed $200,000 for two weeks work. Not bad. *Perhaps I should have celebrated with a swig from the toe drink.*

Cola Loves the Klondike!

Chance Phelps

Lance Corporal Chance Russell Phelps
United States Marine

Image courtesy of John Phelps
www.JohnPhelps.com

Chance Phelps

Although I held many meetings in cemeteries while working on the Dark Side, I'd like to begin with a story about one meeting I held after transitioning to Corporate Counterintelligence. The meeting was scheduled in a poignant setting that involved a potential whistleblower for a major defense contractor.

> ***An aside...***
> There's a Cola Non-Negotiable that reads, "Cola, a Patriotic American, will never knowingly interfere with the activities of others working on behalf of the defense of our nation." Yes, a defense contractor would fall into that Cola Non-Negotiable. However, in this case, it appeared the defense contractor might be working on behalf of himself and against our nation. It was worth looking into, especially if it could benefit the United States of America.

Back to The Whistleblower...

He was a young former Marine who was attending a work-related week-long meeting in Jackson Hole, Wyoming. "Taylor Chantay" (not his real name) was troubled by certain information that crossed his desk at work. He knew that whistleblowers enjoy very well-intentioned legal protections. However, he also knew that reality dictated he take measures to protect himself, since legal protections generally failed to offer most whistleblowers adequate safeguards. Taylor wanted to find a safe conduit for that information. He needed to find someone who could assist him in making the situation right, without undue risk to himself.

Taylor used his Marine Corps contacts for assistance. Those efforts eventually led him to me. Taylor didn't trust attorneys or the legal system to assist him with this matter safely. The young Marine understood Cola was a former Corporate Spy, now working as a good guy Corporate Counterintelligence professional, and might be helpful in meeting his needs. He was assured that Cola was a true Patriot and could be trusted completely. A valued intermediary reached out to me and placed me in touch with Taylor. Once I understood the nature of his need and what he wanted to reveal about his company, I offered to handle the job pro bono. Just another in a long line of efforts by Cola to seek peace through penance. I also promised to do my level best to insulate him, while making the situation known to the appropriate authorities.

After an exhaustive due diligence investigative effort, I agreed to meet with him. I needed to handle this matter carefully, because of his employer's relationship with the Federal government. My meeting with the young man was set near Jackson Hole, Wyoming where Taylor would be a peripheral participant in a high-level meeting related to his employer's business dealings.

Lance Corporal Chance Phelps

Posthumous Promotion to Lance Corporal

I'd recently heard a story about an American hero who'd been laid to rest not far from Jackson Hole. Chance Russell Phelps, a young U.S. Marine, was killed while escorting a convoy carrying 1st Marine Division Brigadier General John F. Kelly, who later became President Donald Trump's Chief-of-Staff. The convoy came under heavy fire. Although wounded in the attack, Chance Phelps refused to be evacuated. He remained at his post manning an M240 machine gun, covering the evacuation of the rest of his convoy. After successfully offering protection for his men, Phelps began his withdrawal. The young Marine suffered a fatal head wound as he evacuated the area.

> ***An aside...***
> On the drive up from Fort Collins, TJ informed me when her son, Coop, deployed on this, his second, "hump" into Iraq he was assigned to be the turret machine gunner in a large IED resistant infantry mobility vehicle called an MRAP (Mine-Resistant Ambush Protected). MRAP's are constructed with V-shaped hulls that are designed to direct blasts away from the underside of the vehicle. While most of the armored vehicle's occupants are well-protected from enemy fire, turret gunners are positioned at the top of the MRAP. The top parts of their bodies are exposed to incoming fire. TJ's husband was very concerned about Coop's assignment.

During a conversation with a couple from Fort Collins, Walt and Brooke, TJ discovered they had two sons serving in Operation Iraqi Freedom. They were all at an event organized by Brooke. The activity was associated with providing care packages for men and women deployed to Iraq. Brooke was trying to raise money for purchases related to the project.

Brook

Brooke was inspired by a woman she knew named Joyce, who lived in the San Diego area. TJ and her husband knew Joyce as well. Brooke also shared her frustrations about hitting so many brick walls in her fundraising efforts. Many people seemed to think of the Iraq War as something seen on TV and didn't understand the realities for those on the ground in that war-ravaged land. For those cozy citizens, it was an afterthought and didn't impact their lives; that it wasn't real.

Not real? Chance and his family are real. People like Brooke and Joyce get it. Too bad more people don't understand the sacrifices these families make on behalf of our nation.

COOP'S HUMMER NEAR COMBAT OUTPOST KUBAYSAH

circa 2008

TJ told me Chance was killed doing the same job in a Humvee that her son would be doing in the MRAP. They were both assigned to the M240 Machine Gun. To his parent's relief, after arriving in Iraq for that 2nd deployment Coop was reassigned to drive the MRAP. Like Chance, her own son went to war in a Humvee during his first Operation Iraqi Freedom deployment. Coop was charged with driving that Humvee. When the battalion commander's staff researched his previous missions during the first deployment, they chose to have Coop's experienced hands on the wheel of the commander's vehicle. TJ and her husband were grateful for that turn of events.

During the drive to Dubois, TJ told me about an event she'd recently attended at the Marine Corps' Camp Pendleton in southern California. It was the Christmas season. TJ, her husband, and Coop's teenage sister, "Sissy," drove to the San Diego area. They had decided to forgo the exchange of Christmas gifts and, instead, show their gratitude to members of our military. TJ and her husband had been at Pendleton a month earlier to enjoy Thanksgiving dinner with their son in the cafeteria. The food was okay, but certainly not a lovingly prepared Thanksgiving dinner with all the trimmings.

They arrived and met with one of the event's organizers. The lady was well-known for hugging members of the military as they were departing or returning from deployments. She was an avid supporter of the military and a Marine mother. Joyce, affectionately referred to as "Hugs" by TJ's husband, was always doing something special for our service men and women. TJ said Hugs once raised a lot of money to assist a young Marine and his wife. He'd suffered a major heart infection and needed a heart transplant. Family finances were strained, and Hugs wanted to relieve financial pressures burdening the young family. Hugs met him on one of her regular trips to the hospital visiting war-torn Marines who'd returned home from Iraq and Afghanistan.

On this particular holiday occasion, four wonderful individuals organized a special Christmas Dinner on behalf of the brand new Marines at Camp Pendleton. Our newest members of the military weren't able to go home for Christmas. They needed to remain behind for training and guard duty.

Oklahoma physician Rachel Gibbs and her husband, attorney George Gibbs, brainstorming with Hugs and husband Curtis, conceived the idea over dinner one evening. Both couples were parents of U.S. Marines. They didn't want the kids to suffer through cafeteria food on Christmas.

George and Rachel worked with a Tulsa barbecue restaurant, Albert G's, to secure a special barbecue Christmas dinner for some of our nation's newest Marines. Chuck Gawey, Albert G's owner, and his team worked several days preparing more than 200 pounds of meat for the meal. The special dinner included pulled pork, many slabs of ribs, as well as an assortment of other meats. They also provided sauces, salads, bread, and dessert. The meal was placed into several large foot locker-sized containers, then flown overnight by UPS to southern California, and delivered to Camp Pendleton. UPS delivered their bill to the Gibbs family.

TJ and her family, Hugs and her husband Curt, as well as many others, young and old, pitched in. They prepared table settings, heated and plated the food, and served that most excellent Oklahoma meal to the young Marines. Sissy told her parents it was the best Christmas she'd ever had. TJ and her husband agreed.

I read an online article about the event. It appears Rachel and George invested many thousands of dollars on the project. Chuck heavily discounted Albert G's bill. *Sacrificial giving at its best!*

People like TJ and her husband, Sissy, Curt, Hugs, George, Rachel, Chuck, Walt, Brooke, and others who support our troops are our nation's unsung heroes. They do these things out of grateful hearts and sincere concern; reaping a form of joy only available through service to others. Cola is eternally grateful for people like you.

Back to Chance Phelps...
I don't recall the details of how the late Chance Phelps became well-known after that battle. I do know, however, the story of his journey home was shared in a journal account penned by Marine Lt. Colonel Michael Strobl. The Colonel volunteered to escort the young PFC home. Strobl didn't know Phelps. Moreover, it is unusual for officers to escort enlisted men back home to their families for burial. However, Strobl and Phelps were from the same hometown. The Colonel wanted to honor Chance by escorting him home.

Strobl's report was widely read and very well received. The account of that journey was eventually told in an HBO documentary, "Taking Chance" starring Kevin Bacon. I later watched that program with my wife on television. To this day, my wife doesn't know I once paid my respects to Lance Corporal Chance Russell Phelps at his graveside.

I chose the cemetery, where U.S. Marine Chance Phelps was laid to rest, for my meeting with former Marine Taylor Chantay. My meeting plan included the requisition of three Watchers, one Cutout, and an Escort. The three Watchers drove in from Salt Lake City. My Colleagues drove two white SUVs and a Nissan 350Z to Jackson Hole. Once there they set up operations. Leaving one of the Watchers behind, the other two ferried the "Z" car to Dubois, Wyoming for later use by TJ. They then returned to Jackson Hole in one of the SUV's.

> ***An aside...***
> An Escort is usually assigned the responsibility of escorting a Subject, usually a meeting attendee, to a specific location to meet with Cola. Not to be confused with prostitution.

Back to Jackson Hole...
We positioned the Watchers in Jackson Hole to shadow Taylor, while I drove Escort TJ and myself from Fort Collins, Colorado to Dubois, Wyoming. TJ, a resident of that beautiful Colorado community, was deeply moved by the story of Chance Phelps. The Operation's success was critical to my young Colleague.

TJ and her husband previously traveled to Dubois to pay their respects to Chance Phelps. She had a good sense of the small town and its cemetery. During our 400 mile drive from Fort Collins, TJ and I discussed how the meeting should unfold.

We intended to transport Taylor to the cemetery in the 350Z. TJ's assistance was critical in choreographing our activities from the time she drove him into the small community, to the moment we revealed Chance's grave to our young Whistleblower-to-be. We developed the framework of a plan on our long drive from Colorado to northwestern Wyoming.

TJ's first duty upon our arrival in Dubois was to assist me with an initial reconnoiter of the small town and the cemetery. We walked the cemetery for about an hour before we settled on the steps we should take once she arrived with Taylor. As you'll see shortly, the choreography was both critical and delicate. The choreographed plans were designed to assist us in determining if

Taylor and the Cola Team were moving forward with the right motivations and having a good understanding of the risks. More importantly, Taylor needed to know, deep in his core, if he really wanted to take the tremendous risks associated with outing his employer. We chose the grave of Chance Phelps to assure everyone involved that what we were planning was the right thing to do.

After finalizing our plans, I drove TJ to Lander Street, where our Watchers previously parked the "Z" in front of one of several large bushes just off the main drag. TJ would be driving 75 miles to Jackson Hole in the "Z" to collect our Client, while I continued reconnoitering Dubois. The stage was set.

> ***An aside...***
> One of the significant benefits of planning meets in cemeteries is in setting Pigeon Memory. Unlike the sensory craziness at NASCAR races and NFL stadiums on game day, the sights, smells, and sounds within cemeteries are relatively static; and easy to imprint on one's mind.

Back to Dubois...
After delivering TJ to the "Z" car, I discretely staged three different bug-out bags in various places outside of Dubois, should I have to egress the area on foot. We weren't involved in anything illegal by meeting with Taylor, but there was always the risk of crossing someone dangerous, and I needed to prepare myself and TJ for the possibility that we might need to make an unplanned departure.

Once I finished my emergency egress plans, I went back to the cemetery and stood by Chance's grave for a very long time; soaking in the sights, sounds, and smells. I thought of the young Marine and his family. I considered Strobl's mission. Words like honor and sacrifice filled my mind. I realized I was standing on hallowed ground, at the final resting place of an American hero who had, in his father's words, "Become part of Americana."

Getting back to business, I noted the direction of the wind and every structure and road I could see. I categorized sounds and smells. I further considered what I'd be saying to Taylor. Then I was ready.

Before driving down the hill to rendezvous with my Escort and her Package, I thought long and hard about Chance, his family, and his buddies. I considered my family as well. Throughout it all, my son was in the forefront of my mind. I realized just how painful it would be to lose him. After pulling myself back from a place of deep and profound thoughts, I realized my vision was occluded. I stood before the blurred image of Chance's tombstone. My face was wet. I'd been weeping and didn't even know it.

> ***An aside...***
> A Package is usually a person being escorted by a Cola Escort, to a meeting with Cola.

Back to Taylor...
Taylor was expecting me to make contact with him in Jackson Hole, with a series of coded knocks rapped on his hotel room door, followed by bona fides, during the wee hours of the next morning. The bona fide for Taylor's ears in this Operation was, "Bellawood." As usual, I wasn't going along with a plan conveyed to a potential meeting attendee; even though the "wee hours" plan was my design. It was pure misdirection.

Game On
Shortly after lunch that day, a Cola Colleague slipped into a restroom where Taylor was taking care of business. The timing was okay for Taylor. He wouldn't be missed. The morning meeting schedule ended with lunch. Participants were freed for the remainder of the day and evening to enjoy the sights and attractions in and around Jackson Hole. Chantay would be back in time for the following day's events. The Operation was officially underway.

When Taylor turned from the urinal toward the sink, My Colleague tucked a folded note into his breast pocket, patted the pocket twice, and quickly departed the restroom. The paper told Taylor to immediately leave the hotel and walk to the building housing "Wyoming Outfitters." He was instructed to go inside the store and take an "urgent" phone call. Before departing the restroom, however, he was advised to tear the note into tiny pieces and drop them into a toilet. The instructions indicated he was to repeatedly flush the toilet until every last remnant of the note disappeared from the porcelain bowl.

As Taylor entered Wyoming Outfitters, he heard a voice call out, "Anyone here named Bellawood? There's an urgent call for Bellawood!"

Taylor took the call and was instructed to walk out quickly and cut across the Jackson Town Square.

As he cut diagonally through the grassy, wooded, park-like town square, Taylor noticed someone standing by a flagpole to his left calling out, "Hey Bellawood! Over here!" Taylor left the path he was on and cut across the grass. It was TJ at the pole. We figured the sight of a woman would assist in putting the young Marine at ease. She told Taylor to continue walking, step over the short two rail fence, and get into the white sports utility vehicle sitting at the curb with two small kayaks tied to the roof rack.

After Taylor hopped in, the SUV drove north on Cache Street, then made several quick turns. On the west side of Miller Park, Taylor jumped out. He was wearing a cheap fluffy beard, held in place by an elastic band, and a red hoodie, with the hood covering his head. The beard wasn't supposed to look genuine. It was intended to draw attention to the beard itself, while simultaneously concealing the man's face who was wearing the beard.

The white sports utility vehicle slowed next to an identical SUV facing the same direction. Dressed in the feature obscuring clothing, Taylor jumped out of the first SUV and into its twin. Neither vehicle came to a complete stop. The transfer was nearly perfect, and the two cars continued in the same direction; taking turns as the lead vehicle. When they arrived at an intersection previously selected for a divergent maneuver, one vehicle turned left and the other drove to the right.

After a few more turns, Taylor's ride slowed and a man with a fake beard and red hoodie jumped out and hopped into the back end of a green and white Grand Teton National Park ambulance.

The ambulance was now carrying an impostor. The fellow who hopped into the emergency vehicle was a Cutout having a build and height similar to that of Taylor Chantay. He neither knew anything of the Operation, nor any of our Team Members. He only knew that he was told to jump into the ambulance. He never saw Taylor's face and didn't know anyone he saw that day. Our timing was critical. The green and white vehicle would get him out of town and drop him off at the airport, where a commercial flight to Denver was preparing to depart.

The ambulance was actually out of service on that day. Someone with access to the vehicle enjoyed five crisp one hundred dollar bills for the quick ten mile trip to the airport, where Taylor's impersonator was dropped off for his flight.

THE ACTUAL HAT WORN BY TAYLOR

A few minutes later Taylor, now wearing a Marine Corps Museum baseball cap, hopped out of the White SUV and jumped into a Nissan 350Z. Moments later the sleek sports car was rocketing down a ribbon of asphalt on US Route 26, heading toward the Dubois Cemetery. At the same time, our three Watchers were returning to Salt Lake City in the two SUV's. The four kayaks remained behind in Jackson Hole, after being anonymously donated to a local church.

Less than two hours later, the white sports car drove into Dubois and slowly wound its way through town and headed up the hill toward the cemetery. I moved in behind the vehicle as it entered Dubois. I was driving a large white Ford Excursion with magnetic door signs advertising, "Two Loons Adventures."

As we headed through Dubois, I hoped this would be my third and final trip to the cemetery today. Turning a corner, something to the right caught my eye. I watched a man step off a curb, walk around a pickup truck, and get in it. I immediately recognized him from a news piece I'd seen about Chance Phelps. It was Chance's father, John. A well-regarded professional artist, Mr. Phelps appeared to be a man carved from the granite cliffs of the Old West. Tall, lean, and ruggedly handsome. That proud father of a great U.S. Marine had just unknowingly crossed paths with a small group of patriotic people on their way to honor his son.

> ***An aside...***
> My heart ached for the man on that day. In fact, that heartache continues to this day. His son and the entire Phelps family paid a terrible price on behalf of our nation. I cannot fathom the emotions and pain endured by the family.

Back to Northwestern Wyoming...
I considered Chance and his final resting place as we began making the trip up the hill. The majestic pine trees, stationed around the cemetery, appeared to serve as vigilant sentries, guarding the remains of those inhabiting that sacred ground. High on the hill with a panoramic view of Wyoming's Wind River and spectacular Absaroka Mountain Range, the cemetery overlooks the town of Dubois. From the small community, the pines appear as evenly spaced spikes.

Mr. Phelps joined our little parade driving toward the cemetery. As we rounded a ninety-degree turn on Boedecker Street, I looked high through the upper part of the Excursion's windshield. The tops of the pine sentries guarding Chance were visible nearly a half mile distant atop the hill. From that perspective, I could simultaneously see the pines through the windshield, as well as the mirror image of John Phelps at the wheel of his pickup truck behind us, as it was eating the dust kicked up by our convoy. The scene was unsettling. What if he was heading towards Chance's grave? Had he keyed on us for some reason? Since TJ and I failed to plan contingencies for John's intrusion into our Operation, how would she react? Did we need to bug out?

My mind raced. I was about to flash my lights at TJ and have her pull over when everything changed. Mr. Phelps turned off and drove east on Mountain View Drive, shortly before our arrival at the cemetery. I finally relaxed.

Ahead of me, the white 350Z came to a stop on the east side of the cemetery. My young Colleague, TJ, exited her vehicle. As instructed, Taylor remained in the little Nissan.

> ***An aside...***
> At the time, TJ was a Blue Star Infantry Marine mother. Her son was working an area in Iraq less than eighty miles distant from Ramadi, where Chance Phelps made the ultimate sacrifice. During the Memorial Day weekend in 2009, she and her husband made the journey to Dubois to pay their respects to Chance. Although this was her second appearance at Chance's grave, the "Bellawood" Operation remained a challenging, albeit rewarding trip, for TJ.

Back to The Dubois Cemetery...
I drove to the opposite side of the large grass covered rectangle, sparsely populated with gravestones and flowers. I parked the huge Ford Excursion in a large triangle shaped parking area, west of our intended destination. My vehicle was facing one of six rectangular burial sections in the cemetery. This area was the intended location for my first and only meeting with Taylor Chantay. Within that section, were a number of headstones. In the near center of the lawn were two upright gravestones bearing the name, Phelps.

I walked to an area about 10' north of, and directly perpendicular to, the larger grave marker and waited as TJ approached my position. When TJ arrived where I stood, I noticed her face reflected a measure of concern. She told me Taylor was a little too flippant about the Operation during their two-hour road trip. I reminded her that our well-planned choreography was intended to address that particular problem. I also pointed out that his flippancy wasn't such a bad thing.

A dramatic turn of events was about to unfold and fall on the young man. An unexpected revelation, if it worked as planned, would catch Taylor entirely off guard. The choreography was intended to, figuratively, knock him off his feet. When asked if there were any other problems, TJ gave me the all clear.

I raised my hand and beckoned Taylor to join us. The young Marine unfolded his frame and extricated himself from the tiny car. He walked briskly in our direction. Keeping his eyes on me, he failed to see the little heart-shaped headstone bearing the single word, Phelps. I didn't want him to connect the dots, just yet.

> ***An aside...***
> Although not sure, I can only surmise the small headstone marks the grave of Chance's older sister who, based on the dates shown on the marker, passed away three and a half years before his birth; after living for a short two and a half weeks.

Back to Dubois...
As Taylor approached, he chuckled and remarked about "all the cloak and dagger" associated with our meeting. That was my opening. I needed to set the stage and erase his light-hearted demeanor before Chance became front and center.

I gave a slight nod to TJ, and without drawing attention to herself, she meandered to the south. He slowed and began to look around the cemetery. Not good. I immediately stepped forward and reached my hand out to shake that of Mr. Chantay.

He was taller than the average Marine. He had the fixed square jaw, flat stomach, and erect posture often seen in active duty Marines. Seeing that, I recalled Taylor received his "Certificate of

Release or Discharge from Active Duty" (DD214) a few months earlier. He hadn't been out of the Corps long, and it showed.

I uttered a few pleasantries about the view to distract Taylor's gaze from his immediate surroundings. As I spoke, TJ positioned herself in front of the headstone belonging to Sarah Katherine Phelps. TJ's role at that point was to make sure Taylor didn't see the word "Phelps" carved into that stone.

I placed my hands on Taylor's shoulder and slowly guided him toward the east side of Chance's upright gravestone. I chose that side because Chance's name didn't appear there. It was, however, tricky. Chance's grave had a second ground level marker bearing his name just 8 feet to the east of the upright stone. It was important to keep Taylor's eyes away from that marker, so I used the grand scenery as a distraction. I remarked about the view over the white flagpoles lining the parking lot to our west; followed by a comment that the area was chosen to provide us with privacy and provide an atmosphere conducive to introspection.

Why Cola? Why keep Taylor from seeing Chance's name? Good question.

I needed to make certain the young former Marine was in for both a penny and a pound. He was taking a big step asking me to work with him and move forward with the whistleblowing plan. Chance would help in more ways than one. Our little performance was expected to take a dramatic and telling turn when Chance Phelps made his dramatic entrance.

Taylor was acquainted with Chance. During our pre-meet investigatory phase, we discovered Taylor knew young Mr. Phelps. He'd blogged about how they met over pizza at Camp Pendleton's School of Infantry (SOI) and hung out once in Oceanside, California while on leave. They also sat on the tailgate of someone's pickup truck in a dirt lot in Twentynine Palms, California eating fast food. Behind the pickup and filling their view was a giant mural of Marines at war, painted on the side of a building on the town's main drag. They discussed war and what the wall meant to them. In the blog, Taylor said he'd prefer to keep the details of their conversation about the large painting to himself. He wrote, "That's something I shared with Chance. Nothing embarrassing or anything like that. Chance and I connected that evening. That brief time was ours and I'd prefer to keep it that way. It's my way of keeping my brother alive to me."

The blog entry mentioned them getting a huge laugh out of watching a short "Boot" come out of the bathroom of the town's best pizza restaurant shaking his head. The Boot was wearing a red shirt splattered with dark spots. They knew exactly what happened. The bathroom in that pizza place had the highest mounted urinal either of them had ever seen. It was clear the Boot had to pee uphill and was splattered by his own fluids as they ricocheted off the porcelain urinal. Taylor penned, "As we laughed at the Boot, I looked across the table at Chance. His trademark smile and uneven dimples were in overdrive. If I didn't know better, I would suspect my grinning mischievous friend was behind mounting that urinal so high on the wall."

> ***An aside...***
> A "Boot" is a disparaging term used by seasoned Marines to describe young Marines fresh out of boot camp. BOOT is said to be an acronym meaning Beginning Of One's Tour.
>
> In the contemporary Marine Corps, especially with infantry troops, new Marines are generally called "Boots" until they've been in combat. Their treatment follows the lines of high school freshmen and fraternity pledges. Once they are seasoned members of the unit, or when a fresh group of Boots arrives, that demeaning title becomes part of their past.

Back to Chance's Grave...
After I finished walking and distracting him with the grand panoramic view from the cemetery, Taylor was positioned precisely where I wanted him. He was standing next to and on the backside of, Chance's upright headstone. Carefully planned misdirection successfully kept Taylor from seeing Chance's name on the lawn level marker eight feet behind him.

Looking down at the back of Chance's headstone, I slowly and softly recited the words engraved on the monument.

SEMPER FIDELIS.
WE'LL ALWAYS KNOW YOU TALL AND FREE,
BEYOND THE GLOWING SKY.
SO FLY AWAY YOUNG WARRIOR,
WE'LL SEE YOU BY AND BY.

Then I read the inscription, carved in all capital letters, found at the base of the upright stone.

UNITED STATES MARINE CORPS BRONZE STAR WITH VALOR

KIA, AL ANBAR, IRAQ. APRIL 9, 2004

Looking Taylor in the eyes, I said, "Young man, sacrifice is tough. In many cases, it cannot be undone. We're standing at the grave of a young Marine, like yourself. Unlike yourself, he paid the ultimate price. The ramifications of his decision to join the military have impacted an untold number of others. Some might argue the price was too high. Others may be grateful for his sacrifice. Military supporters will often say they know he was doing the right thing. Family, friends, and acquaintances miss him, are proud of him, and are glad to have had an opportunity to know this young Marine."

Taking a step toward the young man I said, "The point Taylor is that choices have consequences and the ramifications of difficult decisions will invariably impact the lives of others; especially family, friends, and acquaintances. Are you prepared to take the big step with your desire to become a whistleblower? Have you thoughtfully considered the risks and how they might impact your loved ones with this decision?

Taylor, I'm good at what I do. Very good. However, I'm also human. I will do my level best to protect you in this matter, but I cannot offer the kind of guarantees that will ensure you remain free from fallout."

Then in a dramatic move, I bent over and placed my hand on Chance's headstone and bowed my head. As a cool Wyoming breeze kicked up a little, I whispered. "Son, I'm so sorry you're no longer able to enjoy life with your family. I'm sure you've been missed. I know you touched the lives of many people and your absence has been difficult for them in countless ways.

"I wouldn't be surprised if the U.S. Marine standing beside me lost one or more friends on the battlefield. I'm sure if he lost a friend that made the life-altering decision to go to war, it impacted Taylor's life in unexpected ways. If he lost a brother in the war, it must have left him with heartache and sadness. You made a choice. A decision. It's too late for you to change your mind. It's not too late for Marine Taylor Chantay."

As I looked up, I could see Taylor's stoicism remained. Emotionless and impassive. Was it surface stoicism? Had he resolved to be a tough guy at this meeting? Was his resolution firm and based on solid conviction? Was Taylor's choice to blow the whistle just whimsy? Alternatively, was it cautiously considered? Was he, at the core of his being, solidly behind this course of action? Would he back out when it started getting tough? Would he remain faithful to the decision? Semper Fidelis? I needed to know. I need assurances and firmly believed Chance Phelps would help me know the answers to my questions.

I stood, turned my back to the headstone and stepped into Taylor's personal space. Placing my right hand on his left shoulder, I gently guided him to his right and around the tombstone. As Chance's name on the other side of the handsome marker came into view, I felt Taylor shudder. He froze. I looked into his eyes as they welled with tears. He quickly removed the "National Museum of the Marine Corps" hat from his head, revealing a trademark USMC High and Tight haircut.

Then Taylor's knees buckled, and he dropped to the earth on one knee. A quickly outstretched hand appeared from nowhere and kept him from falling forward. I was instantly reminded of the final scene in Saving Private Ryan when actor Harrison Young, in the role of an older James Francis Ryan, dropped to a knee in front of Captain Miller's grave.

Taylor began sobbing heavily. Racked with grief-filled convulsions, the handsome Marine wilted under the weight of crushing emotion. It appeared his pain was sincere. The passion was overwhelmingly personal. I had to look away.

As I began turning my head, I instantly considered the possibility that I might be falling prey to an act. Needing to be sure of what was unfolding before me, I glanced up at TJ. She had streams of tears running down her face. Confirmation. TJ doesn't get caught up in performances. Taylor's grief was, indeed, authentic.

Then I, too, began weeping. I lost track of time and situational awareness. It seems as though time stopped. The emotion at that time and place was raw, real, and will forever remain with me. A hush descended upon our small gathering. Minutes passed.

I looked down and watched a teardrop fall from Taylor's jaw and disappear into the grass just forward of the grave marker. Taylor began to open his mouth and a thick saliva bubble formed between his lips. Hollywood's best actors could never pull off this performance. It was genuine, heartfelt, and grief-stricken. Taylor whispered, "I'm so sorry Chance. I'm so sorry. So sorry."

Taylor then reached across and traced his index finger in an arc around the first engraved "C" of Chance's first name. Pausing, Taylor quietly said, "Doggone It Dimples. I surely miss you dude. I'll never forget you."

After a few minutes, Taylor stood up and looked at me, then turned to TJ. He said, "Ma'am, thank you so much for bringing me to see Chance. I'll never forget what you've done for me."

As TJ nodded with a tight sad smile, Taylor turned back to me and straightened as if he was about to be inspected by a Drill Instructor. Drawing his shoulders back he looked into my eyes for an uncomfortable pregnant moment. Was he about to back out? His expression changed. A firmness fell over his face. His jaw reflected resolve. I knew he'd made a decision. As his eyes filled with determination, Taylor Chantay cleared his throat. He took a deep breath and roared, “Raaaahhhh!!! Let’s Roll Cola!”

Roll we did. We successfully blew the whistle and exposed the contractor’s misdeeds. Although the matter worked its way through the Pentagon and everything was made right, it neither impacted Taylor directly nor did it go public. I’m thankful Taylor’s role in the matter remained unknown to all involved. He’s a good man, and we have Chance Phelps to thank for ensuring the Operation began correctly; and for the right reasons. *Thanks Chance!*

MEMORABLE LOCATIONS

Most of the time I schedule Game critical meetings and encounters in boring, innocuous, locations such as coffee shops, hallways, elevators, and parking garages. As such, they are unworthy of ink in this book. On the other hand, decades of consulting with Clients, Agents, Assets, Inside Men, Cutouts, and OneSevens have occasionally occurred in intensely memorable meeting places. Venues that, looking back, can be variously characterized as unusual, emotional, weird, interesting, memorable, and unexpected. As such, some of those meeting locations warrant mention in this manuscript; as do a few other notable locations.

In previous chapters, I shared stories involving memorable meetings. There are additional stories and unique venues worthy of discussion. I want to offer Readers a tiny peek into the variety of meeting places and memorable meetings I've had over the years.

The stereotypical park bench meetings between CIA Agents and their Assets are always fun to consider. Two people sitting next to each other in public parks, acting like they don't know one another, and conversing like ventriloquist Jeff Dunham with his little buddy Walter. *hmmm, Which one is the dummy?* Anyone within eye-shot or earshot cannot help but know exactly what they're doing. It becomes increasingly comical when they pick up each other's briefcases or the newspaper their bench mate leaves on the bench when he departs.

That doesn't even begin to describe the various ways spies attempt to cover espionage actions while in public settings. I love it when I see a Spy, decked out in a fine suit, fetching documents out of a trash bin in a park. There's also a perverse pleasure when I observe overweight red-faced Agents straining, while they bend over to covertly remove documents taped to the bottoms of park benches and restaurant stools.

Yes, such activities do occur. Both state-sponsored espionage operators and corporate spies engage in such silliness. I, on the other hand, prefer less obvious meeting places and tactics. My tactical style often requires a more significant investment of time and effort than that of my peers. However, I find a generous measure of peace, knowing I'm leaving as little as possible to chance.

The purpose of this chapter is to share some of my experiences when it became necessary to meet with various individuals associated with Operations involving me. The overarching description that best describes these meeting is "in secret." While obfuscation is a necessary integral part of this manuscript, the locations described in this chapter are accurate representations of sites I've used for surreptitious meetings.

WASHINGTON D.C.

The Land of Equivocation
My work in Washington D.C. over the years has been eye-opening. Few backbones exist in D.C. It's as if politicians and bureaucrats were told on their first day of work, "Your number one priority is to equivocate." Of course, equivocate means to dodge, avoid communicating the truth, and to deceive. Not a good approach for those in positions of power whose words and actions can impact the lives of people everywhere.

Few individuals seem interested in taking a stand on anything. Backbones are a rarity. Some refer to them as Swamp Rats. They are political rodents heavily influenced by the winds of opinion, second-guessing, career opportunities, longevity at all costs, and an overriding thirst for connections, status, and power. Few individuals stand for principle in that land. It's more than disappointing. *It is sick!*

That environment breeds opportunity for political and Corporate Espionage. It's been the setting for more than six dozen first time Cola encounters with potential Clients, OneSevens, Agents, and others; and more Ops than I can count. Here are just a few memorable locations in The Land of Equivocation.

HERBERT RICHARD "DICK" OXNAM

The Korean War Veterans Memorial
My trusted friend and co-author of this book, Ryan Shaughnessy, often used a coded fax transmission when he needed to pass on sensitive information. One morning I received a fax from Ryan with "K-Man" in the "TO:" section of the fax header.

K-Man was his way of telling me he needed an urgent meeting. He and I were in the D.C. area at the time, so I knew the venue would be nearby.

Ryan's coded assignation faxes always contained a number in the first position, in the first paragraph. That number served to alert me to the specific paragraph containing the coded time and location for our meeting.

Here's the body of the fax I received from Ryan:

K-Man,

"I'm sure you remember me telling you about the chance encounter I had with the seven old Marines, who were part of the same unit during the Korean War. I just received a letter from one of those Marines. Even before I received his letter I vividly recalled his name, Dick Oxnam. He's the Colonel I told you about who was at the reunion with his wife, Betty. You'll recall me saying when they first met she outranked the future Bird Colonel. Enjoy!"

"'Ryan, you asked me about my experiences in Korea. Thank you for your interest in the sacrifices we made in service to our great nation. Yes, thank you for understanding why I prefer to call it the Korean War, as opposed to using the term Korean Conflict. Anyone who fought on the ground would tell you it was WAR.

"'Near the end of the Korean War I was sent to command troops in an area that is now part of the DMZ. We were on the front lines for the better part of a year. We were fighting more Chinese than North Koreans. They came at us in unending swarms.

"'My platoon was positioned on a large hill or small mountain peak. If you've ever been to Tucson and seen our "A" Mountain, you know the size of the hill we defended. It was all rock. No dirt. All the soil had been blown away by months of artillery fire. Even the dust. We couldn't dig Marine Fighting Holes for protection. On one occasion our own Corsairs thought we were Chinese troops. They strafed us, dropped bombs, and showered us with napalm. Our only protection was made possible by stacking the bodies of dead Chinese soldiers around us like sandbags. It was tough duty. The stench was terrible and watching them decompose was difficult. Their eyes would bulge out, then later go back inside their skulls.

"'I see by your letter you remember Betty telling you about my injury. It really wasn't a big deal. I was shot in the neck at Outpost East Berlin on July 11, 1953. It was a minor wound, but I was evacuated anyway, under the cover of darkness. I was patched up in short order and sent back to my command, sixteen days before hostilities ceased.

"'Returning home was tough. Vietnam veterans weren't the only ones who suffered catcalls and hurtful words. People called us killers of women and children. The insults were painful. I've never gotten over that. After returning home a draft-dodging fraternity brother asked me, "Oxnam, where have you been?" I couldn't answer him. He, like others, had a hard time believing a man can be both a Christian and a battlefield Marine.'"

"Oxnam recounted one particular patrol, composed of fourteen U.S. Army Soldiers, three Marines, one Navy Corpsman, and an Air Force Forward Air Observer. It was the last official day of the war. The

> armistice was scheduled to take effect that evening. Everyone was dressed in full combat gear, on patrol and surrounded by granite walls and juniper bushes. Although hostilities officially ceased two hours earlier, the mixed group hiked until midnight. At midnight the patrol stopped to build a Memorial honoring comrades they lost in the Korean War. Oxnam received a Purple Heart and the Bronze Star for his service during that time."

My review of the fax made it clear the seventh paragraph contained the coded message. Without question, the first and final paragraphs were of Ryan's creation. A process of elimination revealed Dick Oxnam most likely penned the other paragraphs. The double reference to midnight in the final paragraph was undeniable. Ryan was telling me the meeting needed to occur at midnight that night. The last sentence led me to believe the venue would be the Korean War Memorial. Which one?

BETTY OXNAM

circa 2002

Off the top of my head, I could think of three in the area. The first is on the Washington Mall in D.C. The second is in

Baltimore. The third is somewhere in Virginia. I knew Ryan wouldn't keep me hanging. I realized the composition of the troops described in that paragraph was probably the keystone to solving the riddle.

Not wanting to waste any time, I immediately reached out to my Information and Research OneSeven. She's a young librarian I call Kaylee. I gave her the clues and asked her to research the composition of the military branches and also mentioned the granite walls and Juniper bushes. I told Kaylee I needed to know which Korean War Memorial was involved. I told her I'd call back in an hour.

> ***An aside...***
> Kaylee, like Diamond Dave, is an unwitting OneSeven. She has no idea I am a Spy. She believes I am a freelance ghostwriter and journalist. Unlike Diamond Dave, Kaylee receives regular payments from me. I need her often and usually on short notice.
>
> Kaylee repeatedly tells me she's glad our arrangement is retainer-based. According to Kaylee, if she were working by the hour, she'd go broke. It's almost as if Kaylee knows the answers and information before I seek them from her. Much of the information she provides to me is, surprisingly, off the top of her head. I am spoiled. Her consistently fast responses to information requests serve to raise my expectations unfairly. Now that the Internet is a viable tool, she's even more valuable. The plethora of data on the net needs filtered and condensed into useful data sets. Kaylee is quick in providing what I refer to as "briefing papers" when she researches complicated matters. She saves me loads of time.
>
> Kaylee is a prolific reader, and her retention is phenomenal. I'd like to get her on Jeopardy.
>
> *hmmm, perhaps that'll be my next Operation.*

Back to My Researcher...
Kaylee responded with a laugh. I asked what was so funny. She said, "No need to call me back Cola. I know which memorial you're seeking."

Then she said, "The number and type of warriors, plus the references to granite and Juniper are conclusive. I know the location of the memorial you're seeking. Go visit Abe Lincoln. After bidding Honest Abe farewell, head directly toward the architect of Monticello."

I got it immediately. Monticello is the home of Thomas Jefferson, which he designed. If I could walk in a straight line from the Lincoln Memorial toward the Jefferson Memorial, I would quickly pass directly through the relatively new Korean War Veterans Memorial on the Washington Mall. That call with Kaylee took all of 3 minutes.

After getting off the phone with Kaylee, I marveled at Ryan's ingenuity. He did tell me about Colonel Oxnam quite a few years earlier. I recall him mentioning how Oxnam's children were a patriotic group that, once grown, dedicated themselves to service to others. They work in education, as first responders, in community service, and in defense of our nation. He said Betty was an especially proud mother who repeatedly touted the successes of her children and their extended family. Everyone knows Cola's memory is excellent. Although Ryan's recall is above average, how did he remember the man and his wife's name after all these years? How and why did he remain in contact with Colonel Oxnam?

I parked my car a few blocks north of Lafayette Park about 11:00 PM and made my way east to 15th. The area is a little sketchy that late at night. I traveled south on 15th and began feeling better once I approached Old Ebbitt Grill. A great Washington restaurant frequented by the Cola Team when not operational. A few minutes later I was on the Mall. Turning west, I walked down Constitution until I reached the area just north of the splendid World War II Memorial. I cut across the Memorial and continued west on the south side of the Reflecting Pool.

I knew the Korean War Veterans Memorial was near the end of the pool and off the pathway to the south. As I approached the end of the Reflecting Pool, I began to slow my stride and listen carefully. I turned toward the Memorial. The area was dark and foreboding. Although not entirely dark, visibility was less than desirable. A ground fog was dancing lightly near my ankles. *Weird.*

I turned left and followed a couple of sidewalks until reaching the concrete path that led to the Pool of Remembrance. Turning left, I began a slow, methodical, cautious approach to the pool. The fog thickened. It was rolling in fast from the Potomac. Slowing and quietly shifting and swirling. The hair stood up on my neck. Between me and a massive black granite wall on the southern border of the Memorial, stood nineteen apparitions. Now my hair and goosebumps were screaming, "Fight or Flight Cola!"

The nineteen figures before me were American fighting men constructed of stainless steel, and standing a little more than seven feet tall. It was a platoon on patrol in Korea during the war. The swirling fog was thick and rose above the warriors' knees.

Reaching their lower thighs, it boiled and churned; reminding me of the first Passover in the Ten Commandments movie, starring Charlton Heston, when death descended on Pharaoh's people. Standing there in the fog, I remember the slowly churning vapor vividly. I was experiencing a rare and eerie unearthly surreal event. Nearly reaching my waist at times, it served to deaden sounds; making the entire experience even more unreal.

I felt as though I was there in Korea with the Colonel. Walking through a foggy swamp with a platoon of America's finest. The patrol was precisely as described by Ryan in the last paragraph of the fax. It was composed of fourteen U.S. Army Soldiers, three Marines, one Navy Corpsman, and an Air Force Forward Air Observer. Looking at the scene before me, I couldn't help but think of Dick Oxnam in the winter of 1952 - 1953.

The entire experience left me chilled. I gained a new measure of respect for those young boys who, not so long ago, braved the elements and waves of Chinese warriors in that land so far from home. American Heros!

Ryan tapped me on the shoulder. Instantly coming out of my reverie with a startled jolt, I said, "Geez Ryan! You scared me to death! Look at that, Ryan! Creepy isn't it."

Ryan later told me he saw something just as creepy when he was in Boot Camp at the Marine Corps Recruit Depot in San Diego. He said Drill Instructors roused his Company for a pre-dawn drill on the Parade Deck. As they marched on that enormous asphalt slab, fog rolled in off the Pacific and settled just above their knees. Ryan said it was eerie. Creepy.

MARINE CORPS RECRUIT DEPOT SAN DIEGO

circa 2006

As he marched across the parade deck, officially referred to as Shepherd Memorial Drill Field, he realized millions of men earned the title United States Marine on that sacred ground. Many thousands of them that went to war, never came home.

USMC Recruits in Boot Camp

circa 2006

Ryan said the eerily calm swirling fog in that sea of slowly marching Recruits reminded him of the many souls who toiled upon that hallowed ground. Recruits who later became Marines. Marines who eventually gave their lives on the field of battle. Marines he never knew but honored in remembrance as he marched through the early morning fog rolling in off the Pacific Ocean. Marines like Chance Phelps who, not so long ago, became a U. S. Marine on that very parade deck. Marines like Dick Oxnam and his buddies who became U.S. Marines on that sacred ground, then went on to sacrifice so much during the Korean War.

If you've never visited the Korean War Veterans Memorial in Washington D.C., I heartily recommend it; day or night, fog or no fog, whether you're involved in espionage or not. I believe the Memorial is open twenty-four hours a day.

I encourage you to honor those who sacrificed so much, by visiting that impressive memorial. Just do it.

◇ ◇ ◇

A DISGUISED COLA ONESEVEN AT THE PETERSON HOUSE

Bistro d'OC

Most Americans know President Lincoln's assassination occurred while he was attending a performance at Ford's Theater in Washington DC. Perhaps a majority of those Americans know first responders transported the fatally injured 56-year-old President across the street to The Peterson House, owned by German tailor William Petersen and his wife, Anna. Few people, however, know a delightful French bistro occupied the adjoining building, along the north wall of The Peterson House for most of the first fifteen years of this new century.

Some nine hours after John Wilkes Booth fired a bullet into Lincoln's skull, the 16th President took his final breath in a Peterson House bedroom. Adjacent to the north wall of the bedroom where Abraham Lincoln died is the structure that once housed "Bistro d'OC." Cola Fugelere and others respectfully raised glasses and toasted the teetotalling late President from the bar positioned next to that wall in the small French bistro.

Bistro d'OC served me well for more than a decade, as an excellent rendezvous location in Washington DC. Jo, her husband James, Ryan, Bren, Jon Shayner, TJ, Roy, Skookum Jim, and others met me there in the early days after the quaint little French Bistro opened. It was dark, inviting, comfortable, and exceptionally pleasant. There were several different dining rooms, each with different colored walls, painted with taste. Tastefully adorned with flowers, plants, and other nice touches, the spaces were pleasant and comfortable. Elevated meals and doting servers made the experience inviting. The pleasurable environment beckoned us to dine at Bistro d'OC repeatedly. I found the bar served me well as an excellent subdued late-night discussion venue.

Traveling on foot from the north made it easy for us to avoid being picked up by area surveillance cameras. That is, as of the last time I worked in that area. The rapid proliferation of contemporary video surveillance camera installations suggests that is no longer the case.

Over time the staff began to know us too well. That's when we chose to move to Old Ebbitt Grill for the relative anonymity it provided our small band of espionage professionals and associated individuals. When the necessary relocation occurred, I asked My Colleagues to avoid any future patronage at the bistro.

We also had a few rules for Old Ebbitt Grill (OEG).

- No Spy Games at OEG.
- No Ops conducted at OEG.
- OEG is a business free zone.
- No business discussions at OEG.
- OEG is a meals-only gathering place.
- Mind our own business when in OEG.

An aside...
We enjoyed Bistro d'OC for many reasons. One of which was its proximity to the International Spy Museum. Only two-tenths of a mile apart, our favorite French bistro and the museum opened for business at nearly the same time. Over the years we've laughed and waxed nostalgic when visiting that most excellent museum.

Although Old Ebbitt Grill remains reasonably close to the museum, it's three times farther than the bistro. That small difference is the only reason we can find to explain

> why we visit the museum less often than previous to the change in restaurants.

Back to Bistro d'OC...
A year after we relocated our dinner engagements to Old Ebbitt Grill, I realized Bistro d'OC could serve me well for clandestine meetings with one of my Agents, Patrick Kelly. Pat was an assistant to one of the most successful lobbyists in Washington and realized the business success his boss enjoyed was due, in part, to espionage. In short, his boss was stealing information from other lobbyists and corporate entities in and around the District of Columbia. Pat's boss was actively using non-professional corporate spies to purloin information belonging to others.

Pat is an honorable man. As such, he was exceedingly disappointed with his employer's business practices. He's since moved on, but before his departure, Pat contacted me for my services.

After exercising my usual due diligence practices and thoroughly vetting Pat Kelly, I offered to meet him late one evening at a different Washington area bar. Knowing Pat would be taking a taxi from his Georgetown townhouse, I bribed the dispatcher, who gave the driver specific instructions, via cell phone, moments before pulling up to Pat's residence.

> ***An aside...***
> In my good guy role as a Corporate Counterintelligence professional, I find myself uncomfortable using variations of the word "bribe," both in conversation and in this manuscript. I suppose I self-justify my activities by believing what I'm doing is okay when I offer money to others for certain services.
>
> The activity is no different than that I engaged in while on the Dark Side, but the goal reflects an upright approach; offering an ethically beneficial purpose. It stands to reason that I'm practicing a "the end justifies the means" rationalization for my activities. Sorry, it's

> hard to teach new methods to an old dog with proven tricks.

Back to Georgetown...
Shortly after the taxi departed Georgetown with its passenger, the driver uttered a bona fide I had passed along to the dispatcher. "Pamela Sue loves croquet." Immediately after that, the taxi turned into a large parking garage and stopped at an elevator. The driver informed Pat the fare was paid in full. He was instructed to take the elevator down one floor. The taxi drove away.

When the elevator door opened and Pat stepped in, one of My Colleagues said, "Hiking to the top of a flat mountain makes for good memories."

> ***An aside...***
> As with the "Pamela Sue" bona fide, the "Hiking..." comment was passed along to Pat ahead of time. He was told those phrases to indicate all was going as planned; and, as such, was designed to relax The Subject.

Back to The Elevator...
My Colleague used an elevator maintenance bypass key to redirect the elevator to a specific floor. Pat exited the elevator two floors above and hopped into the back of a waiting panel van. The van departed the garage, meandered for a while attempting to draw out any tails, then drove my young Client to Bistro d'OC. I was patiently awaiting his arrival, knowing the SDR would radically increase his travel time from nearby Georgetown to the area just north of the Washington Mall. The SDR included multiple trips around Dupont Circle and various roads in and out of Rock Creek Park.

Bistro d'OC had two front doors. While Pat was riding in the van, our driver instructed him to enter the restaurant using the left side door. He was further directed to walk straight in and position himself at the end of the bar with his back to the entrance. Encouraged to enjoy a beverage, Pat was told to consume no more than two alcoholic drinks while waiting for me.

He was also advised to expect me any time after his arrival, up to an hour later.

While Pat sat at the bar nursing a cold Corona Light, I discretely observed him from a nearby table. Wearing a disguise, neither the staff nor Pat would be able to describe me to anyone else that evening or beyond. Pat enjoyed his favorite beer, while I finished eating cheesecake with raspberry coulis and whipped cream. After fifteen minutes my Nokia flip phone began to vibrate. One of the Watchers was calling to let me know the coast was clear. No followers or evidence of breadcrumbs were detected.

Picking up my coffee cup, I walked a few short steps to the bar and uttered a bona fide that informed Pat the person greeting him was Cola the Spy. "Hello sir, Molly O' is not a fan of bowling pins."

> ***An aside...***
> Yes, such bona fides are silly. However, they serve a genuinely important purpose. They are so odd and specific, they help avoid accidental misunderstandings that might occur if someone uttered something and it were to be accepted as a bona fide. For example, if a bona fide was "Do you have the time" or "It's a beautiful day" an innocent pedestrian or an evildoer could confuse or misdirect the Target. That is, therefore, the reason spies employ improbable odd phrases.

Back to The Cloak and Dagger...
Pat looked me over from head to toe and asked, "Who are you?"

"As you suspect, young man, I'm Cola. Please accept my apologies for all the cloak and dagger. Understand such measures are necessary for our mutual protection. For what it's worth, we're alone. Nobody followed you to this serious location."

Confusion washed across Pat's face. He asked, "Serious location?"

I responded by letting him know that the path upon which we were about to embark held dangers for each of us. I reminded Pat that the outcome of an Operation designed to expose his employer could result in the lobbyist losing nearly everything he owned. I told the young man to understand the cornucopia of possible ramifications, based upon our actions, could lead to many different outcomes; including the possibility we'd be creating a potentially dangerous foe. It was a serious undertaking, and I wanted to discuss the matter with him in a location that bore an equal amount of seriousness.

A quizzical look crossed his face once more. I lifted my coffee cup and waved it at the bartender. The bartender sauntered over. I ordered a Lagavulin, "Neat."

Once my beverage arrived, I raised my glass in the manner of a toast. Pat raised his Corona. I mimicked the words Secretary of War Edwin Stanton is said to have uttered, immediately after Lincoln took his final breath, "Now he belongs to the angels."

Again confused, Pat asked me to explain. Once more I told the young man I chose the bistro because it is a serious location. "Pat, our toast was lifted in honor of the 16th President of the United States."

I gestured with the whiskey snifter to a small wine racking sitting atop the bar to our left. Moving too quickly, a small amount of the precious golden beverage spilled onto the surface of the bar. Looking at the precious liquid, I said, "I guess this is a place of sacrifice. Abe Lincoln gave his life to our nation. He took his last breath just a few feet from where we're sitting, beyond the wine rack to your left, and on the opposite side of the wall. I accidentally sacrificed some of the world's finest smoky 16-year-old whiskey while attempting to convey the seriousness of the situation by pointing out that our assassinated President died a few feet from here. You're about to embark on a path that could result in equally serious ramifications. If you're correct about bribery, blackmail, and extortion, this could become very dangerous for both of us. Pat, my point is that this is serious business. Are you certain you want to do this?"

He was serious. Over the coming few years Pat and I met at the Bistro d'OC bar many times as the Operation unfolded. Each time we came together we lifted the trademark toast to teetotalling Abe. It was an excellent location, and the memories leave me in a melancholy mood. As of this writing, the most excellent atmosphere of the Bistro d'OC in that location no longer exists. Honest Abe's Souvenir, a tourist-centric gift shop, is the current occupant of that location.

Change is inevitable. Just ask the dinosaurs, the residents of Pompeii, or the former rulers of the Roman Empire. Not only is the bistro gone, but Pat's beer choices have also morphed. He recently told me his favorite beer in his twenties was Heileman's Special Export Light, from the Pabst Brewing Company. When he was in his thirties, a fellow Little League parent introduced him to Corona Light. Now that Pat is in his fifties, his taste in suds is morphing once more. He now likes to drink Chainbreaker White IPA from Deschutes Brewing Company. I sure hope he doesn't transition to fruit-flavored beers once he reaches my age.

I've been happy to stock my refrigerator with his favorites over the years, but fruity beer has no home in our Washington area safe house refrigerator. Sorry, Pat. If you'd like, I'll work hard to track down something else for you. How about a blast from the past? Heileman's Special Export Light?

Restaurants

Politicians, government bureaucrats, lobbyists, and media types gravitate to Washington's hot spots. Area restaurants are more than just great meeting places for Cola insiders. They can be venues for informational tidbits of value.

Invisible restaurant staffers could serve their benefactors well in such locations. Privileged information floating within earshot is undoubtedly available for aggregation in the many excellent restaurants surrounding the centers of power in our nation's capital. The saying, "Loose Lips Sink Ships" is well-known in Washington for many good reasons. Loose lips are commonplace in Washington area restaurants and artisan coffee houses.

While dining at various District of Columbia restaurants when non-operational, I've picked up more than a few valuable tidbits; especially during the later hours when patrons have had too much to drink. On some occasions, I have enjoyed picking the brains of braggarts and others who work for politicians, lobbyists, and media personalities. The excellent selection of alcohol at many of these haunts often loosens the tongues of insiders, seeking opportunities to brag about their role in the Who's Who of Washington D.C. Some want others to believe they have a seat at the table. The plethora of individuals with an overabundant desire to advance and become a somebody in Washington DC results in many who misplace reasonable judgment, in favor of perceived opportunity. While other places will serve just as well with informational diarrhea, the closer one is to the Washington Monument, the better.

I was having a post-Op drink in one such establishment late one evening and overheard a young woman make a regrettable statement. I immediately took a pen out of my pocket and memorialized those words. She said, "You don't get it, I'm advancing my career. I'm connected, I'm moving forward, and I'm destined to impact history. I will become part of the history of this city, this nation, this world. I will do whatever it takes to succeed inside the beltway. I don't care. It'll happen and God help anyone who gets in my way. If you get in my way, I'll run you over. I don't care. I WILL SUCCEED!"

Cola's overriding thought, "At what cost?"

What an empty goal! A hollow ambition! A Fool's Hollow!

There are many choices available if I want to disappear in the clutter and chaos of a busy restaurant environment. I must say, though, it stretches Pigeon Memory to successfully hold clandestine meetings in busy venues without risking exposure to a well-planned doublecross or worse. My antennae work overtime when dining in Washington area hotspots while I'm operational.

An aside...
Restaurants are more than just meeting places and venues for intelligence gathering. They can be excellent venues for exchanges.

I wear black dress Florsheim loafers. When microfiche was a favorite medium for passing large volumes of data, I had one of my OneSevens modify two identical pairs of Florsheim shoes to accommodate concealments in hollowed out heels. I provided the footwear to one of my Agents who wore the same size as me.

NOTE: On one occasion the concealment contained a surprise note. It read, “Cola's spy shoe choice is the most stylish comfortable off-the-shelf shoe in the world. Kudos Cola! Florsheim shoes are the best!”

We'd meet for coffee when an exchange was necessary. My Agent would pass microfiche film, containing blueprint images, to me by taking off his shoes and switching with me. He'd leave the restaurant with the second pair of empty concealment capable Florsheim shoes, and I’d depart with precious purloined proprietary information.

THE UNITED STATES SUPREME COURT

Cola's Favorite Pillar Pass Location

Pillar Passes

I often refer to structural opportunities to conceal Brush Passes as "Pillar Passes." While the term refers to more than just the use of Pillars, I do prefer those vertical structures for passing and receiving information and other items of value.

THE JEFFERSON MEMORIAL

Site of Cola's First Critical Brush Pass

An aside...

Agents generally use a standard espionage Brush Pass with their Handlers to covertly pass information and/or items from one person to another. It usually involves two individuals walking toward one another (sometimes in the same direction), passing very closely, exchanging items, then continuing forward without pause. When done correctly neither person appears to have done anything other than walk by the other person.

My first real critical Brush Pass occurred about one o'clock on a cold winter morning at the Jefferson Memorial. Power to the area was down, and I needed to take possession of a file provided by an investigative journalist. I was planning to pass a manila envelope filled with cash to the journalist while taking possession of a similar envelope filled with documents.

The pass was ugly. We bumped into one another in the darkness, and both of us dropped our envelopes. As we went to the floor to retrieve what we allowed to fall, we bumped heads with force. I saw stars. Once we were back on our feet with the gravity challenged envelopes, it was unclear who had which envelope. I patted down the envelope in my hand and realized it contained cash. He understood as well. We successfully attempted the second transfer then continued walking, after our clumsy delay of ineptitude. Thankfully, the darkness and the Jefferson Memorial's enormous pillars concealed our actions.

After that silly encounter, I've called Brush Passes something different. I refer to them as Pillar Passes. In fact, I prefer opportunities to pass or receive confidential information by using line-of-sight obstacles like pillars, statues, bushes and trees, people, and vehicles.

Back to The Washington Mall...
Years ago I discovered various monuments and structures in the area of the Washington Mall offer great opportunities to do quick Pillar Passes and similar exchanges. The Supreme Court's columns have been used by me, more often than any other location in the District of Columbia. The Jefferson Memorial, the Lincoln Memorial, the National Archives, and the interior of the

Smithsonian's National Museum of American History are four of my favorites after the Supreme Court.

I really enjoy conducting Pillar Passes in front of the Star-Spangled Banner. That flag inspired our National Anthem and is located in a very dim viewing area in the National Museum. Several times in recent years, Pat Kelly and I passed USBs while standing in the flag's viewing area.

LINCOLN MEMORIAL

Although, except for the columns at the Supreme Court's front entrance, I've used the men's bathroom inside the base of the Lincoln Memorial more than any other location for Pillar Passes. That space is small, busy, and offers reasonably discrete exchanges. Surveillance teams would have difficulty positioning themselves to thwart covert transfers or place eyes on Subjects during exchanges.

> ***An aside...***
> Using a trick I learned from a Pickpocket OneSeven, I usually have one or more Colleagues in the area for further passes. Those actions are designed to confuse any Watchers in the area and ensure any incriminating information departs the area quickly. We often drop passed materials into a bag lined with signal blocking

> technologies (a Faraday Cage design) in case tracking devices are incorporated into USBs, SD cards, dongles, RFID cards, or other equipment passed from our Agents to us.

Back to Pillar Passes...

In my early days as an espionage professional, we often transferred photos, files, and folders in manila envelopes. We hid microfiche records in concealments of one kind or another; including cigarette packages, coiled fiche concealed under cigar bands, flattened film taped to the bottoms of Styrofoam cups, and in other everyday objects. We quickly moved from microfiche to disc media. 8", then 5-¼", then 3-½" floppy disks, followed by CDs, DVDs, SD cards, and USBs. Some of those transfers now occur digitally using Smart Phones and computers. Each method carries a myriad of risks. However, as of this writing, SD cards and USBs remain the preferred methods for personally managed physical transfers of data in the Corporate Espionage arena.

> ***An aside...***
>
> I once had an Inside Man, Russ, who was the father of eight lovely daughters. Russ and his beautiful bride have long since retired to the American southwest. Russ was a great guy who lost his high school sweetheart wife shortly after their last child was born. Working hard to make ends meet, Russ was an electrical engineer who struggled with the sacrifices involved in raising, educating, and saving for the weddings of his daughters.
>
> Russ met an extraordinary woman, Soo-jin, who became his second wife. Soo-jin was a very successful administrator in the educational arena and wanted the make sure each of the girls had a healthy college fund. She told Russ she wanted to begin investing the proceeds from her professional life into eight different savings accounts dedicated to the girls' education. Russ appreciated Soo-jin's gesture. It took much pressure off, but her thoughtfulness didn't entirely resolve Russ's financial woes.

The first daughter's wedding costs overwhelmed Russ's expectations, and he realized he was ill-prepared to fund seven more weddings. Russ needed to increase his income, so he invested in a food wagon. He addressed his staffing needs by manning the mobile restaurant with his older daughters. The food cart brought in a little more money but fell short in meeting Russ's goals. That's where Cola came in and helped pick up the slack.

Russ was working on a high-level project for an international consortium. Two of the companies involved were, at the very least, antagonistic to the United States. At worst, they were enemies. My self-justification for helping to steal the consortium's designs was their belligerence toward my country. At the same time, they were attempting to profit from our goodness and free markets.

My responsibility was to obtain blueprints for critical components under development for the project. Russ provided those drawings on microfiche. That wasn't unusual. However, the method of transferring those documents to me was odd, convenient, and tasty.

Tasty? Yep. Russ would work several evenings a week in the food wagon with his daughter, Lea. I would wait until there were no other customers in the area. Then I'd walk up and place an order with Lea for a vanilla ice cream cone.

I didn't want to chance someone else receiving my order. If someone else did, that person would likely return or discard the cone after the first taste. The nature of my order was intended to protect the exchanged information, while also making sure Russ was alerted to my presence.

While Lea had no idea who I was to her father, she did remember me between visits to the food wagon. Russ shared that she dubbed me the "Piggy Bank Guy." Lea never referred to me in person using those words. The

Piggy Bank Guy was a term she used in conversations with her father when speaking about me.

I played the same distracting game each time I arrived, and Lea remained kind and polite during each visit. I'm sure other teenagers would engage in eye rolling and nasty comments. Not Lea. She was a gracious young lady who possessed style and decency.

She would inform her father to prep a vanilla cone with a double dash of salt. That was a heads up for Russ. Once alerted that Cola was waiting outside the food wagon, Russ would prepare the cone by dropping a small plastic bag containing microfiche documents into the bottom of a cone, then load it with ice cream. In the meantime, I would fumble with lots of dimes, nickels, and pennies. My fumbling and Lea's counting served to keep her distracted, so the young lady's father could place the microfiche into the concealment without her seeing his activities.

Russ would load the concealment, then pass the microfiche infused waffle cone to his daughter. Lea would hand it to me, and I'd walk away licking the tasty treat. My car was never too far away. I would drive a few blocks licking the cone. Once I was relatively comfortable knowing I wasn't followed, I'd pull over and engage in a well-practiced ritual.

I'd drop the cone head first into a cup. Then I'd drink from a water bottle to wash the salty sweet taste from my mouth. Following the cleansing of my palate, I'd reach down and shake the bottom of the cone until the remaining soft serve ice cream fell into the cup, leaving me with the cone. About half the time the packaged microfiche would drop onto the top of the ice cream heap. On other occasions, the microfiche treasure would remain inside the cone, after securing itself to the inner sides of the cone. The best part of the entire experience was in collecting the valuable treasure provided by Russ.

Lea followed in her father's footsteps and became an accomplished electrical engineer. Although I've not used her skills in my Counterespionage efforts, she holds a vaunted position on my candidate shortlist for an Electrical Engineer OneSeven. As long as I have Jo, Lea will have to remain on my OneSeven wait list.

P.S. Russ's association with me made it possible for his daughters to enjoy beautiful weddings. Thanks to Soo-jin's gracious educational grants, each of the girls earned their degrees. Soo-jin also assisted the girls in their employment efforts by using her well-developed talents in creating the most appropriate résumés I've ever seen.

The National Law Enforcement Officers Memorial
Located in Washington D.C.'s Judiciary Square, The National Law Enforcement Officers Memorial offers an excellent opportunity for solemnity and focus. The area is busier than I would like, but Pigeon Memory is sufficiently helpful in that location. Besides, it's always an honor to stop there and pay my respects to those fallen Officers who've given so much to each of us.

Manhattan

Katz's Delicatessen
The very busy Katz's Delicatessen in NYC is an excellent meeting location with trusted associates for several reasons. (1) Great food, (2) Anonymity, (3) Ease of Access, (4) Noise (covers private conversations). Katz does, however, offer three downsides. (1) The potential for a long wait to be seated, (2) Pigeon Memory issues, (3) Small World/Chance Encounters (people from around the globe dine there).

Empire State Building
I've held a single uncomfortable meeting atop the Empire State Building. Unfortunately, it wasn't a Sleepless in Seattle dream

meeting on Valentine's Day. I was there to meet a short, gruff, hairy, overweight associate; not a beautiful woman.

The only reason I was willing to meet someone atop the Empire State Building, is because he is a longtime well-trusted associate. I would not plan a first time meeting with anyone at that location. Ingress and egress are difficult. Too many choke points.

Multiple elevators and stairs are necessary to travel to the visitor area and return to street level. Tourists queuing up to get in and out can result in backups and delays. It's confined, crowded, and harbors too many potential pitfalls.

Statue of Liberty

Although a wonderful place, I will only visit the Statue of Liberty alone; and after performing a very thorough SDR. I choose not to meet anyone there. I visit that location for the serenity and history.

The location is well-suited as a setup staging area for anyone intending me harm. The layout and remote location present problems for this espionage professional. Lines of sight and other espionage-related shortcomings exist in that location. Ingress and egress are significant issues; especially if departure becomes an immediate necessity.

There are only two options available for getting to Liberty Island. Both involve a ferry. Private boats cannot dock on the island. One ferry departs from Lower Manhattan and the other from Jersey City. Until 2007 I would use the Circle Line Ferry. Ferries operated by Statue Cruises replaced the concession for the Circle Line. Security measures are reasonable and smuggling weapons onto the island would be problematic. Anyone with decent vision and inexpensive communications devices can alert accomplices in New York or New Jersey that you've just boarded a boat. One of the two disembark points could quickly become an ambush point. Not good options for someone concerned about apprehension or snatches.

In the off-season, Pigeon Memory is not a problem on Liberty Island, but remaining covert and unavailable to onsite Watchers is nearly impossible. Pigeon Memory, however, is a major problem during the high season when thousands of daily visitors set foot on the island. I can't begin to imagine going operational on Liberty Island when it's overrun by tourists.

Battery Park
Pigeon Memory can be somewhat problematic at Battery Park. Ingress and egress are good. I appreciate the setting, and I am willing to meet known associates in that location.

The World Trade Center
Although the Twin Towers no longer exist, I held a couple of CCM meetings atop the south tower, while insinuating myself into tours that included the party I needed to surprise.

Los Angeles Area

Beach Communities
I have rendezvoused with Colleagues at the Malibu Pier, the Santa Monica Pier, and at the Manhattan Beach Pier. Ingress and egress is a concern at those three locations. However, the piers are scenic, enjoyable, and embraced by me for short meetings with known and trusted associates. The settings are pleasant. Also, when large crowds are present, an opportunity for anonymity exists.

NO FISHING

Malibu Pier

An aside...

Located between Malibu Beach and Surfriders Beach, the Malibu Pier reminds me that rules and laws are, at best, optional for many people. One of my associates took a photo at the end of the Malibu Pier. There were "No Fishing" signs posted everywhere on the pier. There are four fishing poles in the photo and a "No Fishing" sign. Many people were fishing that day.

I've come to expect the public to ignore rules and for the government to change the laws. I believe people choose to ignore many laws out of a "Me First" approach to life. That "Me First" or "It's All About Me" philosophy results in justification for many selfish actions.

For example, people wanting to get somewhere quickly, regardless of the speed limit, will often drive faster than allowable by law. Drive your car on the New Jersey Turnpike, and you'll see what I mean. Travel anywhere along Interstate 10 between Santa Monica, California and Jacksonville, Florida. My assertions will be validated. Heck, driving through Phoenix on I-10 in a posted 65 mph zone and you'll find that almost every other driver is leaving you in the dust; often traveling 75 to 80 miles per hour. *Rules don't matter!*

Governments, like people, engage in their own self-serving justifications. Government motives are almost always on a parallel path with money. Remember when police would arrest bookies and numbers runners for facilitating gambling? Remember when running numbers was a primary source of income for organized crime?

Governments wanted their piece of the pie and began running numbers. The various lotteries represent that concept. It's a legislated approach engineered by politicians to funnel additional funds into government coffers. Native American gaming is little different. Except for Nevada, most states had traditionally banned gambling. The remaining 49 states witnessed Nevada cleaning up, so most of them changed state law to permit gambling within their borders - for a slice of the action. *I digress...*

Olympia

I've never met a Client in a more peaceful setting than I discovered in Olympia, Greece. Olympia was the setting for the original Greek Olympics games dating back nearly 2800 years. Beginning as a festival, it morphed into athletic events that included footraces, wrestling, and javelin throwing. Performed in the nude, the idea was to celebrate the male physique.

My trips to Olympia repeatedly pique Cola's imagination. I imagine the ancient sights, smells, and sounds of the crowd, the athletes, and the overall atmosphere. I'm sure it was very noisy. Odd, too, from my 21st-century perspective. The thought of seeing naked men running, throwing, and wrestling with one another seems downright awkward in a public setting.

An aside...

The first Olympians often carried out their athletic pursuits in the buff. While exposed male genitalia was acceptable to be seen in public, the head of the penis (the glans) dishonored anyone shamefully exposing that most private part of his anatomy. In those days, allowing one's glans to be visible to others in public was akin to indecent exposure.

Modest athletes, not wanting to risk offending anyone, would use a string or thin piece of leather to tie off his uncircumcised foreskin. The practice was intended to keep the glans from peeking out. The loose end of the string would be fastened around the waist, thereby lifting the penis upward to reveal the scrotum. It was, indeed, a curious practice and would be a very unusual sight for us today.

I'm a believer in fully understanding situations, and will often experiment to see how things I read and hear about would work in actual practice. *I'm sure you recall my experience with Dumb Cane.* I'm an experimenter by nature. However, tying a string to my privates and running around naked in front of a gathering of people is not for me. Yes, it would be embarrassing. However, the potential for pain and damage scares the pants off of me. *pun intended...*

PEACEFUL OLYMPIA, GREECE

A MEXICAN TOURIST IN OLYMPIA, GREECE

Back to Olympia, with My Clothes On...

However, nowadays Olympia is anything but noisy. It is a peaceful, tranquil, setting. The ruins of Olympia include standing columns and foundations. The site is now a mere vestige of a once vibrant public setting. Today grasses and trees sway gently in the quiet breezes. The beauty and sound of millions of leaves fluttering presents a calm, serene, environment; echoing little of the exciting history of the area. Today Olympia is a perfect setting for a picnic or a quiet CCM. The ancient location enjoys reasonable Pigeon Memory opportunities, except those occasions when sightseeing buses unload scores of tourists.

Denver's Buckhorn Exchange

I once enjoyed a fruitful meeting in a rather strange, albeit tasty, restaurant in Denver, Colorado. The Buckhorn Exchange is a dark, comfortable, eating establishment reflecting a profitable relationship for one or more taxidermists. Founded in 1893, the restaurant's liquor license underscores its continuous operation. License Number 1 was the first liquor license ever issued in Colorado.

INSIDE THE BUCKHORN EXCHANGE

A wide variety of animal mounts are everywhere. The menu also contains a varied list of exotic animals presented to bedazzle patron taste buds. The culinary delights include rattlesnake, bison, alligator, Rocky Mountain Oysters, elk, quail, and other oddities.

The venue is interesting, exotic, and delightful.

Boston, Massachusetts

My first trip to that cemetery was somewhat ritualistic for me. Not unlike my toasting Honest Abe from a barstool in Bistro d'OC, I went to the Beantown Pub across the street from the Granary Burying Ground and hosted a Sam Adams beer in tribute to Samuel Adams. Then I went directly across the street and paid my respects at the grave of Mr. Adams.

Sam Adams, Massachusetts Governor and Founding Father of the United States of America, was a second cousin to fellow Founding Father and President, John Adams. His deeds are worthy of my admiration and a sudsy toast.

Moving on, I dropped in on Paul Revere's grave near the back of the cemetery. Then I turned around to view the greater part of the graveyard I tried to determine the location of John Hancock's resting place. To my right was a large white pillar, much taller than the typical Granary headstone. *hmmm, a perfect tombstone for an ego-centric attention-getter*

I walked across the cemetery and, sure enough, high above my head were the words, "John Hancock."

John Hancock was a wealthy, ambitious, and egotistical merchant. Continually seeking public acclaim and attention, Hancock always stood out in a crowd. Setting his "John Hancock" on the Declaration of Independence is reflective of his desire to be noticed.

Hancock's tall gravestone reflects his immense ego. Set off to one side of the Granary Burying Ground in Boston, the white pillar has been the setting for more than a few Cola meetings.

Ponca City Oklahoma

I was reviewing a possible cemetery meeting location in Ponca City, Oklahoma one cold, dreary, winter day. As I reconnoitered the grounds of Ponca City's Odd Fellows Cemetery attempting to determine the potential for a safe and secure meet with a OneSeven candidate, I stopped and happened to look down on a grave marker. I couldn't believe my eyes.

The words "Leslie McBride Muchmore" jumped off the ground-level marker and hit me between the eyes. It was an unforgettable name. A name I knew.

Not too many years before, I was in Guadalajara, Mexico for some rest and relaxation, a few weeks before an upcoming Mexico City Operation. While there, I shared more than a few cervezas with an American from Oklahoma who introduced himself to me as, "Les Muchmore." When I met Les Muchmore, I remember thinking, "Is he less, or much more?"

LES MUCHMORE

I seem to recall Les was studying in Mexico working on a double Masters. Spanish and Journalism. He was a very nice, soft spoken, and interesting fellow. I vividly remember his wavy blonde hair, wire-rimmed glasses, and the consistently flared nostrils of his nose. He spoke slowly, with an accent that could have only originated in Oklahoma.

It is, indeed, a small world. Here I was looking down on the grave of a man I only knew in another country. I'm sure few people discover someone has passed away by glancing at down and seeing a gravestone, under such random circumstances.

After meeting with the OneSeven, I discreetly asked around Ponca City and discovered Les was a member of the family that owned the local newspaper. He had recently moved to Lake Tahoe, Nevada and was returning home from work one evening, when his car became stuck in the snow. Les was outside his vehicle trying to affix snow chains to the tires. According to local rumors, he was struck by a drunk driver and killed on a cold and lonely stretch of road, up the hill from Tahoe's beautiful lake.

What a tragedy. In another life, Les and I could have become lifelong friends. He was taken too soon and not long after I met him more than 1200 miles away from his home. Les was only 22 years old at the time of his death. So sad.

Pacific Palisades, California

The pristine Getty Villa, just south of Malibu, is a beautiful venue. Cola meetings are common at that location. The Getty Villa reminds me of a visit I once made to Pompeii.

The Getty Villa

If you've ever visited Pompeii, I urge you to visit The Getty Villa. It'll take you back in time to a place before Mount Vesuvius blew its top and covered Pompeii with many feet of deadly volcanic ash.

Anchorage, Alaska

My father's work took him to Anchorage for a time while I was growing up. One particular event in that land will forever stand out in my mind. It occurred many years before I entered the Corporate Espionage arena. However, it was a pivotal chapter in the life of Cola Fugelere, and the effects played a critical a role in my life as a Spy.

That was the first time I experienced what I refer to as the "Hummingbird Effect." Although I was probably too young to appreciate the physiology involved at the time, I nevertheless became conscious of an astounding change in my metabolism. It was all about adrenaline.

> ***An aside...***
> Cola neither runs, nor does he stall, stammer, or blather when something unexpected occurs. His adrenaline kicks in, without any apparent external changes. What happens to me is weird, but helpful. I get tunnel vision, and everything slows down. I continue thinking at my pace, while everything else in the world turns to thick honey and scarcely moves. I feel like I'm inside myself looking out. It's probably akin to Hummingbird experiences, due to their ultrahigh metabolic rate. It can happen to soldiers when engaged in battle.
>
> Again, weird, but helpful. In effect, I can quickly work out issues, without the delays expected by others. My ability to recall those moments is amazing. Unreal.
>
> During adrenaline dumps, I not only remember the tiniest details from my five senses, but my recall is unbelievably vivid; allowing me to remember exactly what I was thinking and other thought processes. My Colleagues find it fascinating. I merely consider it an opportunistic gift.
>
> On the other hand, I get what I call an Adrenaline Hangover when my blood chemistry returns to normal. I get the shakes for a few minutes, then am entirely drained afterward. I'm spent. No energy.

Back to The Event...
On March 27, 1964, at 5:36 pm, a record-breaking 9.2 magnitude earthquake struck Alaska. Lasting nearly five minutes, the Good Friday Earthquake was the most powerful earthquake ever recorded in North America. It is the second most powerful earthquake recorded in the history of the world.

CATALINA "MAMA" FUGELERE

It was Good Friday, and the schools were closed in our nation's largest state. I spent the late winter afternoon in our front yard building a huge snowman. My mother, "Mama" Fugelere, called me inside for dinner. She was cooking spaghetti. My siblings were elsewhere in the home. I'd just finished taking off my hat, gloves, boots, and coat. Standing in the living room, I felt a huge unreal jolt. The entire house jumped into the air. Then everything seemed to slow down. Cola's adrenaline was coursing through his veins.

I watched in awe as our furniture jumped, moved, twisted, and shook. My mother ran into the living room as I watched a red liquid fly through the air. *Blood? Thankfully, no.* Mama had been cooking The Fugelere Family's Old World Red Spaghetti Sauce Recipe on the stove.

> ***An aside...***
> The violent release of energy on Good Friday 1964 occurred when one tectonic plate was thrust under another, along a 600-mile section of the 2100 mile fault called the Aleutian Trough. It was absolutely unbelievable. Approximately 60 miles of lower crust suddenly dove under the upper crust. Six hundred miles of Alaskan earth traveled sixty miles in five minutes!

> According to the U.S. Geological Survey, "If the energy of a magnitude 5.0 earthquake is like snapping a single strand of spaghetti, then a 9.2 earthquake releases enough energy to snap 800,000 spaghetti strands.

Back to The Big One...
The energy of the earthquake lifted my mother's pot of boiling spaghetti sauce, tossed it across the ceiling, and out of the kitchen. Mama reacted quickly and was lucky she wasn't scalded. *hmmm... Was Mama experiencing the Hummingbird Effect?*

As she ran into the living room, I watched her moving in slow motion. She reached out and caught a tall floor lamp as it was falling toward the floor. Just then I watched a younger sister run from the back of the house and dart out the front door. She ran weaving and stumbling like a drunk. Watching out the front window, I saw her stop at the perimeter fence and hang on to a fence post for her life. Above her head, power lines were snapping and jumping. *Yikes!*

GINO "PAPA" FUGELERE

I learned later my father, "Papa" Fugelere, had just departed Peggy's Airport Cafe, after treating himself to ice cream, pie, and coffee. He pulled out of the parking lot, directly across from the Merrill Field airport, and drove toward downtown Anchorage. All of a sudden Dad's car felt like it had a flat tire. As he slowed and looked forward, my father saw a vehicle disappear about a quarter mile away. Then it reappeared, followed by another disappearance. Papa said the asphalt looked like slender black waves on the ocean. The street rose and fell repeatedly.

To his right, Papa saw an elderly woman fall. She'd been walking beside the road. Papa jumped out to offer assistance and fell to the ground. He said it felt as though the earth was sucking and pulling on him.

MY THEN GIRLFRIEND'S FATHER'S CAR

March 28, 1964

Little did Papa know at the time, less than a mile in front of him, and one street to the right, an entire block of businesses and half of 4th Avenue dropped 30' into the earth. One iconic color photo of that downtown scene, owned by UPI, shows Bob Zachry's blue 1960 Chevrolet Biscayne resting on the bottom of that section of the street. Zachry was the father of my, then, girlfriend. One mile directly in front of my father's car, a multistory section of J.C. Penny collapsed onto the street, killing a woman inside her car.

The next day Papa loaded our family in his big black Chrysler Imperial and drove us around town. One of our stops was the area on 4th Avenue where the businesses were gobbled up by the earth. I vividly recall seeing something that's never left my mind.

Standing before our car as we pulled up to peek into the huge hole in the street, were two soldiers standing on an earthquake created ramp of asphalt that dropped into the hole. The one on the left was tall and wearing heavy dark clothing, topped by a fur hat. His puffed up white "Bunny Boots" stood out in stark contrast to his attire. He was holding a rifle vertically. One hand was stretched out toward our car indicating we couldn't go any farther. That wasn't necessary. Papa had pulled the car right up to the hole, with nowhere else to go.

The other soldier, a shorter man, was wearing all gray and had a tin soldier kind of military hat on his head. He pointed his rifle toward, and slightly above, our car. Papa stuck his head out the window and chastised the soldier for aiming the weapon at his family. Then we drove off.

I realized everything was going slow again. I guess the shock and trauma of seeing a soldier with a gun aimed in our direction re-awoke my adrenal glands. From that day forward I realized something was different about Cola Fugelere. I could see the world around me in slow motion. *Wow!*

P.S. My snowman withstood North America's most powerful recorded earthquake. There wasn't a crack on his cold white icy skin. *I should have become a builder.*

MEMORABLE ACAPULCO

Readers of this book have likely concluded Stefano Gino "Cola" Fugelere is a man of contradictions. On the one hand, I'll drive the speed limit and obey most laws. On the other hand, I have a track record of covert after-hours entries into businesses, to misappropriate proprietary business information. I'm a man of well-defined morals and ethically-based non-negotiables. Conversely, I will render havoc in the lives of those who seek my services, then turn on me after I've performed as expected; to avoid meeting previously promised financial commitments.

You recall the Cola Non-Negotiable about discussing my family; then Cola went and devoted an entire chapter to John's belief that I'm a state-sponsored Espionage Agent. In that, I contradicted a Cola Non-Negotiable. There's something about writing an autobiography that has drawn out thoughts, words, and stories I've seldom uttered and certainly avoided discussing in detail.

This chapter will take Readers into an area I've kept close to the vest my entire adult life. It's about love and intimacy. Cola Fugelere is an extremely private man who endured internal struggles, as he worked on this manuscript and attempted to find the most appropriate way to share memories and his perspective concerning two fleshy sensual encounters witnessed while on foreign soil. Those who know me well will understand it is out of character for me to intrude on the privacy of others, much less divulge what I observed in Acapulco. Regardless, I decided to reveal my observations Readers.

Sex is not a comfortable subject for me, so I will employ literary devices to ease my discomfort. I will also attempt to use those devices to provide a modicum of respect and dignity to the entire matter. So you understand, I derived much the Acapulco story from a combination of sounds and conversations I covertly recorded while in Acapulco. I folded in many interviews and eyewitness accounts, as well as public records and purchase receipts. The eyewitness accounts included those garnered from hotel staffers, government employees, taxi drivers, and others. I, too, witnessed my Targets over several days; including the reluctant observation of some private moments.

I conducted the Operation in Guerrero, a state on the western seacoast of Mexico, Guerrero; appreciated for its waters and weather. Acapulco, the setting for my Operation, is a beach resort city in Guerrero that once drew the rich and famous from around the world. The city has evolved into a seaside destination primarily enjoyed by Mexican tourists.

My trip to Acapulco was to conduct a surveillance Operation. The activity involved a couple who had flown from the United States to elope far from home. When the Client sought my assistance with the matter and detailed his desires, I suggested he hire a private detective. I told him I didn't do that kind of work. The Client shared his fears that a private eye, he didn't know and trust, might use the job to blackmail either him or The Subject of the surveillance.

Readers need to understand, when surveilling we sometimes unintentionally witness private moments between others. I would love to tell you the following observations occurred inadvertently. They did not. In this particular case, voyeurism was part of my assignment. I was then, and to this day remain, troubled that I represented My Client in the capacity of a Peeping Tom for part of the Operation. I cannot clear my mind of what I beheld. However, I remain content remembering a special personal interaction I witnessed involving two beautiful people. I was an unintended observer of the pure intimate expression of intensely true love, and am glad for the experience.

I found myself mesmerized by the maturity, romance, sensual pleasure, and genuine affection presented by my Target in that southern Mexican seaside resort setting. To my surprise, I embraced what I witnessed in Acapulco. When a positive learning experience lands on my doorstep, I find ways to use such experiences as tools to assist in making me a better man or a better Spy. In this case, the learning experience hit me between the eyes, captured my undivided attention, and led to improvements in an already healthy relationship with my bride; and in my marriage bed. In that, it deserves sharing.

◇ ◇ ◇

This is the story of Michael and Summer. Summer's father, Mr. Slono, a wealthy automotive industry supplier, hired me to prosecute this Operation. Slono was a very nice man, whom I've always referred to as, "Mr. Slo."

Slo wanted to learn more about the man who was about to marry his daughter. He didn't understand why the young couple didn't want a traditional marriage ceremony. Slo rejected their reasoning. Michael and Summer believed their wedding was theirs alone. They had no desire to involve others. It was about them, and they wanted a private, intimate, time together; before sharing their new lives with others. They promised Summer's father they would have a reception after their honeymoon. Slo wasn't satisfied.

Mr. Slo heard some rumors about Michael, suggesting the young man was a sexual pervert. Michael, who was previously married, planned to marry Mr. Slo's daughter. Any suggestions about kinky sex and Michael didn't sit well with My Client. The entire matter came to a head for Mr. Slo after Summer announced her refusal to ask Michael to execute a prenuptial agreement. Mr. Slo's attorney had drafted a prenup agreement which included specific confidentiality provisions associated with My Client's business affairs.

Summer was Mr. Slo's only living relative. Slo's parents died when he was in high school. He had no brothers, sisters, cousins, aunts or uncles. His wife, Summer's mother, was an orphan without siblings or other living relatives. She died while birthing her daughter; leaving only Summer in Slo's life. It was clear to me there was more than money involved. Slo was about to lose his little girl to another man. He didn't want anything less than the best for his little girl.

The tales heard by Mr. Slo about Michael having a proclivity for kinky sexual encounters with his late wife bothered the man. Rumors are always problematic. First, because people are often willing to capture juicy tidbits and embrace them as fact; regardless of any factual foundation. Second, rumors have a way of growing, morphing, and becoming something distant from any originating truth. In this case, I needed someone to chase the stories about Michael back to their origins. I needed a truth detector. More accurately, I needed three truth detectors.

I enlisted the services of a select group of OneSevens who refer to themselves as The Sisters Three. I affectionately call them the ThreeSevens. They are real-life sisters who were all professional investigators before launching their investigations services business. Lou is a former homicide detective, Lyn's background is in insurance investigations, and the third, Lulu, is a retired forensic scientist. Loaded with personality, they are all smart, skilled interviewers, excellent role players, and crafty eavesdroppers.

> ***An aside...***
> The word "eavesdrop" has been used for centuries to describe someone listening in on the conversations of others. People would literally hang from the eaves of buildings to overhear private conversations occurring within structures.
>
> In the 1500's, King Henry VIII had craftsmen install carved wooden figures under his eaves to thwart eavesdropping. The carvings are said to have worked well in keeping unauthorized ears from hearing what they shouldn't. It was Henry VIII's way of combating gossip.

Back to The ThreeSevens...
I put the ThreeSevens to work chasing the genesis of the rumors about Michael's sexual past. They carried out their responsibilities while I was on assignment in Acapulco. It was only after my mission in Acapulco was completed that I discovered how the rumor started, thanks to great investigative work by The Sisters Three.

Michael, who had married his high school sweetheart, lost the love of his life to adenocarcinoma after three short years of marriage. Best friends since junior high school, they were married at eighteen. Apparently, both of them, like Summer, remained virgins until after their wedding.

According to The Sisters Three, Michael was fascinated with the sexual aspect to a marital relationship and, with visceral determination, decided it should be a healthy priority in his marriage. He wanted to get it right. He loved his fiancé profoundly and believed he owed her his very best. Michael undertook a careful, serious study of sexual relations, marriage, and physiology before his first wedding. He wanted to be the best husband possible, in and out of the marriage bed. His studies led him to a place of understanding. He believed a continual offering of love, energy, interest, and devotion to his bride would sustain both of them with happiness and contentment. He believed in celibacy before marriage and monogamy once married.

The ThreeSevens discovered his late wife was at a bachelorette party sometime after she and Michael were married. At that event, and after drinking a little too much champagne, she told three girlfriends at her table that Michael carefully researched sex before the wedding.

She confided that her wedding night was beyond her wildest expectations. Although Michael was a virgin, his research paid off on their wedding night. She claimed the experience was unbelievable. She told her friends that even after their wedding night Michael was diligent in doing whatever he could to make each lovemaking experience uniquely special.

She didn't say more or offer details. When asked why she didn't say more, she told her friends that Michael's philosophy about sex within the bonds of marriage, and hers as well, is that it is something they should never share with anyone else. It was theirs, and theirs alone. Never to be discussed.

On another occasion a few days later, the three were together again for lunch. Michael's late wife was the recipient of another request for the juicy details of her sex life. She was reported to have responded with the following (paraphrased):

"Once others are aware of the details of our sex life, we've lost something special. It's not unlike having sex outside our marriage. If we go there, it's no longer just ours. Our life, our marriage, and our lovemaking will be forever tarnished if we share either our special moments or our bodies with any other person."

The Sisters' investigation discovered Michael was approached by a girlfriend of his late wife a few months after cancer took her from him. She was one of the three at that bachelorette party. The woman's approach was flirtatious and ignored by Michael. A few days later she attempted to charm Michael once more and, again, he rebuffed her advances. On a third occasion, she appeared at Michael's home late one evening, intoxicated, and wearing very suggestive attire.

According to two close friends, her attire included a very short vinyl skirt and tall high heeled shoes. A matching vinyl jacket accompanied the orange vinyl skirt atop an undersized shirt. A push-up bra forced her breasts nearly out of the tiny white shirt; and also presented an unwelcome offering of unnatural cleavage. She'd overdone her makeup and topped it all off with an orange wig.

The friends said she'd spent the afternoon at a San Diego Nordstrom preparing herself as an offering for Michael. Her friends said she looked like one of the prostitutes they'd seen in San Diego's Old Town during the recent Republican convention. She further prepared for the evening by hanging out with two other women within their circle. They were known as The

Tequila Twins. She consumed courage in the form of margaritas before visiting Michael's home.

The sultry woman stood on Michael's front porch and invited him to share some of his special sexual powers with her. Michael emphatically told her he wasn't interested and closed the door in her face.

The woman's embarrassed anger boiled over, and she began spreading rumors about Michael being a sexual deviant. She claimed Michael's late wife confided in her and shared concerns about his proclivities for twisted sex. Her comments were intended to hurt Michael.

The other two women, who were present when their late friend discussed the value of intimacy and privacy in her sex life, approached Michael to let him know about the gossip the third woman had been spreading. He asked the ladies to ignore the slanderous remarks.

When asked why he wouldn't defend himself, Michael explained that he and his late wife enjoyed a perfect relationship. Their sex life was theirs alone and would remain private. Michael said he would not diminish the intimate relationship he had with his wife by discussing it with anyone. He indicated that sharing sacred private moments he had with his bride, as a way of attempting to defend himself, would prove nothing. He knew his intimate relations with his late wife weren't consistent with the lurid stories spread about by the wicked woman. That was good enough for him.

◇ ◇ ◇

Michael was the nephew of one of Mr. Slo's industry rivals. The uncle, Michael's only living relative, passed away just two weeks after Michael and Summer returned home from their honeymoon. As expected, Michael inherited the business.

Mr. Slo held concerns that his competitor could become the recipient of valuable insider information closely-held by Mr. Slo's company. Summer told her father she loved and trusted Michael, and that was more important than money. She also insisted that Michael's decency and ethics were of the highest order. In a letter to her father, Summer wrote, “Michael is an honorable man who would never take advantage of either me, of your successes, or your company's proprietary information.”

I’d previously conducted a couple of Ops for Mr. Slo. He trusted me fully. He appreciated my approach to both life and Corporate Espionage, as well as my reputation for holding confidences. He wanted me to discover what I could about Michael’s sexual preferences, his relationship with the uncle’s company, and my perceptions regarding his ethics, morals, and habits. I agreed to perform any investigations necessary to reveal that which Mr. Slo sought, but insisted he would receive only general information associated with his requests. I made it abundantly clear I would never provide Slo with details, or other information, that should remain private between Michael and Summer. In that, I would neither betray Mr. Slo’s confidence nor unnecessarily divulge private matters involving Michael and Summer.

◇ ◇ ◇

SLONO CABIN

1992

In a few short months, my agreement with Mr. Slo, involving Michael and Summer, would become null and void; without legal or moral force or effect. All three of them departed this world on a cold winter night when a combination of heat, cold, and moisture resulted in their deaths. Carbon monoxide poisoning tragically took Mr. Slo, Michael, Summer, and an unborn child long before their time. None of them left any living relatives.

Slo owned a luxurious mountain cabin. One cold winter he invited his pregnant daughter and her husband to enjoy an off-season planning session with him at the family retreat. He wanted to chart the future and possible merger of the two family businesses. The cabin's boiler, located in the basement, pumped heated water throughout the structure and under the floors. Slo's newly installed system, referred to as radiant floor heating, was an efficient environmental system that kept the house and floors at a constant comfortable temperature.

A post-accident investigation concluded the HVAC engineer erred when he designed a four-inch vertical flue vent for the initially planned boiler installation, but later failed to modify the flue design when a significant equipment change occurred. The investigation concluded the initial design was acceptable. However, before construction, the boiler was upgraded to a high-efficiency unit. Upgrades of this type require changes to vertical flue dimensions. In some cases, those modifications involve the need for an exhaust fan within the flue system. The more efficient boiler needed a six-inch flue to function safely. Raising the efficiency of boiler units results in a decrease in flue gas temperatures. HVAC engineers realize as flue temperatures drop, there is an increased possibility for the accumulation of ice, as condensation build-up in the flue vent increases and freezes.

During an unknown period before their deaths, moisture in the vertical ventilation system began building up and created layers of ice on the small flue's interior. Eventually, frozen condensation began restricting exhaust fumes. Toxic gases started backing up and moving into the home. In time, the pipe iced up completely, diverting all fumes into the residence. Carbon Monoxide (CO) buildup in the structure displaced oxygen in the circulatory systems of the small family; depriving their hearts, brains, and other vital organs of life-sustaining oxygen. The odorless, tasteless, CO gas appears to have overtaken Slo and his family while they slept. They never woke up, and there was no outward evidence of suffering as they suffocated.

I believe the absence of both legal foundation and heirs, combined with Cola obfuscation and the passage of several decades, allows me flexibility in my decision to share the following account of Michael and Summer's only trip to Acapulco. Readers will never know their real identities, nor discover anything about My Client, Mr. Slo. This is as much a tribute to the family, as well as a lesson for us all.

Again, I employ liberal use of literary devices in the remainder of this chapter. I ask you to trust me as I share the love story of Michael and Summer. The words spoken in the casita on their wedding night are accurate and presented without edits. Please respect and enjoy this wonderful love story, as I step back and allow it to unfold.

◇ ◇ ◇

Michael and Summer flew into Acapulco four days before they hoped to marry. At the airport, they hailed a taxi and traveled high atop a semi-remote location with a majestic view of Acapulco and Acapulco Bay. They checked into two rooms at the luxurious pink and white Las Brisas hotel. This unusual hotel is composed of more than 250 casitas (small houses) dotting the slope of the mountainside. Las Brisas is perhaps the "tallest" hotel in the world, with neither hallways nor elevators. Hotel guests drive trademark pink and white jeeps up and down the mountain's nearly fifteen story elevation, across more than forty acres.

The two lovebirds checked in and spent a few minutes with the hotel's concierge. They were interested in the large white cross at the top of the mountain and asked if they could marry on that spot. The concierge told them "Yes" and offered to make any arrangements necessary. He said he could secure a priest for the ceremony. He asked them to return in the morning to finalize the arrangements.

Michael picked up Summer at her casita the following morning. Before departing the little house with Summer, Michael set his 35mm camera on a table, started the timer, and ran to his fiancé's side for a photo. Little did they know at the time, that photo of them in shorts and tennis shoes would be their only wedding day photo.

MICHAEL AND SUMMER

Wedding Day Photo

The couple departed the casita and enjoyed a pleasant breakfast, then drove their jeep downhill to meet with the concierge. After trying to finalize the details for their wedding, they paused the discussion in frustration, due to some issues associated with their poor Spanish and the concierge's weak English language skills. During their break, they noticed a sign in the hotel lobby directing guests to the British Consular Office. They were relieved to have found a person, likely fluent in both English and Spanish, that might assist with their communications involving the concierge.

Michael and Summer sat down with the Consul and told him of their discussions with the concierge. The Consul laughed and encouraged them to go ahead with the ceremony, but to understand neither the U.S. nor Mexico would recognize their marriage. Confused, they asked him to explain.

The British gentleman shared that in Mexico, unlike the United States, there were two ceremonies. One was a religious ceremony and the other a civil ceremony. The former would marry a couple in the eyes of God. The latter would formalize their marriage under the laws of the nation. What they had planned on top of the mountain would only please God, not the government.

The official wrote an address for them on the back of his business card and told the couple to give it to a taxi driver. The taxi would take them to a federal building, where they would see a Federal Judge who could marry them. The Consul promised to call ahead so The Judge would be expecting them. He also explained the administration of a blood test was necessary and involved a three-day wait for the results before the government would issue a marriage license. They would need to return to the federal building in three days for The Judge to perform a civil ceremony and provide them with a certificate of marriage.

Michael and Summer were aware of the waiting period and excited to get the process started. Thanking the Consul, they departed for a prearranged escorted tour of the hotel and nearby areas of interest. The tour guide drove them around the property and the surrounding area for the next few hours. Afterward, the taxi deposited the couple at the Las Brisas seaside restaurant, located on a private beach, far below the main hotel grounds. They enjoyed a long leisurely lunch before moving ahead with arrangements for their wedding.

After lunch, they took a pink and white shuttle uphill to the hotel's main entrance. Back in the lobby area, they asked a staff member for a taxi. Michael provided the driver with the business card containing the courthouse address. The cab drove off the mountain and into Acapulco.

Acapulco is a deceptively large community with hundreds of thousands of residents. Most of the population lives in an area unseen by visitors to Las Brisas. As the taxi wound farther into the city Summer noticed an increase in poverty, decay, and rubbish. When the party arrived at the federal building, the conditions outside the vehicle's windows were so poor Summer was afraid to exit the taxi. Worse yet, the federal building wasn't visible.

Michael assured her all would be okay and asked the driver where they were. The driver told them they couldn't drive the final distance to the courthouse and to follow him on foot. Summer told Michael she'd get out of the taxi on one condition. When he asked about the condition, his fiancé told him she would exit the cab if he promised she wouldn't have to return in three days. He agreed to her demands and Summer reluctantly exited the livery vehicle.

They followed the taxi driver down a narrow walkway and around the corner. He pointed to the federal building in the distance. Michael paid the taxi fare to the courthouse, then tore a twenty dollar bill in half and asked the driver to remain with the taxi at the courthouse until they returned. He told the man the twenty-dollar bill would be a tip for waiting. The driver agreed and accepted one half of the torn twenty.

Once inside, the couple discovered the building housed Mexico's official welfare agency, a health and medical center, and the federal court system. Poor people stood in lines throughout the facility. After speaking with a few staff members, they were escorted into the office of the federal district Judge and asked to sit down. The Judge was at his desk signing stacks of documents. He spoke no English, looked up briefly, and smiled.

> ***An aside...***
> I returned to Acapulco recently and discovered the building no longer exists. It was razed a number of years ago.

Back to The Old Courthouse...
The Judge's aide eventually entered the office and told them he received a call from the British Consul, seeking The Judge's assistance with their plans. He said he'd be happy to handle everything they needed to become married. Michael told the aide his bride-to-be didn't want to come back in three days and asked

if there were any options. The Judge's aide told them a three-day wait for the blood test wasn't necessary. He paused. Then, with a wink and a nod, he said, "For the right price."

> ***An aside...***
> That was a problem for me. Slo wanted my investigation concluded within that three-day window so he could stop the wedding; if the fruit of my efforts supported his concerns about Michael. As I'm sure you realize, the offer of a bribe and Summer's unwillingness to return to the courthouse in three days was about to throw a monkey wrench into Slo's desires and Cola's plans. *There was no backstop for that unexpected turn of events.*

Back to The Judge's Chambers...
Michael asked about the cost. The aide advised him it would only be one hundred American dollars. Summer quickly told Michael to agree to pay the requested bribe. She really didn't want to return. The fee was paid, as well as funds for the marriage license, the wedding certificate, photocopies, and money for the witnesses. Michael and Summer never saw the witnesses and didn't take a blood test.

As they were waiting for the aide to complete the necessary paperwork, a woman repeatedly entered The Judge's chambers with documents for The Judge to execute. Every so often The Judge would look up and speak to Summer and Michael seated in old wooden chairs on the opposite side of the massive desk. They didn't know what he was saying, so they simply smiled and nodded.

On one occasion The Judge was given paperwork by the woman and, as usual, signed the documents and began chatting it up with the young couple. This time it went on longer than before. He'd speak, then nod at them smiling, saying "Sí?" Summer and Michael nodded and responded likewise with, "Sí."

At some point, the aide appeared at the doorway. The Judge stopped speaking and said something in Spanish to the aide. The young man then looked at Michael and said, "Now that you're married, The Judge is inviting you to kiss your wife."

Michael and Summer were shocked. They didn't realize The Judge had performed a wedding ceremony. They hugged and kissed, enjoying the moment. As they departed the courthouse it dawned on the young bride that she wouldn't be returning to the slums of Acapulco again. Summer was elated.

Returning to the hotel, they canceled plans with the concierge and detoured to thank the consular official. Michael then told Summer she had plenty of time to prepare for their wedding dinner. He'd pick her up in two hours. She departed the lobby and headed to her room.

Michael went directly to the front desk to make special arrangements for their wedding night. He asked the desk clerk about the two packages he shipped to Acapulco a few weeks earlier, and addressed to himself in care of the Las Brisas hotel. The address label contained specific instructions for them to be held at the front desk until he requested them. The young lady, who was assisting Michael, went into a back room and came out with a large flat elongated box and a cube-shaped container on a rolling cart. Michael explained the boxes contained a large crystal vase and a collection of feathers necessary to complete an arrangement in the vase. He requested someone take the items to Summer's room and place the crystal vessel in the middle of the table, then create an arrangement with the feathers.

He also ordered six dozen red roses, a bottle of 1980 Dom Perignon on ice, and a heart-shaped box of expensive chocolates. He provided the young desk clerk with the time for their dinner reservations. Michael also requested his packed bags be collected from his casita while he and Summer were dining, and delivered to Summer's casita.

At that point, Michael made a special request for the delivery and placement of the six dozen roses. He asked staff to place three vases, each containing a dozen roses, in suitable tabletop locations throughout the casita. The remaining three dozen roses were to be dismantled petal by petal. He wanted the petals scattered across the sheets on the turned down bed. The box of chocolates was to be opened and placed upon the pillow nearest the front door. Michael asked them to locate several lit candles on the concrete shelf above the bed, with all the lights turned off. He also directed the staff to the stereo resting in the wall inset near the closet. He asked them to turn up the volume on the portable music device to number three; but to avoid touching any other controls. Michael had a specially recorded compact disc loaded and had set the stereo play setting to, "Repeat Play." It had been playing all day. He just hoped Summer hadn't touched it during the day. *She hadn't.* He asked that all deliveries to Summer's casita occur while they were away for dinner. He left an appropriate gratuity with the staff and departed the hotel lobby for the trip up the mountain to his casita. He was ready for a long hot shower and looked forward to a few minutes rest before his wedding night began to unfold.

Michael arrived at his wife's room two hours later. Before knocking on Summer's casita door, Michael picked a pink Hibiscus flower from a nearby bush. Hibiscus is the official Las Brisas flower. It is also their logo. Hundreds of Hibiscus plants grow on the property. Each day staff members throw two or three fresh Hibiscus flowers into each casita's swimming pool. When Summer opened the door, Michael slid the stem of the beautiful flower into her silky blonde hair and across the top of her left ear. He then gave his new bride a long passionate kiss. Then, stepping back, he invited his wife to join him for a romantic dinner.

> ***An aside...***
> If you turn back to their wedding photo, you can see a pink Hibiscus set into Summer's hair, near her right ear.

Back to Las Brisas...
Their wedding meal setting was at a Las Brisas restaurant high up on the mountain, sporting an exquisite view of Acapulco Bay and the city. A stunning couple, Summer entered the 5-Star patio restaurant wearing a long white dress, custom designed and tailored for her slender figure. Michael wore white slacks and a matching short-sleeved white shirt, highlighting his handsome, tanned face and arms.

Summer enjoyed a well-prepared Fettuccine Alfredo, while Michael dined on frog legs. A bottle of white wine paired well with their meals. The newlyweds enjoyed a long romantic dinner, smiling and laughing the entire time. As they finished two puffed up Grand Marnier Souffles, Michael and Summer slowed their speaking and lovingly peered into one another's eyes. A soft Frank Sinatra tune was playing in the background. The evening out was coming to a close and ending on a very romantic high.

When the check arrived, Michael scarcely gave it a glance, signed it and added his room number, then stood up and reached out for the hand of his lovely wife. Looking into Michael's eyes, Summer stood up slowly. The handsome couple gracefully strolled out of the restaurant, arm in arm. Bathed by the white light of a full moon and moving with coordinated grace, the lovebirds walked down the hill a short distance to Summer's casita.

An aside...

A Personal Note From Steven Fowler

Cola wanted me to present this information to readers and, at first, I resisted. I'm neither a romance author, nor do I find writing about sex a comfortable task. I'm reserved and private regarding such matters. After we went over the material countless times, I realized how I could present this story. I took a cue from Michael's own words, and incorporated a Solomonic approach. Cola certainly helped me, by his actions that evening. He offered the young couple privacy during the most intimate moments; choosing not to witness that part of the evening.

The Bible contains Solomon's words regarding the human body, attraction, sexuality, and sex within the bounds of marriage. I decided, if that subject can be presented tastefully in the Good Book, I could try to follow Solomon's example and use his approach in this chapter. I trust I faithfully presented the love story of Michael and Summer in a respectful reasonable manner; without offending anyone's sensibilities.

Back to The Newlyweds...
The charming couple opened the gate to their private secluded courtyard and entered. As Michael closed the gate, the newlyweds stopped and stood motionless as they marveled at the reflection of the beautiful full moon perfectly mirrored on the still waters of their private swimming pool. Summer told Michael this was, without question, the most romantic evening of her life. He smiled in the moonlight and wrapped his arms around his new bride and kissed her gently.

As Michael stood in that peaceful setting, he broke the mood in an odd way and apologized to Summer. I couldn't believe it when the young groom took the unexpected timeout, intruded on the romantic mood, and spoke to his bride extemporaneously. As you're about to see, Michael had the entire evening well choreographed, carefully scripted, and executed it rather well. However, when he spoke off-script at that moment, he was fully honest with his bride. Textbook Michael.

On the fidgety scale, he was off the charts nervous. Fortunately for both of them, he calmed down after issuing his apology. Here are Michael's actual words (several microphones were placed around the patio and recorded the event):

> "Summer, I love you and want this night to be special. I've done my best to study and prepare it for tonight [sic], to make it very special for you. I hope you don't find it too corny, but it's the best I can do since I'm not a very good Romeo. Anyway, if you find it more of a cliché or whatever you call it than you'd like [sic], I'm so sorry. But anyway, I hope it's okay honey. It won't be nasty or anything like that, just probably a little corny. I really think it'll be okay with you so don't be scared or anything like that. Okay? Okay?"

Summer shook her head sideways in confusion, followed by a firm nod and two softly spoken words, "It's okay."

Michael's shoulders lowered a little as he blew out a relieved "Whew." Then, bending slightly, the strong lean groom carefully picked up his bride and carried her up a few steps and to the entrance to their casita. Using the hand that helped cradle Summer's thighs, Michael turned the knob and opened the door. Music spilled out into their private patio. As the groom was stepping inside, his bride reached down and removed her shoes; dropping them to the floor. Michael used his left foot to push the door closed as he stepped further into the room.

The main entrance to the casita was just to the left of a large floor to ceiling window overlooking their private patio. There were no window coverings over the large window. Unknown to the young couple, a dark-skinned voyeur was standing in the shadows between two large Hibiscus plants in the courtyard directly in front of the window. An uncomfortable and embarrassed Peeping Cola was watching them intently.

As Michael slowly let his bride down to the floor Summer gasped at what she saw in the room. Rose petals on the bed. A red heart-shaped box lid was resting next to an open container of chocolates on one of the pillows. A bottle of champagne was nestled into a chilled vessel on a stand, and candle flames flickered yellow shadows on the walls and ceiling. A carefully selected collection of songs, Michael had someone record on a compact disc, were playing softly on the portable player. Summer said, "Oh Michael! I love you so much, Michael. I love you more than you could ever know. Thank you."

Michael stepped over to the stand and handed two champagne glasses to Summer as she took in the room. He lifted the Dom Perignon from the ice bucket, untwisted the wire securing the cork, and covered the cork with a white towel embroidered with a pink Hibiscus. Twisting the cork slowly, he was careful to avoid bruising the champagne with a pop. He expertly relieved the pressure and removed the cork. Pouring the bubbly liquid into the glasses and taking one for himself, Michael asked Summer if she'd like a piece of chocolate. She said, "Yes."

Her romantic husband stepped over to the bed and removed the open container of chocolates. As he held the box out to Summer, she lifted a single piece of chocolate and placed it halfway into her mouth. She bit down and gestured to Michael with the remaining half. He opened his mouth and closed his moist lips the chocolate. Michael set the box aside, and they entwined their arms as they chewed the exquisite treat. The young groom looked deep into Summer's eyes and told her he loved her. They shared a chocolaty kiss then lifted the champagne flutes as Michael slowly and softly said,

> "Summer my love. I lift a toast to the most beautiful wonderful woman in the world. The Judge didn't give me the opportunity to offer any promises, pledges, [*unintelligible...*], or vows in his chambers, so I shall do so now. I pledge my unending devotion to you. I promise to share all of my love, all of my life, with you and only you, so long as we both shall live. I pray we will enjoy many joy-filled years of faithful love and romance. Summer, I hope and pray our special moments of intimacy, passion, and love will provide us with the large family we've never known. I can only believe God has blessed our union. I trust He and this marriage will enrich us corporately and individually for the remainder of our lives. God bless you, Summer. You are the love of my life, and I will do everything possible to honor you at all times and in all ways. I love you my wife, my lover, my Summer. To our union! In the spirit of this romantic Mexican setting, ¡Salud!"

The handsome couple clumsily lifted their flutes and sipped the expensive champagne. Summer giggled as she twitched her nose. She told Michael the bubbles tickled her sinuses. Her husband responded with, "Mine too" as he unwound his arm and asked his wife to remain where she was standing. Then he whispered,

> "Summer, my love. We are about to enjoy one of the most amazing benefits of marriage. I want this to be an extraordinary evening for you. Indeed, the most romantic and pleasurable night you've ever experienced. You saved yourself for your husband, for me. This will be new for you, and I want it to be everything you'd imagined and more.
>
> "I promise I'll never do anything involving your body, or mine, to offend you in any manner. I'll be respectful

throughout the evening and sensitive to your needs while doing my level best to make the evening sensual, exciting, romantic, and filled with compassionate love.

"I also promise I'll never violate your trust. I'll always speak the truth and never deceive you. When I tell you or our children to trust me, you can know to the core of your being that I'll never violate that trust. Trust is valuable, meaningful, and fragile. I recognize a trust lost, is a trust that can never be fully reinstated. Summer, I will never violate any request of you to trust me.

"Tonight I ask you to trust me and give me the opportunity to make this the most wonderful memorable evening of your life. Okay?"

Summer nodded. Michael gently placed his hands on her cheeks and kissed his bride for several minutes. She responded to his kiss shortly after it began. Summer wrapped her arms around her husband's neck, then used her hands on the back of his head to pull his face and mouth firmly against hers.

As they kissed, Michael dropped his right hand to the center of the backside of her dress and slowly lowered the zipper down her shapely backside until it would travel no more. Michael reached up carefully and placed his hands at the top of her shoulders. Summer dropped her arms to his waist and allowed him to part the dress and remove it from her shoulders. He carefully pushed it down, while continuing to kiss his bride. When the garment reached her waist, she helped him move it over her hips, as Michael lowered his mouth and kissed the side of her neck. The dress quietly fell the rest of the way to the floor.

After a few minutes kissing and exploring one another with their hands and mouths, the newlyweds found themselves fully undressed, standing before one another next to the bed. Bathed in the romantic glow of flickering yellow candlelight, Michael stared deep into Summer's eyes, while gently caressing her unfamiliar body. Then with a soft, sincere voice, Michael shared from his heart.

> “Summer, I love you. I love your face and your smile. I love your heart and your intellect. I love your sense of humor, and I delight in your personality. I adore your honest laugh and am touched when you giggle. Your blue eyes pierce my very soul, and the touch of your long elegant fingers makes my heart beat faster.
>
> “Tonight I’m beginning to learn more about your body. I love your body Summer. Your slender neck is soft and beautiful. It attracts me in ways I cannot describe. The feeling I get when I kiss your neck warms my very soul.”

Gently touching Summer's soft pink lips with his thumbs, he said,

> “The Bible details a sexual encounter between Solomon and his new bride on the day of their wedding. She, like you Summer, was a virgin. Solomon writes about joy, exploration, and how each of his five senses experienced new sensations and pleasures as he explored her body. Her impressions and perspective are, likewise, presented for our edification. The detail and sensual beauty of that encounter, written three thousand years ago, is as applicable for us as it was for the people of his time. I, like King Solomon and his bride, want both of us to enjoy and savor every moment of this first encounter.
>
> “Solomon speaks of tasting honey and milk under the tongue of his wife. I, too, enjoy the wonderment of your lovely tasty tongue. It is pure honey to my lips and serves to warm my very soul. Summer, I want you to know I love the taste of your lips, mouth, and tongue.”

An aside...

The Bible: Song of Solomon 4:11 (NIV)
“Your lips drop sweetness as the honeycomb,
my bride;
milk and honey are under your tongue...”

Solomon couldn't have known about honey under her tongue, unless he used his own tongue to taste the honey. *Correct?*

Back to Summer and Michael...

"Your mouth is so beautiful and inviting. Your sensual voice is music to my ears and excites my very soul. Your lips and your tongue make my mouth happy and bring my taste buds to life. You've moved these wonderful lips to tell me you love me. You've placed them on mine with care, with interest, in exploration, with love, and now with an unmistakable passion.

"I'm excited to know these lips will one day kiss our children and say their names aloud. Your mouth will instruct our little ones and share your love with them. With your lips, you'll comfort them, and me, in times of pain, hurt, distress, and need. Likewise, words will cross your beautiful lips to bring laughter and joy to your family. They have, indeed, already done so in the few hours we've been husband and wife."

Lowering his hands to her shoulders, Michael said,

"Your shoulders are soft but strong. They will help you carry our family into the future and bear the weight of motherhood."

Drawing his hands down her arms, Michael continued,

"These arms that embrace me fill me with an unbelievable warmth and immense joy, knowing I am loved. Loved by you. I'm honored to know one day these arms will cradle my children. Our children."

Grasping her hands in his, he said,

"These hands will hold and caress me for many years. They'll prepare my food, wipe my tears, and mend my wounds. You'll use them to guide me into you on that day you'll conceive our very first child. Perhaps that day is today. These hands will also care for and nourish our babies. Your long slender fingers will touch each member of your family on the outside, and your touch will bless us all on the inside; in ways you'll never know."

Michael released her hands and moved them to her breasts.

"Until this night, I've never touched this area of privacy, and I recognize the privilege I enjoy as your husband. I'm enjoying an opportunity to become intimately familiar with your beautiful breasts. Breasts are meant to attract and please your husband, as well as provide nourishment to your children. They are an important, wonderful, part of your beautiful body and bring joy to my hands, eyes, mouth, and heart. They are neither too large, nor too small. They are just right. They are you. Thank you for sharing them with me."

Reaching around her back he said,

"You have a strong, beautiful back. It is smooth and feels good in my hands. I feel a special strength in your back. A strength that tells me you'll always be the strong backbone of our family. Your back reminds me you're a person of purpose, a woman with resolve, and a strong lady with an unbending sense of right and wrong."

Dropping his hands down her back, he reached an area he'd still not seen with his eyes, and only touched now for the very first time. He said,

"Wow! Your round perfect bottom is so warm, so smooth, so firm. I've dreamed of this moment, and my hands are happier than I could ever imagine. Your face, eyes, smile, neck, and breasts will always capture my attention when you're facing me. Now I know you'll forever bring back this wonderful moment when your backside is all I see of you. Thank you for this wonderful moment, this wonderful feeling."

Then Michael slowly lowered his body to one knee, while softly drawing his hands down beyond her thighs, knees, and calves until he reached her ankles. Then the young groom gently clasped her ankles for a few moments. Slowly. Ever so slowly, Michael drew his hands up and caressed her calves. Continuing upward as he rested on one knee, the young man passed his hands across the back of her thighs and pulled her legs into his face. Michael kissed the front of each thigh, just above Summer's knees and said,

> "These legs will push our children in their strollers and on their bikes. They will take countless treks to the grocery store, as you gather ingredients to prepare fine meals with good nutrition for your family with loving hands. You will part these beautiful legs to accept me into your body and, likewise, part them to bring our children into this world. You'll wrap them around me in love and in times of passion. Your legs are beautiful, and you'll use them in beautiful ways on behalf of your loved ones."

Then Michael asked Summer to close her eyes and trust him. Without hesitation, she immediately acquiesced. Michael asked her to bear with him for a moment, as he stepped over to a low table on one side of the room. He carefully removed two of the twenty-four-inch white Ostrich wing feathers from the feather bouquet. The long feathers were very soft and wispy.

Stepping back in front of his wife with his arms behind his back, Michael said,

> "Summer, sex between a husband and wife is wonderful. It's a time of gentle sharing, intense pleasure, and an expression of our love for one another. It can be a time of exhausting athleticism as well as overwhelming emotions. We'll laugh, cry, weep, smile, kiss, hug, squeeze, taste, and more. We may whisper, whimper, and moan.
>
> "Nerve endings are awakened and exercised. Muscles and skin react in different and unexpected ways. Juices will flow, and our bodies will sweat. Breathing will become heavy and, in many ways, we will become one.

> "Tonight is your first night, and you're not prepared to receive me just yet. I want this night to be special and without discomfort. If you're not quite ready for me, it could hurt. Therefore, please enjoy new and unusual feelings as I work to prepare you to receive me. My actions are intended to awaken dormant nerves, relax certain body parts, and encourage blood and juices to flow into the right areas so that you can enjoy this first experience with your new husband. Are you with me?"

She nodded, and her eyes remained closed. As Roberta Flack's song, Killing Me Softly With His Song began playing, Michael launched into a series of long-practiced Tai Chi movements. Holding a long Ostrich feather in each hand, Michael's arms, legs, and body began moving like clouds across the face of a majestic mountain. The feathers first passed close to her head, and her chin lifted slightly. Michael continued his Tai Chi form, and the two descending feathers nearly touched her breasts. The air was disturbed, and her bare breasts rose ever so slightly as Summer drew in a short breath.

On the next slower pass each feather gently touched her soft nipples as they passed. Going through Tai Chi moves, Michael repeated that series of movements many times as her nipples began to rise and harden. Summer's chest started rising and falling as Roberta Flack's lyrics quietly echoed off the concrete walls of the casita. In this case, Michael was killing his wife softly with the soft sensuous feathers as they gently moved across Summer's naked body.

Michael continued his Tai Chi feather movements as he worked his way around his wife. He drew the feathers down her bare back and through the middle of her naked bottom. It was clear other parts of Summer's body began to awaken when she shuddered and quietly moaned. Michael went around and around his wife for a little more than ten minutes, as the feathers lightly danced all over her skin. She began breathing heavy as Anne Murray's hit song, "Could I Have This Dance" came to an end. Michael sat the feathers down and approached his wife from behind. He gently whispered into her ear, paraphrasing the lyrics of the song, and asked,

"Summer, will you be my dance partner every day throughout eternity?"

She answered,

"Yes. Yes. Please don't stop."

As the next song began, Michael replaced the actions of the feathers as he carefully began exploring the body of his nervous young virgin with his hands. After five or six minutes of sensual caressing, the happy young man said, "It's your turn Summer."

Summer reached up and held Michael's head in a firm, gentle, caress while she kissed her husband with a passion he'd never experienced before that night. As her tongue began exploring her husband's somewhat familiar mouth, her hands began a path to new and exciting destinations.

As she explored his body with her hands, Summer's body began flowing like water across her husband's body. At first, the graceful movements were slow. As Michael responded, their sensual pace increased. They glided in unison, rubbing their bodies against one another.

Eventually, Michael determined it was time for Summer to receive her husband for the first time. He gently applied pressure to her lower back with his left hand and guided her to the bed. Summer sat down on the sheet adorned with fresh rose petals and, as her husband placed his hands behind her back, she lowered her head to the pillow. Then she lifted her feet from the floor and onto the sheets. She moved and wiggled farther into the bed. Michael resumed kissing his bride.

Thirty minutes later all movement in the small casita ceased. The only sound louder than the Pacific Ocean's waves crashing against the rocky coastline far below was the breathless aftermath of a post-nuptial encounter.

Catching her breath, Summer told Michael she'd never imagined anything as wonderful as the lovemaking she'd just experienced. She never knew making love could be such an enjoyable experience. Summer thanked him for being so careful, gentle, and considerate. Then she quieted, and they both fell into a deep sleep.

◇ ◇ ◇

Once they were fully asleep, I carefully extricated myself from my hiding place in their private courtyard. I knew I'd just witnessed something special, albeit extremely private. Words elude me. The ineffable emotions I experienced that evening were profound. I couldn't help marveling at what I'd seen and heard. I replayed the events of the previous hour in my head repeatedly. I'm thankful I maintained my resolve and kept my head turned during their most intimate moments. Although their room contained electronic eavesdropping devices and I heard everything that occurred in their little casita during that phenomenal hour, I successfully refrained from visually intruding on their night, while they were in their wedding bed. That time was theirs, and I avoided involving myself further as they made love.

The following morning a paid informant notified a Cola Cutout that Michael and Summer had booked a "Safari." Although scheduled for a dozen participants, a crisp fifty dollar bill encouraged the excursion representative that an additional person wouldn't be a problem. I was given a map and told I needed to have my pink and white jeep in a specific location at a particular time. From there, I could join the parade of Las Brisas jeeps as they journeyed to the destination.

I don't recall a lot about the earlier part of the safari, except that we ended up in small boats on a lazy river. We were deposited onto an island, located in the middle of the channel, for a unique lunchtime adventure. Excursion guests were informed our main course needed to be collected and cooked. Guides stretched a large seine to its full length, as one of their number slowly entered the river holding one end of the rectangular volleyball-like net. He walked into the current and extended the fishing net perpendicular to the flowing waters. After a few minutes, he began moving up the river in a wide arc, gradually curving the net back toward the island. As the guide came ashore, two additional guides started pulling the seine net ashore. My fellow guests were both surprised and delighted to see a hundred or more small fish wriggling and thrashing about in the net.

The guides used skewers about 2 feet long to impale the small five and six inch fish. After adding three whole fish to each skewer, they placed the skewers into one of several small fires. Once fully cooked, they withdrew the shish kebabs from the flames and handed fish-laden sticks to their guests. One of the guides laughed, and in heavily accented English, referred to them as "Fish Kebabs."

I recall sitting directly in front of Michael and Summer at a long picnic table. Summer had been beaming throughout the day. She was head over heels in love with Michael and everybody on the safari could see it in her face. An elderly Canadian woman asked when they were married. Michael spoke up and said they were married the previous day. Murmuring and quiet giggles erupted along both sides of the table. It was as if everyone knew Summer experienced something new and special in the hours leading up to the safari. Michael and Summer's embarrassment was written all over their blushing faces. They reminded me of turtles as their necks and heads dropped into their shoulders. Moments later, after they'd recovered, Summer's beaming resumed.

When a guide handed Summer's kebab to her, the beaming suddenly stopped. A terrible face replaced her rosy-cheeked smile and twinkling eyes. The corners of her mouth dropped in an unbecoming manner as she eyed the three small fully intact fish on the stick in her hands. Michael and the rest of the excursion's guests dove right in and ate the fish on their sticks. Summer just stared at the scaly corpses.

> ***An aside...***
> Ever since that day, I picture Summer's three fish on a stick whenever I hear the term, "fish stick."

Back to Summer and The Fishy Lunch...
Summer dropped her fish stick and exclaimed, "How can you people eat those nasty fish. They're looking at you as you eat their intestines. That's just gross!"

Laughter erupted. Everyone was laughing. After a few moments, the young bride added to the noisy mirth. I don't believe she ever picked up the fish stick again. I seem to recall Michael downing her three fish, before going back to the fires for a few more skewers.

After lunch, we were transported downriver to the beach. As we arrived, I saw about fifteen of the skinniest horses I'd ever seen. To a horse, their ribs were all well pronounced. The scene disturbed Summer, but she put on her game face as a guide lifted her onto one of the skinnier horses. In a few minutes, we were all galloping down the beach bareback. As we all slowed to a trot to look at a dead dolphin on the beach, I heard Summer tell Michael, "My bottom is hurting. This horse needs some padding."

Michael asked her if she wanted to stop. She said no. Later I'm sure she regretted giving Michael that answer.

The following evening I made my way into their private courtyard for a final check on the young couple, before drafting my report to Mr. Slo. Michael was in the middle of the bedroom performing for Summer. Wearing his swimming trunks, he had a plastic cap on his head, with a long tube hanging down. I believe it was an accessory for a hairdryer. He began acting like an elephant, swinging the long tube like an elephant's trunk. Summer's hair was wet, and she had a comb in her hand. Michael appeared to be making fun of her primping her hair. He then launched into a well-memorized skit.

My recording device picked up about 8 minutes of Michael performing the skit. Much later in the audio recording and long after his performance concluded, Michael told Summer he called the skit, "Baldness." Michael said he memorized the words and performed it on many occasions while he was in high school for both drama and speech class events. Michael appeared to recite the entire skit from memory. Here's a small taste of Michael's performance.

> "What do you ladies do to your hair? I'll tell you what you do to your hair, and correct me if I'm wrong. You dye it,

> fry it, curl it, swirl it, roast it, toast it, oil it, boil it, spin it, pin it, stuff it, puff it, mash it, smash it, hack it, shellac it, scent it, and cement it. You cut it poodle, noodle, apple strudel. Every way but Yankee Doodle. You pinch it with pins and stuff it with cotton. Good times there are not forgotten. Look away, look away, look away, Dixieland. I wish I was in Dixie, away, away... Pardon me, friends. Sometimes I get carried away.
>
> "Lots of girls like to give themselves a home permanent. So they run down to the local drug store, you know, and buy themselves a chemistry set. Why as soon as they've given themselves a home permanent, they stay home – PERMANENT."

It was dark, and lights were on in the casita. I enjoyed seeing Summer having so much fun. I couldn't hear what Michael was saying until I listened to the recording later that night. However, once Michael finished his act, I knew everything was well. I would be reporting as much to Summer's father.

I watched Michael bow as he concluded his performance and walked into the bathroom. Cola's work was done for the night. I was stepping out of my hiding place behind a large bush and heard the gate open. I froze, then silently withdrew into the bushes.

A young woman and a middle-aged housekeeper entered the courtyard and began making their way to the front door of the casita. I later discovered the young woman was an unmarried nineteen-year-old; in training for a housekeeper position. It appeared they were carrying fresh towels and bottled water.

As the two women approached the front door in the darkness, Michael stepped out of the bathroom, after removing his damp swimming trunks and quickly rinsing the pool's chlorine from his body. Michael was dripping wet and naked. Summer, was laying on top of the bed. She wore both a wry smile and a Las Brisas monogrammed terry cloth robe. She stared at her husband's nude body.

As Michael stood naked in the middle of the room, Summer was admiring her hunk. He was standing in front of the large picture window overlooking their dark private courtyard. The floor to ceiling window was positioned next to the wooden front door, and directly in front of the brick pathway leading to the casita's entrance. As Michael was speaking with his bride, he became aroused. An erection quickly revealed the fullness of his manhood.

The ambient light was sufficiently bright and permitted me an opportunity to witness the eyes of the young housekeeper as they grew wide. Her lips took on the shape of an "O." She raised her right hand to cover her gaping mouth. The older woman crossed herself, then reached over with a long slender arm attempting to cover the eyes of the young housekeeper who was staring in innocence and astonishment. The teenager quickly moved to her left to keep the supervisor's hand from successfully obstructing the amazing view of Michael's glorious naked body.

I glanced back at Michael and, at some level, felt oddly jealous. I, too, marveled at the sight of Michael's family jewels. I didn't look long. Within moments I was distracted by a scuffle near my position in the bush.

The older woman was pulling on the young housekeeper, trying to get her to leave the courtyard. After some tugging and harsh whispers, they seemed to settle their differences. They worked out a plan, then immediately marched up to the casita's front door.

Michael heard a knock on the door and quickly retreated into the bathroom. Summer said, "Come in" and the maids entered the tiny home, delivered the towels and water, and quickly departed. As they walked through and exited the courtyard, the senior housekeeper berated the young girl for her behavior and reluctance to depart. As they walked out of the courtyard, I heard her say to the young girl, "Ten cuidado con lo que deseas, porque puede hacerse realidad."

I believe those words are from an old Mexican proverb. I think it is translated correctly as, "Be careful what you wish for, as it could become true."

When the two servants departed, Michael emerged from the bathroom wearing a white robe. He was thoroughly embarrassed. He looked at Summer and told her, "My gosh. I thought our courtyard gave us more privacy than that. I never dreamed anyone would be dropping in this late at night. That giant picture window makes it painfully obvious I exposed myself to an old lady and a young girl. I wonder how long they were standing there while I scratched myself. I am so embarrassed!"

Summer began giggling, then laughing out loud. She was trying to tell her husband she didn't know anyone would be delivering anything either. The more she attempted to say as much, the more she laughed. She became almost hysterical. Within moments Michael joined her in the laughter. It was clear, his embarrassment had really keyed him up, and now he was letting out that tension. He looked at Summer and said, "Wow! I've kept my privates private for a very long time. Here I am on my third day of marriage, and three women have gotten a good look at me, saluting the world with a giant erection meant only for you."

Michael began laughing again, before realizing the sound coming from Summer was sobbing. He became quiet very quickly and asked Summer what was wrong. Summer was sitting on the bed in a white terry cloth robe, adorned with the single pink Las Brisas Hibiscus logo. She untied the soft robe, drew her knees up, then parted the robe while spreading her legs apart. The dark complected man positioned a few feet outside the large picture window in a thick bush gasped audibly. Michael gasped as well, and the sound was easily picked up by the audio bugs hidden within the casita's bedroom.

The entire inner area of Summer's legs, from her knees up, was black and blue. Her private parts suffered thorough bruising as well. The blackened area was greater than the width of my hands, and traveled upward from her knees and fully into her crotch. Only once have I seen anyone as severely bruised as Summer.

The sight was shocking. The pain must have been excruciating for her.

No, Michael's wedding night activities notwithstanding, the fault wasn't his. Summer's bruising resulted from riding a bony horse without a saddle. So unfortunate. It was only her second full day of marriage. Further lovemaking wouldn't be possible until Summer healed.

> ***An aside...***
> As I've mentioned previously in this manuscript, my father was a contractor. When I was a teenager Papa Fugelere won a contract for the installation of a high-pressure water transmission line. Project engineers decided the water line should be placed approximately eighteen feet below the surface of the roadway. Not only was the ditch deep, but it was also unstable as well. The entire area was saturated with underground water and composed of heavy clay.
>
> Papa was in the very deep trench one rainy, dreary, summer afternoon. Papa was inspecting the pipe at the bottom of the ditch when one of the unstable banks collapsed. The collapsing earth slammed him to the bottom of the trench and into a pool of water. The impact of the water-saturated clay crushed my father and immediately broke twenty-six bones in his body; shattering the lower part of his rib cage and spine. Breaks continued all the way down to his feet. The only part of Papa's body not covered by the heavy earth was his head.
>
> My father's mouth was at the same level as the pool of water. Papa was sputtering and spitting water, trying to keep from drowning. He stretched his neck to keep his mouth above the rising water. Above him, another massive section of the clay trench was teetering and close to collapsing.
>
> My father had a faithful employee, Jerry, who risked his own life by jumping into the dangerously unstable ditch. Jerry did his level best to keep Dad's mouth above water,

while simultaneously trying to remove the heavy earth from my father's body. Jerry was a hero.

Eventually rescued from the ditch, Papa wasn't expected to make it through the night. Emergency room physicians considered his internal bleeding irreparable. Papa proved them wrong and survived.

I was permitted to visit my father in the hospital several days later. He was lying in a hospital bed. Tubes and wires covered his body. Surgeons had drilled holes through his shins and inserted pins to support a sandbag traction system. The weight of that system continually pulled my father down into the bed. When I entered his hospital room, he was flat on the bed. Papa using his powerful arms he grasped a bar above the bed and pulled himself up into a sitting position. Pain washed across his face. Other than a grunt, he was silent as his pain centers rebelled against the action.

At one point Papa lifted the sheets and showed me his bruised naked body. An area from five inches below his clavicle, all the way down to his feet, was completely blackened. Not one square inch of normal skin color remained in that area. His bruises represented the many broken bones beneath the surface.

Doctors said Papa would never walk again. Papa is a hard-charging determined man with true grit. True Grit is more than just the title of a movie starring John Wayne. It is also descriptive of my extremely tough father.

Thirty days after the accident, Papa convinced his physicians to release him from the hospital. A broken healing man, he stiffly walked out of that life-saving institution, leaning on a cane and limping badly. Papa nearly lost his life that summer. Today his back and lower skeleton are filled with arthritis. In spite of his ever-present pain, Papa never complains. He is a tough, tough, man. I am proud of him for his resolve, his

> determination, his grit, and his guts. Gino Fugelere is my hero!

Back to Summer and Michael...
At first, Michael thought he'd gotten too rough with his bride and apologized for his athleticism in bed. Summer laughed and said, "No silly, it wasn't you. It was that skinny horse. The bruises happened because we trotted and galloped that bony nag down the beach for many miles."

Once more Michael's embarrassment was palpable. He really believed he caused the bruising. He just stood at the foot of the bed and stared. It was quiet in the room for a few moments, then Michael broke out laughing once more.

Summer asked what was so funny. Michael said, "I hope the housekeepers aren't standing out there anymore. The young one would be so afraid to have sex with a man she'll run away, break down the door of the nearest convent, and beg to become a nun." Summer joined her husband and began laughing again.

The dark man departed the courtyard during the laughter and never saw the young couple again.

◇ ◇ ◇

I caught a flight out of Acapulco early the next morning. That afternoon the ThreeSevens reported the rumors about Michael were baseless. That evening I hand delivered my report to Mr. Slo. The report contained a single sentence containing a dozen words. Each word cost Mr. Slo more than three thousand dollars per word, and he was thrilled to write the check. Here's the full text from that report:

> "Mr. Slono, Michael will be the perfect husband for your beautiful daughter."

They were a cute couple. After the lovebirds returned home from their two-week honeymoon, Slo told me they purchased matching tennis shoes. After a couple of days, they bought matching jackets. Two weeks later they bought matching SUV's.

Slo quoted Forrest Gump when he said, "They are two peas in a pod."

◇ ◇ ◇

The world lost three extraordinary people, far too early; as well as an unborn infant. Michael and Summer were two of the finest individuals I've ever encountered. I learned much about life from those two kids half my age. I appreciate Mr. Slono for giving me the opportunity to have known them. He was a good guy. I salute them all.

London and Beyond

London's Albert Memorial

My first trip to London was memorable in a number of ways. Not long after The Quick Lube Job, I planned a trip "over the pond" to visit The United Kingdom and the European Continent. I intended on touring The UK, then taking a ferry to the continent to travel that historic land.

On the afternoon of May 25, 1979, American Airlines Flight 191, from Chicago's O'Hare International Airport to Los Angeles International Airport, crashed mere moments after take-off. An NTSB investigation concluded the McDonnell Douglas DC-10's left side engine separated from the aircraft, causing an uncontrolled descent from 325 feet. The accident resulted in 273 deaths (271 souls on the plane, as well as two on the ground).

Less than two weeks after the accident, on June 6, 1979, the Federal Aviation Administration grounded all DC-10's under its jurisdiction. The FAA's ruling effectively banned DC-10's from flying in U.S. airspace. That move prevented foreign-owned DC-10's from flying within the U.S.; to include those owned and operated by Laker Airways.

I know. You're wondering why the DC-10 and Laker Airways are relevant to this chapter. Bear with me. I'm getting there.

Two weeks before the DC-10 went down in Chicago, I decided to travel around Europe with a backpack. Just a vacation. An opportunity to see the world. No espionage plans.

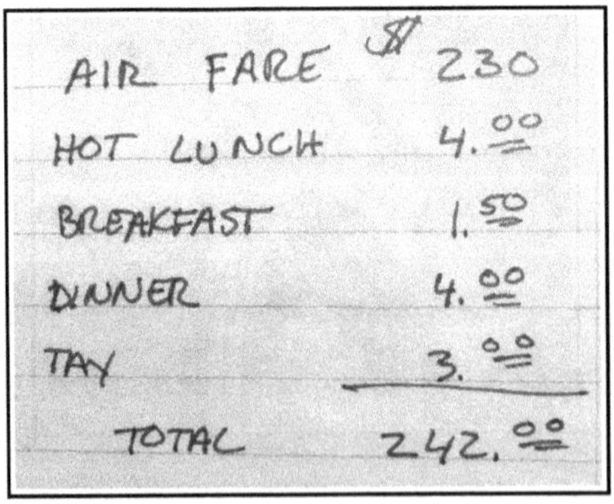

	$
AIR FARE	230
HOT LUNCH	4.00
BREAKFAST	1.50
DINNER	4.00
TAX	3.00
TOTAL	242.00

COLA'S JOURNAL NOTING LAKER'S FLIGHT COSTS

Clearly, Young Cola's Addition Leaves Much to be Desired

I was able to set aside enough money for the trip, courtesy of Uncle Frank and my first steps into Corporate Espionage with The Quick Lube Job. That said, I still needed to maintain a budget. I found a cheap flight on Sir Freddie Laker's no-frills discount airline, Laker Airways. Laker regularly flew a DC-10 into Los Angeles International Airport. Perfect. Europe, here I come!

A few days before the FAA suspended DC-10 operations, I purchased a ticket to Los Angeles. Once there, I could catch a Laker Airways flight to London's Gatwick airport. When the DC-10 fleet was grounded, my trip entered a holding pattern.

During the period after DC-10 flights underwent suspension, investigators discovered maintenance issues were responsible for the accident. Five weeks after the ban's imposition, on July 13, 1979, DC-10's were once more permitted to fly in U.S. airspace; subject to enhanced maintenance protocols. Airline personnel were required to follow new maintenance procedures, designed to address the safety-related issues that resulted in the loss of Flight 191. That was, indeed, good news. My life had been on hold awaiting the resumption of DC-10 flights. Now I could begin my journey.

A day after the ban lifted, I was permitted to exchange my previously purchased ticket for a domestic flight to Los Angeles. My bags were packed, and I was ready to go. When I heard the news that Laker received a green light for flights from LAX to London, I was on the next plane for Los Angeles.

After unsuccessfully attempting to sleep on the hard tile floor at LAX that night, I joined a small group of other young people queuing up for the first post-suspension Laker Airways flight to the UK. The huge McDonnell Douglas wide-bodied jet had very few passengers. The ground crew quickly loaded a small quantity of cargo into the big bird. I'd be surprised if it were anything more than 20% full. My journal record states, "The aircraft is only about 1/5 filled." The entire row where I sat in the wide-body jet was empty. As were the rows directly fore and aft. I took a window seat and sat there hoping the big jet's engines would remain affixed to the aircraft.

The pilot's pre-departure announcement informed all aboard that the regularly scheduled refueling stop in Bangor, Maine wouldn't be necessary. According to the Captain, the small number of passengers combined with an unusually fast atmospheric jet stream made it possible for a non-stop flight and an early arrival into London Gatwick.

If we'd not received the briefing, the takeoff probably wouldn't have made sense. Thanks to that knowledge, I understood what was about to follow. The pilot was hard on his brakes as he pushed the thrust levers forward; perhaps to the stops. As the engines wound up, the giant jet began vibrating, but not moving. That was very unsettling. An experienced flyer, I knew something was radically different as we sat at the end of the runway shaking like someone about to participate in their first television interview. Hang on engines, don't let go! Once the pilot appeared to achieve his desired thrust goals, he released the brakes.

The giant aluminum tube lunged forward, roaring down the runway toward the Pacific Ocean. I knew a full load of fuel would require more runway, but the takeoff roll was lasting longer than I expected. It was very unsettling. The fatal O'Hare crash was filling my thoughts. It seemed to take forever before the lumbering jet began to lift from the asphalt runway. *Hang on engines! Hang on!*

I've never experienced a takeoff like that, before or since. My theory has always been that the flight plan change, to skip the refueling stop in Bangor, Maine, resulted in a need to fill the big jet's kerosene tanks to the brim. Doing so added considerably more additional weight, offset at some level by fewer passengers and baggage than usual. To achieve a safe takeoff with a full load of fuel, the pilot needed to bring the engines to full, or nearly full, throttle before releasing the brakes. The act of keeping the plane stationary until it reached takeoff thrust, permitted the big airliner more initial speed and a safer distance to rotation, before climbing out over the campfires of Dockweiler Beach and the dark evening waters of the Pacific Ocean.

> ***An aside...***
> That entire experience came back to haunt me when the movie "Pearl Harbor" made its debut, and we watched Alec Baldwin, in the role of Lieutenant Colonel James

"Jimmy" Doolittle, fight to get his heavily laden B-25B bomber off the short flight deck of the aircraft carrier.

Baldwin said, "Max power! Come on! Come on!" Someone on the flight deck said, "Oh please!" Baldwin's co-pilot, a Catholic, was busy crossing himself.

I understood it all. In some fashion or another, that was the scene aboard that heavily laden DC-10, trying to lift off for its 5,400 mile non-stop flight to London.

Back to Cola's Flight...
After takeoff, I stretched across the five contiguous unoccupied middle section seats. I was exhausted after unsuccessfully trying to sleep on LAX's hard tile floor the night before. I slept well as the big jet hummed.

Hours later I awoke to find we were over a bright blue sea. I was seeing the Atlantic Ocean for the first time, as an adult, flying in an aircraft. The view was not unlike the one seen years before by Charles Lindbergh, on his quest to become the first human to fly across the Atlantic. Although, as I recall, Lindbergh's weather was not as clear and the ocean as blue as that enjoyed by me that morning.

Walking down the aisle, I stopped to visit with an acquaintance from my evening, and the following day, at the Los Angeles airport. Her name was Ann. Ann had an interesting job. She worked in an unusual capacity. On the staff of a dictionary company, one of Ann's responsibilities was to discover new words and new uses for existing words. Interesting.

She asked me where I'd be staying in London. I told Ann I hadn't thought that far ahead. She and a tall fellow named Andy, I'd met the night before in Los Angeles, were staying at a London Bed and Breakfast called The Warwick House. Giving me the address, she invited me to hang out with them the following day. *Great.*

An aside...
A few years later I recall thinking back with wonderment about the planning for that trip, or a lack thereof. In

retrospect, there were no plans. I had no thoughts in mind associated with visiting any specific tourist destinations. I'd given zero consideration to lodging or specific transportation; beyond my desire to purchase a motorcycle, at some point, from the BMW factory in Germany. When my flight lifted from California soil, I had no idea how I was going to get from London to Germany and didn't even consider it at the time.

Little did I know, over the next few weeks I'd be visiting The United Kingdom, the Netherlands, France, Germany, Sweden, Denmark and other countries; without prior planning. A failure to plan, however, left me sleeping with a protective knife in my hand on one occasion. I'd taken shelter under a bush in a drug-infested Amsterdam park when I couldn't find anywhere to stay. I was afraid and didn't sleep a wink.

On the other hand, one thing I considered ahead of time was the security of carrying a wallet, connected to my belt with a chain. That chain saved my traveler's checks in a Paris train station when an old Gypsy man sprayed my rear pocket with an unknown liquid. Likely an acid. The leather wallet fell from the tattered pocket, only to be caught by the chain tether. I whirled around, realized what just happened, then took off running with a funny looking multi-thousand dollar tail swinging behind me. I was surprised to discover that nasty acid didn't penetrate my clothing sufficiently to injure my skin.

I now call such cavalier adventures, "Young People Planning" (YPP). I don't permit Cola Associates to approach Operations with YPP. We continually remind associates that safety, security, and success are all dependent on cautious and methodical prior planning.

Associates are consistently coached to embrace and understand "π" (Pi, aka 3.14159.....), in the context of planning and executing espionage operations. The mathematical irrationality of Pi is in its failure to be expressed with exactness.

> Planning for success in espionage is, at best, irrational. There are just too many variables in life and espionage for exactitude. However, the Cola Team can reasonably increase the odds of achieving success in Operations, to near perfection, with continual reasoned iteration.
>
> I suffered a few avoidable hiccups during my first European trip because of my failure to develop plans. Fortunately, those hiccups were, by in large, minor. They did, however, provide a good foundation for understanding the need for proper prior planning.
>
> I tell my Associates I speak from experience, by sharing how I flew to Europe as a young person without prior planning. In fact, I'm surprised just how anal-retentive I've become. Now I plan everything.

Back to Cola's Trip Across the Pond...
After landing at London Gatwick, I caught a train into the city. The train's final destination was London's Victoria Station. Arrival there was followed by a trek downstairs to the London Underground (the city's subway system), where I caught The Tube (subway) to a Bed and Breakfast in Kensington, where I was to meet up with Andy and Ann.

> ***An aside...***
> While in London on that trip for several weeks, I traveled using a motorcycle, The Tube, trains, bipedal locomotion, and London's famous red double-decker AEC Routemaster buses.
>
> Riding a motorcycle on the "wrong" side of the road was harrowing. It was especially discombobulating when I approached those odd intersections with five connecting roads, without a roundabout. I never really grasped the subtleties of operating a motor vehicle on the "wrong" side of the road.

Back to Kensington...
I really loved the speed and charm associated with the London Underground. It offered upfront and close peeks into the

everyday lives of everyday Londoners. Ingress and egress were especially notable at some of The Tube stations. Escalators then and now offered smooth, speedy transport from the surface to the underworld. Some of the escalators were unbelievably long. A number of them were wooden tread escalators of the type used long ago when the London Underground launched.

My wife and I flew to London for a winter visit four years ago (business and pleasure). She'd never been there before, and I wanted her to see the historic wooden escalators. I was disappointed to discover only one such escalator remained. It was on the Central Line, far from any destination we had planned.

Less than a decade after I was delighted to discover my first wooden moving stairway in London's Underground, a fire broke out at King's Cross Station, killing more than 30 people and injuring a hundred more. That tragic fire, caused by a lit match dropped onto the mechanical wooden stair, resulted in the dismantling of all similar devices serving Tube stations. The remaining Central Line escalator was dismantled shortly after my wife and I departed from that fun trip to the city.

> ***An aside...***
> **Speaking of Lit Matches...**
> I must share one of my unique Tube experiences on that first trip to London. I was sitting to the left of and facing an elderly man who was missing his right arm. Looking at him, I decided he must have lost his arm in World War II.
>
> He was wearing an unbuttoned, button up, sweater. I watched him stretch his left arm across his waist and reach his left hand into his right side pocket. After fumbling for a brief moment, the hand returned to his left side with an unfolded cigarette paper. He then dropped that hand into his left pocket and appeared to be digging and churning within the pocket. After about 30 seconds his hand came out with a perfectly round rolled cigarette. He lifted the tube to his lips, then licked and sealed the round unwrinkled cylinder. The old smoker

then lit his masterpiece and began puffing on the smoky treat.

I was very impressed. Have you ever tried to roll loose tobacco or marijuana into a rolling paper, and accomplish it perfectly? I've never witnessed a two-handed person perform such magic. I learned a valuable lesson that day. Practice does, indeed, make perfect. Thereafter, when an Operation required difficult tasks, I made them less difficult through practice practice practice.

Back to London's Underground...
When the subway stopped at the Earl's Court Underground Station, I stood up and exited the subway car. As I was emerging I nearly knocked over three huge men. Embarrassed, I looked up to apologize, then had the shock of my life. Before me was the first person I'd made eye contact with since landing in The UK. Standing there on the subway platform was a man I knew. I'd last seen him a couple of days before I began my long, disjointed journey to London.

I was a member of a fraternity at my college. One of the three men before me was a member of a rival fraternity. He was wearing a tee shirt with our university name and logo. I'd seen him last at a college beer drinking competition just a few days earlier. He'd downed an entire pitcher of beer in one quick pour. He was a slob and a jerk, so I didn't bother to either apologize or say hello.

Wearing my huge orange backpack, I turned sideways and passed beside the three giants. Then I walked over to an incredibly long wooden escalator and rode away from that surprising scene; only to get another huge surprise.

An aside...
Small World Chance Encounters
The girth of the globe upon which we live is large, sporting a nearly 25,000-mile circumference. Earth is, nevertheless, a relatively small satellite. Populated by more than seven billion human beings. It's absolutely

amazing just how easy it is to bump into people we know thousands of miles from where we'd expect to see them.

Chance encounters with someone we know, far from home and in unexpected locations, can be simultaneously surprising, amazing, and disconcerting. In espionage is can be downright dangerous.

Although Cola becomes suspicious when coincidences occur, I recognize some just happen. That small world encounter on the subway platform occurred after my quick decision to catch the next unplanned flight to Los Angeles. Then there's that last minute in-flight decision to meet Andy and Ann at a B&B few could have anticipated. Then catching an unplanned subway ride to the platform where the timing had to be perfect so I would bump into a beer guzzling Sigma Alpha Epsilon frat boy I knew. No, it wasn't planned.

Small World Chance Encounters will happen. Good spies need to keep that in mind, knowing such events can ruin a well-planned and well-executed Op.

Back to My Next Huge Surprise...
As I stepped out of the Earl's Court Underground Station, I looked up, across, and around the intersection in front of me. I was viewing above-ground London for the very first time, and I couldn't believe what I was seeing. Moments ago I physically bumped into someone I knew, six thousand miles from home. Now my vision was filled with the nighttime lights of a McDonald's and a Pizza Hut, and if memory serves me correctly, a Kentucky Fried Chicken. It looked like a street in the town where I went to college.

What? Wrong Way Corrigan? Did I leave Los Angeles? Did the pilot take a cue from Douglas Corrigan?

An aside...
In 1938 a Texan pilot, Douglas Corrigan, earned the nickname "Wrong Way" after flying from Long Beach to Brooklyn, New York. He didn't receive permission to fly

to his desired destination in Ireland. Corrigan's flight plan reflected his stated intention to make a round trip from California, to New York, and back to California. Later Corrigan claimed heavy clouds and navigational errors resulted in his unauthorized flight to Ireland. Therefore, the sobriquet "Wrong Way Corrigan."

Back to The Twilight Zone...
Shaking my head in wonderment, I recall glancing to my left and watching someone approaching and about to pass by the entrance to The Tube station. It was a young female. She had a series of odd black spots on her face and several large ugly blue hickeys on her neck (called love bites in England). A huge safety pin pierced her right cheek, and she had a chain running from her right ear to her right nostril. The chain ran inside the safety pin. Her skin was extremely fair. The contrast between her jet black hair and her overly white skin was a sight I'll never forget. Set back inside an egg-sized field of painted black, her eyes reminded me of the heavy metal music star, Vincent Damon Furnier. Better known as Alice Cooper, Furnier's black eyes sported vertical lines rising and descending from the center of his optical orbit. Her blackness was oval and smudged. The woman was wearing a short shiny leather skirt and tall shiny leather boots. I seem to recall something odd about her arms and hands, but I don't remember what it was. She was, indeed, a sight to behold.

I'd never personally witnessed anyone who looked that intentionally unusual. The young punk rocker who'd just passed by on the sidewalk reminded me I was in a very different place. Clearly, America was a land far far away.

Although the faux America in my vision faded when the punk rocker strolled by, young Cola Fugelere learned very quickly that his world was much smaller than he'd ever imagined. In a few days, I'd experience a reinforcement of that "Small World" lesson.

London's population in 1979 was approaching seven million people. I was about to discover once more that millions of people cannot fully insulate an individual who doesn't want any chance encounters.

Ann, Andy, and I spent our first full day in London visiting some of the major tourist attractions in and around Buckingham Palace. The next day we went our separate ways, never to see one another again, except...

I was walking by Victoria Station one afternoon eight days later and noticed the familiar backside of a young woman pushing a bicycle. It was Ann! Another chance encounter in London! What are the odds?

I caught up with Ann and discovered she was on her way to Germany. We spoke about our experiences since that touristy day with Andy. Then we said goodbye. I've not seen Ann since.

LESSONS LEARNED ON MY FIRST LONDON TRIP

It's a Small World

We live in a very small world. I took a series of planes, trains, automobiles, and subways as I traveled to a place very far from home. Once I was stationed thoroughly within the midst of millions of people, I saw individuals I knew, and places I'd frequented. I experienced my own CCM's and realized if I continued to pursue a career in the espionage arena I needed to remain mindful that such encounters could jeopardize my safety.

The Butterfly Effect

The temporary cessation of DC-10 flights reminded me that circumstances could quickly change, due to matters entirely outside of one's control. Like the "Butterfly Effect," someone turning a wrench far away can impact your comings and goings. My Associates are used to me harping about the "B.E." the aka Butterfly Effect.

> ***An aside...***
> The Butterfly Effect was a term coined by twentieth-century meteorologist and mathematician Edward Lorenz. Using a branch of mathematics called Chaos

> Theory, Lorenz postulated a tornado's formation could have been influenced by, and theoretically traced back to, the flapping of the wings of a tiny butterfly several weeks earlier. Small issues can result in significant changes.
>
> In my cloak and dagger world, seemingly inconsequential external influences can impact espionage operations in tremendous ways.

Back to Lessons Learned...

The Best-Laid Plans of Mice and Men

Plans, such as they are, are subject to change. I've learned through experience, no matter how well we plan Operations, they are still subject to change. Things can go wrong, the unexpected will probably occur, and Butterfly Effects are always possible. *Expect the unexpected!*

Cultural Differences

While in The UK, I did much more than push a dead motorcycle for miles around that old city and visit tourist attractions. I spent much of my time studying the people, customs, and the city. I quickly learned those in the UK didn't do things quite the same way we do back home.

For example, at that time, many public places didn't have a product similar to what I knew as toilet paper. The product reminded me of wax paper. I wasn't impressed. In a few short years all that changed. Subsequent trips over the pond proved that waxing one's bum was no longer in vogue. Thank heavens.

I recall going to a park on a sweltering day. Thirsty, I sat down at an outside restaurant and ordered iced tea. I was informed iced tea wasn't available. Only hot tea. I opted for a Coca-Cola instead. When it arrived, I was confused. The vessel did, indeed, contain the requested Coke. However, there was no ice. To my dismay, I discovered iced drinks in London were a rarity. Of course, times have changed and the iceless beverages of those days have largely vanished.

No worries. I decided to duck into a pub and enjoy a cold beer. As I entered the dark, cool pub, I saw a chalkboard at the entrance encouraging patrons to drink Guinness Stout. I decided to give Guinness a whirl. *When in Rome!* A dark, thick beer with a frothy white top arrived at my table, I picked it up with anticipation and took a big swallow. *Surprise!* It wasn't the ice cold beer I wanted and expected. It was cool. Not warm (that's an old wives' tale). However, I was thrilled with the taste of that creamy Irish beer, the temperature notwithstanding. I've enjoyed Guinness ever since.

Tradecraft 101

Shortly after arriving in London I witnessed an event that, along with The Quick Lube Job, jump-started my career.

While on my first trip to London I discovered, what was then, a fascinating section in Hyde Park dedicated to protests and free speech. The location was appropriately referred to as, "Speaker's Corner." Lively public speaking, animated discussions, and vigorous debate filled the ears of those in the area. Covering a range of subjects, it was a fascinating experience.

> ***An aside...***
> Speaker's Corner, on a Sunday afternoon in 2019, is far less interesting and considerably more hostile. The central theme and consistent topic is religion. Muslims have become a dominant force at the Corner. One Christian, Jay Smith, has been attacked repeatedly when trying to debate Muslims. I've been told that Bobbies don't protect anyone there, except the Muslims. That's both unconscionable and potentially dangerous. Gays, Jews, or Christians are at risk in that environment.

Back to Speaker's Corner and The Interesting Event...

From Cola's Journal:

"Speaker's Corner has to be the most interesting place I have seen yet. There were thousands of people gathered around dozens of speakers (all standing above the crowd on ladders & boxes). There was an Australian speaking on the Mideast, people, and religion. A Socialist speaking about the Working Class. A Jesus Freak, a Catholic Promoter, many Arabs and Indian speakers. Many others I did not get to hear. They were all nuts, inciting trouble, although none succeeded in making violence occur. Catcalls everywhere, from old ladies to punks. People were arguing among themselves.

"There was one very well dressed man calling people queer, ugly, stupid, and many other unprintable things. He would go from speaker to speaker making waves and eventually taking the entire crowd with him. He was pretty strange. He would say he was going to be the next Prime Minister. He would call religious speakers Jesus. He would call Jews, Arabs. He would tell Pakistanis that he would stick his umbrella up their snot-filled Pakistani asses. He asked an old lady, easily over 85 with white whiskers, if she had shaved today. Then he would tell everyone that she was his wife. He would turn to people in the crowd and embarrass them. I was shocked and think he's crazy."

That man was particularly obnoxious. He was an overweight bald senior citizen who showered his audience with vile comments and lurid accusations. His subject matter shocked me. The rude orator was disgusting, demeaning, and demanding. The man's words included threats and profanity. He was well dressed and reminded me of a diminutive Winston Churchill, complete with a black umbrella. He was smoking a large cigar like those smoked by Sir Winston Churchill. At one point I looked around and noticed two Bobbies standing directly behind me.

An aside...
"Bobbie" is a term commonly used when referring to London's Police Officers. During the American Revolution British Home Minister, Sir Robert Peel, managed the creation of London's first organized police force. The new police force was designed to replace the infamous military "Red Coats," along with the occasional constable and watchman.

> The old system did little more than attempt to quell violence and maintain a modicum of order. Having scant structure or accountability, it was an inadequate approach to addressing crime-related needs. The new professional metropolitan police agency was set up for crime-fighting while remaining fully accountable to the citizenry.
>
> These newly organized constables quickly earned two different nicknames. Bobbies and Peelers. Sir Robert Peel's first and last names were the genesis for these two monikers. Bobbies, derived from the commonly used nickname for Robert, "Bob," quickly became the sobriquet that survives to this day.

Back to Speaker's Corner...
As I was saying, I noticed the two Bobbies at my six and decided to ask them about Little Winston. "What is his story? Is he serious? Is he a regular speaker?"

One of the Officers responded to my query. I noted his words in my travel journal while sitting in a restaurant about fifteen minutes later, and know I correctly transcribed his statement, word for word. Unfortunately, that was my only totally accurate record of words spoken that Sunday. I cannot accurately recall what was shared by anyone speaking publicly at Speaker's Corner.

"That man is incarcerated in a local lunatic asylum. Every Sunday the white coats deliver him to Hyde Park for an outing. They'll be along shortly to collect their charge and return him to the asylum."

If nothing else, Cola is a curious guy. Thanking the constable, I moved away to an area where I could maintain a visual on Little Winston, but where the Officers couldn't see me. I wasn't buying the Bobbie story. However, if it was true, I wanted to witness the "white coats" "collect" that ranting nut job.

After a while, Little Winston finished speaking and wandered out of the park. Cola the Neophyte Spy followed as discreetly as possible. It was a challenging task, given the fact that I was wearing my bright orange oversized backpack. As I ducked from doorway to doorway, sidewalk to sidewalk, I told myself if I was going to be a professional Spy, I needed to learn how to surveil without being nailed.

> ***An aside...***
> Not long before my departure to Europe, my mother shared a Gerald Seymour novel with me. Called Harry's Game, it was set in nearby Northern Ireland. The story was about British Army Officer Harry Brown's efforts to track down an IRA assassin in the streets of Belfast. As I read the book and became fascinated by the Harry Brown's activities, I realized state-sponsored and corporate spies have a cornucopia of parallel needs; to include the ability to conduct surveillance on, and successfully tail, a Mark.

Back to Little Winston...
Peering into a storefront window, I discreetly observed a reflection of the Target crossing the street behind my back. At that moment I felt like I was back in the game. The familiar Quick Lube Job juices coursed through my veins as I watched the waddling orator make his way toward some unknown destination. Here I was, in the land of 007, working on my Tradecraft.

At that moment, I remember audibly telling myself, "The die is cast. Cola the Spy lives!"

"Cola the Spy" was Born

Henceforth, my activities would be espionage-centric. My efforts going forward would be to develop my skills and fully immerse myself into doing that which was necessary to launch a successful career in Corporate Espionage.

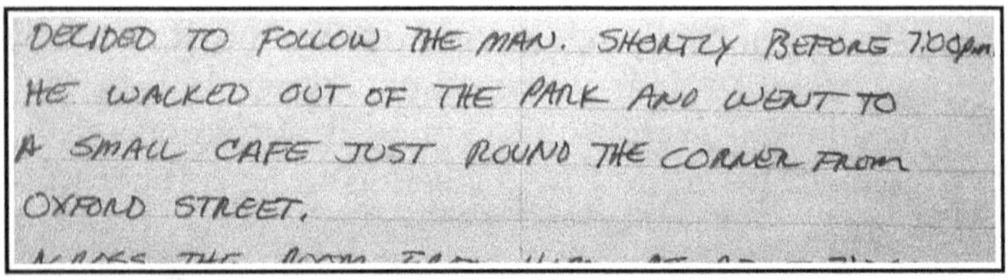
DECIDED TO FOLLOW THE MAN. SHORTLY BEFORE 7:00pm,
HE WALKED OUT OF THE PARK AND WENT TO
A SMALL CAFE JUST ROUND THE CORNER FROM
OXFORD STREET.

JOURNAL NOTES FROM TAILING LITTLE WINSTON

Little Winston ducked into a small restaurant just around the corner from Oxford Street. I decided to follow him in. He was seated when I entered. I took a table across the tiny room. As I recall, there were mirrors on the wall, so I could watch him well, without appearing obvious. He ordered. I had something small, quick, and inexpensive along with a cup of tea; thinking I needed the ability to vacate the premises on short notice. I took time to journal the Bobbie's words and otherwise record the events leading up to that moment.

I discovered my prudence wasn't necessary when a well-filled plate of Bangers and Mash arrived at his table. This Yankee watched in amazement as Little Winston ate his peas. Using a knife and the back of his fork, Little Winston would use the knife to roll one pea at a time up the backside of his fork, straddled between two tines. Once positioned where he wanted it, he'd gently lift the fork to his mouth and munch his minuscule snack.

One pea at a time? He certainly didn't devour his meal in haste. The entire process was curious, not to mention painfully slow. I had to modify my eating speed radically, to keep food on my plate and maintain some justification for lingering in the restaurant. That didn't work well enough. I recall ordering an additional item and a second cup of Earl Grey to buy myself some time.

Once Little Winston finally consumed his pile of green peas and appeared to be finishing the meal, I jumped up and paid my bill. Hiding between two lorries parked nearby, I waited for my Mark to exit the restaurant. I considered the possibility that he'd be heading directly back to Hyde Park for his return trip to the mental hospital, so I positioned myself accordingly. That rookie planning didn't work well for his next move.

To my surprise and chagrin, he moved farther into the neighborhood across from Hyde Park. After a few blocks, he turned left and up 3 or 4 steps. At the top of the steps, he stood at the entrance to a residence. Then Little Winston produced a key, unlocked the door, and strolled inside. That was that.

The Bobbie's words echoed in my mind as I turned and walked away. The story about the white coats was pure fabrication. I believe the Bobbie was embarrassed that a free man, who wasn't committed by the State to a mental institution, would say such horrible threatening words in a public venue and get away with it. That was huge. My gut was right on the mark. Since that day I've learned to listen to my gut. I've lost count of the times my inner thinking and instincts have saved me. Just another in a long line of lessons learned in Londontown.

Lesson Learned

Here's another lesson I learned and took to heart. I had more than a few difficulties using payphones on that trip. Those experiences taught me Cola the Spy needs to understand more than just venues, ingress and egress, and other location related items before running an Op. I needed to be aware of communication options, laws, customs, accents and languages, modes of transportation, tool availability (e.g., lock picks, electronics, etc...) and more. I learned the value of keeping a large quantity of coins on me at all times for payphones and parking meters. That, in turn, helped me understand the necessity of maintaining a large variety of bills on my person so I could quickly pay at restaurants and stores, then duck out with little delay.

Trust me when I say, an Operation can go sideways quickly and ultimately fail, over something as simple as not being able to use the telephone. Lesson learned. Lesson shared.

Subsequent Trips to the UK

Over the years I've made many beneficial excursions over the pond.

Outside the City

Although I've traveled out of the city for personal interests, my only business trip outside London was for a successful CCM. I surprised the owner of a North American precious metals refinery who was visiting Stonehenge while on holiday. He was on an excursion that required train and bus transportation to the site from London. I, on the other hand, made the trip in a rented car. Ingress and egress for tourists using the combined railway, followed by bus transportation to the ancient monument can be problematic. Pigeon Memory is pretty much a non-issue. It's a peaceful, remote location that's easy to reconnoiter.

Inside Londontown

London is a busy, vibrant city. A hub of espionage activity. State-sponsored, as well as corporate. As such, my business interests have called me to London many times over the years. I've found the atmosphere, food, drink, privacy, darkness, and general atmosphere of some local pubs to be perfect locations for surreptitious meetings. Ingress, egress, and Pigeon Memory are pretty darn good in the dozen or so pubs I use for business activities.

My favorite UK pub for espionage-related meetings is in Notting Hill on Campden Hill Road. Campden Hill is a sleepy street located three or four blocks from the Notting Hill Gate and a circuitous one-mile walk from Kensington Palace, into a low-key Notting Hill neighborhood. The location is a pub called The Windsor Castle. That setting has served me very well on many occasions.

> ***An aside...***
> We now only conduct Good Guy Operations as Counterintelligence Consultants. Regardless, the privacy of Cola meetings remains paramount. I guess this book will end The Cola Team's Counterintelligence meetings at

> The Windsor Castle. However, our Team will continue to frequent the pub in a non-espionage capacity.
>
> After all, sharing is caring. I relish the opportunity to thank The Windsor Castle for their excellence over the years by encouraging my Readers to frequent that fine establishment whenever they're in London.

Back to The Windsor Castle...
I've exercised many ingress and egress options, running complicated SDR's every time I visit the pub. I have variously entered Kensington Park via the Lancaster Gate, Marble Arch, The Albert Memorial, and Hyde Park Corner. Pigeon Memory is reasonably helpful late in the evenings when I usually try to meet Contacts at The Windsor Castle.

As Readers might suspect and should know by now, I don't provide Contacts with the actual address and ask them to rendezvous with me there. One hundred percent of the time the meet is set up with false starts, location changes, a Watch Team, other avenues of subterfuge, and many evasive maneuvers.

> ***An aside...***
> I NEVER reveal detailed information regarding egress strategies, tactics, and SDR's. That's my insurance policy if a quick safe unexpected departure becomes necessary.

Back to The Best Pub in London...
The Windsor Castle has an excellent menu and atmosphere. A superb staff. Excellent ingress and egress on the grounds. The dark paneled hardwood floor decor and donut shaped layout offer convenient line-of-sight options; to include an exterior eating area with several egress accommodations. It is an excellent Pigeon Memory venue.

COLA AND A COMPANION'S WINDSOR CASTLE MEAL

GLIMPSE OF THE BACK ROOM

I prefer to use the small room at the back of the donut. From that vantage point, I can see the back patio area, the kitchen door, and access to the front, from both the eastside and the westside passageways.

The Castle carries a ten-year-old Laphroaig, which I've enjoyed on each visit. Unlike my accident with the golden nectar at Bistro d'OC in Washington D.C., I've never wasted a single drop of that famous Scottish brew in The Castle. Laphroaig pairs exceptionally well with their most excellent pot pie. Everything on the menu is well-prepared and goes above and beyond in pleasing my palate. I heartily recommend the dining experience available at The Windsor Castle.

The London Silver Vaults
I've engaged in a few Pillar Passes deep inside the London Silver Vaults. Those are generally dicey activities offering good security while presenting some risk-laden issues. Fortunately, I have a well-regarded high-level Contact within the vaults that serves me well in offsetting some of the risks.

The Tower of London
The Tower offers excellent opportunities for clandestine meetings and Pillar Passes. After using the facility for more than a few operational activities, memory and access issues have become very manageable.

Westminster Abbey
I tried using Westminster Abbey for a few operational necessities, but a considerable security issue all but ruled out any future espionage-related involvement within that facility. I invite Readers to tour the Abbey. Consider it a field trip.

Those of you with good espionage sense will understand my reservations 15 to 20 minutes after entering. If you don't figure it out, no worries. It's neither obvious nor something necessary for Readers to know. It merely offers a glimpse into your own observational skills and perceptual strengths.

Looking Back at My First Visit to London

When I look back over the years to my initial venture onto the soil of that historic town, I cannot help but be surprised it has become a reasonably frequent location for my work-related efforts. Memories of my first visit there are filled with some disconcerting and unexpected experiences.

I ended up backing out of my desire to purchase a BMW motorcycle at the factory in Germany when I discovered direct low markup sales no longer occurred at the factory. I decided to buy a motorbike in London instead, and transport it to the continent later.

I purchased a used lemon. I'm not mechanically inclined and discovered a full fresh battery would drain in three or four hours. Then the bike would die. The selling company wouldn't help in any way. I then went to a consumer advocacy group for help. They were unable to assist with my problem. The U.S. Embassy, too, had nothing to offer.

I took it to a mechanic who fiddled with it (recharged the battery), charged me the pound equivalent of forty dollars, and sent me on my way. Following the established pattern, I broke down miles from anywhere. I was used to that. I parked the oversized paperweight and, as usual, found my way back to one of the various youth hostels I frequented in London. I would get into bed and plan my next morning's push with my bike.

Over the course of a week, I pushed that broken Honda many miles around London, before selling it back to the company where I originally purchased it. I recouped only pennies on the dollar. Oh well. Lesson learned.

It was an interesting, memorable adventure. I harbored no ill will toward anyone over the fiasco. Life is not without risk, there are no real guarantees in life, and many people are merely hustling to put Yorkshire Pudding on the table. It's a dog eat dog world out there. My naivety and youthful inexperience ultimately consumed many hundreds of my hard earned grease and oil dollars from The Quick Lube Job.

Over the following weeks, I worked to improve my fledgling Tradecraft skills. I learned to use reflections in store windows, shadows, lines of sight, changes in attire, distractions, body language, feigned indifference, activities, and background noises to improve my skills when tailing unsuspecting individuals surreptitiously. Unfortunately for me, nobody I was following had any reason to suspect they were under surveillance by a tail. Plus, I was alone. There was no opportunity to perform LeapFrog or Picket Surveillance. It was just Cola and randomly selected soft targets of opportunity. Regardless, the exercises permitted iteration and improvement.

> ***An aside...***
> **LeapFrog and Picket Surveillance Techniques**
> These are surveillance options often used when tailing individuals to help avoid discovery by The Subject of the surveillance. LeapFrogging works better in vehicle surveillance scenarios. Pickets are helpful in many situations but generally require larger teams.

Back to Espionage 101...
Over time I learned to allow my Targets to see me on multiple occasions and become somewhat suspicious. Then I'd fall back and begin tailing them from afar. On one occasion a Target broke into a run, screaming, and I had to scramble into The London Underground and take The Tube away from the area.

A few days later, one Target approached two Bobbies. As he was speaking to the constables, the man turned and pointed directly at me. I heard the Target say, "Him!"

I didn't break my stride and kept on walking toward the problem. That proved to be a good move for me. I didn't falter, run, or look guilty.

I was, however, a little concerned. I was wearing my orange backpack when the previous Target screamed and ran away. As I approached the Bobbies, I realized the risks associated with another orange backpack-wearing young man haunting one more British citizen. What if the earlier Target reported my actions and the orange backpack? Did these Bobbie's get a heads up about me during this morning's roll call? Another rookie mistake. I had a lot to learn.

I did learn a valuable lesson when the Police Officer challenged me in the back of my van during The Quick Lube Job. You'll recall me saying that night I learned the value of having a backstop story and props to support my assertions. I might be a little slow, but I do learn from events and mistakes.

While I was tailing this Target, I was entirely in character with a carefully considered backstop story, as well as props appropriate for the situation. A good backstop, designed to protect me in an event just like this.

One of the two Bobbies stopped me with an, "Excuse me, sir. May I have a word?"

I stopped. "Yes, sir?"

The Bobbie informed me the citizen at his side was concerned that I was following him. I feigned surprise and shook my head, saying, "No sir. I don't even know this man."

I was asked to produce my identification. After the Bobbie reviewed my passport, he asked what I was doing "in this part of London."

I told him I stopped by the London School of Economics to visit a friend from the states. A girl named Robin Z*******. She is a real person actually named "Robin," and was, at that time, a student at the London School of Economics. Classes were out, and I couldn't locate Robin anywhere (true story). I told the Bobbie I then decided to visit the British Museum. At that point, the man I was following called me a liar and insisted I followed him from the London School of Economics, where he had business, then on toward Fleet Street where he had further business. Then back beyond the school toward his home.

The route from the London School of Economics to Fleet Street was in a nearly opposite direction as the route from the London School of Economics to the British Museum. I knew that, but was ready with a planned riposte. I agreed with the Target. I said I had, indeed, departed the school and headed down Fleet Street, on my way to St. Paul's Cathedral. I told the Bobbie I was looking at a travel book as I was walking there but realized my backpack was too large to ascend the tiny stairway to the top of St. Paul's dome.

Yikes! Another mistake! I called attention to my backpack! Not smart.

I informed the Bobbies I doubled back toward the London School of Economics. I passed by the school on my way to the British Museum. The museum was in the opposite direction from the school, as was St. Paul's Cathedral. The school, the cathedral, and the museum were all circled on my map. When I showed my materials to the Bobbie, he bought my story. Hook, line, and sinker.

The other silent Bobbie finally spoke up. He told my accuser it was merely coincidence and to, "Run along now. There's nothing to worry about. Our friend from the colonies is simply a wandering tourist visiting our treasures."

The Bobbies told me to go about my business and advised they wouldn't be as understanding if this man has further issues with me, or if another citizen brought me to their attention. I thanked the Constables and went directly to the British Museum.

My backstopping plans worked that time, but the entire matter suggested I had a long way to go before I developed competency in my tailing skills. I also realized it was time to move on. I'd worn out my welcome in this world-class city. It was time to travel to the European continent.

The Second Leg

That night I found myself on a ferry from Dover, England to Calais, France; where the second leg of my European adventure began. As with the first leg, the second leg offered learning experiences and opportunities to fold my newfound knowledge into skill sets as a professional Spy.

Amsterdam
In Amsterdam, I attempted to sleep in a park, under a bush, with a protective pocket knife in my hand. That helped reinforce my understanding that making plans ahead of time is necessary in life. Espionage is no different. I realized unexpected, and unplanned issues, could be the harbinger of danger and disaster.

That city also holds dear, the building many of us came to know when we were school children as we read the Diary of Anne Frank. Visiting that location, I thought back to the story of that young girl. Being there assisted me in learning about patience, perseverance, and the value of having trusted associates. Many remarkable people have come into my life and maintained the confidences necessary to keep me safe and free. Patience, like that seen in the person of Anne Frank, has helped me endure many long, tedious stakeouts. The perseverance I learned has assisted me in taking each Operation to its logical conclusion.

Adjusting to Circumstances
While in Amsterdam I purchased a single fee, all you can travel, Eurail Pass.

> ***An aside...***
> My journal records it as an Interrail Pass, but my memory is convincing and suggests it was then called, "Eurail." Sorry, for the confusion. *Heck, I'm confused.*

Back to Traveling The Continent...
After my fitful night in the park with my tiny knife, I decided it was wishful thinking for me to discover a youth hostel with vacancies every night. The Eurail Pass provided a welcome option. Travel at night and sleep on the train. Wake up and visit another great European city. Repeat the process. Every couple of days I'd find a public bath so I could clean up. I was learning to adjust to unforeseen circumstances. That ability is key to success in the espionage arena.

I arrived in Copenhagen, Denmark one morning. I found an extremely tasty fresh Danish for breakfast, then found a place to bathe. Entering a local public bath, I paid the fee, then found my way into a private room with a locking wooden cabinet. I undressed, placed my valuables in the locker, then secured both the locking cabinet door and the changing room. Walking down a short corridor, I discovered a room with two long rows of sinks where I could shave and brush my teeth. Afterward, and a little further along, were the showers. *Great.*

The Straw Man and My Six

While I was brushing my teeth, I learned another valuable lesson: *Watch my six!*

While I was shaving and unaware of anyone behind me, an elderly man approached with a pail of soapy water and a handful of straw. Without my knowledge, the old man stood directly behind me, dipped the straw into the warm soapy water, and began scrubbing my back. *Yikes!*

It happened as I was drawing a razor across my face. I nearly jumped over the sink. Startled, I turned quickly and saw the old man with a sheepish smile on his face. He lifted the pail and showed it to me. He raised his other hand so I could see the straw, then dipped the wadded stalks into the soapy brew. The Straw Man nodded his head in a manner suggesting I turn my back to him. I complied, and he finished scrubbing my backside.

Nothing untoward occurred, but it was an odd awkward event for young Cola Fugelere. The Straw Man only scrubbed for about thirty seconds, then disappeared, never to be seen by me again. I finished at the sink and headed to the showers, never once forgetting to be aware of my six o'clock position.

> ***An aside...***
> **Situational Awareness**
> I learned a valuable lesson that day, thanks to an old man and a bundle of soapy straw. Never forget my six. From that day forward, I've been vigilant and successful in maintaining good situational awareness. My Danish experience in that bathhouse taught me the dangers associated with dropping my guard. Not just in unfamiliar settings.

Dropping one's guard in familiar settings is, likewise, dangerous. In fact, it is easier to become lulled into situational complacency in familiar and seemingly safe settings. I learned that the hard way in a different time and place.

In all situations I am acutely aware of where I sit, routes to exits, my position relative to walls, to the locations of others, their mannerisms, what their hands and eyes are doing, body tension suggesting they are about to spring into action, the positions of their feet, their footwear, what's above my head, smells, sounds, and more. I habitually sit and stand with walls to my back, when and where possible. If not possible, my eyes, neck, torso, and feet become unpatterned swivels, continually adjusting to assist me with situational awareness. I track shadows and seek reflective surfaces so that I can spot movement and the unseen.

In The Arch and The Needle chapter of this book, I mentioned the government agents positioned themselves to trap me upon my arrival at the Space Needle. In my humble opinion, they committed many errors including the fresh haircuts, their clothing, and footwear. However, their most egregious error was committed as they continually scanned the area. Most of them swiveled their heads in a predictable pattern. In that, they became apparent and readily noticeable by an inexperienced Cola.

My preferred method of scanning involves following pedestrians, birds, cars, squirrels, aircraft, buses, dogs and other moving objects with my head. In that, the likelihood of patterns decreases. Reasons for my head movements appear natural and unthreatening. Often, especially when dark glasses conceal my eyes, I'm able to track objects like cars with my head, while keeping my eyes on something else. It's taken many years of practice to perfect that skill.

> Additionally, I employ other proprietary Cola actions designed to reduce patterns of predictability somewhat further. Uneven, unpatterned, and unpredictable camouflage systems are designed to break up the visual appearance and shape of a face, body, vehicle, or building. Likewise, the use of unpatterned movements become helpful in rendering me less noticeable.

Back to The Public Bath...
As I dressed and considered my need to improve my situational awareness skills, I silently thanked The Straw Man for revealing a weakness needing addressed. Later that day I began working hard to undo a lifetime of situational complacency. I knew my desire to pursue professionalism in my newfound career required much work on my part. I needed to practice, learn, improvise, and adapt.

Later that day I visited one of the world's oldest, busiest, and most beautiful amusement parks in the world. Copenhagen's Tivoli Gardens. Filled with impressive flower gardens, it is a beautiful setting. Smiling tourists, running children, and the remarkable flower gardens create an odd mix of serenity and sensory overload. It was a perfect place to work on my situational awareness skills. I didn't realize it at the time, but the days I spent there taught me about the value of Pigeon Memory. It was a great experience, and since that fateful day with The Straw Man and my early efforts to develop my Situational Awareness skills in Tivoli Gardens, I've never stopped working to improve and enhance my Tradecraft abilities.

Cola's life in espionage started with The Quick Lube Job and began maturing in Europe. The maturation process continues to this day. Maturation is all about learning. Never stop learning. Never stop growing. Be all you can be, no matter your profession.

BLACKMAIL AND EXTORTION

Over the years I've learned a successful approach to surreptitious corporate review, where access to C-Level staffers is unusually difficult, is to focus my efforts on the secretaries and assistants of corporate officers. Those staff members frequently have access to nearly all of the same information as their bosses, but often without context or organized clarity. On occasion, I possess sufficient understanding of Client needs to apply context myself.

On other occasions, especially where information is highly compartmentalized, I've found it imperative to aggregate data from several well-placed sources. Once sufficient purloined intelligence is collected, it is necessary to organize it into a cohesive, understandable final product. Client involvement is usually required to guide us with structuring the collection process, as well as arranging that information into a recognizable product. It's not unlike assembling a jigsaw puzzle, but only having a vague idea of the final image. If a piece is missing, it's often difficult to know until late in the assembly process. We'll try to determine what is missing and who is best positioned to provide the needed materials. We will then adjust targeting and tactics to achieve our goals. One particular case comes to mind.

In the 1980's I was contacted by the majority stockholder of a sizable biomedical product development company. My contemporaries and I referred to him as "Napman," because of his habitual napping during high-level conversations.

> ***An aside...***
> Napman suffered from, Narcolepsy, a sleep disorder. Those with Narcolepsy, an autoimmune disease, have a wake-sleep cycle problem that often results in muscle weakness and a sudden onset of the sleep cycle.

Back to Napman...
Napman was a Napoleonic figure who seemed to compensate for his under average stature with a dominant aggressive personality. Winning was everything to him.

Napman previously contracted with me to help him place a quisling inside a competing biomedical research and development entity I'll call "Company X." Napman told me he didn't care if the Operation yielded little in the short term. He was looking at the play from a long-game perspective. He wanted me to provide him with a player who had staying power and would benefit him in the long term. I settled on a reasonably good candidate and positioned him well within the competing company as an Information Technology (IT) professional. Over a three year period, Napman benefited from periodic information dumps provided by the IT Insider. The information held value, but never really amounted to anything sufficiently significant to have warranted the IT man's placement in the competing organization. *Until...*

One evening Napman received information from his IT Insider that a staff attorney for Company X was given a priority project searching patent records. The IT Insider said the search was related to a highly compartmentalized project at the company. He had information that the attorney was seeking "Prior Art," using terms the IT Insider had recently seen on The Project Director's whiteboard in a well-secured section of the research lab. Prior Art is information presented to the public as part of a previous patent filing. The attorney discovered no such filings, and a giddy atmosphere seemed to envelop the lab.

Napman believed Company X was close to final development of a patentable product, representing a potentially huge medical breakthrough. The IT Insider told Napman the level of excitement among lab staffers suggested a breakthrough product was under development. Napman agreed. He said, based upon keyword search parameters for Prior Art, the product he envisioned could be worth millions to the patent holder. Napman wanted to know everything about the research, the findings, the product, the estimated patent submission timeline, and when they expected to take the product to market. He enlisted me in his quest to beat Company X to the patent office.

My father was a builder who taught me the importance of a good foundation; especially when constructing something substantial. Espionage efforts also require a structurally sound foundation. Our foundations are informational, rather than rebar and concrete. They're composed of validated information.

The initial task in constructing a foundation for an espionage action targeting Company X would be to refresh my knowledge of that company. I decided to review notes I compiled during my first Operation for Napman when I secured placement of the IT professional inside Company X. The Op was successful, and the IT Insider periodically passed helpful information to My Client. After spending a full afternoon reviewing those documents, I set up a meet with Napman for the following morning.

Napman joined me in my hotel suite for the entire day, and late into the evening. I picked his brain for every single tidbit of information about Company X that Napman could recall. I poked and prodded. My assault included questions, prosecutorial in nature, trying to poke holes in everything he said. That approach was necessary to separate fact from opinion; rumored innuendo and speculation from supportable data. To better understand my Target, I needed a fact-based foundation. Napman's biases required revelation and discounting. Once I was satisfied I'd gathered as much as possible from My Client, I planned the next phase necessary in constructing a firm informational foundation.

The following week I rented a rural tourist resort facility and spent a four day weekend with the IT Insider. I wined and dined

Napman's Agent. I separated fact from fiction. I discovered Cola needed to determine the difference between actual insider data in the Agent's information dumps, and Agent added informational spice. It was apparent many of the Agent's reports contained intelligence he believed Napman would be happy to hear but wasn't actually authentic actionable data. The IT Insider was trying to please his master, and keep the healthy stipend coming in from Napman. Not good. Not helpful.

Much of the weekend was spent educating myself about staff members; their roles, personalities, proclivities, habits, passions, ambitions, relationships, inhibitions and weaknesses, loyalties, personal lives and more. I also invested time learning about the company culture, policies and procedures, centers of information, and Power Dynamics (PD).

> ***An aside...***
> Power Dynamics are a potentially large vessel of opportunity for spies. Knowing who is weak and who is strong is vital in espionage. Ethical issues, honesty problems, affinity for gossip, and misplaced loyalties are arrows in my quiver. An unethical manager can be powerful. On the other hand, ethics or other issues can weaken such managers. Power and strengths need to be identified, quantified, and cautiously considered. Knowing how power is amassed and applied is very important to me. Is it gained by title, fiat, successes, theft or deception? Is it used judiciously? Is it squandered? Does it further the interests of the company? Would it enhance espionage opportunities?
>
> Power Dynamics are fundamental to a solid foundational construction for in-depth espionage activities. I find value in assigning a Power Dynamic Quotient (PDQ), of Cola's design, to each person I evaluate. Developing a workable PDQ isn't an exact science, but if carefully constructed it can add tremendous value to an Operation.
>
> Nearly every organization has staff members driven to do that which is necessary to enhance their status,

opportunities, income, and job security. Middle managers, like most people, seek ways to expand their workplace opportunities. These personality types are common and most such staffers seldom risk their positions or employment by straying too far afield.

However, most medium to large organizations have a few insecure narcissistic "it's all about me" mid-level managers who engage in activities that initially, and often incorrectly, appear consistent with corporate priorities. They are generally good candidates for insider information and trouble. Their drive for power will often cloud ethical considerations. They tend to focus on short-term benefits and ignore long-term costs. They often fail to weigh many of the risks associated with their behaviors, while building their little fiefdoms. I refer to these power grabbing narcissists as Empire Builders.

In short, Empire Builders have a single loyalty. It is a self-centered loyalty to themselves. They are number one. Everyone else is secondary.

Empire Builders artfully mask their behaviors and are often passive aggressive. Empire Builders generally construct their own unscrupulous ongoing operations. They engage in a plethora of game playing activities as they work to garner power and prestige. Vanity and drive will often cloud their judgment and magnify their risks. They habitually dissemble to disguise their actual attitudes and real motives. They are phony, devious, and dangerous. Empire Builders are master manipulators who thirst for credit at every turn; and will throw co-workers under the bus at every opportunity. Their behavior is often sycophantic, but only when their target is positioned to enhance the Empire Builder's agenda and career path. Their self-serving interests trump corporate needs and budgetary concerns. Empire Building activities are unpredictable and continually result in altered responses by unwitting colleagues beguiled by power grabbing Empire Builders. If left to their own devices Empire Builders will squander company resources in their driven, narcissistic quest for power and control.

Power plays, corporate ladder climbing, and empire building are all counterproductive unhealthy workplace activities. They are counter to healthy collaboration and harmful to team-centered efforts. Once identified, senior management should take preemptive action to discourage and, if possible, terminate these destructive individuals. Ordinary organizational Power Dynamics are fluid but aren't generally destabilizing. However, rogue waves of uncertainty are often conjured up by Empire Builders and can result in unpredictable behaviors and outcomes. Fortunately for me, I've learned to recognize their indicators, cautiously value their potential as operational Assets, and can reasonably manage a majority of the Empire Builders that cross my path.

Understanding organizational Power Dynamics offers opportunities. Recruiting Empire Builders in their roles as operational insiders also harbors considerable risk for an Op. I've known more than a few ladder climbing power players to turn on their handler and kill an OP. They can create a complicated and thorny path to a successful play. However, a well-vetted Empire Builder and a well-structured plan can present a tremendous opportunity for a Corporate Spy. If handled correctly, Empire Builders can be set up to take the fall if the Op goes south. They are, indeed, excellent targets for intelligence gathering purposes. In the matter of the this Operation, one Empire Builder paid dearly for her hidden agenda after Cola uncovered her real intentions while on staff at Company X.

Back to The IT Insider...

Much of my time with the IT Insider was devoted to revealing the Power Dynamics of empire building middle managers associated with the research project. My goal was to identify them and determine how they might be of value to my efforts. As with Napman, I had to carefully weave my way through the IT Insider's biases and speculatory conclusions. His own PD needed filtering to enable me to discover the reality behind his disclosures.

By Sunday morning I had a comfortably clear picture of the players and politics associated with the research project. Information gleaned from the IT Insider suggested neither the C-Level staffers nor their assistants or secretaries, would be helpful to my efforts. However, The Project Director's assistant, I'll call "Maura," was a power grabbing empire building narcissist with substantial ethical issues. While in the office she appeared composed and professional. When away from work and with coworkers, she often feigned a whispering gossipy persona.

Maura was successful in recruiting several key allies in short order. She'd only been with the company for six months but appeared to be a solid insider with tremendous knowledge, as well as coveted responsibilities and allegiances. Maura was smart, mean, and dishonest. She cautiously sidestepped most on-premises gossiping. The bulk of her information gathering appeared to take place after hours. She also had money troubles. Those and other factors led me to believe Maura's Power Dynamic Quotient (PDQ) was a perfect fit for my needs.

As the Operation unfolded, our focus turned directly to Maura. She had access to The Project Director's cornucopia of research secrets and more than a few gossiping lab staffers to provide background, context, and nuanced details. I discovered a large measure of her Empire Building efforts occurred after hours, as Maura worked the phone from her patio; while consuming adult beverages. That information led me to target Maura's patio for electronic eavesdropping.

◇ ◇ ◇

The "Patent Play" had many moving parts, but there is no real value in detailing most of the mundane actions we took on Napman's behalf. However, Maura's activities played a crucial role in my successful prosecution of The Patent Play. Unbeknownst to me, Maura was more than just the key to achieving my goals. Her actions, unrelated to my plans, enabled me to conclude The Patent Play Operation quickly. Her Empire

Building efforts unknowingly provided everything Napman was seeking, and at a considerable price for Maura.

◇ ◇ ◇

Maura lived in a curious subdivision. It was a gated community, and each home was attached to the residence on each side. Described as "Patio Homes" with shared walls between every unit and every rear patio, they weren't overly private.

Fortunately for me, Maura's rented house was on the outer perimeter at the bottom of a cul-de-sac. As a result, her home's placement was offset and set back from the two adjoining properties. The design placed her patio area reasonably far from those of her neighbors. Maura had additional hedging between her two neighbor's block walls and her backyard, offering excellent privacy. The developer positioned Maura's home near a golf course, but provided a substantial greenbelt between the residence and the fairway. A nearly impenetrable hedge of large trees and bushes occupied the space between the properties, spanning approximately 50' from her wall to the golf course. The walls were about 6' tall and the thick high foliage provided Maura and nearby residents with a considerable margin of privacy and noise abatement.

I'm guessing the trees and thick foliage, as well as the 6' stuccoed block wall, were installed to protect the house from the little white projectiles that littered the dense underbrush. The cul-de-sac's design resulted in Maura's home sitting too close to the fairway. The "bottom of the sack" jutted out into the fairway, a few yards too far. The addition of barrier vegetation choked the fairway's dogleg into an odd undersized golfing bottleneck.

Perfect for me. No gate entry or guardhouse actions necessary. Moreover, the neighborhood had a no pet policy. Therefore, no barking dogs. Privacy and seclusion. A perfect layout for my needs; and, as you'll see, for Maura's activities as well.

My initial visit to Maura's home was from the golf course approach, about 3 o'clock one morning. I carefully reconnoitered the area and quickly determined, if necessary, I could sit on

Maura's home daily with little exposure or risk. Evidence indicated golfers chasing lost balls gave up before going very far into the thick vegetation. Lost golf balls littered the undergrowth.

Although I planned on leaving autonomous listening devices behind, operational considerations suggested I make additional arrangements to remain onsite surveilling Maura, as necessary. To that end, I made several offsite trips to prepare The Hide for any long-term surveillance needs.

A Colleague assisted me late each afternoon and into the early evening for several days, moving equipment into the area near Mara's patio. Timing was critical because of certain beneficial transitional light levels we wanted to use as dusk unfolded.

> ***An aside...***
> Dusk is an excellent time to move on a Target location. The cones in our eyes provide humans with sight during the day. Rods provide us with peripheral and nighttime vision. As the sun begins to set and light diminishes, cones turn off and rods begin to awaken. That period between full cone activity and complete rod takeover occurs at dusk and dawn; when vision is least effective. That's when Cola likes to strike.
>
> Although Cola and his Colleagues have the same rods and cones as anyone else, we found that wearing prescription glasses with an anti-reflective coating gives us an edge; and not just any prescription. Our Optometrist OneSeven provides us with a "Sphere" that's designed for dusk-only conditions. The diopters are just a little different than called for in a normal prescription (plus or minus, I can't recall which), and calibrated for that time-limited light levels conversion we experience at dawn, and again at dusk. The Cola conceived prescription system marginally enhances our ability to see better during day-to-night and night-to-day transitions.

Back to The Golf Course...
Riding a golf cart, we "played" the back nine several days in a row. Each time we approached the dogleg near our Target patio,

I intentionally drove my golf ball into the bushes surrounding Maura's house. My Colleague would park the golf cart in a well-concealed void between two large bushes. We'd off-load our gear and I'd moved it farther into the foliage while My Colleague acted as lookout. It was in that foliage where I'd be constructing a Hide.

> ***An aside...***
> A Hide is a hiding place where a Spy will position himself and/or his equipment, as needed, to surreptitiously collect information and/or items necessary to successfully prosecute the Operation. When constructed outdoors, it is common to use camouflage materials for concealment. When indoors, a Hide might be as simple as a closet or bathroom stall.

Back to The Hide...
My Colleague and I stocked The Hide with water, plastic bags for hygiene-related purposes, trash and physical evidence removal, as well as foodstuffs. We also brought in 3 Betamax Camcorders with about a dozen fully charged batteries, as well as audio recording devices and a small periscope. Still cameras and a few other tools were included in the deliveries we made into the foliage.

> ***An aside...***
> Most Readers are probably familiar with VHS players, camcorders, and tapes. The original video player, Betamax, beat VHS to the marketplace by a year. Although Sony introduced Betamax systems to the consumer world, they ultimately lost the video format battle to VHS. Most people knew Betamax had superior resolution, better sound, stable imaging, and was better constructed. However, consumers opted for the lower priced, but nearly as good, VHS system; eventually forcing Betamax out of the consumer market.
>
> Cola preferred Betamax systems because they were well-built. The rugged devices would stand up to rough and tumble operational needs better than VHS. The higher quality audio and video was a bonus for me. Another

> bonus was the smaller recording media dimensions and resulting cartridge size. Over the years Video 8, Hi-8, and Digital 8 emerged. Those smaller tapes became my new standard until I transitioned fully to digital flash memory systems.
>
> At first, I had a standalone Betamax recording device, a large external battery pack, and a separate camera. The system was bulky and awkward to deal with in the world of clandestinity. My first self-contained recording system, a real camcorder, was the Sony Betamovie BMC-100P. That device changed the espionage game and made using them much more comfortable and improved espionage outcomes.

Back to Cola's Hide...
Once The Hide was stocked with items necessary for the operation, I rolled up my sleeves and went to work. The following two days presented unexpected discoveries. During the installation of my listening devices, I discovered there were already several wired microphones hidden on the patio. The microphone wires were connected to an audio recording device affixed to a bushy tree just inside the wall from my position. The recording media in the device was a cassette tape. The tape was identical to the blank tapes I planned on using to record whatever my microphones picked up. It was also identical to the media I used in my Sony Walkman.

> ***An aside...***
> Stakeouts require patience and can sometimes involve many hours or days of waiting. For me, stakeouts are very difficult. If I was on a stakeout for hours, then had to act quickly and focus on a task, I often turned to my Walkman to focus. Hitting "Play" provided me with the Mission Impossible score and visions of Barney concentrating on his responsibilities and activities in time-critical situations. Barney was one of the characters from the original television series. Even in life and death situations, Barney remained calm and completed his work without panicking. However, when in those situations both Barney and I could turn on the sweat. A

> salty deluge would often drip off the end of my Sicilian nose as I worked. The music and thoughts of Barney at work assisted me by providing focus and calm when I needed it most.

Back to Cola's Unexpected Discovery...
Yikes! This was an unexpected turn of events. I needed to go the extra mile to ensure my equipment wasn't discoverable by whoever had planted the devices on Maura's patio. The discovery of the existing bugs notwithstanding, my immediate concern was, WHY?

Why did Maura have sophisticated listening devices on her property? Was the FBI, DEA, or another espionage professional surveilling Maura? What had I gotten myself involved with on this job?

While sitting in my "Hide," I considered these and other questions. I finally decided I was probably in the clear. Not compromised. I moved forward with surveilling Maura's patio carrying out my activities with a heightened sense of concern and awareness. I also decided it would behoove me to physically stake out the location, rather than rely solely on unattended recording devices.

I moved my recording equipment, food, water, and camouflaged materials farther back into the underbrush. I pulled back the camera equipment I'd installed near the patio and set up several more cameras deeper into the brush. It took a few extra trips to collect the additional Betacams and charged batteries, but the effort paid off in the long run.

Extra cameras were necessary because the nearly impenetrable foliage further from the wall reduced observable viewing angles. I also removed wired microphones I'd installed on the patio and replaced them with directional microphones positioned high in the trees. Those actions left Maura's courtyard free from any equipment belonging to me. Then I waited.

I didn't have to wait long. That Friday afternoon when Maura came home she was joined on the patio by The Patent Project

Director a few minutes later. According to information I'd collected, The Project Director was a happily married man. Why was he joining Maura on her patio?

Information came to me some weeks later that Maura asked him over to assist in planning his wife's surprise birthday party. It appears he was okay with the delay in going home, but I didn't know it at the time. His wife and daughter were on a plane, flying to the Midwest for a week-long visit with her parents on their farm.

It was clear. Maura had other designs for the meeting. After he'd been on Maura's patio for about an hour, I dubbed him "Snare." At that point, I realized she was an evil predator, and her boss was about to become an unwitting victim.

Although I didn't see how she did it at the time, I was under no illusion. Maura drugged Snare. Subsequent video review revealed her adding something to a margarita I watched her blend for Snare on the portable patio bar. I discovered the drug she added to Snare's drink was something she referred to as "Hipnoseed."

The substance was probably the Benzodiazepine drug: Flunitrazepam. More commonly known today under the brand name Rohypnol, it carries the street name Roofie - the Date Rape Drug. I believe Maura derived the word Hipnoseed from Rohypnol's Grecian brand name, "Hipnosedon." The drug has sedative and hypnotic effects, as well as powerful amnesic properties. Unwitting victims are sedated and usually become unresponsive, while later having an inability to recall what occurred while medicated.

Contemporary Roofie manufacturing techniques include a dye designed to turn liquids blue when adding the drug. In the 1980's adding Roofies didn't alter the appearance of the fluid. Regardless, I'm not so sure The Project Director's blue-green margarita would have alerted him to the drug, if Maura used today's formula to alter his beverage.

Once Snare was entirely unresponsive, Maura called out to someone inside her home. I was more than surprised when a naked man appeared on the patio. I immediately recognized him as one of the security staff from Maura's workplace. My head was spinning, and I was at a loss to understand what might be going on. However, it didn't take long for them to reveal their purpose.

They went into the house and carried out a large folding Byōbu screen. Japanese households use Byōbu screens as room dividers. The Byōbu had images screen printed on it showing Kama Sutra sexual positions. They also carried out lightweight imitation Japanese plants. A bamboo rug was placed on the patio pavers, followed by a mattress, covered with red sheets. Perhaps satin. Finally, Maura put two matching red pillows on the bed.

They undressed Snare and positioned him on the bed. While The Security Guy was adjusting the props and Snare, Maura ducked inside and returned with a 35mm camera on a tripod. She also placed a Polaroid SX-70 on a nearby table. The SX-70 was capable of producing developed photos in 60 seconds.

Maura removed all of her clothes. Then she dressed in a kinky-looking leather outfit made with a few fine strips of black leather. Little, if anything, private was covered by the sadomasochistic costume. She put on a pair of black knee-high leather boots with extremely long stiletto heels. Maura placed sunglasses on Snare's face, bound his wrists with an elastic bandage, and climbed atop her victim. She held his bound hands to her cleavage, arched her back and looked toward the sky. *Bizarre.*

Following Maura's directions, The Security Guy adjusted the 35mm camera's view to include Snare and Maura's body. He was careful not to show Maura's face or Snare's bound wrists in the viewfinder. From my vantage point, it appeared as though The Project Director was conscious and actively participating in the kinky encounter. He was neither awake nor a willing participant.

The Security Guy took a couple of photos with the Polaroid that appeared to show the same perspective as the camera on the tripod. He showed Maura the developed Polaroid photos. She was satisfied with the angle but insisted The Security Guy get it correct. She kept saying something about the adhesive bandage on her back and advised The Security Guy to avoid including it in the shot if he could. A little while later, after the photography session was over, she had her cohort remove the adhesive bandage. It had been covering what appeared to be a birthmark.

After The Security Guy shot photos of Snare and Maura with both cameras and the two conspirators were satisfied with their efforts, Maura removed the leather costume and boots, then donned a robe. The naked Security Guy put on a skimpy leather costume, aroused himself, and took his turn in the obscene photography session. Using both cameras, the two schemers took many photographs I've never been able to comfortably describe when discussing the events of that afternoon with others. Let's just say they were extremely inappropriate lurid images. The conspirators positioned the victim's bound wrists behind The Security Guy's back, and later around his neck, for various photos.

Just when I thought it couldn't get any worse, they began using super glue to stage even more explicit photos. Maura removed the elastic bandages from Snare's wrists. Then they glued Snare's fingers together in a manner to make it appear the unconscious man was actively participating in the sexual encounter with The Security Guy. The activities of that late afternoon were disgusting. I was troubled, but Snare's defilement was beyond the pale. Rape is undoubtedly the single word that best describes the events I witnessed that terrible day.

When they were done taking photos, Maura applied an unknown substance to her victim's hands and, along with a single-edged razor blade, worked to separate Snare's super-glued fingers. One of his hands was left bleeding.

Snare was dressed and placed back into the chair. Immediately afterward the two conspirators retired to the satin sheets for their own sexual activities. I couldn't believe my eyes.

I was appalled at what I'd seen. Who were these people? What did they want from Snare? Such tactics were unfamiliar to me.

I've never engaged in activities of that kind. It was appalling and immoral. Maura was out for blood, but I didn't know why.

It was obvious Maura and The Security Guy were setting Snare up for extortion. After they'd finished taking their blackmail photos and had their own tryst, the conspirators removed all evidence of what they'd done. I discovered later that they'd carried the folding screen, the artificial plants, pillows, the bed with the satin sheets, cameras, tripod and other evidence to a small van hidden in Maura's garage.

Earlier it dawned on me that Maura was also setting The Security Guy up for blackmail. The microphones could have easily captured their conversations while Snare was out cold. I also witnessed Maura turn up the music, before taking 35mm photos of The Security Guy while he was making adjustments to the scene with the unconscious victim. The music easily drowned out the shutter sound coming from the camera. It was clear that Maura included both The Security Guy and the unwitting Project Director in the photos. *Maura is One Nasty Bitch!*

Very late that evening The Project Director began coming around. Maura gave him coffee and water. He was disoriented. He kept asking questions that Maura dismissed. He told Maura he had to leave, but Maura said no. She told him when he passed out Maura called his wife; and that she would be arriving shortly.

Maura was buying time until The Project Director could process the situation better. She must not have known his wife was on a flight to the midwest. He tried to get out of the lounge chair, telling Maura she was on a plane. Maura placed her hands on his chest and pushed him back into the chair.

Her victim's face morphed into a mask of foggy confusion. He muttered, "But, but, but..." over and over.

She too began muttering. It appeared she was scrambling for a proper response.

hmmm... No backstop story? Sign of a rookie!

After a few moments, Maura composed herself and told The Project Director that the aircraft had mechanical problems. She said it returned to the airport. She informed her victim that his wife was rebooked for a flight the following day, and she would be arriving at Maura's home any minute. With that news, The Project Director relaxed and slumped down into the chair.

After a few minutes, Maura decided he was sufficiently alert and asked The Security Guy to come out to the patio. Fully dressed, the formerly naked conspirator walked over to The Project Director and handed him a stack of Polaroid photos. The man shot up straight and gasped loudly. The Security Guy reached over to a large plant and removed a Louisville Slugger from the bush. He held in menacingly in both hands. The Project Director's eyes widened, then he vomited and broke down crying.

After 5 or 6 minutes, his wailing and sobbing became a quiet whimper. When he was reasonably calm, Maura walked over and told him to review each of the photos carefully. He did.

Then Maura took the photos from her victim and sat down beside him. She apologized for her "necessary" handiwork and told The Project Director she could make the photos disappear if he provided her with information relating to the lab's patent project. He began crying again and shaking his head. Once he calmed down, he said, "Ok, you win. Bitch!"

Maura told him if he persisted with the attitude, she'd hold off on destroying the photos. She said if he came clean, she'd burn the pictures in his presence. The Project Director demanded to know if there were other photos. Maura and The Security Guy shook their heads simultaneously, indicating no other images existed.

Maura nodded to The Security Guy. He moved toward my location, but I wasn't concerned. I knew where he was going. While Maura distracted The Project Director, The Security Guy walked over to the bushy tree and turned on the recorder.

Satisfied that no other photos existed, The Project Director spilled the beans on the project. He spoke with deliberation for more than an hour. Once he had finished, Maura showed one particularly lurid photo of The Project Director. It was a photo of him seemingly engaged in oral sex with another unidentifiable man. I knew the unidentifiable man to be The Security Guy and had video proving it.

Maura told The Project Director she was going to make sure his children saw that photo if he didn't "keep quiet." She said she would then copy the remainder of her photo inventory and disperse them throughout Snare's workplace and the community. He protested loudly, exclaiming they had a deal. Her retort was something about the folly of making a deal with the devil.

I've never before or since encountered that particular brand of evil I witnessed in Maura.

Maura handed the photos to The Security Guy. She then showed The Project Director three rolls of 35mm film. She said those canisters contained many other images of his unconscious activities. Maura told Snare viewers of their excellent photographic work would believe he was both conscious and actively participating in a myriad of kinky sexual activities. The Security Guy took the photographic evidence and walked into the house. I never saw him again. Too bad. I would have enjoyed taking out The Project Director's humiliation and pain on that clown.

Once The Security Guy was gone, Maura told The Project Director to compose himself and go home. She threatened him, saying if he uttered a word to anyone about what happened on that patio, she would do exactly as promised. She advised him to show up to work on Monday and act as if nothing had happened, "or else!"

Maura escorted the man from her patio. Believing I only had a few moments, I slipped out of my hiding place and rushed to the wall. Pulling myself up and over the wall, I quickly replaced Maura's tape of The Project Director's coerced revelations with my Mission Impossible tunes, after first wiping the cassette down to remove any fingerprints. I fast-forwarded the tape for about twenty seconds, then set it to begin recording again. Knowing it was laying down audio, I remained characteristically quiet. She'd rewind the tape offsite and see if The Project Director's words recorded as planned. At least I hoped she'd wait until then to review the tape. I was taking a risk but figured Maura was going to bug out and remove the audio evidence of her scheme as quickly as possible.

Boy, was she going to be surprised...

Retracing my steps, I rapidly returned to my hiding place and called in The Operation's Cola Team for my evacuation. Two Colleagues would arrive shortly riding separate golf carts. I would depart with the recorded media on foot and they were responsible for collecting all the equipment I used for the Op.

As I awaited Maura's return, I considered the possibilities. Was Maura working on her own? Was she part of a larger conspiracy? Was she working for a third entity? Was she working for Napman?

That final thought was especially disturbing. Napman knew better. He, like all Cola Clients, understood my Non-Negotiables and was very well aware that "Clients are not permitted to simultaneously enlist others for the same services I offer."

My priority, upon removal of all my equipment from The Hide and sanitizing the area, would be to get to the bottom of the bizarre events that unfolded over the last few hours. My concern was more about self-preservation, rather than operational success. I was in dangerous territory and needed to know why. Moreover, I needed to determine how I could extricate myself from dangers associated with Maura's blackmail scheme.

> ***An aside...***
> Situations like that are precisely why I rely heavily on Cutouts. Cutouts are persons or companies spies use to insulate and protect parties involved in passing goods or information. They are, simply put, unaffiliated middlemen. Proper usage dictates multiple Cutouts and is generally structured to keep one of the parties from identifying the other party. Even my best Clients know little about me and my life. They are only privy to what I

cautiously share. Most of that sharing is smoke and mirrors. They don't know my actual identity, where I live, how to find me directly, or how to point law enforcement in my direction. Again, it's all about self-preservation.

For example, Napman had no idea of my whereabouts, unless I was with him. He knew neither my given name nor my family name. He only knew me as Cola. Payment was wired to an account number associated with an offshore shell corporation. I always set up the meets (meeting times and places), and faithfully shifted them at the last minute.

Huge blocks of time were also invested by My Colleagues and me running SDR's (Surveillance Detection Runs). SDR's were so critical, if I discovered a Colleague shortcutting an SDR, I dropped him or her like a hot rock; and never worked with that individual again. SDR's are the lifeblood of operational safety.

Conducting surveillance on Clients is also part of the equation. With whom is My Client meeting? Is My Client being square with me or involving me in something nefarious behind my back? Are they attempting to set me up in some manner? Is My Client being followed to one of our meets? These and other thoughts filled my mind as I awaited Maura's return.

Back to Maura's Patio...

When Maura returned to the backyard, she went directly to the cassette recorder and unknowingly retrieved the Mission Impossible tape. She retreated to the house, and a short time later I heard her car leaving the premises.

I rapidly dismantled my gear, followed by a careful inventory. Cola's trash was included in that inventory. Everything was consolidated onto a single tarp, for later collection by Cola Colleagues. Once I was satisfied no other evidence remained of my activities, I departed the dense foliage and darted across the fairway to await the arrival of My Colleagues.

My investigation over the next couple of days determined Maura was, indeed, working on behalf of a third entity. Her secret employer occupied a medical development space similar to that of our Target company. It became clear they, like Napman, caught wind of something big being developed at the biomedical research company, far earlier than Napman. That gave them time to position Maura within the company.

They no longer had access to The Project Director's words stored on the cassette tape, but Maura and The Security Guy might still be able to give them sufficient information to beat Napman to the patent office. I needed to thwart their efforts and take them off the stage.

I had a OneSeven edit the various video recordings I made and create a short video showing what Maura had done, but without revealing any of the research information disclosed by The Project Director. The footage showed her demands for the research project data. The OneSeven also added in some of the still photos I captured. The final product made it abundantly clear that Maura engaged in criminal activities on her patio. Thanks to the video, The Project Director, as well as his employer, were clearly shown to be victims in a plot to steal patentable information.

I had a copy of the video delivered immediately to Maura. I needed to shut her down. That move worked well. Maura departed the community within 24 hours of receiving the damning video. Without notifying her employer, she quietly abandoned her rented home and relocated to another region of the U.S. Two Cola Colleagues had the sinister woman under continual surveillance as she drove a rental van across the country.

Two months later I used Cutouts for delivery of the video we produced. Deliveries to The Project Director and The Project Director's employer went as planned. The Operation was, at that point, a footnote in Cola's history. Several years later I made a discreet inquiry into the matter and received a few crumbs of unverified information.

I heard Maura was arrested. I don't know the charges, but did hear she spilled the beans on a third medical development company. It is my understanding a plea deal with the prosecution put legal matters to rest. I do not know to what end, except that Maura's handler at the third company went to prison.

I did hear about an out of court settlement. The information I received indicated the civil liability borne by the third company resulted in a few million dollars paid to The Project Director and many more millions to his employer. The settlement included a contractual obligation for the third company to remain out of that particular development space for at least 25 years.

All the data I uncovered regarding the patent was turned over to Napman. I have no idea if he ultimately secured a patent, or if The Project Director's company secured it. To my knowledge, Napman never knew anything about the bizarre events on the patio that fateful evening. I certainly didn't share any of that with him.

My only hope through it all is that The Project Director adjusted sufficiently to go on and have a good life. He certainly didn't deserve the treatment he received at the hands of the two blackmailing extortionists. I trust I did the right thing by doing what I could to assist him in bringing Maura, The Security Guy, and the third company to justice.

THE HOLE AND THE TOE

When I was a young Spy, I occasionally pulled a few Wally-like stunts. This is a story about one particular embarrassing faux pas. One reason it is *embarrassing* for me has to do with the year. I was well seasoned and more than ten years into my espionage career.

I accepted a contract requiring me to record certain confidential corporate communications. Those communications were telephonic and took place between the home office of a Wealthy Industrialist and his corporate offices. His home and office security was state-of-the-art and presented many problems. It would be nearly impossible for me to install a straightforward phone tap within the given timeline. We needed to come up with a different method of capturing high-level internal communications.

As we were looking into options, one of My Colleagues discovered the Wealthy Industrialist had weekly conversations with his partner, a brother. They were equal partners in the business I was targeting. I was initially under the impression the brother was not a working partner or engaged in the day-to-day affairs of the corporation. It appeared he carried out responsibilities in an apparent advisory capacity with the company's top-level management. The man was blind. Information we gathered indicated he preferred to remain at home most of the time. The Wealthy Industrialist failed to consider his brother's house a potential target for Corporate Espionage. All of that gave the brother an aura of invisibility; even with the Cola Team (for a time). It was a soft target. We decided to tap the blind brother's phone.

A Colleague and I approached his home early one morning. We had a backstop story at the ready, suggesting ties to the local water utility. The residence was a small, unassuming single story cottage built atop a low two-foot high crawl space. Dressed like plumbers, with a plumbing truck and plumbing tools, we crawled under the home. As expected, a telephone cable we needed to tap ran under the building's floorboards. We needed to tie into that cable, connect to a power source, and install the devices necessary to capture and record phone calls to and from the residence. As I feared, spiders and cobwebs were everywhere. I really didn't want to be there.

Did I tell you Cola is deathly afraid of spiders? *Yikes!* As I said, I really didn't want to be there. I'm sure arachnophobia played a role in distracting me, resulting in my Wally-like mistake.

We also installed a Pen Register to record the telephone numbers he dialed. If memory serves me correctly, we attempted to use, for the first time, a device largely unknown to us. It was a Trap and Trace device, designed to record the phone numbers of those calling into the residence. It was similar to the first few iterations of Caller ID systems. I don't recall that device ever working for us. We believed if the brothers failed to discuss anything substantive during calls to the blind brother's home, perhaps those devices could assist us in determining if other phones were potentially tappable and not located at either the Wealthy Industrialist's home or his office.

O^2H

As My Colleague was completing the installation of those devices, I told him I needed to get O^2H as soon as possible. He was aware of my disdain for spiders and agreed to finish.

> ***An aside...***
> O^2H is a term I picked up during my college years. My fraternity brothers and I would say, "O^2H" when we wanted or needed to get "Out Of Here." If we finished something, like a meal, we might ask others, "Are we O^2H?" as a way to know if everyone was RTR (Ready to Rally aka "Leave").
>
> *What can I say? It's the way we spoke in college. Now people talk like that when texting. LOL*

Back to The Crawlspace...
I connected a bundle of wires to the existing water meter and strung the cable along the ceiling of the musty crawl space. The home, while only one story, was built with many different levels that varied by inches from room to room. As I affixed the wires above my head, I kept a tape measure handy to assist me in calculating the ups and downs so I could drill a hole in the exterior wall, in the appropriate location.

The exterior hole required drilling from the outside. If drilled from the interior, I ran the risk of splintering the man's beautiful tongue and groove redwood siding. The entrance to the crawl space wasn't anywhere near where the wire needed to come out of the structure. That's why I was running calculations to make sure when I walked down the side of the home I drilled a hole in the correct spot.

Once the wire was out, we needed to install a box used for remote readings from water meters. Although we called it an Alias Box, it was, in fact, a real remote reading port allowing meter readers to remotely access water usage data originating at the water meter. With that box in place, one of My Colleagues could return to the residence from time to time, pretending she was with the local water utility. She was young and pretty. Non-threatening. If approached, My Colleague would confidently inform her audience she was there to read the meter. The "reading" device she carried was genuine. She would read the meter from the exterior of the residence and add that data to an official-looking form she carried on a clipboard. Then she'd crawl under the home to read the meter itself, to confirm the numbers displayed outside the residence. My young Colleague would review data visible to her in the analog readout window of the water meter and add that information to the form. Skookum Jim would probably call a comparison of those two pieces of data, Checksum Verification.

> ***An aside...***
> Good backstop stories are far more believable and accepted more often when the story is fact-based. Reading the meter, both outside and under the residence, was insurance. It was a fact-based activity to ensure believability and acceptance. As with insurance, you never want to need it, and hope you don't. You do what you can to avoid triggering its need. However, when you need to call your insurance provider, you certainly hope your policy has sufficient coverage for the issue. Reading the meter was smart coverage.

Back to Reading The Meter...
Her sub rosa duty while under the house was to retrieve a cassette tape from the recording machine and exchange it with a fresh cassette. She'd transfer the cartridge to a Colleague using a brush pass in various crowded public places. The receiving Agent would return to our safe house where we'd play and transcribe the phone conversations captured by our surveillance equipment.

Unfortunately, my mind was in a spidery realm. I clearly erred when calculating the location for the hole I was about to drill from the outside of the home to the top of the crawl space where my wire was coiled; ready to be pulled through the exterior wall and connected to The Alias Box. I vividly recall drilling the hole using a flat half-inch spade bit. Spade bits (not the same as those used for horses) are designed to produce holes in wood.

When I felt the bit complete the hole, I quickly pulled the bit out and looked in. I expected to see a faint glow from the flashlight being used by My Colleague on the other side of the house. That I didn't see. What I saw shocked me. My head instantly jerked backward, away from the hole. The situation required a quick-thinking Cola to come up with a salable excuse. Our planned backstop story wouldn't begin to cover this situation. I needed to adapt and improvise. *Forthwith!*

A Bare Hairy Toe

When I peered through the hole, I saw a bare hairy toe. We had no plans for that. I stood up quickly. Peering through the glass in front of me, I saw the blind brother. I'll refer to him as Mr. Toe. He was sitting at his kitchen table next to the window eating breakfast. The table was small and rectangular, made for two people. Mr. Toe was seated in one chair. The other was empty. I'd accidentally drilled a hole at floor level. It should have been about three or four inches lower and under the floor. Oops! Without delay, I jumped up and knocked on the back door to his kitchen.

> ***An aside...***
> As a result of that experience, I had Jo fabricate a "PMS" device (Pinhole Marking System). The PMS device drills a pinhole through a wall from the inside. The PMS then shoots a gas carrying fine green powder through the tiny hole. That permits installers to drill from inside to the outside; without worrying about splintering the finished side of the wall. Then installers transition around the wall and locate the green powdery residue, deposited by the PMS, in and around the pinhole. The pinhole becomes the intended location for drilling inward, so installers can avoid splintering surfaces and/or perforating bare hairy toes.
>
> On occasion when both sides of the wall are finished, a short full-sized hole is drilled, followed by a PMS perforation. When drilled again from the opposite side, we can accurately hit the full-sized hole without worrying about splintering or otherwise damaging the opposite side. We use this method when both sides of a wall are finished and maintaining a pristine condition on both surfaces is important.

Back to The Perforated Kitchen...
Cola neither runs, nor does he stall, stammer, or blather when something goes wrong. His adrenaline kicks in, but it doesn't result in external changes. As mentioned previously, what happens to me is weird, but helpful. I tend to get a form of tunnel vision, and everything seems to slow down. I continue thinking at my pace, while everything else in the world turns to thick honey. Again, weird, but helpful. I can quickly work out issues and react properly, without any apparent delay noticeable by others. My Colleagues find it fascinating. I merely consider it an opportunistic gift.

Mr. Toe invited me to "Come in and take a seat."

Cola calmly entered the little house. The simple, clean kitchen and dinette belied the wealth of his family. It was a pleasant room, but very weird. I felt like I'd entered an episode of the Twilight Zone.

The wooden dining chair was painted white and had a white vinyl seat cushion. I sat down and looked around. The white decor didn't stop with the chair. In fact, everything was white. White white white. The floor, ceiling, cabinets, walls, appliances, window coverings, and table were all nearly the same shade of white. Two white placemats sat on the small table. The silverware, seated on a white cloth napkin next to his white breakfast plate, had white plastic handles. The plate contained egg whites and a half eaten piece of untoasted white bread. The brown crust had been removed from the bread. A white bowl contained white hominy grits, diluted with white cream or milk. A single slice of yellow butter on top of the grits looked out of place. The salt and pepper shakers were white, as was a sugar bowl containing white sugar cubes. h*mmm, did the pepper mill contain white pepper?* A white coffee cup, resting on a matching white saucer, sat on the table near the man and the liquid was white. Next to the cup was a small white container. In short order, I would discover that it contained heavy cream. A white carafe, filled with coffee, sat in the middle of the table next to a white plastic water pitcher. A single light fixture hung from the white ceiling, suspended on a white cord. The device was a small white globe. A red-tipped white cane leaned against the white window sill.

Mr. Toe *(or should I call him Mr. White?)* wore a white Izod polo shirt and white slacks with a white belt. White socks and white deck shoes sat on a white area rug near the door. The man had a plain white baseball hat on his head, along with white framed sunglasses. White curly hair protruded from the bottom of the cap, above his ears. A white-faced watch, held securely to the blind man's arm by a white leather band, adorned his left wrist. *Weird! A blind man wearing a wristwatch!*

I'm assuming Mr. Toe's blindness was in some manner responsible for the genesis of the kitchen's weird color scheme. It was a bizarre scene, and I was about to add a white wire and white caulking to the mix. If black is the absence of color, this had to be the most colorfully weird room I've ever seen. It was airy, bright, and infinitely odd. I can't say it enough, that was one weird room!

White Elephant

Cola wondered if he should address the white elephant in the room. I wanted to mention, or ask something about, the whiteness before me. I didn't want to be rude, but would it be rude to mention the obvious? Did he want his kitchen to be a conversation starter? Or, was it a quirk that should be observed, but ignored. I chose the latter; moving on to why and how I ended up sitting in the albino dining room.

I quickly apologized for nearly drilling a hole in his big toe. He politely asked what I was doing. I told Mr. Toe I worked for a contractor charged with installing equipment to help meter readers with their duties prior to a federally required equipment testing phase began. The installations made it for meter readers to avoid crawling beneath every home in the community to collect waster usage information. He said he paid a flat fee for water and asked why it was necessary to read the meter.

That was true and not unknown to us. I informed Mr. Toe a decade earlier the federal government underwrote a significant portion of the expenses necessary for the installation of the area's water supply and distribution system. Federal funding requirements included certification for every home to prove the installation of a water meter; even though abundant water supplies existed in that area. Moreover, the city had no intentions of ever charging for metered water. Regardless, the feds made our activities necessary before the water utility could receive the final federal money transfer for the project.

The information about federal funding for the project and the requirement for water meter installations was accurate. As such, it provided me with good backstop information. Backstopping with verifiable facts is always preferred to fictional backstopped stories.

> ***An aside...***
> While writing this chapter, I reached out to the water utility in that community. As I suspected, although water meters were installed in every residence and business, as part of a federal project decades ago, the residents there continue to pay flat rate water bills quarterly. I ran some numbers and estimated the Feds wasted many hundreds of thousands of dollars on that wasteful project involving the installation of hundreds of superfluous water meters.

Back to Mr. Toe and a Touch of Cola Fiction...
I told Mr. Toe a testing program was underway to ensure the meters would provide accurate information to the box at the exterior of each home. It was an early stage pilot program necessary before every home and business had exterior water meter readers installed. The federal government designed the program to gauge water usage, calculate waste and leakage, and otherwise review the efficacy and necessity of meter-based billing. The ultimate goal was to encourage water conservation.

I further informed the blind man the project wouldn't affect current billing practices. His bill would remain unchanged for the foreseeable future. For the time being, testing would only impact a few dozen buildings.

That's where our backstop story ended. The rest was an extemporaneous response to my faux pas. If I failed to convince Mr. Toe with a good line of bull, it could doom the entire Operation.

I informed the nice man that the wiring couldn't come directly from the crawl space to the exterior of the home. I said a code issue required us to mount the box outside his home at a specified height. Moreover, no exposed wiring was allowable on the exterior of the home; therefore, the reason I drilled into this kitchen. I added that the unfortunate perforation was right at floor level inside his breakfast dining area, and would instantly turn ninety degrees and drop directly into the crawl space. I said only a half inch of wire would show on his kitchen floor. I told Mr. Toe the cable and baseboard were both white, as was the caulking I'd be using, so it would be nearly invisible.

Then I compounded my faux pas by saying, "You'll never see it."

I'm such an idiot!

More than just a silly comment, I left it sitting there like a fetid turd. I didn't realize what I'd said to the sightless fellow until My Colleague and I had departed and I was providing My Colleague with my After Action Report. *Ugh!*

Believe it or not, Mr. Toe, like the Police Officer on my Quick Lube Job, bought my line of bull; hook, line, and sinker.

He was a kind man and invited me to join him for a cup of coffee and a treat. The coffee was great. Additionally, Mr. Toe had one of the best homemade apple turnovers I've ever eaten. They weren't normal. Each turnover had a thin layer of white frosting, covered with powdered sugar. He made those white Apple turnovers himself. Amazing. I had a delightful visit with the man and learned something valuable that morning.

Mr. Toe told me as a young blind man he realized he could see sound. During his teenage years, friends would stop by to visit him. He began to notice some of his possessions in the bedroom went missing about the time those visits occurred. As his suspicions grew Mr. Toe noticed one particular boy's voice would continually undergo nearly imperceptible changes when he was in the room. The blind teenager realized the pitch was changing because the boy was turning his head, looking all over the place. His turning neck created structural changes in the boy's neck, thereby modifying pressures and tissue positioning. Also, sound echoes off walls, furnishings, and other items differently as the head turns.

Armed with the discovery, he keyed on that particular teenager. Mr. Toe began inventorying his room before and after the boy entered his home. He also kept a mental map of where the kid was looking and in what parts of the bedroom he ventured. In short order, the blind teen nailed the boy for the thefts.

He told me he liked and trusted me. When I asked why, Mr. Toe said I kept my eyes on him the entire time we were talking. Interesting. He didn't realize I was, indeed, looking around the kitchen and small dining area.

It's a Cola thing. I'm always surveying rooms. That weird room was captivating. I was unable to keep from looking around and taking it in. Regardless, the blind man was partially correct. I did keep my head aimed directly at Mr. Toe. It's an old habit I picked up during hours and hours of specialized surveillance.

> ***An aside...***
> When doing what I call, In Your Face Surveillance, the setting was often in an outdoor restaurant, a sports stadium, or park. I would hide behind my sunglasses and sit absolutely still, facing my head in an expected or a neutral direction; while keeping my eyes roving. Sometimes I carried a white cane and pretended I was blind. Most of the time though, I was acting as a sighted man just sitting there wearing sunglasses. In those situations, I was generally within a few feet of my Target and often within his or her line of sight, while trying to remain unobtrusive. If possible, invisible.

Back to The Very White Room...
My experience with the blind man was merely a good habit that unexpectedly paid off. That habit endeared me to Mr. Toe and got me off the hook that day. After thanking him for the treats, My Colleague and I departed. I couldn't wait to tell My Colleague about the weird room. I never saw the blind fellow again.

The Operation was a great success, in spite of my Wally World mathematical shortcomings and the near piercing of a blind man's foot. We garnered reams of valuable information from the brother's conversations. An unexpected piece of low hanging fruit also landed in our basket. We discovered the blind hairy-toed brother was a micromanager who faithfully called into the office each day to speak with the VP of Sales, the General Counsel, the VP of Marketing, and the VP of Finance and Accounting. Once a week the two brothers closed out their week with a call discussing the prior week, the upcoming week, and other corporate business.

The recollection of that hairy white toe, seen by a surprised Cola through a freshly drilled hole, will forever bring a smile to my face. That was, indeed, a Candid Cola Moment. I'd love to have a photo of my face as I jerked back from that hole. Heck, I'd really really love to have a picture of that weird room to include in this book. Alas, it's not to be.

HE DIED IN MY ARMS

JACK LEE AND MARK WINFREE
Front to Back

Jack
One of my cover jobs, having nothing to do with Corporate Espionage, holds a particular solemnity for me. I was working in a small community. The contract my partner and I had with the

city required a close working relationship with the City Manager. Jack was a nice old guy who befriended my coworker, Mark, and me. We had meetings in Jack's office at City Hall on several occasions. Here's what happened one sad morning.

Mark and I had an appointment with Jack to review the status of the project. We wanted to discuss an issue we discovered on the blueprints. Jack greeted us and invited Mark and me to sit down in front of his desk. The desk filled the large room nicely. The office had high ceilings and equally high windows. The structure was built in the 1800's and served as both City Hall and the local jail. The wooden floors creaked, and the building was drafty. However, it was both historic and charming. The massive desk was an antique and was a perfect fit for Jack's office.

Mark and I sat down in front of the desk, and we exchanged pleasantries with the old fellow. While Jack was telling us something about his weekend, Mark began unrolling our set of blueprints on Jack's desk. We were there to point out a particular problem on the prints that would result in a minor delay for the project. Mark and I had choreographed how the meeting would unfold. Jack was going to be disappointed, and we wanted him to fully understand the issues, as he would be issuing a report on the matter for a City Council meeting later that day.

According to our pre-planned script, when Mark began unrolling the blueprints, I moved to get into position so that I could point something out to Jack. I stood up and walked around the desk, stopping at Jack's right side. I was slightly behind the old fellow. When I arrived next to his chair, I recall Jack engaging in small talk. He asked, "How were the girls over the weekend?"

At that point, Jack yawned and slowly lowered his forehead to the desk. Mark and I looked at each other. We both shrugged. All of a sudden Jack began shaking and convulsing. I quickly reached my arms under his and straightened him up in his chair. His convulsions lessened. Mark rushed around the desk, and we carefully laid Jack's heavy frame on the cold wooden floor. He was no longer convulsing or breathing. Jack was unresponsive. CPR was unsuccessful.

That was a difficult day. A sad day. I'd never witnessed a person pass from this earth before that day. Worse yet, he passed away in my arms. A medical professional said nothing could have been done to save Jack. He had a bad heart. According to the medical authorities involved, whatever occurred inside Jack's chest would have taken him even if he was in the world's best hospital that morning. I certainly hope they weren't just trying to make me feel better.

SAD FOOTNOTE #1

Jack's Funeral

Although I wasn't present at Jack's funeral, I heard the graveside service held tragedy and angst for the family. Second-hand information I received suggested Jack's poorly constructed pine coffin came apart as pallbearers were carrying him to his grave. Funeral participants were shocked when Jack's body dropped from the broken box and fell to the ground.

> ***An aside...***
> When Jack was pronounced dead in his office by first responders, Mark and I assisted the two medics, and one or two others, when it was time to lift him off the floor and place him on a gurney. Jack was about 5'8" and weighed well north of 200 pounds. I was amazed at the level of difficulty we had lifting Jack. While I cannot speak for the others, I suspect they had the same issues as me. It was challenging to gain purchase on any part of Jack. The skin, fat, and muscle simply rolled as I tried to raise him. Positioned near his waist, I felt weak and inadequate to the task. Sometime later, someone told me that kind of problem is not unusual when attempting to lift the dead weight of a lifeless overweight body.

Back to The Cemetery...
I cannot imagine the pain borne by Jack's family that day. I knew his wife. My heart went out to her.

MARK WINFREE

SAD FOOTNOTE #2

Mark

About ten years later I received a late night phone call from my Uncle Cash telling me Mark died in an automobile accident. Ten years after receiving that call from my uncle, I received a call from my father telling me Uncle Cash was dead. Shot by a stranger.

David

A few years before Jack's death, I was with my friends Teo and Lorenzo when we discovered the body of a college friend, Dave, several days after he ended his life. He had been despondent and took his life by self-immolation. The young man drank a bottle of brandy, poured a can of gasoline on his head, then lit himself on fire. So painful. So sad. So tragic. So final.

Life is a Gift

Jack, Mark, Uncle Cash, Mr. Slo, Michael, Summer, and others no longer enjoy life in this world. I'm sure they'd all agree, Life is precious a gift. It shouldn't be squandered or wasted. It should be embraced, relished, enjoyed, valued, and enriched.

As I've lived the Cola life, and other people and events have touched me in various ways, I've become an armchair philosopher. I continually remind myself that life is short and am thankful for my Christian faith. I believe we should regard each day, each relationship, and each opportunity to create positive memories as nothing less than extremely important. We should never forget life is, at best, fleeting. We should laugh more, have more adventures, hug longer, and never fail to remind loved ones they are precious.

COUNTERINTELLIGENCE

Which came first? The chicken or the egg? Not the easiest paradox to solve. On the other hand, placing the cart before the horse is clearly understood by most as being in the wrong order. In my world, as with the cart and horse analogy, one “counter” should come before the other.

Counterintelligence vs. Counterespionage
In short, Intelligence should come before Espionage. Counterintelligence is an activity that occurs BEFORE espionage activities are underway. Counterespionage activities are efforts designed to thwart or counter actions involving espionage, AFTER the discovery of espionage activity.

Oh? You don’t believe you have espionage problems in your business? Trust Cola. You do. The question is, “How bad is it?” Are your competitors merely keeping an eye on you and passively collecting information about your company, or are they actively co-opting your family, er business jewels? It doesn’t matter if it’s on the ‘Not Bad’ end of the spectrum, or on the ‘Terrible” side, I recommend the same response. Close the gate. *CLOSE IT NOW!*

There’s a certain futility in closing the barn doors AFTER the cows have escaped. I consistently recommend that business owners, having secrets others desire, avoid future problems by engaging in Corporate Counterintelligence activities. Doing so could help prevent the damage and costs associated with espionage and reactionary Counterespionage efforts.

A successful international company once hired me for a highly unusual assignment. I often refer to that company as "H2O." When I received news they wanted to consult with me, I went to work learning as much as possible about the company. H2O had recently concluded a series of focus group and community-wide marketing tests related to a product considered for large-scale manufacturing. A rumor within the industry suggested H2O's product development pipeline had kicked out a winner. Media reports heralded expectations for a corporate windfall involving many dollars and considerable market share. As I would soon discover, all of those rumors and reports were true.

Company leaders chose to follow the example of Coca-Cola and NOT patent their formula, but keep it a trade secret instead. They did that to avoid the twenty year time limitations offered by patent protections. Coca-Cola's decision has proven prescient after more than one hundred twenty-five years of secrecy as they've closely guarded their formula. Likewise, H2O wanted similar opportunities and hired Cola (no pun or parallel intended) to provide the foundation for keeping their new trade secret, SECRET.

The product's confidential manufacturing process would require an inordinate amount of water. Knowledgeable competitors could conceivably reverse engineer H2O's proprietary processes. Competing companies, knowing either the quantity or realizing the unexpectedly large volume of water necessary for the product's manufacturing process, could conceivably produce a similar product. H2O's Chief Product Engineer calculated an apparent 50% reduction in the water used in manufacturing could successfully confound any competitor's attempts to co-opt H2O's highly valued proprietary information.

The local water utility metered consumption at their new facility. H2O's CEO was concerned for the privacy and security of their water usage data. They didn't want to risk someone accessing records at the water company serving their soon-to-be-launched facility. Nor did they believe it was prudent to inform water utility officials of their concerns. Doing so could prompt one of them to peddle H2O's numbers to competing organizations.

The CEO approached me for my assistance. He asked if I'd work with H2O by going to the water company and hacking their computer system to make it appear as though H2O was using less than the actual consumption. I informed The CEO I'd look into the matter. However, I first wanted to meet him face to face. He agreed to fly in from his corporate offices and meet me at the newly completed manufacturing plant.

We met, and he detailed his needs. I studied the situation with the water company for several days and realized The CEO's goal was a big mountain to climb. The hacking route he proposed presented many risks. The water company kept meticulous hard copy and computerized records. A simple hack wouldn't work. Moreover, a full-fledged hack would be risky, and the resulting numbers wouldn't stand the scrutiny of the water utility's internal auditors.

Those bean counters reconciled water usage by comparing hard copy field records made at the meter, and the electronic data entered into company databases by a team of clerks using those field records. I discovered later, the dangers of trying to pay off meter readers or clerks were higher than expected. Acting as a workers compensation investigator interviewing the company's internal audit team, one of my Agents uncovered a revealing fact. The water company employed redundant measuring and reporting systems, designed to validate water consumption by their larger customers.

I returned to the factory to engage in a brainstorming exercise. I reviewed every aspect of the manufacturing process. My investigation began at the manufactured end product. From there, I worked my way back to the beginning. My journey ended in the mechanical room, at the water meter. Nothing. No helpful ideas. There wasn't anything I could find within the facility to engender a solution. I knew a fleet of water tankers could bring in water, and take it out; thereby assisting efforts to conceal actual water usage for the manufacturing process. The presence of water tankers and trucks would send up a figurative red flag to others, thereby drawing unnecessary attention to H2O's water-related activities.

I was considering an "invisible people" solution to H2O's water consumption. I pondered options while standing in the mechanical room, staring blankly at piping and that rascally water meter. Then, Bingo! I had an idea; and it didn't require any invisible people.

The solution I considered could save me much time and prove to be the perfect solution. If I could get the water meter to report less water usage than actual, then my problem would be solved. Closer inspection revealed a metal tamper-evident serialized security seal protected the device against tampering.

I needed to find two critical components necessary for solving the problem. First, I needed a couple of water meters identical to the one in the mechanical room. I would fly out and see if my favorite OneSeven, Jo, could help me understand the inner mechanism and find a way to reduce indicated usage. Second, I needed Jo, and the indirect assistance of metallurgist daughter Kat, to assist me in counterfeiting an identical duplicate security seal made of the same metal. Jo would handle the need to have the same serial number stamped into the new seal.

I took a series of measurements and photos of the meter and its seal. Using controlled lighting, my OneSeven photographer and I photographed the meter's security seal to determine the precise color with 100% visual accuracy. We took several scrapings of the seal and, with the assistance of a color wheel and a color corrected lighting system, ascertained the exact color for the security device. I saved the scrapings so Kat could do a metallurgical analysis on them.

A Colleague tracked down three new water meters identical to the newly installed meter in the factory. Each one had identification plates. Jo worked through me, with another OneSeven, to accurately duplicate the plate on the factory's meter. My Colleague purchased the three new meters and shipped them to a trusted Cutout. I retrieved the meters from the

Cutout and boarded a plane for the quick flight to collaborate with Jo.

Moments after Jo opened the meter's housing, I proudly beat her to the punch and quickly announced a possible solution. Jo was deathly quiet for about thirty seconds. I thought she was going to tell me I was an idiot. I began to doubt myself and started squirming. When Jo spoke, she said, "Double 'o' Genius!" She was complimenting Cola by calling me a Double "o." It felt smarter than being called 007. *00Genius! I liked the sound of it.*

My idea was to remove the larger of the internal worm screws and slice off 50% of the mechanism's threads. Shaped like a screw, by removing one side of the worm's raised threading, it would only make contact with, and turn, the worm drive wheel during ½ of the worm screw's full 360-degree turn.

Jo took measurements with a caliper and another strange device. Then she looked at me and smiled. According to Jo, one of her initial concerns dissipated when she measured thread spacing and angles. If the design had been slightly different, the turning worm's ridges wouldn't have seated into the wheel's gears correctly as it turned. That could have jammed and damaged the mechanism.

Jo removed the worm screw from the meter and attached it to one of the computer controlled machines in her high tech machine shop. The device, a metalworking lathe, allowed Jo to carefully remove the screw-like surface from one side of the worm. The final product was so perfect; it appeared factory made.

> ***An aside...***
> While on that "worm drive" trip to work with Jo, I appreciated and accepted an invitation by James and Jo to join them for Sunday breakfast. It turned out to be a large gathering.
>
> I thought I would be joining James and Jo, perhaps with Hank, Kat, and Gary coming along as well. To my delight and surprise, James invited his parents Mr. JK Bottles

and his lovely wife, Marta. Jo also asked her delightful father, Kenneth, and his new young bride, Jacquelyn, to meet us as well. Juan and Bambi Tips, close friends of James and Jo from Florida also dined with us that morning. The Tips brought along their kids Shay, Amby, and Tracy. I'd met them all over the years. Great people!

Every single person attending that large breakfast gathering unexpectedly witnessed a performance we won't soon forget. Jo chose a restaurant owned by one of my former Client's, Gwen Jeffries. Jo hoped her family and friends would rekindle relationships, while enjoying an excellent morning meal. She expected everyone would benefit from lively interesting conversations. Instead, it turned into a gastro-centric memory-creating adventure unparalleled in Cola's experience.

As we were being seated, a rather large woman was placing a breakfast order at a nearby table. I overheard the woman ask the server for "a triple order of flapjacks, two pitchers of orange juice, a breakfast bowl filled with butter, and three bottles of maple syrup."

I recall thinking, "No wonder she's overweight."

Her immense girth made even more sense after the server delivered the most massive stack of pancakes I'd ever seen, along with the pitchers of OJ, a cereal bowl piled high with whipped butter, and three syrup dispensers. *Yikes!* Delivered to the table on a large metal pizza platter, the carbopacking stack was about 16" in diameter and nearly a foot high. That platter and the other breakfast components easily contained more than 5,000 calories.

The round woman picked up a butter knife. As she began licking her swollen lips, she dug into the large bowl of butter. Then she thoroughly coated the top cake with about a quarter inch of butter.

Kenneth looked around to see why JK was working hard but failing to contain his laughter. JK's face was beet red. It looked like he'd overdosed on betanin, the red pigment found in beets. As Kenneth turned toward the focus of JK's attention, his eyebrows rose high on his forehead. His eyes and mouth opened wide in astonishment. JK's entire body began bouncing up and down as he worked to contain himself. Kenneth slowly said "Wow!" and broke out laughing.

JK looked at Kenneth and managed to blurt out, "You think?"

Bambi was laughing tears onto Juan's ear, trying to contain her giggles. Juan's mouth was agape and, like Kenneth, his eyes were wide in disbelief.

As Marta told JK to "Shush!," Jacquelyn implored her husband to act like an adult when in a public place. She should have ignored her husband and, instead, focused her disdain on the big woman's next actions.

As we watched in astonishment, the woman poured far too much maple syrup onto the butter covering the top pancake. She made multiple circular paths around the hotcake, while dramatically raising and lowering the glass and chrome syrup dispenser. It was the kind of container that requires users to press their thumbs down on a lever, necessary to slide open the familiar trap door; thereby releasing the sweet nectar.

My shock turned to horror as she completed her sugary pour and brought the syrup dispenser to her mouth. As it neared that gaping fleshy hole, a giant pink tongue lumbered out between her fat lips. That swollen tongue left a long shiny trail of saliva on the dispenser as she licked off syrup remaining on the rim of the container. I was reminded of the slimy trail left by a snail crawling across a leaf. There was a collective inhalation of air at our table.

At the same time, Marta dropped a white ceramic mug and spilled hot coffee across the table. About half our party witnessed the mating of the woman's tongue and the syrup dispenser. The other half gasped as Marta's coffee cup crashed to the table, without a smidgen of response from Marta. The spilled coffee ran to Marta's right, where Jacquelyn was sitting. Bambi began waving her hands and jumped up with a white cloth napkin as the hot fluid started dripping onto Jacquelyn's lap. Jacquelyn didn't seem to notice as Bambi busied herself, cleaning up the hot mess. Bambi barked at Juan and told him to "get with the program and give me your napkin." Juan wasn't paying attention. He, too, was mesmerized by the theater at the adjoining calorie-filled table.

I glanced at my other breakfast mates. Kat sat frozen in her seat. She'd been watching the obese woman's actions. Kat had been about to decorate her own pancakes with the contents from an identical syrup dispenser when the uncivilized woman licked the chrome-colored container. Kat looked like a seated mannequin, with a frozen look of disgust on her face. The dispenser in her hand was stock-still in time and place. If I didn't know better, I might have thought Kat was staring at a plate of rotting intestines. In slow motion, Kat sat the container down and began to repeatedly wipe her hands on the cloth napkin resting on her lap. Then she brought both hands back up to the table and slowly pushed her breakfast away.

After a few moments, Juan noticed Kat. He erupted into a big belly laugh as Kat's frozen body reflected shock and pure disgust. Between his belly laughs, Juan whispered "Jabba the Hutt!"; then our entire table erupted in laughter. Miss Lid Licker didn't seem to notice.

Each time she finished eating the pancake at the top of the heap, the giant woman repeated her dramatic lathering of butter, as well as the pouring and slobbering lick routine. Miss Lid Licker repeatedly lathered, poured, masticated and licked her way, layer after layer, to the bottom cake. She finished with a loud prolonged watery belch.

The disgustingly predictable routine gave everyone at our table an opportunity to watch the woman slobber all over the restaurant's syrup jar. We were all witnesses to that utterly disgusting performance. As I recall, few at our table finished eating breakfast that morning. Most of us never touched our food.

I'll be perfectly honest with my Readers. I've not been inclined to use one of those dispensers since witnessing that disgusting scene; and don't believe I'll ever do so again. *Yuck!*

Back to The Meter...
After my plumbing OneSeven installed the reengineered meter and tested the metered flow against the gallons received post-meter, he determined that 1000 gallons actually received was recorded as 502 gallons. The CEO was thrilled. So much so, he sweetened my contract by throwing in a family vacation for Treena, the kids, and yours truly. I felt guilty and gave the same vacation to My Colleagues, Jo, and the other OneSeven's involved in the project.

Before leaving the factory that weekend, a thought crossed my mind. I know if I were in the business of selling vast quantities of water to a factory, I'd hedge my bet by making sure I wasn't under billing the client. To satisfy my curiosity, I walked to an area outside the facility near the mechanical room. As I surveyed the area, I discovered a rectangular concrete and steel cover resting in a steel frame embedded in the asphalt, just outside a nearby fence. It was near the property line but within the utility company easement.

Lifting the heavy lid by its handle, I discovered another water meter, identical to the mechanical room's model, ensconced in a steel box. *Ah Ha! Two meters on the same water service line!*

I'd left the remaining water meters with Jo. A quick phone call to my favorite OneSeven brought her up to speed. I provided her with a new serial number for the seal and information from the second meter's identification plate. I also transmitted several digital photos to Jo so she could appropriately age the new meter. I knew she'd be shipping out a perfect counterfeit the following day.

After finishing with Jo, I decided to contact The CEO at his hotel. He was in town for final pre-launch activities associated with the new factory. I told the man we needed to meet and said it was an urgent matter.

The CEO joined me at the manufacturing facility. I directed him to the outside water meter. The color drained from his face. He thanked me profusely for considering the need and taking steps necessary for replacing the second meter. I informed him, in addition to swapping out the exterior meter, we should modify one or two additional meters. He stammered something about the number of meters the "&%#@ water company" needed to monitor a single factory.

Once he calmed down and I had an opportunity to apologize, I told him it was clear the water company took water consumption seriously, and wouldn't be happy if they discovered what we'd done. I said we wouldn't use the additional meters for the factory. I informed him they were for his farmland in the same county. He told me the company didn't own other property in the area; especially farm property. I agreed but followed up by letting him know he needed his Chief Product Engineer to figure out the number of acres he needed to purchase to handle a specific rotation of crops.

He asked why. I told him he'd be in considerable trouble if the water utility discovered he was stealing water, by only paying for 50% of the factory's volume. He was advised to purchase a farm and plant crops, with a water consumption volume approximating H2O's factory consumption. If he used "Cola Meters" to increase apparent farm water usage to levels to make up for the theft, he might be better positioned to assist himself if he became a defendant in a lawsuit brought forth by the water utility. Modified "Cola Meters" registering water usage much higher than actual could reflect a positive justifiable intent on

H2O's part. In fact, that might result in the water utility deciding to void any post-discovery legal action against H2O.

I reminded The CEO that Cola is a problem solver. He had a problem and purchasing a farm would solve a potentially critical problem. He stood there looking down, nodding. Then he raised his head and focused his gaze on my eyes.

After a moment he relaxed and appeared relieved. The CEO smiled and thanked me. He said he had been having a difficult time sleeping. He said, "Cola when I met you and shared our need, I was reticent to make the commitment and sign your contract. I'm not comfortable working with a Corporate Spy, and I'm not comfortable stealing from one of our vendors. That screwed up my ability to sleep well. My wife told me I need to see my doctor and also change whatever is going on at work.

> "I went to my doctor, and he sent me to a heart specialist. The cardiologist scolded me for drinking too much coffee. I've been making up for my lack of sleep by drinking more than a dozen cups of coffee every day. Too much caffeine triggered atrial fibrillation. You know what that is, right? The A-Fib was making my heart jump like a bowl of jello, and the doc said I was going to spin off a clot and clog my brain. I'm at risk for a stroke.
>
> "Realizing my wife and the heart doc are correct, I almost pulled the plug on the project. Now I'm glad I didn't. You've given me an excellent opportunity to make things right before I damage the reputations of H2O and myself. You're a real prince Cola. Thank you.
>
> "I want you to know. I underestimated your honesty and professionalism. Please forgive me. Your involvement and this additional proposal will go far in securing our commercial interests while helping this tired old company officer get some much-needed sleep. Thank you. Thank you."

It felt good, knowing my logic and ethics coincided to assist the CEO with his medical needs. Gratifying.

An aside...
I was challenged by a Client some years before when he disputed what I'd said in a private meeting. He convinced himself I promised something I had not. After that, whenever I met with Clients, I recorded our conversations. Those recordings cleared up confusion on more than one occasion. In this case, the recording of The CEO's appreciative remarks provided Readers of this book with an absolutely accurate account of the words he spoke that day.

Back to The Factory...
The CEO showed his appreciation by tripling my contract before I even replaced the concrete lid on the exterior water meter. I recommended The Engineer's calculations include an increase in reportable water usage. I suggested H2O's overall consumption be at least 10% more than farm + factory actuals. Doing so might obviate any post-discovery outrage. After all, who can complain when being paid 10% more than expected? It's a Baker's Dozen approach.

An aside...
A Baker's Dozen = 13
There are many theories regarding the origin of "A Baker's Dozen." Most have their foundation in medieval England, where bakers often misrepresented their goods. An underlying theme in many theories is related to cheating, involving weights and quantities. To avoid a beating, a baker selling the King a dozen loaves of bread would throw in a 13th loaf to make sure he remained in the King's good graces.

Back to Water Consumption Manipulation...
H2O's Chief Product Engineer redesigned the worm drive's tooth count for two new farmland water meters. The calculations provided by The Engineer were, according to Jo, nearly perfect in balancing water usage between the farm and factory. The Engineer considered crop types in a rotation schedule, usable acreage, average annual precipitation, and a few other factors to reasonably predict yearly water usage at the farm. He then increased his recommendations for the new water meters to reflect higher consumption, to account for the under-reported

water used at the factory; and an additional ten percent was added in for good measure.

Jo went to work, ran a plethora of calculations to verify the recommended tooth count. Once satisfied with the engineering design, she constructed two new worm screws and worm drive wheels for the two replacement water meters.

The entire project came off without a hitch. The farm, just like the factory, had redundant metering systems. I'm thankful I discovered the meter doubling activity by the water utility and am glad The CEO agreed to my recommendation to purchase a farm, to offset the theft resulting from the altered factory meters.

More than a decade has passed, and the company's formula remains intact and private. We closed the gate BEFORE the cows began scattering, in a shrewd Counterintelligence move. If a competitor had successfully obtained water usage data and reverse-engineered the formula, the costs to H2O would have been excessive. At that juncture, H2O's options would have been inadequate; and Counterespionage efforts would have been risky, costly, and of minimal value. As you can see, H2O deftly placed the horse *before* the cart, by taking steps to leverage his Counterintelligence opportunities.

I've not done any other work for H2O, but receive an anonymous "Thank You" card each January. There is no return address, and each postmark is from a different city. I suspect the sender travels a lot and sends the Thank You card from different cities as he or she travels for business. The person signs it, "Water Worm."

hmmm, I wonder who that could be...

Afternoon Delight

The Only Human Being on Waikiki Beach

Skookum Jim and I have rendezvoused, laughed, and reminisced all over the United States. From Hawaii and Alaska, to New York, New Jersey, and Connecticut, south to Texas and Mexico. We've visited friends in Belize and traveled to Arizona and Las Vegas in the desert southwest. We've cruised with our wives in the Caribbean, jet skied lakes, hiked Nevada's deserts, skied scenic Lake Tahoe, and traveled to World Series baseball games.

I'd like to briefly share one particular event with you that involved my dear friend Jim. Four close friends landed at Oahu International Airport on Tuesday, November 23, 1982. We traveled to Hawaii to enjoy a Thanksgiving vacation in the Hawaiian Islands.

As our taxi was traveling to Honolulu from the airport, we heard an Emergency Broadcast System announcement on the taxi's AM radio. Unknown to any of us before that moment, a hurricane was bearing down on the volcanic island chain. Named Hurricane Ewa, it was expected to make landfall later that evening. Residents were advised to prepare for a loss of electricity lasting several days, beginning that night.

While the livery vehicle continued toward our accommodations, we realized we had a problem. Our hotel was a high rise tourist property a few blocks from the beach. According to the emergency announcement, most population centers should be prepared to be without electricity during and after Ewa's landfall. Dark hotel, no food, no working elevators, and other issues became part of our conversation.

Then one of our group came up with an idea. Jim suggested we put our brains and backs to work by volunteering for the Red Cross. We had the taxi driver stop briefly at our hotel so we could check in and drop off our bags. The taxi driver was asked to make a second short diversion, for a brief visit to Waikiki Beach before proceeding to Oahu's Red Cross headquarters.

We took turns walking out to the beach. I believe it was about 3:30 in the afternoon and sunny. No clouds were in sight, although there was plenty of wind.

When it was my turn, I remember thinking it felt like I was standing in a sandblasting booth. An unrelenting horizontal onslaught of flying salt water and sand tore into my skin. It was very uncomfortable. However, as I look back on that afternoon visit, I always do so with a smile on my face. I vividly recall the minute or two I stood on the beach, looking in one direction toward Diamond Head, then turning the other way toward downtown and the harbor. For that brief period, I had the distinct experience of being the only human being standing on Waikiki beach at 3:30 in the afternoon. Nobody was on the beach in either direction.

Afternoon Delight

We were directly in front of the famous Outrigger Waikiki Hotel on some of the most famous sands in the world. I stood there and wondered how many decades had passed since anyone, on a sunny afternoon, held the distinction of being the only person visible in either direction from that area. The view was extraordinary. I lingered just a little longer to relish my moments of absolute solitude on the sands of Waikiki Beach that afternoon. It was a most unusual delightful experience.

ACTUAL REGALIA FROM COLA'S RED CROSS GIG

As Cola and his buddies entered the Red Cross, we discovered the frenzy had not yet started. We introduced ourselves to a beaming Red Cross representative who assessed our backgrounds and skill sets. They split us up, and we didn't see one another until after Ewa had passed. It's been many years since that day, and the details have become a little fuzzy. I believe Jim's assignment was similar to mine. I don't recall what the others were assigned to manage.

Red Cross officials instructed me to commandeer an elementary school in the pineapple fields on the west side of the island. Showing me a map of the area, I was told to familiarize myself with the area. The Red Cross intended to use the school as a shelter and medical triage facility. They assembled a team and placed Cola in command. I had two paramedics and two nurses under my charge; as well as an ambulance. Our convoy included a police escort and two other vehicles. One carried a large emergency generator and the other included food, water, and miscellaneous items.

After loading our vehicles with supplies and everyone was ready, the convoy headed out. The patrol car in the lead and our ambulance had the emergency lights flashing and sirens wailing. The generator truck was directly behind us. I don't recall if our little convoy had a police car in the rear, although I do remember a second police vehicle later on our trip when a downed electric line blocked the road. If memory serves me correctly, a few uprooted palm trees littered the highway. I recall driving into fields to get around some of the obstacles.

We arrived at the elementary school safely. I went about organizing my Team, as well as locals already onsite who volunteered to assist us with setting up and securing the shelter. I recall redirecting a large group of indigenous farm workers, after noticing that a member of my Team had positioned them at tables and chairs near potentially dangerous glass windowpanes. Not good. I reminded everyone on my Team about our pre-mission brief; and the importance of following the guidance we received. We relocated everyone to a kitchen and another area that didn't have windows.

A RED CROSS VOLUNTEER

Red Cross Hurricane Ewa Planning Meeting November 1982

The indigenous people coming to the shelter were poor, scared, and grateful. Some were hungry, others very thirsty. Fortunately, in addition to our medical supplies, we also had food and water.

It was a long, noisy night, and most of the injuries we treated were minor. The next day, Wednesday, we returned to Red Cross headquarters. Once there, we were directed to do whatever we could to round up generators from retail businesses that sold generators, from government entities and military bases, and construction contractors. That day is a blur to me, after a long sleepless night managing the pineapple field shelter.

The following day was Thanksgiving. We spent most of the day driving the island in a rented car, trying to find something to eat.

We finally rounded up hamburgers on the far side of the island in Kailua or Kahaluu (I cannot recall which community). After satisfying our hunger, we returned to Waikiki and marveled at beach-side hotel storm damage. Water and sand filled most of the underground parking facilities. It was like a ghost town. We turned in our rental car and went back to our hotel. We climbed many stairs to reach our rooms, changed clothes (no water for showers), and headed back down in the darkened stairwell.

A few hours later we finally enjoyed a bit of touristy Hawaii when we took a Thanksgiving Day Sunset Dinner Cruise on a sailboat. Finally. Food and drink. It was a beautiful calm evening and a most excellent cruise in Mamala Bay.

◇ ◇ ◇

Then the fun started. There was a mass exodus from the islands. We took a bus to the airport daily, for nearly a week, trying to get a flight out - anywhere. We were young and disheveled. Day after day airline personnel boarded families, people wearing ties, and other respectable looking travelers. Finally, Skookum Jim and a fellow named Steve boarded a flight. Two of us remained for two more days.

On the fifth or six day, Cola had had enough. I was already a Corporate Spy with a proven track record. At that point, I had amassed many successful Operations involving my need to perform before an audience of one, or more. That morning I decided to put Cola on stage.

I told my buddy Rick to sit on a chair where everyone could easily see him. I told Rick to "Look retarded."

Be nice people. It was 1982. We spoke differently back then.

I told Rick to drop his chin and drool a little. Not too much. Just enough to be seen. Then I approached the podium.

I got into character by repeating words said to have been spoken by the 19th Century Sioux leader, Chief Sitting Bull.

> "Inside me are two dogs. One is evil and mean. The other is good and kind. They fight with one another all the time. When someone asks me which one wins, I tell them, 'The one I feed the most.'"

At that moment I decided to feed the mean dog. Cola's not an evil man. I can, however, get mean on occasion; and this would be one such occasion. Looking angry and shaking my finger, I loudly addressed a woman I'd seen every day working that podium for the airline. I said, "Ma'am, you've seen my retarded brother and me every day for the past six days. We come early in the morning and don't leave until the last flight of the day is boarded, late into the evening. I've been pleasant and polite the entire time. However, this cannot continue, and I'm done being nice.

"Look at my retarded brother over there. He and I finished our last pineapple this morning. We're out of food. He is wearing his last diaper. He's out of diapers, and I'm out of patience. I don't care how you do it, but I'm telling you and everyone within earshot (that included many people, because I was projecting my voice and it carried a long way), I've had enough. I'm tired of being treated like a second-class citizen. However, all of that is changing right now. You WILL board us on a flight, TODAY! Do you understand?"

She did, and we were on the next flight out. It was heading for the Pacific Northwest. Too bad the destination wasn't southern California. Heck, I was proud of Rick and know we, with a little Cola Magic, could have gotten him a gig in Hollywood. His Academy Award performance, without question, was the reason we had seats on a big beautiful bird leaving that Hurricane ravaged island.

Taking Charge

Cola's various adventures often turned into great learning experiences. Success in espionage requires self-control, correctly assessing situations, reasoned reactions, and the ability to take charge when necessary. Those are ingredients for leadership. Great leaders never accept the "I've arrived" falsehood. Leaders never arrive in the land of perfection. Although great leaders continually seek perfection, they recognize their flaws. In spite of failures, they continue learning and bettering themselves.

My hurricane adventure in Hawaii was successful in many ways. I learned a lot and found value in helping others. However, many years later I discovered I'd lost some of my youthful initiative.

The discovery was painful when I realized I'd done absolutely nothing when I could have helped. Two young men burned to death, while I waited for somebody else to step up and help. That experience reminded me of my flaws. I failed to act and squandered my leadership abilities because I'd mothballed a measure of Cola's self-starting initiative.

My family was returning from a wonderful camping trip, that doubled as an opportunity for a clandestine meeting with a Colleague. Our campsite and the risk-laden critical meeting were in a setting far from the grid, away from electronic surveillance, and in a perfect location for Pigeon Memory. The Great

Outdoors. My secret work-related meeting lasted a mere thirty minutes. The camping trip provided three or four days of excellent rest and relaxation for the Fugelere family.

The drive home took us down a slightly narrow winding mountain road. It was the end of a long holiday weekend. Although traffic was relatively heavy in the direction we were traveling, traffic coming toward us was anything but light. As our truck and camp trailer rounded a corner, several cars coming toward us were flashing their lights. Curious. Were they trying to tell us a ticket-writing Police Officer was around the corner? A wild animal stopped in the road? An accident?

As we rounded the corner, I received the answer. Heavy black smoke rose above the trees. A pickup truck was in a low area off the left side of the road, a few hundred yards ahead. The sedan in front of us sped up as if he were rushing to the accident. Then the car came to a quick stop a mere hundred yards from the crash. The driver jumped out of his car and ran toward the smoke. As I slowed and came up behind the man's car, I recall commenting to my wife about people sticking their noses into situations they shouldn't.

"Look," I said. "there are five cars in front of his and more than a few people standing around the burning truck. He shouldn't be getting in the way. He just wants to see it up close. A rubbernecker!"

Treena said, "Cola, he could be a doctor or a relative of the people in the accident."

My wife was correct. Not about the man's profession or his relationship to those involved in the car crash. She was right to address my cynicism.

A few moments later the man ran back to his car, opened the trunk, and retrieved a hammer. Leaving his trunk ajar, he sprinted away, returning to the burning truck. I watched him vault into the bed of the pickup truck. He beat out the back window with the hammer. A few minutes later he had finished cutting the seat belts off three children, and removed them through the rear window of the burning vehicle. Once the kids were safely in the arms of onlookers, The Good Samaritan returned to the truck. He tried, but failed to remove the two kids remaining in the front seat.

He and others were standing a short distance from the driver's door when I heard sirens wailing. A fire truck and ambulance passed by us and approached the burning vehicle, as fire poured from the engine compartment.

A few firefighters moved onlookers back while others assessed the situation with the truck. Medics were busy checking out the three children and an older couple. All of a sudden I heard a whoop whoop whoop and watched a helicopter touch down. Several firefighters jumped from the chopper.

As I was watching those activities, someone walked by my truck. I was just sitting there doing nothing; trying to stay out of the way.

I asked the passerby what was happening. The passerby informed me five kids in the small pickup truck were traveling in the same direction as us. According to the passerby, the pickup's young driver tried to pass a vehicle. It appeared to be a no passing zone, with limited forward visibility. A large SUV was coming from the other direction, resulting in a head-on collision.

The passerby said people were standing around watching the truck burn when a guy appeared out of nowhere. He confirmed what we thought we'd witnessed. Without assistance from anyone else, The Good Samaritan had, indeed, pulled three younger kids from the backseat of the truck; but couldn't get the two older kids out of the front seat. The collision pushed in the front of the truck, jamming all four doors and pinning the legs of the two boys.

According to the passerby, the two boys still trapped in the vehicle were conscious and aware of their circumstances. My heart went out to them. That's a painful memory for Cola. That ache in my being remains to this day.

I asked why the firefighters were just standing there. The passerby told me heat from the fire was keeping them away from the trapped boys. According to the passerby, the truck's engine block was made out of magnesium and couldn't be put out with water. Adding water to a magnesium fire only makes it hotter. The passerby also told us some "Hot Shots" were flown into to make sure the vehicle fire didn't turn into a wildfire.

We wanted to know about the people in the SUV. The passerby said they weren't hurt very bad and should be okay. Same for the three kids pulled from the back seat. I thanked the passerby for the information, and he departed.

THE GOOD SAMARITAN SAVED THREE

Terrible. It was an awful scene. We sat in our truck and watched those two boys burn alive. The pickup eventually became fully engulfed in flames. Once the fire extinguished itself, the operator of a large commercial truck winched the charred vehicle onto his truck's flatbed. As the truck slowly passed by us, we prayed for the souls of the two kids.

Shortly after that, The Good Samaritan returned to the trunk of his car. I got out of my vehicle and walked over to him. I thanked him for taking the initiative and saving the three kids. After applauding him for his quick thinking, I asked him what prompted him to take action.

He told me some years earlier he watched someone die as a whole bunch of people stood by, including him, just watching. Afterward, he was ashamed of himself. He said he kept waiting for someone to do something, but nobody did anything. He said his guilt resulted in a personal promise to never again be a stationary part of the scenery. One thing he learned about people through that earlier situation was reinforced as he was working to save the kids in the truck. Human nature is to stand by and wait for somebody else to do something.

He taught me a valuable lesson that day. I, too, vowed never again to be mashed potatoes just sitting around doing nothing. That decision to never be a lookie-loo bystander was more tangible than I could ever imagine.

Twice in the coming month I would be put to the test. I'm happy to say I didn't fail and was successful in possibly saving the life of a woman. I'm not sure if a man involved in an accident I tried to help survived or not. Here's how it all unfolded.

On a sunny, beautiful morning two weeks later I was traveling in a mountainous rural area. I was about to merge onto a steep divided highway with two lanes for each direction of travel. A large tractor-trailer passed by, as it traveled downhill.

Heavily loaded with giant copper anodes, the semi was uttering a deep base sound caused by the compression engine braking system, referred to as Jake Brakes, as it traveled down the steep grade. The driver was slowing the vehicle on the steep drop toward the Colorado River far below. Sometime later, Justin, an expert in the copper ingot business community, told me the three bundles of anodes on that rig weighed more than 15,000 pounds each. The total load topped out at a whopping 46,000 pounds.

Ten or fifteen seconds after the big rig passed, a pickup truck fully loaded with tables, chairs, and a big cabinet flew by. Both vehicles were traveling in the right lane. As I pulled onto the highway behind the pickup, I realized it was moving much faster than the eighteen wheeler in front of it. I was wondering when he was going to slow or change lanes. He was approaching the trailer far too fast.

All of a sudden, without seeing any brake lights at all, I watched the pickup truck hit the back of the trailer. The back end of the small truck flew up into the air, then came crashing back down. Although the semi's trailer never appeared to move at all, the big truck's cab jerked, twisted, and jumped. The driver of the big rig tried to stop, but his weight and momentum carried him a considerable distance down the mountain before it came to a standstill.

I stomped on my brakes and slid to a stop behind the pickup truck. Remembering the lesson I learned by watching the kids burn to death, I hit the hazard lights, jumped out of my car, and ran to the pickup truck. The front end was smashed and partially shoved under the truck's cab. The horn was stuck and blared incessantly. Through smoky white steam, I could see the truck had a single occupant. His head was resting on the steering wheel, and I could see he was either unconscious or dead.

As people began to gather around, I pulled out my flip phone and dialed 9-1-1, while simultaneously trying to open the driver's door. It wouldn't budge. Jammed. After watching the pickup truck burn two weeks before, I was concerned about a fire. I wanted to get the door open, so I could remove the man if a fire broke out. I ran around to the other side of the truck as the 9-1-1 Operator answered the phone. The passenger side door wouldn't open either. I noticed a cantaloupe-sized rock nearby.

Running back to the driver's door, I tried to break the glass by gently banging the rock against the window. My fear of hurting the driver with the rock, or flying glass, kept me from hitting it harder. I couldn't get the window to break or crack.

Running around to the passenger side once more, I noticed about a dozen people standing within a few feet of the truck, doing absolutely nothing. That was me, two weeks earlier. I didn't give the rubberneckers much thought, because my priority at the moment was to try and save the driver. Holding my phone in one hand, I struck the window as hard as I could with the rock in my other hand. Boing. The heavy stone just bounced off the window. At that point, the 9-1-1 Operator possessed all the information she needed. I told her I had to go. Then I hung up.

Now I had two hands to use in my quest to break the window. Boing, boing, boing. I couldn't break that silly window. Later I learned a small sharp object can be more effective than a large round rock, when trying to break a window.

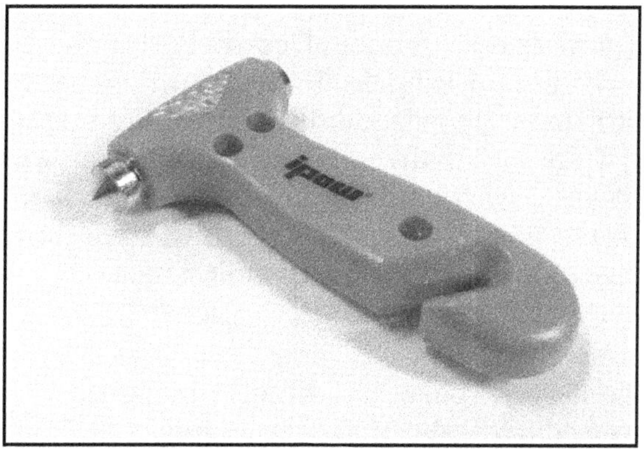

IPOW Hammer and Seat Belt Cutter

> ***An aside...***
> My entire family and many close friends are aware of my failed attempts to break the truck's windows that day. Our vehicles now carry quick escape tools that have a pointed hammer and a seat belt cutter built into a single device.

Back to The Accident...
I dropped the rock and ran around to the back of the pickup truck. I noticed the rear window had been partially broken out by the furniture. It must have happened when the back end of the truck stopped suddenly and flew up into the air. After throwing a dining room table and a few chairs out of the pickup, I pulled a china cabinet out of the way. I tried climbing through the hole in the window. I cut my forearms and elbows as I entered the broken window. Small pieces of glass, embedded in the rubber window gasket, were sticking up and made the tight fit even more difficult. Backing out, I broke a chair and used one of the legs to widen the hole. Climbing back in, I cut myself further, but that was the last thing on my mind. Seeing white smoke and

fearing fire, I worked quickly as I fought claustrophobia and an oppressive fear that I might become trapped; then burned alive.

I placed my legs behind the man's back without touching him, then kicked the door until it popped open. Cola thought the driver might have a broken neck. I feared I might accidentally nudge him and sever his spinal cord. Fortunately, that never happened. My phone rang as I was crawling back out of the truck's cab through the jagged hole. Thinking it might be the 9-1-1 Operator, I answered the call. Sure enough, it was the same Operator. While I was running around the truck to get to the injured driver, I passed the growing crowd of bystanders on the way. The Operator informed me an ambulance was en route. She asked about the man's condition.

I felt his wrist for a pulse. Nothing. Moving up to his neck, I carefully pressed my index and middle finger against his carotid artery. Nothing. I told the 9-1-1 Operator he was gone and suggested she inform the medics. As I was saying that, I felt a very slight change in his neck. Focusing on my fingers, I felt a light pulse and immediately informed the 9-1-1 Operator.

She and I agreed I wouldn't move the man unless it became critically necessary. It was about then that Cola realized the steamy white smoke I'd seen was probably a combination of airbag powder and steam from the radiator. I relaxed a little and awaited the arrival of first responders.

In this case, I guess I was the actual first responder. The Medics, Firefighters, and Police Officers that arrived a little later were second responders; and the bystanders were 100% MIA (Missing In Action). If nothing else, watching those two boys leave this world had a thin silver lining. I would never again be an MIA bystander.

When help arrived, the emergency officials all rushed to help me. My arms were bleeding all over the asphalt. I told them I was okay, but the man in the truck was in bad shape.

An aside...
Crawling through that shattered truck window left me with a small raised scar near my right elbow. Now and then I catch myself massaging the scar. I'm glad it's there. It warmly reminds me that being a Good Samaritan is both noble and necessary. Rubbing that scar also saddens me, because it symbolizes the lives lost, leading up to the creation of that scar tissue.

Back to The Overcrowded Accident Site...
As I stood there watching the professionals address the needs of the helpless accident victim, I realized emergency vehicles filled the entire right lane; as well as bystander vehicles, my car, and the two trucks involved in the accident. People were everywhere, and traffic was flying by in the left lane.

I was shocked. Here was a terrible accident and people were standing everywhere, yet the self-centered drivers shooting by were more interested in getting to their destinations without delay, than cautiously approaching and passing the accident site. To this day, I'm amazed at the narcissistic behavior I witnessed on that crowded highway.

After affixing a collar to the man's neck, he was removed from the truck and laid on the ground. His heart stopped. CPR was started by a medic, as others placed wires on his chest and performed additional duties. I don't recall how long they worked on him before transport to the hospital.

After the ambulance took the man away, I walked over to the truck driver impacted by the pickup truck. He introduced me to his wife. They were understandably upset. She said when the pickup hit the heavy trailer, it hit them so hard it knocked her out of her seat.

While we were talking, a firefighter pulled me aside. He said my wounds needed bandaging. During my treatment, the first responder said, "Nothing you did could have improved the situation."

He believed the driver of the pickup truck had a heart attack, or some other major medical issue, before hitting the back of the eighteen wheeler. Although he couldn't be sure. According to the firefighter Cola's observations, those of another driver that was coming up behind me in the left lane before the accident, and the big rig driver, suggested the injured man was in trouble before the crash. He said that would explain why the pickup accelerated rapidly down the mountain and into the back of the trailer.

A few days later I looked up the Officer that took my report. I asked how the man was doing. The Officer apologized. He told me privacy laws and department rules prohibited him from telling me anything about the man. He then dropped his chin to his chest. I often wonder if that was his way of saying the man didn't make it or that he wasn't doing well.

◇ ◇ ◇

Cola was tested once more, about two weeks later. I was inside a retail store next to a busy highway. A fellow approached me and said something unusual was going on down the road. Looking out the front window I couldn't believe my eyes. A car was in the middle of the highway, perpendicular to the flow of traffic. Vehicles were not slowing down and simply swerved around the stalled vehicle. The stalled car took up both lanes on the northbound side. I was a few hundred yards away but could see someone's head face down on the steering wheel.

Without hesitation, I jumped up and ran to my car. I could have sprinted to the stopped vehicle faster, but after watching traffic blow by the smashed pickup truck two weeks earlier, I wanted a barrier to protect me from the glass and steel missiles barreling down the highway. I shot out onto the road and came to a stop about twenty feet from the stationary vehicle. Angling my car to cover about half of each lane, I hoped it would protect the lady I could see in the stationary vehicle. Of course, I was worried about Cola's well-being too.

Jumping out of my car, I rushed to the stopped vehicle and opened the door. Although it was a sweltering day, I discovered the inside of her car was freezing. No telling how long it had been stopped there with the A/C running. I touched the skin of the person. She was ice cold and unresponsive. I feared she might be dead. Checking her neck, I felt a pulse and called 9-1-1.

The Operator asked me a series of questions. As I was answering one of her questions, she suddenly interrupted me. The Operator directed me to the back of the car and asked me to give her the license plate information. After I complied with her request, she said, "Okay. We know what's going on. We know her. The woman has diabetes and is likely hypoglycemic. Low blood sugar. She's probably in insulin shock. Please standby. The medics are almost on the scene."

I watched the medics roll up as she was thanking me. They jumped out of their rig and quickly assessed the situation. One of them had a small packet similar to those filled with ketchup that comes with french fries at fast food restaurants. I think the package was either white or earth tone in color. The medic tore the end open and began squeezing a brown substance into the lady's mouth. After a minute or so she began to stir. A few minutes later she was woozy but conscious.

I'm thankful I had an opportunity to help the woman. Fortunately, nobody broadsided her while her car sat in the middle of the highway. Here was another silver lining that grew out of lessons learned from The Good Samaritan on that tragic day when two young souls departed this earth far too early.

◇ ◇ ◇

The most important lesson in all of this? Somebody needs to take charge. I don't sit back and allow others to guide my destiny. I'm not a lemming.

Cola is a leader who will take charge when necessary, even if taking action means placing Cola at risk. It's the right thing to do. I suggest others learn from my experiences. By doing so, you might have an opportunity to save someone's life.

Take Charge!

◇ ◇ ◇

A Personal Note from Steven Fowler

Shortly after publishing the first edition of this book, I had the misfortune of coming upon a terrible accident. Taking a cue from Cola's "Take Charge" Chapter, I didn't hesitate and did my level best to assist the victims of that accident. Here are my recollections and impressions relating to the events of that evening:

> *For the record, I did not consume any alcohol on that day, either before or after the accident.*
>
> *Moreover, I do not use mind altering medications, illegal drugs, or any other related substances; either prescribed or recreationally. My thoughts and memories are clear. The actions I took occurred with deliberate sober seriousness.*

THE MASS CASUALTY INCIDENT

Generally Speaking...
When most people hear the phrases, "Mass Casualty Incident" and "Multiple Casualty Incident" they often think of school shootings, horrific traffic accidents, and airplane crashes; involving dozens, if not a hundred or more, casualties. To be fair, that is a good general term for such events.

More Specifically...
The accepted definition of a Mass Casualty Incident (MCI) in the emergency response arena is:

> "Those incidents where available resources and personnel are overwhelmed by the number and type of casualties involved."

Yes, it could be a downed airliner. On the other hand, an MCI could be a small plane accident, involving three critically injured occupants, attended to by a 2 person emergency response team.

I'm a conscientious person who has an innate desire to help others, where and when I can; especially when physical or mental stresses may be involved. Recently I became an active participant in a Mass Casualty Incident (MCI). The NY Times, USA Today, the Washington Post, and many other media outlets reported on the accident. While personally painful, the horrific incident is important for me to revisit and share.

I'd spent the evening visiting my two adult children and, after taking them to dinner, I was returning to my home. The route I took included a nearly 40 mile stretch of a relatively straight two-lane roadway (one lane each side); having few bends and elevation changes. My son lost a friend on that road, and my brother-in-law knew a couple of people who also died nearby. In fact, the worst accident in the county's history occurred on that same roadway, less than five miles from the MCI I'm about to share with you. My wife and others know I don't like driving that road and that I consider it dangerous.

There's just something about the road that continually reminds me that a head-on collision is always a possibility. My son often visits my wife and me, after driving that route. Likewise, Tracey and I use the same roadway because of the time and distances involved. It's simply a faster, shorter route than taking the nearby divided interstate.

As I drove home, I recall thinking, "There aren't many vehicles on the road tonight." I chalked it up to the afternoon and early evening rain in that part of the state. Although it was overcast, dark, and foreboding, I believed the road might be safer than usual due to low traffic counts. The asphalt was dry, and I was relaxed. Setting the cruise control at the posted speed limit, as I habitually do, I instructed Siri to begin playing an audiobook through my Apple Airpods.

After a few miles, I noticed a vehicle behind me. They'd closed the distance in the past minute or two, and I realized they were driving faster than me. Although we'd been traveling in a 65 mile per hour zone, the speed limit dropped to 55 mph, as we approached the intersection at the junction of two state routes. The approaching car didn't appear to slow as the speed limit dropped. The separation between us closed quickly. I'm not particularly fond of headlights in my rearview mirror. I slowed and pulled to the right side of the road, allowing the vehicle behind me to move ahead. Shortly after the car passed, I reentered the roadway and continued toward my home.

Perhaps five or ten minutes later I noticed a white apparition appear out of the blackness. The shape was odd and seemed to be changing. Moreover, it was close. Too close. Slamming on my brakes, I came to a stop much closer to the object than was comfortable. A few more feet and I would have collided with a vehicle that was just involved in a horrific automobile accident.

I realized that strange image before me was a white car with a crushed front end. I think it was the same vehicle that passed me a few minutes earlier. Something I'd initially seen was, indeed, changing. Once stopped, I believed I was seeing dust, radiator steam, and airbag powder filling the air above the vehicle and settling to the ground. *Yikes! A car accident!*

Quickly looking in my rear-view mirror, I determined it was safe to exit my vehicle. Dialing 9-1-1 as I jumped out of my car, I realized screams and pleas for help were coming from different directions. It was overwhelming. Looking to my immediate left, I saw the unfamiliar shape of a dark smashed vehicle resting on its side in the mud, just off the asphalt roadway. The separation between the cars was about 20 to 30 feet.

Directly between the two vehicles, I saw a woman laying on the asphalt, and in the periphery of the beam of my headlights. I later discovered her name. I'll call her "N" for this discussion. She was pleading for help. I ran to her and quickly determined her injuries were very severe, perhaps life-threatening. It was cool outside, and I knew she was going into shock. "N" needed to be covered quickly. I told her I was sorry and I'd do everything I could to assist her. I promised help would arrive shortly.

I knew I didn't have either a jacket or a blanket in my car. I looked around quickly. On a lark, I ran to the white vehicle on my right and peered into the rear passenger side window. I noticed a laundry basket resting on the backseat. The basket appeared to contain freshly laundered clothes. Reaching through the broken window, I collected an armful of clothing and darted back to that poor lady. Throughout those moments cries, moans, and pleas filled my ears.

All the while I was trying to get 9-1-1 on the phone. My phone readout indicated, "No Service." *Yikes!*

I unfolded and carefully draped the laundered clothing on the victim, taking care to avoid even touching her. It was clear, "N's" injuries were severe. I wanted to pat her lightly, as a way of comforting the dear lady. My heart hurt for her. However, I was afraid doing so might cause discomfort or harm her further.

After doing all I thought I could do for her, I ran to the cries of help coming from a woman to my left. As I approached the side of the dark vehicle, I could tell it was on its side, and the roof was facing me. Looking down toward the cries for help, I saw a dark haired lady laying on the ground. I'll refer to her as "K." I could only see the upper half of the lady, as the vehicle was resting atop the lower half of her body. To her left was another person. However, my instincts told me that person was beyond helping. *Oh, my! A fatality accident!*

She told me her name and asked if I could pull her out from under the vehicle. I know better than moving an accident victim. I didn't have the tools, knowledge, or experience to undertake such an activity. Using her name, I apologized and told her we needed to wait until help arrived before moving her. Just then I heard something on my phone and realized the call to 9-1-1 just went through.

I stepped back toward my car and informed the operator I was at the scene of a terrible accident. Although I'd only seen two victims, I could hear someone crying. Another was moaning. Someone was banging on metal somewhere. I told the operator many were hurt. I don't recall if I mentioned one or more might be dead. I said we were located between two waypoints on a 40 miles stretch of road, but I didn't know where. I may have narrowed her understanding of the accident location to a twenty-mile area. Not close enough. Then, the call dropped.

Looking at the iPhone's oleophobic screen, I noticed I still had a signal; even though the call had dropped. *Thank you, Lord!* I immediately phoned my wife and briefly informed her I was "okay," and the accident was "terrible." Then I directed her to use the iPhone tool, "Find iPhone," to figure out where I was, then call 9-1-1 and let them know my location. Hanging up, I went back to work.

I ran to the back of the dark vehicle. Standing at the sideways back end, I realized it was a Chevrolet Suburban. The damage and darkness kept me from knowing earlier what kind of vehicle was lying on its side. The only light back there was coming from my iPhone. The headlights from my vehicle were pointed directly at the white car.

Overwhelming anguish was reflected in the moans and cries for help echoing within the large Chevy. Wanting to open the back door, I stopped myself. I was afraid if I attempted to open the back gate/door I might cause the vehicle to shift and possibly topple onto "K."

I suddenly remembered my wife purchased stocking stuffers for family and friends last Christmas, after hearing about Cola's experiences. Those gifts were IPOW combination Window Breaking Hammers and Seatbelt Cutters. I recalled one nestled in my glove box. I ran to my car and retrieved the tool.

> ***An aside...***
> The IPOW tool I used that night to break out the back window of the Suburban is the same one pictured several pages back in this book. That photograph was taken several months before the accident described here. It is also identical to the model Cola keeps in his vehicles.

Back to the Accident...
When I returned to the rear of the Suburban, I whacked the back window with the tiny orange hammer. The Suburban's rear window shattered instantly and fell to the ground in a heap of thousands of black glass particles. As the rubber window molding swung away from the vehicle and hit me in the chest, my light pierced the darkness. The sight shook the core of my soul.

I can only offer the following to best, albeit briefly, describe what I saw: Seven broken people who had been playing Twister in the heart of a tornado.

I don't mean to be flippant with that statement. It certainly wasn't a game. However, that's the best description I can come up with, using as few words as possible, to describe the tangle of broken bodies in my view; a few in very unnatural positions.

I don't believe I've ever felt more alone in my life. Frustration and helplessness descended on my soul. Empathy for the victims filled my heart. Then I realized the victims were far more alone and fearful than me. I decided to redouble my efforts to console the living and remind them help was on the way.

As I discovered later, eight people involved in that accident would be dead before sunrise the following morning. The only individuals who would survive beyond that night happened to be directly in front of me as I peered into the rear of the Suburban.

The scene I recall inside that large vehicle is painful to consider, and describing it is beyond my ability to share comfortably. Moreover, out of respect for the three survivors, it is better that I avoid further discussion regarding what my eyes beheld when the glass window disintegrated.

> ***An aside...***
> Throughout all of this, a pall of overwhelming fear weighed me down. The only useful visible light in the area was coming from my little Toyota Prius. I feared anyone traveling down the road might think the car was going slow and try to pass at high speed. If that happened, this already terrible situation would become far worse. The danger was equally concerning if any cars came from the other direction. The wrecked white car blocked my vehicle's headlights. I considered moving the Prius. However, the only place I could reasonably relocate it, to alert oncoming vehicles, would result in the beams of my headlights shining directly upon the lady I just covered up. I didn't want to stress "N" further.

Back to the Rear of the Suburban...
There was nothing I could reasonably do for anyone in the seatless back end of the Suburban. They were either dead, dying, or terribly injured. Tangled as they were, untangling them was ill-advised. Fortunately, the dank air and fumes were replaced by fresh air, after I used the IPOW tool to break out the glass hatch at the rear of the vehicle.

I then moved back toward the lady I'd covered with the clothes from the laundry basket. I believe, at that point, "N" was gone from this world. Moving beyond her, I approached the white vehicle and failed to discover additional survivors. After that, I quickly ran a perimeter check to see if anyone else had been ejected away from the accident scene. Looking carefully, I saw nothing of concern - neither people nor children's car seats. *I'm thankful there were no children involved.*

After completing my circuit, I returned to "K" to see how she was doing. She was incredibly calm and brave. When I asked that poor trapped lady if she could describe any injuries, she told me she couldn't feel her legs but was otherwise okay. "K" then asked if I could call her daughter. Looking at my phone, I informed her the signal was gone, but I'd call if it came back.

Just then, I noticed a car coming from the same direction I'd traveled. The emotion at that moment was an overwhelming fear that another vehicle would impact the accident site. I quickly returned to the Prius, turned off the emergency flashers, and repeatedly turned my lights on and off. Then, with my lights off, I turned the flashers back on, followed by the headlights (even though the oncoming car was approaching from behind). *Anything to garner the attention of the oncoming driver.*

The arriving vehicle slowed and came to a stop. Three other cars approached behind that first arrival. In a few moments, I saw a vehicle approaching from the other direction.

I jumped back into my car and began flashing my high beams. Over and over, until the approaching vehicle slowed and stopped. I believed the accident scene would be okay and that particular type of danger had passed. I relaxed and was relieved others were arriving that might help me care for the victims.

I was ashamed and embarrassed. I didn't have a flashlight or flares. Taking advantage of new arrivals, I ran down the line of cars, asking for road flares. Nobody had any.

To my dismay, over the next few minutes, the last three vehicles on one side and the new arrival on the other turned around and drove away. I heard the first arrival speaking. He was sitting in his car with the window down. The man was on the phone speaking with 9-1-1. I'd completed that task minutes before and really needed some help, but received none.

Noticing the cell signal had returned, I quickly returned to "K" so she could speak with her daughter. I reached her daughter and placed my iPhone on speaker mode. None of us realized it at the time, but "K" would pass away shortly.

Finally, flashing lights appeared in the distance. Real help was about to arrive. I ran the circuit one more time to make sure I could relay the current status of the accident victims when help arrived. I briefed the first arriving officer and, over the next few minutes as other first responders arrived and took charge, my involvement receded into the background.

It was a very sad difficult evening.

Unlike Cola's success helping others at accident scenes, I felt totally useless. I was ashamed and disappointed I didn't/couldn't do more for the victims. Over the next few days, I shared that evening's tragedy with family members, close friends, and associates. Included in that group were a couple of professional first responders dear to me, as well as one well-regarded notable physician. They all reminded me that, on occasion, it's just not possible to help everyone; sometimes anyone. To a person they suggested it was likely they couldn't have done anything more than I did; their training and experience notwithstanding. It was a Mass Casualty event, and I had few resources at my disposal.

Looking back I realize I wasn't successful. I didn't save anyone, other than those who might have perished if I hadn't called 9-1-1 when I did or slowed oncoming cars. In all honesty, I've never felt more alone, helpless, or frustrated. Other than trying to comfort the victims with my words and promises, set up the call between the daughter and her dying mother, as well as calling 9-1-1 and slowing approaching vehicles, the only practical thing I actually did for any of them individually was cover the dying lady and pray. I felt so inadequate, but now accept that I did everything possible given the horrific circumstances. Sometimes things are just out of a person's hands. Knowing that, I wouldn't hesitate to jump in again and try to help.

"LG" is a dear friend and a retired physician. He and I discussed the matter of others not stepping up to assist me that evening. He said he believes that's a typical response to such situations.

LG shared that he and his bride were flying to California for a medical conference when a flight attendant announced a medical emergency and asked if there were any physicians aboard the aircraft. LG knew doctors comprised a majority of the passenger manifest. He estimated that two-thirds of the passengers were physicians.

He and his wife, a registered nurse, were seated near the rear of the plane and were shocked when nobody forward of them raised a hand. After all, physicians filled the aircraft. Seeing nobody else willing to involve themselves, LG and his wife jumped up and attended to their fellow traveler.

I asked my friend if he thought the doctors aboard the plane refused to get involved because of liability exposure concerns. LG said, "No Steve, I believe it boils down to human nature. People don't want to get involved. They are often afraid to take the steps necessary to assist others in times of crisis."

Cola Fugelere agrees with LG's assessment of the human nature component in these situations. I learned that lesson first hand, during the aftermath of that awful Mass Casualty Incident. Now you know, and I trust you'll step out of your comfort zone and "Take Charge" when others are in dire need of your assistance.

Take Charge!

AT THE RACES

If I were discussing professional football, baseball, or basketball in the U.S., it might not take my Readers long to figure out which league, team, or player is involved. In this case, The Subject is set in a foreign venue and involves a type of racing not commonly understood in North America. Therefore, I don't need to be as oblique as I would if the sport in this matter involved competitive pastimes popular in the U.S.

This is a story about cheating; and could involve danger for any person who might reveal anything beyond that which I'm about to present to Readers. I recently discovered the disclosure of certain facts in this situation might result in a myriad of problems for a very nice couple. Therefore, I'm writing this story very carefully; in response to a specific request to protect the identities of those two extraordinary individuals, while continuing to share what happened. Cola's concerns were elevated recently when a relative of the antagonists in this story threatened the safety and well-being of My Clients.

This particular situation involved an international boating competition many years ago. I'll avoid mentioning the name of the nation associated with the venue. *With that in mind...*

Misha and Tatiana

The services of my primary Underwater OneSeven became necessary when a wonderful couple flew to the States and asked me to address a problem involving a competing team and cheating. I fondly refer to that particular OneSeven, a former Navy Seal, as WetSeven.

The couple seeking my assistance, Misha and Tatiana, were honest participants within the racing community. They were very wealthy, as were their competitors. Winning wasn't about the money. It was all about friendly competition within their small racing community. Whenever their boat won, they donated the purse to charity.

Over the previous couple of years two surly men, with limited resources, joined their racing community. They were said to be brothers, so I called them the "Surly Brothers." That sinecure team was winning more races than any other team and seemed focused on the money, rather than friendly community stature like everyone else. Rumors regarding cheating swirled about the racing circuit. Misha and Tatiana suspected the rumors had a basis in fact. As we eventually discovered, the fraud involved a propulsion system impermissible under the event's rules.

After watching them closely, Misha asked if my organization could determine if cheating was taking place. If so, Misha wanted it exposed and the cheaters expelled. Tatiana wanted more than that, but the laws of her country forbade what she wanted Cola to do to their private parts. Of course, I wouldn't have done that anyway. *Ouch!*

I accepted the challenge. My young OneSeven translator Роман, whom I refer to as Roman, became a necessary member of the Operation. Roman, WetSeven, and I beefed up our frequent flyer miles getting to the racing venue. Roman acted as my translator, and I posed as his client, an independent sports journalist from Washington State. WetSeven was charged with wet work (underwater work, not the spilling blood type of wetwork) and used his trained roving eyes to assist me topside.

Race organizers adopted strictly defined prop design specifications. It had to be a cleaver style propeller. I don't remember how many blades were permitted, but I'm thinking four. I believe the cheaters were using three-bladed props for better speed. Many years have passed, and I cannot recall all the particulars.

We discovered the Surly Brothers employed an underwater goon whose activities helped us figure out how they were cheating. His name was Igor. Fact. *That was actually his given name.*

All racers underwent engine, keel, and propeller validation before each race to ensure conformity with race rules. There were many days of qualifying competitions and elimination heats, before the real races started. After preliminary heats over the first couple of days, WetSeven reported his suspicions that Igor was switching the Surly Brothers' propeller, subsequent to prerace inspections. This occurred only minutes before the heats began. I asked him how that was possible.

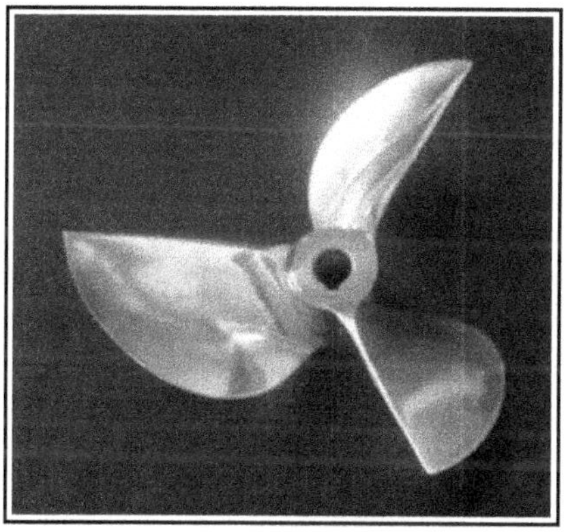

Misha and Tatiana's Prop

According to WetSeven, he discovered Igor stationed aboard one of two nearby boats. They were two innocent looking 2655 Bayliner Ciera Sunbridge model boats. A large rubber-edged platform was secured between the boats and covered with a framed tarpaulin; under which stood a large studio television camera secured atop a beefy pedestal. WetSeven conducted what he referred to as a “nighttime recce (reconnaissance)” of the area the prior day. He discovered a large trap door on the deck of the small barge, behind where the camera operator stood for filming. Curious, he began surveilling the barge. Later that evening he watched Igor step off one of the boats onto the barge. Someone handed Igor something substantial, followed by a few smaller things. WetSeven recognized the items right away. Scuba equipment.

> ***An aside...***
> We later discovered the studio camera was non-functioning. It was broken and obsolete. The Surly Brothers were merely using it as a prop to disguise the platform's actual intended purpose. It was, in reality, a diving platform. Not a filming barge.

Back to WetSeven's Suspicions...
I asked WetSeven why nobody noticed any bubbles when Igor was at work. WetSeven explained that Igor was wearing a rebreather, like those WetSeven used as a Navy Seal. The device was a closed circuit scuba system requiring a mixture of pure oxygen and a diluting gas. WetSeven explained that rebreathers are potentially dangerous because users could end up getting too much oxygen (hyperoxia) or not enough oxygen (hypoxia).

The camera operator removed the framed tarpaulin just before the race began, revealing a large television camera mounted on a professional studio pedestal. The faux cameraman pretended to film the event. The tarped framework was more extensive than necessary for the camera and its pedestal. However, now we knew why. We knew Igor needed the space to prep for his underwater adventures.

I reported our findings to Misha and Tatiana and asked what they wanted me to do. The simple instructions I received covered it all. Tatiana responded with, “Make lose. Make them caught.” [sic]

Our plan was simple. It was all about sabotaging the cheater's propeller. WetSeven had a small window of opportunity to perform his magic, because of the short timeline between propeller inspections and the start of the race.

Once the prop was raised and inspected, the Surly Brothers would lower the propeller back into the water. Igor had to quickly change out the regulation propeller and install the illegal prop. He needed to complete his work before the prop began spinning. Igor's work was fast and efficient. WetSeven had seen enough heats to know the Surly Brothers were timing the engine start. After the prop returned to the water, they waited the same amount of time, on each occasion, before starting the engine they argued and stalled for a time; continually irritating race officials. That left WetSeven a small window of opportunity to get his job done.

After Igor completed his job and slithered away in the green waters, WetSeven came out of hiding and swam up to the propeller with two large long handled adjustable wrenches. The former Navy Seal sheathed the jaws of the wrenches in heavy leather, so those tools wouldn't leave marks; or result in noise or vibrations when used. The long handles provided adequate leverage so WetSeven could do his job. The jaws of each wrench, opened to a calculated width, allowed sufficient space to slide the open jaws neatly onto the propeller; while remaining sufficiently narrow to permit a reasonably good grasp on the props.

> ***An aside...***
> Adjustable wrenches are usually called by the brand name, Crescent, in the United States and Canada. In most of the UK, they are referred to as "adjustable spanners."

Back to The Propeller...
WetSeven would place one wrench on the leading edge of the cleaver prop, and the other on the trailing edge. He'd use the leverage offered by the elongated wrenches and his bulging biceps to bend one prop blade just enough to cause severe vibrations, without making it easy for the cheaters to discover the sabotage. I'm guessing he learned that trick when he was an active Navy Seal. The timing was tight, but WetSeven was successful in ruining the Surly Brothers' chance to win the races

he sabotaged. He said Igor's mistake was never looking back as he swam away.

WetSeven twisted three different props, before three different heats, and successfully nixed the Surly Brothers' chances to win. They were in a foul mood, shouting at each other and others nearby. They were loudly cursing one another. Their words and actions resulted in other racing teams quickly learning they were having vibration issues. They once got into a pushing match on their boat while race officials considered whether or not to inspect their propeller to ensure compliance with regulations. One senior race official nixed any secondary inspections; stating it wasn't necessary and outside the scope of the rules. "After all," the race official said, "the team failed to qualify during those heats."

We later discovered the Surly Brothers began shoving one another as they discussed their supplier. Believing they'd received a bad batch of props from their supplier, one brother exclaimed he wanted the supplier's head on a stick. The other brother was trying to settle him down. Loudly demanding he quiet down.

They had one more opportunity to qualify, and that's when we decided it was time to reveal their cheating ways.

On the last occasion, Igor switched out a regulation propeller and installed the illegal prop. WetSeven, who was hiding nearby, swam over and wrapped a short heavy anchor rope around the prop. When the Surly Brothers started their boat, the prop spun and yanked the anchor up. It tore into the bottom of their boat. The vessel began taking on water. A volunteer, realizing the prop pulled something up into the hull, jumped aboard and hit the switch to raise the prop out of the water.

> ***An aside...***
> That quick action earned him the four crisp American one hundred dollar bills I promised earlier, if he successfully raised the prop clear of the water.

Back to The Cheaters...
When the prop came up, the gig was also up. They were caught red-handed with an illegal prop. Knowing the two Bayliners were associated with the Surly Brothers, race officials had the boats searched. Illegal props, the rebreathing gear, the real purpose for the barge, the fact that the television camera was non-working, Igor's role, and the rest of their cheatfest was exposed. The Surly Brothers received a stiff penalty for their activities, beyond being barred from the sport for life. Government prosecutors charged them with various crimes for their fraud; making accommodations available for them in prison after their trial.

Word got out that Misha and Tatiana were behind the effort to expose the Surly Brothers. People came out of the woodwork to applaud their actions. One ninety-year-old wife of a farmer enjoyed the races. She arrived the next day bearing gifts. She presented two pies she personally baked the night before, along with two prized laying hens. One ninety-two-year-old race veteran offered to stop racing and spend the remainder of his days advising and assisting the young couple. He was a skilled longtime champion of the sport. His knowledge and experience was a priceless gift. He said Misha and Tatiana saved the sport he truly loved, and he wanted to be part of their team.

Did the Surly Brothers learn that cheating doesn't pay?

The lesson learned by Misha and Tatiana? Cola knows the ins and outs necessary to fill their pantry with fresh eggs and tasty pies.

IT'S A SMALL WORLD

Many years ago I was approached by a security official with a technology company to validate the character of a businessman. The Security Professional was a friend of an existing Cola Client and received an excellent endorsement from My Client. The Security Professional told me I came highly recommended. That's always nice to hear. It appeared the matchmaking Client served both parties well.

The Security Professional needed my services because his superiors wanted to know whether or not the businessman, a Public Relations Professional (PR Pro), could be trusted with their closely held proprietary information. The Security Professional's company was seriously considering a business relationship with The PR Pro. Their need involved highly valuable internal materials. The PR Pro, headquartered in the Bay Area, had additional offices in the States, in Europe, and in Asia.

We thought The PR Pro might be a good candidate for surveilling on long international flights, as his offices would require time to penetrate. We had no idea at the onset of our investigation into the habits and practices of The PR Pro that he was highly protective of his work while traveling. Disproving his professionalism was going to be an insurmountably hard nut to crack, but Cola's Team was turning over many stones to make certain our initially positive assessment was spot on accurate.

Our research revealed The PR Pro avoided discussing clients while in public settings. That included restaurants, sporting events, taxis, airplanes, and airports. He was a wise and cautious businessman. The more we dug, the more we came to appreciate that The PR Pro was a prudent ethical businessman, protective of his valued clients and their information. He was, indeed, professional.

During the course of our investigation, a young female Cola Team Member became acquainted with one of his associates. We nicknamed that person "CV the Bear." Her "accidental" encounter began with a series of friendly backgammon games on a pleasant Saint Patrick's Day. The setting was a popular restaurant, furnished with many backgammon tables dedicated for customer use. CV earned the nickname Bear because of his backgammon prowess and many gaming victories over our Agent.

Before involving "The Bear" in our research, we believed The PR Pro was, indeed, of the highest caliber and served each of his clients with professionalism and honesty; handling each situation with full confidentiality. His internal company protocols went a long way in extending his character traits and ethics onto his staff. CV was helpful in unknowingly validating everything positive about The PR Pro.

One final face-to-face was necessary before I would sign off on our conclusions and report back to The Security Professional. We knew The PR Pro had a flight scheduled in a few days. Destination China. I wanted to assess this guy and validate our findings personally. I have a sense for people. I made certain The PR Pro and I would be seated next to one another on that upcoming trans-Pacific flight. I created a situation that would serve as a conversation starter on the aircraft.

My Team followed him for several days seeking the best opportunity for me to be in the same room as The PR Pro. On one occasion he met his lovely wife "Feather" for lunch in downtown San Jose, California. I nicknamed his wife Feather, because of the designer purse she was carrying; tastefully embroidered with a colorful, albeit subdued, feather. The restaurant was perfect for my needs. It was small enough that he might remember me three days hence, while in a restaurant sufficiently large so that bumping into me later wouldn't seem particularly odd.

The restaurant, Mucho's, offered patrons a menu centered around pollo (aka chicken). As I entered the small restaurant, I recognized it was a typical older downtown retail layout having narrow frontage and a deep floor plan. To my right was a roasting wall oven with a dozen or more chickens rotating on skewers that were, in turn, revolving around an axis and being cooked by a fiery flame. There was a long bar on the right and tables down the left side of the elongated restaurant. Various bottles of hot sauce were everywhere.

I took a table next to The PR Pro and Feather. I ordered a chicken burrito and a beer. Watching the young couple, I was impressed with Feather's obvious affection for her husband. Her eyes sparkled as she spoke with her man. She giggled, smiled, and otherwise seemed to enjoy his company and the casual setting. He, too, was enamored with his woman. She was charming. A class act.

EL YUCATECO

As I covertly watched the handsome couple, I fidgeted with a bottle of hot sauce. I'd never seen the brand before and decided to give it a try when my meal arrived. Reading the label, I saw something I'd not seen before and was quickly attracted to the notion of tasting that hot fluid. Nowhere on the label did I read the word "Vinegar." Great, I was sick of tasting different brands of hot sauce that all carried the same flavor – Vinegar.

I've become a longtime fan of the red product I discovered in Mucho's. It was called El Yucateco Chile Habanero. I drive several hundred miles once a year to refill our pantry with a case of their larger eight-ounce bottles.

> ***An aside...***
> I once ordered five cases of El Yucateco. When our UPS guy made his delivery, he came through the door and said, "Whooooo Eeeeee, my hands are on fire!"
>
> "Ed," asked if he could use our restroom. He apologized for the request and told us it was against UPS rules, but said his hands were hot and he needed to put out the fire. Ed said he needed to wash chili powder from his hands right away. *Chili Powder?* As I pondered Ed's words, I heard him in the back room. Just before the bathroom door closed, I heard Ed say, "Whooooo Eeeeee" for the second time.

The product I ordered was liquid. I hoped the supplier didn't get the order wrong. Confused I opened the box and discovered a broken bottle. The contents dried out long ago. It had turned to a powder. Poor Ed. I gave him a bottle of that spicy nectar, and he went away muttering. A few weeks later Ed came by again and thanked me. He said his wife really liked the hot sauce, but it was too hot for him. I called him a panty-waist, and he went away chuckling.

After that, I decided to make sure I didn't do that to Ed again. I've been purchasing the lovely liquid in grocery stores ever since.

Back to Muchos...
When my meal arrived, I purposely made a scene. Using my right arm as a lever, I reached for a bottle of El Yucateco Habanero and intentionally knocked my beer to the painted concrete floor. In the same fluid motion, I tipped the hot sauce to the floor. Both bottles broke and some of the red liquid splattered on one of Feather's leather boots. That part was unintended. I felt terrible and quickly apologized to the classy lady. Staining Feather's boots was not part of my plan. I took a napkin from their table and wiped off Feather's stylish boot. I looked directly at the incredibly urbane PR Pro, just shy of a suspiciously pregnant moment, allowing him to imprint my face on his mind. I gushed and apologized with sincerity. He said, "No worries" and I returned to the mess beside my table.

Three days later I purposely waited to board my flight to the Far East. I waited until The PR Pro marched down the jetway with the other First Class passengers. I knew he had the aisle seat and I wanted him to get comfortable before Cola boarded the aircraft. I was assigned to the window seat, next to my Mark. I was going to be asking him to allow me to crawl over him in a few moments and wanted his undivided attention.

He scarcely looked up when I apologized and stepped over his feet. As I passed by, I said, "Hey. Ah.... nothing." He looked up, and I noticed a glimmer of recognition. As I was sitting down, he was looking directly at me, trying to place my face. I put the same look on my face and said, "Sorry, I thought you looked familiar. My mistake."

He said, "No you're right. You look familiar as well." He paused then chuckled and said, "You're the hot sauce guy."

I feigned both realization and embarrassment. I repeated my apology first uttered to him three days before. He repeated the words he spoke to me at Mucho's, "No worries."

I introduced myself saying, "I'm Hollis Kenburg. I told my sister Ruthie about splattering your wife's shoes. She looked at me as if I were a simpleton. Ruth said, 'Marvelous move, you dolt. Just Marvy!'"

The PR Pro laughed and said, "Sisters can be a tough crowd. I'm always telling Barbara and Janet to cut me some slack. They'll respond with something like, 'Sure, Jerry' as in Jerry Lewis."

> ***An aside...***
> That exchange successfully broke the ice. Cola was in, but felt guilty the entire time. Working Marks like 3X and Maura was easy. The older I am, the more shame I experience working Good Guys like The PR Pro.

Back to My First Class Window Seat...
After that, we struck up a conversation. I mentioned it was a small world and he laughed. He said he'd recently heard a small world story involving his sister and wanted to know if I was interested in hearing what happened. I was. I told him to go ahead.

The PR Pro told me his little sister, I believe her name is Barbara, was working in a Safeway store as a checker (checkout clerk). Barbara was a high school senior at the time. As she was running the cash register one day, checking out groceries, the next person in line blurted out, "Barbara! Barbara! I can't believe it's you. It's been more than sixty years, Barbara."

Then the woman stopped speaking, dropped her head, and apologized. Embarrassed, the old woman said she'd mistaken

Barbara for a teenage girl she knew in Pittsburgh and hadn't seen in "more than three score years."

She told the checker her friend from many years earlier looked exactly like the Barbara standing at the grocery store's cash register. Of course, the only image the old lady could remember of "Barbara," was as a young girl more than a half-century before. The gray-haired senior citizen had no reference point allowing her to visualize the long lost friend as an elderly person.

At first, Barbara thought the mistaken identity might have been because of her Safeway name tag. A boldly embroidered "Barbara" appeared in large letters on her uniform. Then Barbara considered something else. Was it possible? Could it be?

Barbara was the spitting image of her grandmother and named after her as well. Grandma was from Pittsburgh Their family moved west when Grandma Barbara graduated from high school. She asked the old lady, "What was the last name of your friend?"

The woman looked up and answered Barbara's question. As suspected, the woman was a childhood friend of her late grandmother. That old lady hadn't seen Barbara's grandma in more than six decades. Small world.

I took the opportunity to share my London trip small world story with The PR Pro. We chatted a little more during the flight, and I realized My Client would be privileged to have this PR Pro on his team.

One of the final things The PR Pro said to me when we landed in Tokyo, before we went our separate ways, has always stuck in my mind. He told me he and his wife had three kids. He chuckled and wondered aloud if one day in the distant future Cola's son would spill habanero sauce on one of The PR Pro's kids. It's a small world! Who knows?

Small World Dangers

In the early days of my espionage career, a female Cola Team Member and I enrolled in a Nevada-based card dealing school, so we could quickly learn the basics of dealing Blackjack and Hold'em Poker. I had no interest in working for a Nevada casino. I merely needed to be good enough to get a job on the staff of a gambling parlor on the other side of the country.

We believed our efforts on the Client's behalf would necessitate us getting close to one particular high powered Union Official. The man was a big gambler who frequented an illegal after-hours gambling establishment we called "The JC." He was a blackjack aficionado, but he played poker as well. My Team discovered he continually bragged to card dealers, especially the females, about his title, responsibilities, and activities. Cola Team Members alternately called him "The Union Official" and "Blabbermouth."

My Client needed to know union plans, strategies, and tactics for an upcoming contract negotiation. We believed The JC offered us an excellent opportunity to learn more about the union's negotiation plans; and, if necessary, get the goods on Blabbermouth. Who knows? A subtle reminder to him of his failings might have proved helpful at a later date. We hoped it would be easier than that. We had faith in his loose lips and desire to consume excessive quantities of Dewar's and soda.

My Colleague and I both secured positions as JC card dealers. The House assigned her to the blackjack tables because she was very attractive and had a wonderfully engaging personality. Her assignment, beyond dealing cards, was to make sure player drinks remained filled. She was also told to remain conversationally engaged with players, to discourage them from wanting to leave the gaming tables. I became a Hold'em dealer and occasionally subbed at the blackjack table. Blabbermouth gave me the nickname, "Rookie" when he figured out I hadn't been dealing cards very long. The nickname stuck. Before long everyone was referring to me as Rookie. Every so often My Colleague and I would take breaks together. During those breaks, My Colleague would pass along what The Union Official was saying. The gig lasted several months, and we successfully provided our Client with months of valuable information.

A couple of months after that Operation ceased, I was in Atlanta, Georgia meeting with a Client at the top of a tall hotel, sitting in a revolving bar that offered a three hundred sixty degree view of Atlanta's downtown Peachtree district.

When our meeting concluded, I walked to the elevator. As I was about to press the call button, the door opened. Standing before me was The Union Official with a scantily dressed girl in extremely high heels hanging on to each of his hairy arms. They looked identical. Twins. The first thought that entered my mind had nothing to do with the twin hookers. I thought, "Geez, Blabbermouth knows what I did! He knows I undermined the union's negotiations." I quickly pushed that nonsense out of my head.

There was a look of absolute shock and pure fear on The Union Official's face. I discovered later that he was in town on his honeymoon and snuck out for an evening with the twin prostitutes. I knew the woman he married. He'd brought her into the casino a few times when they first began dating. Her father was an even bigger big shot in the union. Blabbermouth was afraid I'd tell his wife about the twin hookers.

Whew! I thought he nailed me in some way, but in actuality, I'd nailed him. I filed that scene away, knowing it might hold value sometime in the future. After we greeted each other, Blabbermouth stepped out of the elevator with his escorts, and I hopped into the waiting car.

As the door began closing, Blabbermouth hit the doors with the palms of his hands and reversed their travel. He quickly dug into a pocket and pulled out a wad of money. Peeling off two one hundred dollar bills, Blabbermouth winked at me and said, "Have a good time Rookie."

The elevator door closed and Cola was two bills richer for his troubles.

When I reached street level, I decided to take a walk. As I walked down Peachtree Street toward Palisades, I thought back about my time at the after-hours gambling joint. A shiver went down my spine when I recalled the night I believed my fate was sealed and Cola was about to be silenced. Permanently. Murdered in the 1st Degree. Not a pleasant memory.

◇ ◇ ◇

I'd been dealing blackjack late one evening. Long after most of the players departed, I started my break. I needed a cup of coffee. I was tired, and it was very late. It was probably four in the morning. I left the card room. Passing between the craps table and the poker room, I headed for the lounge. The lounge had couches and soft chairs. There was also a dining area and a small kitchen around the corner from the living room area.

While in the kitchen I heard The JC's guy buzz the front door, granting entry to two men. I overheard one threatening the other. It sounded really serious. I decided it would be wise to remain near the coffee pot.

A guy named Tim was threatening the other, JB. I knew who they were. They'd come in on occasion to play blackjack. Rumor was that Tim was a cocaine mule who transported the illicit white powder from Florida up the east coast to the town where I was working. The other guy JB was, supposedly, a local distributor. Word had gotten around that JB was using more of the addictive powder that he was selling. Buyers were complaining that JB was cutting the coke, even more, to make up for him snorting the inventory. I heard JB was diluting the cocaine further by adding baby laxative to the mix.

I overheard Tim complaining about JB having someone steal his coke. Tim told JB. "The syndicate won't let this stand. They are going to put a hit out on someone over this. Either you or I will be dead within a week. If I don't kill you or get the coke back JB, they are going to kill me."

Yikes! Cola needed an O^2H exit plan.

I was in a kitchen cul-de-sac with no way out. I didn't want to get involved and certainly didn't want them to know I was hiding in the small room. As they argued, I was trying to figure out how to fit my body into an empty coffee cup and hide there until they were gone. The cup was the largest hiding place available. Cola had no ready answer for this situation.

With nothing else to do, I listened. It appeared Tim motored up the coast with the goods in his trunk. When Tim pulled into town, he drove directly to JB's apartment. He and JB stashed the cocaine under JB's bed and went out on the town. At one point while they were at a bar, JB disappeared. Tim accused JB of calling one of his girlfriends to have her remove the coke from the apartment. When JB and Tim returned and discovered the cocaine was missing, Tim immediately suspected JB. JB told Tim they should head to the casino and see if JB's girlfriend was there. As they sat in the chairs and argued, Tim accused JB of stalling by coming to the after-hours joint, to give his girlfriend time to hide the dope.

As I was standing there listening, the pit boss entered the lounge and asked the two guys if they'd seen Rookie. *Yikes!* They told him no. The boss peeked around the corner and saw me wetting my pants in the kitchen. *Well, not really.*

He peeked, but Cola didn't actually soil himself. I trust you wouldn't be too hard on me I had done so. *It was that scary!*

Wetting my pants wasn't in the cards. I was actually thinking about that huge stainless steel revolver I'd gotten a glimpse of in Tim's shoulder holster one night a few weeks earlier when he'd had too much to drink... or snort.

The pit boss yelled, "Hey Rookie, I see you hiding in there. Your break is over. Get back to work before you get fired!"

I was worried about losing my life and here was a guy trying to scare me over losing a crappy undercover job! The only "fired" that concerned me involved the big stainless steel revolver.

As I rounded the corner and headed back to the card room, I saw the two drug dealers staring at me. Their eyes pierced my back as I turned and walked away. My own eyes were fixated on the rearview mirror as I left and headed back to the motel that night. I never returned to the casino.

Two of my Team Members continued to work the place after I called it quits. I told them we could pull the plug on the Operation, but they declined my offer. They remained on station for about four more weeks, until the union negotiations concluded and our presence there was no longer warranted.

During that four week window, we heard law enforcement officials discovered Tim's headless body in one of Florida's drainage ditches. His fingers were gone. Tim's head remains missing, but all ten fingers were found nailed to a barn door, just off the New Jersey Turnpike. He was rumored to have been executed by the mob.

In a way, execution by mobsters was good for me. JB didn't kill him, so I wasn't a threat to him. The syndicate probably didn't know what I overheard while I was trying to crawl into that small coffee cup. Heck, who would ever guess getting a cup of coffee in a little kitchen would end up becoming the prelude to an execution. That was a scary time.

◇ ◇ ◇

As my thoughts drifted back to my walk down Peachtree Street, I looked around. Really Cola? Are you still looking over your shoulder?

I thought about my evening and the grand view from the revolving restaurant. I thought about running into Blabbermouth in Atlanta. Another small world situation, but I scored a few bills on that occasion. I also thought about Tim and JB. A shiver shot up my spine. *Did I say "shot?"*

As you can see, small world situations combined with a life in espionage, can be very dicey. For most people, chance encounters can be exciting, awkward, or fun. In the espionage arena, small world encounters can be dangerous. What if it was JB in that elevator instead of The Union Official. I shivered again.

JERRY AND THE BAG

I was interviewing a potential Client, Belle, in Los Angeles one beautiful morning. I call her Belle because our introduction occurred at Belmont Park in Elmont, New York. That year I had a contract involving a wealthy Playboy who loved to attend horse racing's Triple Crown each year. I met Belle in the lounge of an upscale area hotel a day or two before the Belmont Stakes, the third leg of the Triple Crown.

The Playboy and I were discussing his delight in fulfilling his father's final wish, to have his ashes scattered on the track at Churchill Downs in Louisville, Kentucky; just a few weeks before the running of the Kentucky Derby. Belle was seated nearby and overheard our conversation. She, too, had recently scattered the cremated remains of her mother.

Belle and her husband nearly lost their lives on Memorial Day, about ten days earlier. They were on the return hike from a prominent landmark in the western United States where they'd scattered one-third of her mother's ashes. Belle and her Beau were suffering from heatstroke, even though they were consuming a lot of water and Gatorade. Their core temperatures rose to dangerous levels, and they became delirious. Belle said her husband saved their lives using a small sheet of Mylar and a few bushes to create shade in an area lacking respite from the deadly desert sunshine.

Belle told The Playboy and me the past week was far more pleasant. She'd traveled to the Kenai River in Alaska, and to her mother's childhood home in Wyoming, to scatter the remaining two-thirds of her mother's remains. She said her mother loved Lilies, so each time she spread some ashes, she left a single Lily behind.

During that discussion, she shared that her own business was about to be cremated by a hostile competitor. The more she shared, the more intrigued I became. Over the next few weeks, I decided to look into Belle and her affairs. I discovered her competitor was, indeed, hostile. Moreover, I knew the guy. You'll remember him too.

We'd crossed paths some years before. The clown was Antonio. I called him Archie 3X. You'll recall him from the St. Louis Arch story I shared in the chapter, The Arch and The Needle. I jumped at the chance to assist Belle, without her asking. That's why we were meeting in southern California that morning.

We were seated at a Pasadena area restaurant called Julienne. In my opinion, Julienne is one of the better restaurants in Los Angeles County. Located in the small upscale community of San Marino, Julienne has outstanding food, an excellent interior restaurant, a unique gift store, and delightful curbside dining.

I've eaten at Julienne over the years when work takes me to Los Angeles. On this occasion, I was seated outside near the curb and enjoying a nice meal with Belle. My Team had already vetted Belle extensively, and I was reasonably comfortable making her acquaintance at Julienne. *That was, until...*

As we were chatting over our breakfast, something concerning occurred; setting off Cola's alarm bells. A tall man stopped by our table, catching me entirely off guard. He looked directly at Belle and said, "Nice Brighton." *What? Who?*

Cola's fight or flight klaxon alarm was screaming at full tilt. Brighton? Nice? Who does that? Code Words? A Trap? My Cola Color Alert Levels shot from Yellow to Orange, bordering on Red! What just happened?

Obviously, Cola failed to maintain good Situational Awareness. I didn't even see the guy until he was right on top of us. Geez, Cola! What were you thinking? Actually, you weren't thinking. You weren't aware Cola.

> ***An aside...***
> **Cola Color Alert Levels**
> Homeland Security, law enforcement agencies, and others have a system of color-coded alert levels. Spies do as well. In Cola's world, I use White, Yellow, Orange, and Red.
>
> I'm only at condition White when sleeping in my own bed. You might think Cola is relaxed and in Condition White while inside secure facilities (e.g., on a White House tour or beyond TSA screeners in airline club lounges). However, even there, I'm not in Condition White. In those situations, I'm usually relaxed but continue scanning for adversaries, unwelcome officials, and others. I call that, Condition Yellow.
>
> Condition Orange is when I suspect a potential threat or am beyond relaxed, and without any specific or obvious threats. Condition Red is when a situation becomes threatening and Cola is in unmistakable jeopardy.
>
> Wally spent too much time in Condition Red. Although Red is sometimes unavoidable, proper prior planning will reduce the possibility of Condition Red and a failed Op. Sometimes an Espionage Professional can get out of trouble when Condition Red appears, but repeated Reds reflect poor Tradecraft, and will ultimately doom a Spy.
>
> My dumpster diving Red situation, when the Police Officer said, "Police, open up!" was saved by a backstop. However, even the best backstop will not save a Spy who spends too much time in Condition Red. Wally is an excellent example of that.

Back to The "Nice Brighton" Guy...
I quickly asked Belle, "What was that all about? Brighton? Who was that guy?"

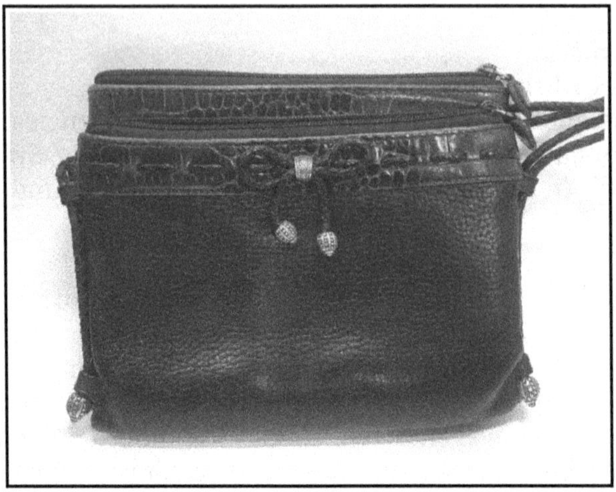

BELLE'S BRIGHTON PURSE

Belle responded by telling me she had no idea as to the identity of the man. She pointed at her necklace and said, "This is a Brighton, and so is my watch and purse."

"Belle, why would a stranger approach you and compliment your purse?"

"I have no idea Cola, except that it's a well-regarded brand name. I suppose they're recognizable to a trained eye."

That wasn't good enough for Cola. I jumped up from the table and told Belle I'd be right back. Looking around, I spotted the man sitting in a nearby Mercedes Benz. As I approached the car I noticed he was on the phone. I didn't wait. Tapping on the window, I drew attention to myself, and the tall man gestured for me to hold on a moment.

After a half minute, he opened his car door. I squatted down at his door, attempting to appear non-threatening. That said, I was positioned to spring into action and either attack or flee rapidly. Fortunately, neither action was necessary.

As the door opened, I asked the man to excuse my intrusion, followed by a question. "Excuse me," I said, "You stopped by our table and said, 'Nice Brighton.' It appears you complimented her for the purse, necklace, or perhaps her watch. I find that odd and am curious. How did you know the brand?"

He smiled and responded with, "I made the purse and recognized it as I passed by."

"You work at their factory?"

"No, I'm Mr. Brighton."

I said, "Smart business."

We chatted for a short time, then I took my leave of Mr. Brighton and walked up to the table.

As Readers know, Cola takes little at face value, especially when either my personal safety or operational security is at risk. I needed to clear the woman with whom I was meeting. I told her he was Mr. Brighton, then said I needed to use the restroom. I stepped inside the building and positioned myself in an area near the gift store's refrigerators, between the champagne and prepared salads. From that position, I had multiple quick egress options.

Using my phone, I quickly researched Brighton. That short exercise provided sufficient information about Mr. Brighton to put me at ease. Mr. Brighton aka Jerry Kohl was, indeed, genuine. The charming man I met on the curb was the same man who, along with his high school sweetheart Terri Kravitz, founded Brighton in 1991.

I returned to Belle and finished our fantastic Julienne breakfast.

P.S. ...and yes. I ended up launching an Operation against Antonio, aka Archie 3X, on Belle's behalf. I'll summarize the Op against Antonio by saying,

> *It'll be a decade before Antonio will exit the penitentiary wearing the same cheap suit he was wearing when he entered.*

TOOLS OF THE TRADE

The purpose for this chapter is to give Readers a glimpse into my toolbox and those of others in this field; and not intended as an exhaustive shopping list for people who may want to outfit their workshops. It's designed to give Readers a sense of some tools once used by corporate spies, as well as some currently used in business-related espionage activities. I will largely avoid discussing tools already described in this manuscript.

Entire books could be written about tools used in Corporate Espionage. My options are varied, in presenting the Reader with information about the tools of my trade. I could have provided Readers with an exhaustive list that would read more like an inventory or book index, but I have little interest in putting Readers to sleep or providing too much information to wannabe spies. An additional issue with that approach would be to leave Readers wondering about how those items are used. To further the randomness of the information I decided to share, I chose to document spy gear as it randomly came to mind; rather than carefully construct a comprehensive alphabetical list.

> ***An aside...***
> Yes, I could bore Readers with techno-babble about things like VPNs and Firewalls, but I won't. That kind of espionage detail is outside the scope and purpose of this book.

Back to The Tools...
Ingredients we use in our recipe for "Grunge" includes a proprietary mixture of coal, food grade diatomaceous earth, graphite, sulfur and a few other items. If you saw "Grunge" on a "Tools of the Trade" list, as well as things like coal, talc, and white glue you'd be perplexed. No worries. It makes more sense to offer examples of how I used "Grunge," rather than merely providing Readers with the recipe.

Another route I could have taken was to have Mr. Fowler methodically list many items and give brief descriptions of their use. I opted to skip that approach. The purpose of this book is to offer Readers a glimpse into the world of Corporate Espionage; not provide Readers with an detailed encyclopedia of items and their uses.

Steve and I settled on condensing the list and, in many cases, providing some context of usage through the presentation of adventures and anecdotes associated with tools I've used in my trade. I trust you'll find this chapter interesting and, at times, potentially unbelievable. Some of my adventures have been funny, others merely interesting. Scary, iffy, and complicated are also words associated with events described in this chapter. As indicated earlier, there is no particular order. Steve Fowler just wrote out my thoughts and memories as they came to me. Enjoy.

Tool Number One: HUMINT
Human Intelligence (HUMINT) is the bread and butter of my business. HUMINT involves personal relationships, face-to-face encounters, trust, mouth-to-ear information sharing, etc. An example of HUMINT would be a Spy, sitting in a Starbucks with a Tall Flat White or Iced Green Tea, engaged in the act of recruiting or debriefing an Asset.

Smartphones
Without question, Apple's introduction of the iPhone was the genesis for the most potent evolutionary tech-centric advancement in the espionage arena in human history. Modern smartphones contain recording devices, cameras, communication tools, global positioning systems, and other

technologies that radically changed The Spy Game. In that, the work of the professional Espionage Agent became far more manageable. Moreover, it mitigated many operational risks we once accepted as wholly unavoidable.

My very best all-time favorite tool for copying documents was my Minox Spy Camera. Today, however, I'd have to say an iPhone is probably the best all-around spy tool in an espionage professional's toolbox. Still camera, video camera, voice recorder, communications device, research tool, and much much more in a single concealable device. *Thank you Steve Jobs!*

Pretending to be Homeless

Appearing homeless, in many areas, serves to create an aura of invisibility. Homeless individuals for many people are, indeed, invisible. They are ignored, deemed either ignorant or deaf, and in some quarters considered relatively harmless.

I have a triple plastic bagged suitcase with smelly homeless undercover costumes. Filthy hats, heavily soiled bulky coats, fingerless gloves, and nasty shoes are among other items in that offensive suitcase. The following is an approach I'll use to ready myself for an appearance as a homeless person.

Many charitable organizations have retail stores that sell old coats and other items necessary to disguise a Spy, at low prices. Most of the things I purchase at those locations are used to assist me in dressing like a homeless person. They are often old and out of style. I'll head to my workshop with an old clean coat purchased from a well known non-profit secondhand store. I prefer bulky coats to hide my frame, any recording equipment or tools I might have, and to make me more uncomfortably intimidating.

Snot

Looking for spies wearing tuxedos (Bond) is fun in the movies. Spy clothes described in the Simon and Garfunkel song "America" are also fun to consider. However, stereotypical spies are anything but invisible. They stand out and draw attention to themselves. Picture 007 at high society embassy events or a gaming table in Monte Carlo. He stands out like a sore thumb.

In my world, dressing down has many more advantages. Appearing homeless in larger urban centers offers better espionage opportunities than the fun characters given life through the writings of Ian Fleming and Paul Simon. A homeless persona will only get an espionage professional so far. Spies need the ability to adopt many personas and character types. That said, in some Ops, there are very nice advantages to appearing homeless, so I keep my homeless costume smelly, ugly, and ready to wear.

One of my tricks is to smear white glue into the fabric on the top of the sleeves, from the back of the hand to the inside of the elbow. If applied correctly, dried white glue appears to be snot. It appears as though the vagrant repeatedly wiped his runny nose onto his sleeve. The purpose is to provide a sensory diversion, intended to draw the attention of onlookers to the disgusting substance on the jacket. Increased focus on other parts of a homeless person's body, means a reduced interest in his or her face; thereby, offering a dimension of invisibility.

> ***An aside...***
> It's helpful that human nature assists with our homeless invisibility efforts. People aren't comfortable looking into the eyes of those they deem disgusting or might have a communicable disease. Arrogant individuals who have little empathy for others are often our Targets. Therefore, the power of homelessness enhances our efforts by leveraging the prejudices of the Mark. People like that become weapons, targeting themselves.

Stink Repellent
I use a homemade sulfur-based aerosol, smelling similar to raw sewage. I'll lightly spray a small amount on the backside of my pants when pretending to be homeless. People are less likely to hang around when their noses are in full rebellion.

Grunge
There is also the human repellent recipe I developed and improved upon over the years. It contains ground rubber from tires, coal dust, talcum powder, food grade diatomaceous earth, sulfur, cheap brandy or cheap wine, rabbit urine, cigarette and cigar ashes, as well as soured milk, ammonia, and one crucial secret ingredient. I'll splash that revolting mix onto the coat, then let it sit in the hot sun until dry.

Once I appropriately prepare my coat, the smell is effective in deterring anyone from approaching. When prepared correctly, it reeks terribly in no wind situations. I refer to how near a person can be to me before smelling my homeless odor as the Reek Radius. It needs to be far enough away, so they don't get too close. I certainly don't want the person to whom I'm listening to, to believe I'm either a threat or so repulsive my Mark will depart. However, the Reek Radius should be sufficiently close so that I can overhear conversations, without making The Mark depart the area. The combination of ingredients and their quantities is critical. So too is the freshness, or lack thereof, of some of the recipe's components. I'll also adjust the recipe based on environmental variables like wind, rain, and temperature. This professional Spy relies heavily on weather forecasts in preparing the execution of Espionage Operations.

Filthy Fingers
Fingerless gloves are also very helpful as a visual deterrent. People don't want to be touched by someone with filthy hands. If someone gets too close, I want to be able to reach out with disgusting hands to encourage others to back off. I'll "wash" my hands in a recipe of grime containing a combination of food grade diatomaceous earth, sulfur, powdered graphite, brake shoe dust, and two other ingredients. Then I'll put on once white and now filthy blackened fingerless gloves.

Blending Into The Background
My favorite locations for a homeless gig are smoking areas near entrances and back doors to businesses and high rise office buildings. I'll usually pretend to be sleeping or intoxicated to lessen the fears of my Target. It took me a while to become

convincing, but two weeks working out the bugs in LA's Skid Row, studying the homeless, successfully educated Cola on how to blend and become a believable vagrant.

Hundreds of homeless individuals clustered together near LA's 5th Street and San Pedro provided excellent opportunities to analyze behaviors, attitudes, and what they did with items like plastic bags, food, and shopping carts. I learned how to conduct myself so that I could blend into their environment. No matter my success with Cola's homeless appearance, many within that community knew something wasn't right about me. I honed my skills by imitating their behaviors and smelling like a homeless man. However, they knew. They just knew. Fortunately, people who aren't part of the homeless community don't have a clue. They really don't "see" me when I morph into just another urban landscape ornament.

The Big Reach

I once used a piece of heavy equipment to duck into a second-floor office quickly. It was a Caterpillar Telehandler; best described as forklift forks connected to a very long boom. I believe the boom's reach exceeded 30 feet; either vertically or horizontally. That permitted a Colleague to lift a basket containing Cola the Spy across a water-filled ditch, over a wall, and onto a second-floor balcony. I jumped out of the basket, darted through a sliding glass door, and ducked into an office. In that office, I quickly photographed documents exposed on the desk, as The Mark sat in the next room eating lunch.

Burner Phones

These are cheap prepaid mobile phones purchased by an unaffiliated third party, for cash. The phones come loaded with an advertised number of minutes before it becomes necessary to reload the phone with additional time. Prudent espionage operators never refill burner phones. They'll smash and discard the phones when the minutes run out, when they are no longer needed, or when they become a liability to retain.

USB Sticks

These are phenomenal devices for a Spy. USBs are helpful, fast, and versatile tools for quickly copying valuable information. They can be used for surreptitious after-hours entries to pull data off computers or a myriad of information snatches. I've used them on multiple occasions for quick data pulls at a coffeehouse, when the Target takes a bathroom break and foolishly leaves the laptop screen open and unlocked.

I've seen USBs housed within more than a few excellent concealments. One of my OneSevens (Jo) placed a USB system within passable hearing aids (mini USB), pocket knives, dummy car fobs, and sunglass temples (mini USB). We also had a number of concealments for mini USB adapters.

If you're concerned about spying in your company, you need to know this and take it to the bank:

> Cola believes USBs and smartphones are the most significant threats to most SMB's (Small to Medium-sized Businesses) aka SME's in the EU (Small to Medium-sized Enterprises). Larger enterprises are pretty good at locking down USB connectivity to their computer systems and restricting employee access to smartphones while in certain areas. *Is your business vulnerable?*

Drafting

Spies commonly employ free email accounts for communicating with each other, as well as their Assets. Professional Espionage Agents don't send any emails containing sensitive information. They'll set up an account and provide access information to their Assets.

The most common Corporate Espionage system using shared web-based email accounts allows both users equal access to the account. One of the users will create a single draft email. It is never sent and remains a draft. A common practice to ensure they don't accidentally send the email is by keeping the TO, CC, and BCC fields intentionally blank. The Subject Line remains blank as well. Communication is performed using that single draft email. The system is referred to by some of us in the espionage community as "Drafting."

In a Drafting system, the draft email is used to write a message from one person to the other. The email isn't sent but is, instead, saved as a draft. After that person logs off, the other party logs on to read the "draft." Then the reader replaces the body of that email with a response; and so forth. Good Tradecraft suggests each iteration is selected and deleted; then replaced multiple times with text copied from the web (e.g., news articles, privacy statements, or Lorem Ipsum Text). The system is very helpful, hard to track and breach, and an excellent surreptitious communications system. I don't personally use Lorem Ipsum Text because it looks curious or suspicious, rather than innocuous.

> ***An aside...***
> Spies will use multiple iterations of Lorem Ipsum Text, or other text copied from the net, to obfuscate earlier versions of information used by them and their confederates in espionage communications. More commonly, Lorem Ipsum Text, aka Greeking, is often used as placeholder text for graphical design, printing, and website design. As placeholder text, it serves Readers by showing how text might appear when formatted in a document or online (see "Lorem Ipsum Text" in this book's Glossary for details).

Intuition

There is no substitution in the espionage arena for trusting one's gut. Doing so has saved me on countless occasions. Here's one example:

> I was once contacted by a man who somehow heard of my activities. The man was a wealthy dentist nabbed by a Fish and Game Officer as he was transporting a tarped trophy elk head in the back of his pickup truck. The Wealthy Dentist told law enforcement investigators he'd killed the elk the prior season and had a tag for that season's hunt. He claimed the head had been in a freezer

until the day before he was apprehended with the elk's remains.

The Wealthy Dentist did not have a legally issued game tag authorizing an elk hunt during the current hunting season. Poaching is illegal. If taken illegally, it would result in charges and other ramifications. If proved to be previously frozen, the poaching suspect could avoid prosecution.

The Wealthy Dentist asked me if I would break into a nearby university and steal the head. Time was of the essence. He approached me on a Friday, before officials could have a necropsy performed. Testing was scheduled for the following Monday to determine if The Wealthy Dentist's assertions about the head's previous freezing were supportable under forensic examination. It was an easy enough job for Cola, and the money was attractive, but something in my gut told me I shouldn't get involved; besides I never go up against the government.

I learned later that law enforcement officials received a tip informing them The Wealthy Dentist was asking around, trying to find someone willing to break into the lab at the university and steal the head. A successful theft would cost Fish and Game critical prosecutorial evidence and require prosecutors to vacate the charges levied against The Wealthy Dentist. The Fish and Game Department, along with other state law-enforcement officials, were lying in wait, hoping to catch whoever would be stealing the head. I don't know the end of the story, but I do know that Cola did the right thing by trusting his gut.

Intuition has value. *I trust Cola's gut!*

An aside...
Just so you know, Cola is a believer in layered defenses. In the aforementioned example I didn't rely solely on a single system to protect myself. A Cola Non-Negotiable AND Cola's intuition worked together to protect me. If

one failed, the other was at the ready to help in deciding what I should do.

Playdough

Although we don't see them often anymore, many hotels and motels once used room keys that were essentially plastic cards containing a specific pattern of holes that permitted the card's user to access the room. We'd use photographs of the cards, carbon paper, or would press them into flattened clay, to capture the pattern for later duplication. The best cards to copy were the Masters, used by maids and management personnel.

Playdough still has applications in today's Spy Games. One such application is for quick key impressions.

Pigeon Memory Items

We often duplicated items or used existing expected items within rooms to perform surveillance tasks. If a new article appeared out of the blue or didn't fit the setting, it might compromise the Operation. However, if the item belonged, or seemed to belong, it might go unnoticed long enough to run the Op to its logical conclusion.

Audio Studs

No, I'm not referring to playboy disc jockeys.

An audio stud is a device Jo designed for me. It is meant to be inserted into the headphone jack of a computer, thereby telling the speakers to shut down.

I'd stick an audio stud in a laptop on a desk in a hotel suite, while the owner snored in the adjoining room. Then I'd start up the computer. The audio stud muted the familiar startup sounds. Great device and extremely small. I keep one on my key ring next to a high capacity USB. *Besides, it nicely doubles to help me avoid waking Treena.*

FATC
My favorite Dark Side tool, when cybersecurity was the primary activity a company used for their Corporate Counterintelligence efforts, was to use the "Fugelere Alternative To Cybersecurity" aka FATC. Using FATC meant Cola was going to engage in On-The-Ground (OTG) espionage tactics. If a Target went techno for self-protection, I focused on HUMINT and other tactics.

Monocular
I always have a monocular at the ready. They are much smaller than a pair of binoculars, easily concealed, and have paid off for me many times. I thought I was the only Spy who carried a monocular until I saw Jason Bourne use one in the Bourne Supremacy to look down onto a bridge from a tall building. He later used that tool in the Bourne Ultimatum when he zoomed in on a document in a government building.

For example, I'll use a monocular to capture a debit card pin used by a Mark at the grocery store checkout counter or at a gas pump (my preference). People often use the same digits to unlock their iPhone, Android phone, iPad, or computer. They are golden numbers when they match, as they usually do. They're more than golden when they match security system disarm codes on alarm panels at work or home. At times, they also unlock and open secure access systems like interior and exterior doors.

I've discovered garage door keypad numbers are often easy to capture with my monocular. Moreover, those codes often provide access to many different devices and areas. People may as well have the code written down on each device and at every location where that code is used.

During one Operation, my monocular helped capture a garage door keypad code. Using that code we accessed a security gate, an alarm system, a computer, and a man-door at a Target's home. Afterward, we went to his business and the same code provided access to those same items and areas again (gate, alarm, computer, and man-door). *What a dummy!*

The Mission Impossible Song

The theme song for Mission Impossible is important to Cola. It has a calming effect when I'm in time-critical and tense situations. I'll catch myself humming that tune often for its therapeutic value. It gives me focus and allows me to tune out unnecessary internal and external distractions. I call it "Barney Focus." Barney, one of the characters in the original television series, was often working under immense pressure. I liken myself to Barney when pressure mounts. Like him, Cola works to maintain focus and get the job done. The song assists in ways few can understand.

Integrity and Reputation

Although it may not initially sound correct to you, I repeat the following important truth often and with emphasis:

"Successful Spies Must Have Integrity"

A tremendous amount of honesty is vital to anyone engaging in the business of Corporate Espionage. It actually makes sense. Read on.

Remember these words as I discuss Integrity and Reputation. Integrity is who you are on the inside. Reputation is how others see you, and not necessarily a reflection of your internal character.

There are huge implications associated with the loss of trade secrets and other information that could irreparably bring harm to those who hire corporate spies. When someone like Cola is engaged in Corporate Espionage, they need to have integrity. That integrity assists them in doing their very best to maintain a stellar reputation, so those who need that information can make sound value judgments. Nobody wants to be double-crossed or blackmailed. When seeking someone to garner information held by a competitor, the hiring party must have a high level of confidence in whomever they hire. If a Spy co-opts information from a competitor, that data is going to be in the hands of the Spy for a time, and they must be trusted to protect that information.

◇ ◇ ◇

The following is an example of Integrity and Reputation involving me. In the late 1980's I was contacted by an aide to a member of the Saudi Royal Family. The Prince, a royal playboy, wanted to find out if he had been, as suspected, cheated at a blackjack table in an underground European gambling casino. The Aide told me I had a stellar reputation and knew I could be trusted. He set up a meeting for me with "The Prince." Meeting participants included The Aide, The Prince, and My Trusted Client who referred The Prince to me.

As we were about to begin the meeting, I collected everyone's undivided attention and informed them my reputation meant nothing. I told my audience, "Cola's reputation is terrible and he cannot be trusted."

Shaken, My Trusted Client jumped up and demanded to know what was going on. The Prince stood to leave and The Aide, standing behind The Prince, was dumbfounded. The Aide stared at me, wide-eyed and in shock. I calmly asked them to take their seats and listen carefully.

I explained that reputations were all about what others say about someone else. "Some," I said, "believe me to be a terrible person. Their beliefs notwithstanding, I AM a man of character and integrity who pursues a good reputation. However, Cola isn't always considered reputable.

Likewise, the men who ran the blackjack game have reputations as well. In their case, I discovered they are reputed to be dangerous, evil, and avoided at all costs."

I told the men slowly and with emphasis, "We are about to enter a dangerous arena."

I'd done my homework and knew those involved in the blackjack games were not exactly Citizen Joe's. They were dangerous underworld figures and were reputed to be adept at removing rivals and troublemakers from the surface of this earth.

The Aide stammered. He couldn't understand how I knew the Who and What of the situation. He looked at The Prince and said, "I told him nothing! Truly nothing, Your Highness!"

I made it clear I was a Spy. I said, "I'm a professional that does his homework before signing on with a potential client."

In that, I hoped to boost my reputation even further by attending the meeting prepared. I followed those comments with a question, "Is Cola's reputation validated by My Trusted Client's recommendation or by Cola himself; through his deeds?"

Someone said, "Both."

Ignoring the statement, I told them my point was that I, in fact, validated the reputation of the mobsters. Their deeds and words confirmed huge character flaws, and certainly didn't show them to be men of integrity. I told the assembled men that the mobsters were dangerous, cunning, and to be avoided at all costs.

I took a chance and informed The Prince he was a sucker, but a living sucker. I insulted him, but the pampered royal playboy really needed me to be candid, honest, firm, and to the point. Yes, based upon those involved, he was probably cheated; and if he preferred to cheat death, The Prince should forget about the entire matter. On the other hand, if he wanted to meet his Maker, he should find someone else to look into his losses at the casino.

I turned down the job and advised The Prince to go away wiser for the experience. He thanked me, and I was rewarded handsomely for my time. Cola did not request the staggering sum promised for the Op. My Trusted Client was happy with my approach, The Aide was both appreciative and stunned, and The Prince calmly accepted my advice. Although, he didn't give up immediately. Again, The Prince asked, "How was I cheated?"

I told The Prince if he loved life it was better he didn't find out.

The Prince was, indeed, cheated. So was everyone else who played blackjack at that casino. I knew, but he didn't need to know, how he was cheated.

My investigation revealed the casino had a couple of card sharks who could deal something called, "Seconds." That is when a player says, "Hit me." The dealer (aka Mechanic), knowing the top card, could intentionally "Hit" the player with the second card. Therefore, dealing seconds.

> ***An aside...***
> A "Mechanic" in the gambling world is a card dealer who manipulates playing cards in a manner to change the outcome in the dealer's favor. There are a few individuals who can manipulate dice when tossing them, increasing the odds in their favor. They are also referred to as Mechanics by some people.

Back to Marked Cards...
I also discovered dealers knew the top card because someone marked the cards using an American nickel, creating an almost imperceptible shine on the edges of higher valued cards. The dealer could see the shine from his perspective, but the player's angle kept the shine invisible to them.

The way I handled The Prince boosted my reputation with My Trusted Client; and, hopefully, with The Prince. Perhaps I'll never know. I've not seen him or heard anything about him in the decades since that interesting meeting.

Pattern Recognition

A helpful tool in espionage is the ability to recognize patterns. Most Targets don't realize they have developed deep-rooted habits and follow patterns unrecognizable to them. Astute spies will spot complicated patterns involving human behavior when others will not. Moreover, canny spies will exploit those behaviors in ways that go unrecognized by Targets and their security teams.

Money, Ego, and Power

While lazy, inept, spies will rely on blackmail and extortion to steal information, successful espionage professionals leverage money, ego, and power to elicit much-needed cooperation and valuable information. Remember Maura's efforts to extort information from Snare?

Misdirection

Magicians aren't the only professionals who rely on misdirection. Misdirection is an invaluable tool in Corporate Espionage. It is so valuable, I am reticent to offer either examples or details. As I mentioned in the front matter of this book, this is NOT a "How to Become a Corporate Espionage Professional" study guide. Trust me when I say, it is one of the most valuable tools in my arsenal. Any magician will confirm the power of misdirection.

The Art of War

The Art of War, written by Sun Tzu about 2500 years ago, is a tremendous resource for espionage professionals. It's really a primer on human behavior in the world of war, deceit, avarice, and espionage. Success in the espionage arena requires a thorough understanding of human behavior. Here are a few excerpts from that great read and variously related commentaries.

> "...it is impossible to obtain trustworthy spies unless they are properly paid for their services."

> "In the enemy's country, win people over by kind treatment, and use them as spies."

> "Worthy men who have been degraded from office, criminals who have undergone punishment; also, favorite concubines who are greedy for gold, men who are aggrieved at being in subordinate positions, or who have been passed over in the distribution of posts, others who are anxious that their side should be defeated in order that they may have a chance of displaying their ability and talents, fickle turncoats who always want to have a

foot in each boat. Officials of these several kinds should be secretly approached and bound to one's interests by means of rich presents. In this way you will be able to find out the state of affairs in the enemy's country, ascertain the plans that are being formed against you, and moreover disturb the harmony and create a breach between the sovereign and his ministers."

"Spies are attached to those who give them most, he who pays them ill is never served. They should never be known to anybody; nor should they know one another. When they propose anything very material, secure their persons, or have in your possession their wives and children as hostages for their fidelity. Never communicate anything to them but what is absolutely necessary that they should know."

"We ostentatiously do things calculated to deceive our own spies, who must be led to believe that they have been unwittingly disclosed. Then, when these spies are captured in the enemy's lines, they will make an entirely false report, and the enemy will take measures accordingly, only to find that we do something quite different."

"...spy must be a man of keen intellect, though in outward appearance a fool; of shabby exterior, but with a will of iron."

"When you have attracted them by substantial offers, you must treat them with absolute sincerity; then they will work for you with all their might."

"Be on your guard against the possibility of spies going over to the service of the enemy."

"Just as water, which carries a boat from bank to bank, may also be the means of sinking it, so reliance on spies, while production of great results, is oft-times the cause of utter destruction."

Sun Tzu's 2500-year-old advice is as valuable and applicable today as it was thousands of years ago.

Rectal Cavity Transport vs. Ultraviolet Messaging

Some spies will use anal cavity insertions to sneak documents out of high-security facilities. However, I was never in favor of, and have never used, that approach.

One of my favorite approaches was to use a special fountain pen that would produce invisible lettering. The writing would remain invisible until, and unless, viewed under special ultraviolet lighting. The wavelength of the light would render the hidden image, visible. The system worked rather well.

For example, we would have our Asset produce a list of names we needed. They were instructed to photocopy that list. We would not have Assets take originals to the restroom. We would have them take a photocopy to the bathroom.

They would enter a toilet stall. We instructed Assets to pull their pants down to their knees or raise their dress, then sit on the toilet. Doing so exposed the front part of each thigh, where they would record the information we needed. The Asset would then transcribe what was on the photocopy. They could not see what they were writing for long, but the lettering remained sufficiently wet enough for a time, so the fresh writing was viewable, and not accidentally overwritten.

When Assets finished transcribing the information from the photocopy onto their skin, they were told to carefully fold the photocopy as we'd trained them to do. Then Assets would unfold the photocopy. Once unfolded, we would have them open a small plastic bottle of water and dampen the seams on the copy paper. That process permitted easy, near silent tearing. Once the water softened the creased seams, they tore up the photocopy. Then the Asset deposited the pieces into the toilet. Assets were explicitly instructed to tear the paper carefully, but to avoid doing so while anyone else was in the restroom. Then they were told to drop the small invisible ink cartridge from the pen into the toilet bowl. Next, Assets were instructed to flush the toilet; and repeat as necessary, until no more paper remained in the bowl. Finally, Assets would place a regular ink cartridge into the pen. They'd wrap toilet paper around the business end of the cartridge pen, lower it below the rim of the toilet bowl, and shake until the TP began to show the ink's visible color. They were instructed to drop the inky toilet paper into the water and flush until all evidence of the ink was gone from the bowl.

An aside...
We eventually transitioned away from cartridge pens. After a time they became a curiosity and people wanted to try writing with them. A OneSeven experimented with many concealments and writing systems that included tampons, fingernail polish brush tubes, bra concealments, removable heels on high heel shoes, lipstick, and key chains. We eventually settled on removable temples for eyeglasses and shoelaces. The plastic ends of shoelaces gave us a writing instrument and an inkwell. Shoelaces turned out to be our best option for an invisible ink pen, but they did have drawbacks.

Shoelaces laces were suitable for one-time use, so they required changing after each document dump. Also, while sitting in a bathroom stall, our Asset's feet were exposed and generally within view of others in the bathroom. We successfully devised a way to temporarily remove and replace the plastic ends on shoelaces to overcome the inherent operational weakness involved with taking the laces entirely off and replacing them while in a bathroom. After a time, we transitioned to a plastic shoelace tip that, when removed, left a plastic tip remaining on the shoelace. Once the removable tip was used, it could be flushed down the toilet.

We had one particular Asset who claimed he liked to remove a shoe, set it on his lap, and use the lace while still connected to the shoe. We didn't want Assets to use that process, because someone outside the stall might get curious about someone wearing a shoe on one foot and a naked sock on the other.

Back to Spies Thighs...
After work, they'd usually meet their Handler in a private setting. The Handler would photograph the front of their thighs with a 35mm camera, using an electronic ultraviolet flash. The flash generated light just outside the visible spectrum at a wavelength of 380 nm. After the film was developed, the secret information we sought was easily visible and readable if the thighs were viewed upside down (because Assets had been sitting on a toilet and recorded the secret information by starting at their knees and moving toward their upper thighs).

Dry Ice
Dry ice has many uses in the espionage arena.

On one particular occasion, I needed to raise the heat in a building located in a large industrial park. After gaining entry, I found my way into a large cold room. A brief search led to the thermostat's location. However, I was disappointed when I discovered it wasn't readily accessible.

The controls sat within a heavily perforated box, secured by a tubular lock. I didn't have my tubular lock picks with me, so I attempted to pick the lock using standard lockpicks. I couldn't successfully manipulate the otherwise pickable lock. There was an issue with my tension wrench getting in the way as I attempted to move two of the key pins.

I didn't have time to play with the lock and considered beating the box with a hammer to gain access to the thermostat. That was a non-starter. Noise would have alerted the nighttime security crew, plus doing so might damage the thermostat. Besides, I didn't want to leave evidence of my presence.

I stood there calmly for a few moments considering options. Then Cola hit upon an idea. I remembered a sizable commercial extermination firm was just around the corner in the industrial park. Businesses serving the nearby container terminal, used for unloading shipping containers from around the world, dominated the industrial park. Exterminators serving shipping companies often need to eradicate rats aboard ships. Dry ice is a common extermination protocol for vermin-infested vessels.

I looked back at the box and made a decision. Bring in dry ice. Yep, I'd use ice to raise the heat. Oxymoronic, but true.

The security box was covered with small perforations so the room's ambient air could flow around the thermostat while keeping unauthorized persons from adjusting temperature controls. As any science teacher would tell his students, heat rises, and cold descends. If I placed a block of dry ice, aka cardice, atop the locked box, cold carbon dioxide gases would descend and envelop the thermostatic sensor; thereby lowering the temperature within the box. The cold gases would be much colder than the current setting on the device. Then the thermostat would do what thermostats do, and fire up the furnace to warm the thermostat. Then Cola could perform his spy duties.

I left the building and successfully penetrated the extermination building. Within three minutes I located a freezer containing small brick-sized blocks of cardice and placed a single block into a small cardboard container sitting on a nearby shelf. Picking up that frozen treasure, I headed back to the Target facility. Once inside the building, I removed the frozen toll from the cardboard box and positioned the brick of dry ice on top of the metal thermostat box. Within a minute the heater kicked on and began warming the facility.

I was able to proceed with the Op, thanks to a small block of frozen carbon dioxide (-109.3° Fahrenheit). According to my calculations, the frozen gas would have completely burned off about two hours before anyone was scheduled to arrive at the facility the next morning. That evaporative sublimation process covered my tracks and turned evidence of my deeds into invisible dissipated vapors.

> ***An aside...***
> Dry ice undergoes "sublimation" when it transitions from a solid to a gas, without passing through an intervening liquid state.

COLA'S PICKS

Lock Picks
I possess more than three dozen various lock-picking tools. No Spy worth his salt can conduct his affairs without a good working knowledge of locks. Cola has re-key kits, an assortment of safe change keys, and other specialized equipment I'd rather not mention. Whether it's picking locks or cracking safes, a good Spy should be an expert in both areas.

> ***An aside...***
> TJ's son can quickly spot a faux Marine. A few insider questions about MCRD, the Fleet, and other obscure USMC details will quickly separate a real Marine from a counterfeit.

Back to Espionage Tools...
I've met more than a few who claim to be espionage professionals that cannot name the parts that help secure a safe (e.g., drive pin, fence, tension washer, drive cam, re-locker, etc...) or tools to assist in cracking safes (e.g., graph paper).

Espionage professionals? No.
Phony or a Wally wannabe? Yes.

Car Washes

We've used car washes on many occasions to plant bugs into vehicles driven by Targets. That approach works well if the Target tends to take care of business within their cars AND has a pattern of washing their vehicles regularly, while habitually choosing an interior service option. We'd plant a short Confederate on the staff at a car wash. Our Cola plant was responsible for vacuuming and cleaning the interior. They would plant recording devices and retrieve recordings.

> ***An aside...***
> Short Confederates were used because of their inability to reach far enough to dry windows, roofs, and hoods. That made the inside cleaning position a logical option. Management usually saw the logic in placing our small people inside automobiles, without coercion from our Team.

Back to Planting Bugs...
One consideration when planting a bug is to be sure sufficient power is available for the device. When vehicles are involved, unlike buildings and exterior locations, power needs are a no-brainer. Cars have 12v power everywhere, allowing spies easy installation of 12v listening devices and recording systems.

Shredders

Spies love shredders. Most people mistakenly believe shredders protect their secrets. Here's a secret. They don't.

In fact, shredders can be very helpful to spies. If the shredder is not a cross-cut shredder, even rookie spies have extremely high success rates recovering information on those shredded documents. Even cross-cut shredders work well for patient professional spies.

I'll try not to disturb the placement of shreds and, if not already bagged, I'll carefully bag them. I have a gifted OneSeven who suffered a brain injury as a teenager and, in the years since, has excelled in detecting, integrating, and completing complex patterns. If I provide a bag of shreds to her, even the cross-cut variety, she'll carefully remove the shreds layer by layer and reconstruct the previously shredded documents. She's amazing. However, based on my observations, even Cola's gifted OneSeven has difficulty reassembling shredded documents if the quantity is large and they undergo thorough mixing.

When I shred my own documents, I'll mix documents truly needing to be destroyed, with three or four times more rubbish records containing benign non-identifiable non-sensitive information. Then I mix and separate the shreds into multiple trash bags. I'll also toss in foods scraps, raw broken eggs, milk, raw chicken juices, raw fish, raw hamburger, and other food items usually destined for the garbage disposal. I'll mix everything thoroughly. Food items that rot quickly and produce noxious odors and nasty residue work best. Then I'll dispose of the bags in separate locations. After all, I recognize shredding isn't the privacy cure-all people believe it to be.

Beware! Shredding documents shouldn't necessarily give you peace of mind and the false sense of security you're feeling. Skookum Jim recently told me about a new software program that can reassemble tens of thousands of shreds into complete documents within minutes. Millions of pieces within a few hours (depending on computer processing power).

The shreds are placed blank side down, not touching, on a flat lime green surface (as opposed to a glossy surface). Diffused room lighting is required. No hot (bright) spots are permitted. Shred placement isn't important so long as the back side is blank. If two-sided documents are involved, technicians photograph both sides with care. The software removes all the black from the image, leaving only pieces of shreds. Then the software performs its magic, and document reassembly occurs in mere minutes (depending on the font sizes, number of shreds, etc...). *Wow! Scary amazing!*

> NOTE: I don't usually burn shreds. There are many issues associated with that practice. I'll save that discussion for another time. However, because of the new software, my system of choice is evolving into a mixture of putrefaction and liquidation. That's a nasty way to go, but necessity is

> the mother of my inventive processes. A chemist OneSeven has just about perfected a recipe for me. The main ingredient? A mixture of cheap high fat beef hamburger and raw chicken hamburger. *Yum!*

Yes, even good guy spies who've transitioned from the Dark Side of espionage need to protect their secrets.

3" HEADLIGHT RFID

RFID Access Stickers

Radio Frequency Identification (RFID) Stickers contain information stored in a unique computer circuit, designed to react to electromagnetic fields. When RFID Stickers breach an electromagnetic field, the circuit's identifying information is read by a receiving device, allowing a computer to identify and track RFID Stickers. Those stickers are attached to objects for various tracking and access purposes.

RFID Access Stickers are not uncommon on the headlights of vehicles often transiting certain types of controlled vehicular access systems. RFID allows easy entry when an RFID equipped vehicle approaches a controlled access area. The RFID sticker's unique signal is read by a computer. The computer then queries its database to see if the car or truck has authorization for entry. If authorized for admission, the computer grants access by opening gates or dropping retractable bollards into the asphalt. Many systems record the unique RFID Sticker number in an access database (log file), with the time and date. Some systems will affiliate RFID log file data with video surveillance records, for computer controlled retrieval of video captured when the vehicle passed through the electromagnetic field.

One of my Counterespionage Clients had an RFID sticker removed from his front headlight. He didn't realize he was targeted by a Spy who removed his RFID sticker. That action allowed the Spy into a secure area at one of My Client's manufacturing facilities. He suffered losses due to that unexpected security weakness, and cleaning up the mess was lengthy and difficult for Cola. The gates were open and the cows long gone. My Client now appreciates the value of locking the gate BEFORE the cows can bolt.

Designated Smoking Areas

As I mentioned when discussing my homeless persona, smoking rooms and outside smoking areas are excellent environments for eavesdropping. On occasion people will drop their guard entirely; even if the audience does not have a repulsive smell or grungy appearance. They'll relax and speak candidly about things they would never discuss in other areas.

Video Surveillance Systems

Why hack into a computer network, when it is often much easier to use video cameras with HD and high-quality lenses having zoom and pan capabilities? Why hack a computer, when an excellent well-positioned camera can capture everything on a computer monitor? A second camera focusing on the keyboard is even better. A third camera with an overview of the room and any players is best.

The IT guys will never know how the breach occurred. As is often the case, people look for the expected. In the case of network and database breaches, IT people will usually seek that which is familiar to them. They'll invest time and other resources looking for evidence of Trojan Horses, phishing, firewall hacks, digital fingerprints and other artifacts.

It Takes Money to Make Money

I once assisted a Client, Pat Richards, with a small deal that Readers may find interesting. Pat's tire business failed. He needed to leave the leased premises within a short time-frame. Pat Richards approached a trucking company to gauge their interest in purchasing his remaining tire inventory. He provided them with a huge discounted price if they'd complete a paid-in-full purchase right away. They agreed and gave Pat a check for $30,000. The tires were loaded and transported to an unknown destination.

My Client took the check to the issuing bank. He asked if they'd exchange the trucking company's business check for several Cashier's Checks. Mr. Richards wanted the Cashier's Checks so he could pay his debts to a few key vendors. The teller informed him the business check from the trucking company was "Not good." It was NSF (Non-Sufficient Funds).

Leaving the bank, Pat drove to the offices of the trucking company and discovered they were no longer at that location. He tried calling the number on the check for several days. No answer. His father-in-law, Perry Anderson, was a longtime Cola Client. Perry recommended Pat contact me.

It didn't take long for Cola to discover the trucking company's accounts were overextended. The entire process took me less than six hours. I found they'd sold all the tires purchased from Mr. Richards. The Trucker carried a lot of high-interest credit card debt and was behind on his house payment. The trucker's company was also in arrears on his semi-truck loan payments. He was in financial trouble.

On the good news front, Cola discovered they'd just received a significant wire transfer into their checking account. That transfer appeared to be associated with Pat's missing tires.

I told Pat, "Get to the bank to try and cash the check, NOW!"

Unfortunately, his was a wasted trip. Same story as before. Non-Sufficient Funds.

I decided to find out just how much cash was in The Trucker's account from which he wrote the check to My Client. As I recall, the bank had nineteen branches. I began calling various branch offices to "verify funds on a checking account." I began by telling whoever answered the phone that I had a check for $15,000 on the account. The bank employee said the check was "good." Phoning another branch with the same approach, I told them I had a check in the amount of $20,000. It was also said to be "good."

After a series of calls, I determined the account carried funds sufficient to cash a check for $28,500, but a check for $29,000 would bounce.

The deal I had with Pat Richards was that I would spend no more than $3000 (10%) to try and recover his funds. If successful, my compensation would be 20% of the $30,000 check. If unsuccessful, he would reimburse me for my actual expenses. Armed with an approximate current balance in The Trucker's checking account, I hatched a plan to cash the check that day.

My Client and I entered one of the bank's branches. I filled out a blank deposit slip in the amount of $1,500, while Pat stopped to eat a cookie on a table near the front door.

> ***An aside...***
> Pat Richards informed me later that he poured himself a small Styrofoam cup of coffee but decided to pass on the cupcake. Curious, I asked why he didn't enjoy a tasty sweet treat. As Treena would say, "They looked yummy." Pat informed me two little girls were manhandling each one. They licked all the sprinkles off the top of each cupcake, then returned the cakes to the serving tray.
>
> Laughing, I told him about my plumber friend, Rick Pepworthy, and the nasty donuts (see the Invisible People chapter).

Back to The Bad Check...
Taking a chance, I walked up to a teller window and deposited $1,500 in cash. That should have raised the available balance on

the account to at least $30,000. I told the teller to post the funds immediately. She did and confirmed the posting. When I received that information, I used a prearranged signal designed to alert Pat of the posted deposit. Pat knew that meant he should queue up and cash the check without delay.

We were in the main branch of the bank. It was midday on a Friday. Payday. I knew they'd have plenty of cash on hand, and that's why we chose that branch.

I'd instructed Pat to ignore any offers of a Cashier's Check. I told him to take it all in cash, so there wouldn't be any issues later. It's rare for a bank to process stop payment requests on Cashier's Checks. However, a bank can refuse to honor a Cashier's Check if they believe fraud may be involved. Alternatively, they can make cashing such checks difficult by invoking forced delays in the remittance process. One excusable delay is to allow bank officials sufficient time to investigate a potential fraud.

Pat Richards successfully cashed the check. He reimbursed me for the $1,500 Cola deposited into the account. My Client added $6000 for my services. Not bad for a day's work.

You know that old saying, it takes money to make money. My activities that day underscore the fact that cash can be a valuable tool in my business.

Can you imagine the look on The Trucker's face when he discovered his checking account was nearly empty? Maintaining an account balance below the amount of an outstanding check does little good when Cola rolls up his sleeves.

> ***An aside...***
> Cola's small world encounters are sometimes simply mistaken identity. I was in the Twin Cities during a cold snap about ten years ago. As I was passing through downtown Minneapolis on a time-critical cross-country road trip, my car began acting up. Ahead and to my right was a car repair facility called Bobby and Steve's Auto World.

I pulled in and a fellow with a knit ski hat waited on me. Nothing about him was familiar. He was a cordial fellow with a frozen red face. His name was Dan. He appeared sincerely concerned about my deadline and promised to get right on it. Dan invited me to enjoy the comforts of Bobby and Steve's spacious waiting area.

Entering the building, I realized the facility was huge. Food and drink options were everywhere. I was hungry and grabbed something hot to eat, along with a black coffee. When I paid for the food, I was directed upstairs to relax while they addressed the problems with my car.

Bobby and Steve's Stairway

There was something unusual about the stairs leading to the upper level (see the photo above). It was impressive. In fact, the entire store (especially the upstairs) was tastefully appointed. The walls sported fine art, there was a restored fifty's something Chevrolet in the waiting area, and more. Two Police Officers were taking a meal break in that area. I was captivated by the setting. *Until...*

You Can't Prepare for Everything!

Until I had the shock of my life. I looked up from my meal and standing before me was Pat Richards. Then he began speaking. No, it wasn't Pat. The voice was wrong.

Way wrong. It was actually the Service Writer I met outside named Dan. Without his coat, frozen red face, and knit ski hat he looked exactly, I mean EXACTLY, like Pat Richards. Didn't sound like him, but he was the spitting image of My Client.

When asked, he told me his last name was Richards. Amazing, the same last name as Pat. I asked him if he had a relative named Pat Richards, and he said no. However, the man told me his wife's name is Pati Richards.

Since Pat Richards is a Client and I hold our relationship in the strictest confidence, I stopped the interrogation. Dan informed me they'd repaired my car. He went over the services performed by his mechanic.

In short, the cost was reasonable, the service was excellent, the food and atmosphere was amazing, and the small world encounter was unbelievable. Perhaps it's true. Perhaps we all have an identical twin somewhere on this planet. Dan Richards and Pat Richards sure made me think twice about that old wives' tale.

Itching Powder

I am reticent to offer much in the way of details on this one. Although I'm sure it was interesting, perhaps funny, to a knowing observer.

Cecil, a Spy specializing in sports wagering and throwing games, was hired to help an underdog team win a basketball game. There was wagering associated with the matter.

An aside...
Throwing games is as old as sporting events. "Throwing a Game" has a number of synonyms, to include event fixing, game fixing, race fixing, point fixing, match fixing, and sports fixing. An associated phrase is, "The fix is in." Other related words include dumping, tweeking, tanking, squeezing, sabotaging, spreading, hustling, sandbagging,

> shaving, throwing, point management, fix management, and outcome management.
>
> Throwing games is big business and nearly impossible to stop. Even more difficult to address are actions associated with point fixing, point spreading, and point shaving.

Back to The Big Itch...
Here's what Cecil did to one team's star player:

Cecil snuck into a hotel room to access the sports bag belonging to the team's Star basketball player. When Cecil entered the room using a manager's master key, The Star was dining in the hotel restaurant with his teammates. The sports bag contained three jockstraps. Cecil sprinkled a healthy dose of Itching Powder into the "junk" pouches of the three pieces of underwear.

When the game started, everything appeared fine. After a few minutes of play, The Star's sabotaged jockstrap began bothering him. The Star began sneaking opportunities to scratch his crotch in front of more than ten thousand fans. By halftime, he was in apparent distress. I'm told he showered and changed into a fresh jock during halftime. When he came out for the second half, it was a repeat of the first half, but worse.

The Itching Powder served its purpose and irritated the basketball player's private parts. The Star's concentration evaporated, and he failed to produce for his team. It was a huge upset. The other team and Cecil's wagering clients won that day.

> ***An aside...***
> Itching Powder is essentially ground glass. It's like a powdered form of the pink insulation found in homes. When placed into the jockstrap of an active person Itching Powder creates problems. First, movement of the thighs and testicles begins to rub small glass particles into the scrotum. As the wearer becomes more active and starts sweating, salts in human sweat will work its way into thousands of microscopic cuts caused by the ground glass. Salt contact in the wounds promotes itching. The

victim begins scratching the area, thereby creating more cuts as he moves and presses the powdered glass into the already uncomfortable sweaty itching area. No real damage, just a lot of irritation.

I've heard powdered sugar will achieve similar results in jockstraps. I have no firsthand experience in that area. If it works though, it's a rather 'sweet' approach to causing distraction for ball players.

Back to The Fixed Basketball Game
To be clear, sabotaging The Star's basketball game was NOT a Cola Op.

False Identification aka Fake ID's
I enjoy an excellent relationship with a OneSeven having exceptional skills in duplicating identification documents. His artistic skills, attention to detail, and perfectionism have served me well for nearly three decades.

There are more than a few unprofessional spies who hit the streets to purchase passable, albeit low grade, false ID's. A common destination for more than a few Wally-like spies is to one of several counterfeiters working on the west coast. The Westlake area of Los Angeles is a popular Fake ID acquisition location. Westlake is on the periphery of downtown LA, a short distance to the west. It is a popular place for securing inexpensive ID's very quickly. I've known several spies who were nailed after attempting to use documents from those ID mills.

My experience and understanding of identity document duplication techniques go back to my high school days. When I was sixteen, my father won an auction bid for a dishwasher box filled with unused, albeit dated, Polaroid film for cents on the dollar. We had film to burn.

In the state where we resided at the time, driving certificates (aka Driver's Licenses) were pretty cheesy. DMV took driver photos in front of a blue background. The remainder of the license was shiny, had uneven lighting, and was printed with odd looking, sometimes faded, characters. That system was easily duplicated. In fact, the entire license was merely a photograph. DMV clerks took driver photographs and all accompanying information at the same time. The captured image included the layout, text, and the driver's image. DMV offices shipped finished film canisters to a lab for developing. Finished photos were die-cut into standard size licenses. Drivers received their finished licenses in the mail.

My buddies Willie and Philipe, along with yours truly (Cola) decided to duplicate the license, using Dad's Polaroid film. We did that so we could buy beer at the local liquor store (although Willie didn't drink, and doesn't to this day). Using similar versions of our names, we constructed a huge white cardboard license matching the state's version and entered William Philip Stephens (for Willie, Philipe, and Stefano) onto the giant poster.

The poster had a cutout for the photograph. The dimensions were such that when we placed our heads in the cutout while holding the poster in front of us, it looked like a giant Driver's License. We affixed wooden poles to the back for the subject to use to hold up the enormous license without showing his fingers on the poster's edges. Not only did it assist by keeping our hands out of view, it also permitted our shoulders to remain in a somewhat natural position.

> ***An aside...***
> Appearing natural when holding up a large sign is difficult. As Readers know, Driver's Licenses have the photo offset to one side. Holding the sign level, while keeping one's head in the center of the cutout, was difficult and unnaturally altered the angle of the holder's shoulders.

Back to The Poster Board Driver's License...

The only differences on our licenses were the height, weight, hair color and eye color. Those blocks remained blank. We used smaller white pieces of poster board material, that would fit within field borders, containing different height, weight, hair and eye color information. We'd roll up a small portion of clear plastic tape and affix it to the back of the little cards, then press them into place. Doing so allowed our single Driver's License to be used by all three of us. Willie had blue eyes, while Philipe and I had dark brown eyes. Willie was a blonde, Philipe had brown hair, and mine was nearly black. Willie stood two inches taller than me, Philipe was about 5'7", and I'm an even six feet tall.

We'd stand outside Philipe's home in the country. A large hill near the house rose above the surrounding farmland. We'd carry the license materials and Polaroid camera up the hill for photos. The subject for the next driver's license would stand at the hill's apex, with the blue sky behind him, and have his picture taken. It took some adjusting to get the size correct, but once we had that figured out, we could make a Fake ID for ourselves in mere minutes. In fact, both Philipe and I still have one of our Fake ID's made with that Polaroid film.

> ***An aside...***
> One afternoon we were up on the hill manufacturing Fake ID's and saw a dust cloud in the distance. A pickup truck was coming our way. *Yikes!* We quickly laid down the giant Driver's License and stood there looking stupid. The vehicle stopped at the bottom of the hill and a middle-aged man emerged. He said, "Hey, I see you up there with the giant Fake ID!"
>
> *Uh Oh! We were busted!*
>
> He continued, "Using a Polaroid camera? If so, cool idea. Would you mind making me a Fake ID too? I want to be twenty-one again!"
>
> Then he laughed and ducked back into his truck. Before leaving he rolled down the window and said, "Have fun boys. I'm impressed!"
>
> He drove away, and we never saw him again.

Back to Our Fake ID's...
An adult Cola remains very impressed with the ingenious approach employed by those three teenagers, as well as the quality of those photographs, nearly fifty years later. The color and image still look the same as they did on the day we took the

photos. No fading or color change. That was a phenomenal point-and-shoot system. In fact, Cola used Polaroids for much of the first decade I spent in espionage, continuing to use the film Papa bought at auction. Thanks, Papa!

Manufactured Identities

Manufacturing an identity is wholly different from making a counterfeit Driver's License. A well-manufactured identity will permit the New You to get a real license from the state. There are two approaches, the legal way, and illegal methods. The unlawful routes to a new identity are risky propositions and recognized by most people as dangerous. There is a third way that is almost entirely legal, but with a few illegal twists. I call them Twisted ID's or TID's.

A small company I once worked with was launched for the sole purpose of manufacturing and supporting TID identities. They used courts, DMVs, phone banks, drafted and backstopped resumes, and employed other tools to create and support new identities with excellent cover stories and personal histories. Their services included borrowed, manufactured, and cyber-only identity creation. Their specialty clients were battered women. They never knowingly worked with criminals. No, they didn't know what I did. They thought I was on the run from a drug dealer I'd turned into the cops.

One summer my wife and I went on a camping trip vacation out west with several other couples. We were all good friends. We visited and camped at the Grand Canyon, Zion National Park, Lake Powell, and a lake in northern Arizona near a town called Springerville. I believe it was called Big Lake.

While at Big Lake we met a nice Israeli man camping next to one of our RV's. We invited him to join us one evening by our manly "Kelly Fire."

> ***An aside...***
> Cola and friends refer to large campfires as Kelly Fires. The name Kelly is said to have originated on the Isle of Man; a 220 square mile island in the Irish Sea. The Isle

> of Man rests halfway between Great Britain and Ireland. Originally spelled "Celli," it means "Man of the Woods."
>
> Our camping companions and the Fugeleres believe any "Man of the Woods" knows how to build "a real fire." A big fire. "A Kelly Fire."
>
> To be clear, a Kelly Fire is neither a bonfire nor an Indian fire. It's in between. Large, safe, beautiful, and warm. Roaring, but not an inferno.

Back to The Camping Trip...
Over the course of the evening, we discovered "The Nice Israeli" was a diamond dealer from New York, now living in Israel. He shared with us that a U.S. division of an Eastern Bloc criminal enterprise kidnapped and held his wife for ransom. The Nice Israeli said they threatened to perform a radical mastectomy on her, without anesthesia, if he contacted law enforcement for their assistance. He knew of the gang's terrible reputation and believed their threats. The Nice Israeli didn't call anyone for help and quickly paid the ransom. His wife was released, and they immediately moved to Israel for the security it offered his family.

With lips loosened by tequila and the relaxing great outdoors, The Nice Israeli told us he and his wife wanted to move back to the States, but far from New York. He was traveling the west coast states to find a new place to settle, but continued to fear a repeat by the Eastern Bloc gang. The Nice Israeli wanted to remain in the wholesale diamond business but wanted a new identity for his wife.

He wanted a different name for her so she could buy a home, set up bank accounts, secure utilities, and so forth. He wanted a name the gang couldn't easily trace. I told him if she changed her name, it was usually a public event with postings in newspapers. He said he was stumped and didn't know what to do.

The next day, when nobody was around, I told him I might be able to help. He provided me with his contact information, and I had my background checking OneSeven, "Rearview," check him out. The Nice Israeli had a clean background. No red flags.

Rearview verified the kidnapping story through contacts in Israel and Belgium.

Two months later I arranged a meeting with The Nice Israeli in Las Vegas. I introduced him to the Identity Manufacturing Guru I've known for decades who specializes in TID's. My camping friend was well taken care of by the TID company and secured a new identity for his bride.

During the TID manufacturing process, I put the diamond dealer in touch with a former government official who is an expert in escape and evasion tactics. Cola's Nice Israeli camping friend needed to learn how to spot tails and other forms of surveillance. They worked together for several weeks so The Nice Israeli could reasonably ascertain if apparent dangers existed for him on his return home, after traveling the globe selling diamonds.

Eight years have passed, and I understand it's been a positive experience for The Nice Israeli couple. I'm glad I could help.

> P.S. One of the validation points for the kidnapping story is his wife's body. One of her little fingers and an ear were mailed to the diamond dealer while the kidnappers were holding her. He has those body parts preserved in formaldehyde, to continually remind him of the dangers involved if he drops his guard. I personally reviewed those items in his home, where he keeps them in a gem safe. Although I've not met his bride, Rearview confirmed she is without one ear and one little finger. She doesn't know her husband kept her severed body parts.

Reflectors and Tail Lights
Back in the day, before GPS devices were available to corporate spies, I used an assortment of reflective materials and lights to assist me in tailing Targets.

TOC
We would use special TOC light bulbs on one side of the rear of a vehicle. TOC stands for "Tracking with Ordinary Candlelight." Light levels on TOCs were outside the norm for automobiles and

served our needs well. Mismatched taillights on a car make it easier to tail. The same held true for headlights. If you didn't have time to change out a head or tail light, the next best thing might be to break that light. Tailing a vehicle with a single brake light or running light, or watching for a single oncoming headlight, offered certain advantages. Headlights were easily dispatched with the pellet gun I kept in the trunk of my car. The pellet pistol didn't work as well when we needed to make broken brake lights visible from a distance.

Occasionally it was necessary to follow big rigs so we could do things with the cargo. We'd mark the top of a trailer so that it could be tailed by a light plane in the daylight. Sometimes we'd do things to the tail lights, but on other occasions using something like a small adhesive strip of green reflecting tape was good enough.

Today, even when spies use GPS tracking systems, they employ redundant measures to track vehicles by using some of the lighting tricks we used in the old days.

Signage and Props

As mentioned elsewhere in this manuscript, magnetic signs offer great access and invisibility opportunities. Beyond signage, we've also found some props to be extremely useful for access and invisibility needs.

For example, I own a giant cockroach with a magnetic base. I'd place it on the roof of my van, along with other magnetic signage, to suggest I was in the pest-control business. That offered opportunities I wouldn't have otherwise enjoyed. It gave me the freedom to walk around homes with an insecticide sprayer in my hand. Sometimes I almost believed Cola was a real exterminator. *Just kidding.*

On other occasions, I would carry a clipboard. If anybody asked what I was doing, I'd tell them I was identifying the types of bugs, weeds, and rodents in the area so I could quote my services to neighborhood homeowners, or real estate agents representing buyers and sellers.

Hardhats, Measuring Tapes, and other Tools

I carried hardhats, measuring tapes, gas sensors, levels, clipboards, forged documents, and other items when I needed to enter buildings under construction or renovation. I'd carry a variety of business cards to identify Cola as a fire safety consultant, a construction materials supply salesman, or a contractor of some kind (e.g., painting, plumbing, drywall, etc.).

I would NOT pretend to be a government safety official, a law enforcement or fire department professional, or a postal employee. That would be contrary to Cola's Non-Negotiables.

Coffeehouses

If I were currently engaged in Dark Side Corporate Espionage, I'd be actively working a coffeehouse near a Target's business. It's incredible just how much information a Spy can pick up by merely sitting in a busy coffeehouse, listening to people converse with one another. It's often easy to look over people's shoulders and observe or photograph laptop screens. People speak louder on the phone than they realize and picking up tidbits from phone calls is powerful. It is amazing what people will reveal while they're sitting there with a cup of Joe, exposed to the entire world without even thinking about it. I'm sure this has been an enormous problem for Apple.

Coffeehouses are also great locations to engage in Corporate Counterespionage and Corporate Counterintelligence activities. I've used them more than a few times in my Counterintelligence and Counterespionage roles to plant utterly false or somewhat inaccurate information. After all, spies are using those prime locations as they collect proprietary business information and company gossip.

You may have heard about the push in California's Bay Area to stop tech companies from providing free on-campus meals for staff members. There are many good reasons for tech companies to keep their people on campus as much as possible, to include mitigation of espionage efforts by outsiders. I wouldn't be surprised if espionage enabling confederates are playing a role in those efforts.

Repairman

There are many kinds of repairmen that enter businesses. I've played them all but found one of my favorites was as a copy machine repairman. That offered me opportunities to copy internal documents without raising suspicions.

Cola went to school long enough to learn the basics and became pretty good at it. The design functions of most machines are so similar, it was unusual for one to stump me as I carried out my espionage duties.

Copy machines are often located next to fax machines. I've planned to be onsite on more than a few occasions when an Op critical incoming fax was expected. I'd simply copy the hot-off-the-presses fax and return it to the fax machine's bin.

Fishing (Telephonic Phishing)

Calling someone at home in the middle of the night catches them off guard. A Cola Call to a Target at 2:00 AM would begin with an introduction. I'd tell the Target I was calling from their security company's central station and needed to reset a trouble code coming from their alarm panel. I'd say I needed to verify their identity before proceeding, then ask for their passcode.

Luke Skywalker would probably have called that "An old Jedi Mind Trick." I was asking the sleepy person for security information they shouldn't be providing to a stranger on the phone. Of course, the intended victim should turn the tables to confirm my identity. You'd be surprised just how often I easily received the information I was seeking.

A moment later I'll ask them to confirm their disarm code. After receiving what I needed, I'll inform them the trouble code cleared okay. "Have a good night."

Many call recipients will not remember receiving a call. Doesn't matter. Their home phone's telephone line would be temporarily disconnected immediately thereafter and reconnected when the entry was completed. Near the end of my Dark Side involvement, we'd also use an electronic cell phone signal jammer to keep them from using mobile phones. If they lived close, we'd also make it difficult for them to use their vehicles for a quick trip to the office. Cola would have departed before any effective response could be initiated. Of course, as I said, that's when I operated on the Dark Side.

If a Mark became suspicious and I knew I was about to have a problem, I'd allay their concerns by saying something like, "The trouble codes originated in the jewelry cases at the front of the store. I'm guessing the problem was caused by the mall's electrical junction box again." I would use statements like that if I were calling the owner of a business totally unaffiliated with jewelry.

If calling the owner of a jewelry store, I might say, "It appears smoke from the deep fryer in the kitchen is interfering with the high-temperature sensor in the grill area again." I'd follow that quickly with an, "Uh oh!" and tell the sleepy person I made a mistake. I'd apologize, say something about dialing the wrong business, apologize again, and hang up."

Ping-Pong Balls

Ping-pong balls were occasionally used to make a Mark think he or she was having car trouble. We'd place a few of the balls in their gas tanks. As they ran low on gas, usually a quarter tank or less, a ball would get sucked down to the gas tank's sump outlet. That would cut off gas flow to the engine. Once the car died and pressure at the tank's outlet relieved, the ping-pong ball would float up, clearing the outlet sump. The car would start once more and travel a few hundred yards, then die again when the gas pedal was depressed for acceleration. We did that successfully on many occasions to feign engine trouble and insert ourselves into the Mark's life.

> ***An aside...***
> Ping-pong balls became more difficult when vehicles were built with the smaller gas filling holes associated with unleaded gas. Ping-pong balls are larger than those holes. We eventually transitioned to an inflatable system designed to overcome that problem.

Back to Engine Trouble...
We'd do this to either offer roadside assistance, then have Mark's car towed to a repair shop where we could plant bugs, remove objects from trunks, etc. We'd also do it to make our Target's late for meetings and events.

Thigh Paper System
I once had a system in place to assist Assets attempting to remove sensitive documents from high-security environments. We called it the "Thigh Paper System" or TPS. We used TPS when sneaking in photographic equipment wasn't a viable option.

The product used was an ordinary household plastic wrap. We'd instruct Assets to place documents inside a plastic wrap envelope they created, set the envelope against their thigh, then bind the plastic envelope further with several layers of plastic wrap.

Early on we had some problems associated with the system. If the bottom wasn't secured correctly, papers could slip out of the plastic wrap, and end up around the ankles of a courier. If the top wasn't secured tightly, the entire TPS could fall down around the ankles.

During one of our first attempts to use the plastic wrap system, we needed to sneak three sheets of 20 lb. bond out of a secure facility. The papers came out of the plastic wrap and fell to the floor. Fortunately and by coincidence, at precisely the same moment there was an issue with someone trying to breach security in that same area. That action was fortuitous, drawing away the attention of the assembled security guards. Although not a planned diversion, it worked out for us and saved the day.

After that mishap, we revised the TPS. We also discovered it was much better to perform offsite dry runs with each Asset. We taught them a better way to wrap their legs and the documents, to minimize issues. We learned to limit documents to three or four sheets of 20 lb. bond. Additional weight on the upper thighs increased risks. We also learned to evaluate thighs for adequacy with the system. Some shapes serve well for plastic wrap transport, and others are not good candidates at all. Wearing pantyhose over the TPS added additional insurance against losing the TPS to gravity.

There was also a problem of plastic wrap sticking to itself and everything else it shouldn't. However, over time we worked out the bugs and found this to be a reasonably effective system. We never lost an Asset who was trying to move papers out of a secure area using the Thigh Paper System.

Today USBs, voice recorders, and smartphone cameras have obviated most TPS deliveries.

Professionally Made "Novelty" Teeth

I'd use expensive custom-made fake teeth manufactured by my Dental OneSeven, Dr. Brara. His skills have provided me with various realistic looks. Those custom appliances help modify my appearance by altering the underlying structural contours of my face. Sometimes I'd add to the phony facade by inserting cotton balls into my cheeks. Add a hat and a false mustache, and I'd look like an entirely different person.

Airport VIP Lounges

My toolkit contained airport specific VIP lounge membership cards from all the major airlines. Like coffeehouses, those airport lounges offered many eavesdropping opportunities. Listening to face-to-face conversations, as well as one side of active phone calls, provided many golden nuggets. Peeking at legal pads and laptop screens also served me well.

Executives should do a better job when in those lounges. For them, most of the other lounge guests are merely part of the landscape and entirely invisible.

Poker Peering

I've used the term "Poker Peering" for decades to describe reading faces and body language. I do it to discover information behind "Close to the Vest" conversations. I call them C2V's. They are exchanges in which the Target is purposefully attempting to conceal valuable information. Corporate spies seeking unspoken information have devised many tactics to assist in revealing what Targets are trying to avoid disclosing in C2V's.

One Poker Peering tool I use to flush C2V information into the open is called, "Shotgunning." Some pheasant hunters will fire their shotguns blindly into bushes, intending to flush prey into the open. Shotgunning is a conversational tool I use that doesn't focus on anything in particular but gives me the opportunity to steer conversations based upon my Target's reactions. My questions are initially vague and become more focused as I near the goal. They are intended to help me find my way through a psychological maze, to achieve the prize my Mark is trying to avoid revealing.

More often than not, in C2V's I have to rely on subtle reactions and expressions on the Target's face. Microexpressions, also referred to as micromomentary expressions, are involuntary facial expressions that are short-lived and often overlooked. It helps to have baseline reactionary information on an individual before shotgunning. Prior engagements assist to understand facial nuances when engaged in probing prospects. Those previous engagements help establish baselines.

Fortune Tellers and Astrologers are, in my humble opinion, charlatans determined to fleece their clients. They will often use a combination of shotgunning and The Barnum Effect (also referred to as the Forer Effect). The Barnum Effect explains how and why charlatans (and spies) extract sufficient information to encourage a continuation of the information dump.

> ***An aside...***
> My first recollection of engaging in a C2V conversation occurred when I was in the 4th grade. I didn't have a name for what I did. However, the shotgunning approach I used was essentially the same as that I'd refine over a lifetime.
>
> I was in school on a Friday, and a classmate asked me if I was too afraid to "make out" with a girl I liked.

Fortunately for me, immediately after he asked the question, a teacher told us to stop talking and continue reading our assignment. I was fortunate because I had no idea what it meant to "make out" with a girl. Cola didn't want to look like an idiot who didn't know what everyone else seemed to understand. Therefore, I set to work planning an approach that would educate me, without revealing my ignorance.

After school, I went home and developed a plan to have an acquaintance unknowingly educate me. The kid, Mike, was also in my 4th-grade class. Mike and Elsa had been an item for a few months and recently broke up. Mike was mad at Elsa because she liked Joey too.

I called Mike on Saturday and pretended I was trying to figure out parents. I told him my cousin's mother was mad at her son because she discovered he'd been making out with his girlfriend. Mike laughed and said he was glad his mother didn't catch him making out with Elsa. I asked if there were any close calls. Mike told me there was one time when his mother found them in his bedroom. Mike said he heard her coming down the hall. He jumped up and was swinging his Louisville Slugger on the other side of the room when his mother opened the door. He was scolded for swinging the bat in the house and for having his door closed with a girl in his bedroom.

What did he jump up from doing?Was he kissing her? Did he have his hands under her shirt? What was Mike doing?

I asked Mike what his mother would have seen if he hadn't heard her approach and open the door. I'll never forget the sweet words Mike shared with me.

"I was sitting on the bed with my arms around Elsa kissing her."

I asked, "Did you have your hands up her shirt?"

"No, I was just kissing her."

Yes! Cola now knew for sure that "making out" meant he was kissing Elsa. Nothing more. My first shotgunning C2V attempt was 100% successful!

Back to Poker Peering...
I play poker at a semi-professional level. It is Cola's way to keep microexpressions on the forefront of my mind and as a way to further develop my micromomentary expression skill sets. Poker players are an interesting lot. Surviving successful older players have learned over thousands of hours of poker playing to keep their poker faces maintained and functioning at the highest levels possible. Youngsters who play poker wearing low slung hats or hoodies, along with dark glasses, are at a severe disadvantage. They never learn the art of facial control. When they are in a situation without the benefit of those tools, they become easy prey for people like me. Seasoned players that once had such skills will discover their facial control skills atrophy after they begin using dark glasses and hats.

Chinese Wall Compartmentalization
"Chinese Wall" is a term used in business describing an information barrier. It's a figurative wall that acts as a communications barrier, designed to secure specific information and keep it under wraps. It's a valuable tool when working in the espionage arena. "The Art of War" discusses this very matter. It reads, "...nor should they know one another."

I've done everything possible to erect and maintain a Chinese Wall between OneSevens and other moving parts within Cola's world, thereby compartmentalizing my organization and Cola's Operations. If too many people knew too much about my organization, it could spell doom for my entire team; as well as past, current, and future Operations. Compartmentalizing Cola's Operations, and insulating our activities, has saved my bacon on many occasions.

I employ additional terms to convey and support my philosophy that Chinese Wall Compartmentalization is critically important.

"Need to Know" and "Unauthorized Access" reflects my belief that security comes through obscurity.

I enjoyed a pleasant breakfast one morning with Air Force Lieutenant General David J. McCloud and his wife, Anna. General McCloud was a former official with the Joint Chiefs of Staff. During our meal, we discussed how the United States government developed the Lockheed F-117A Nighthawk in total secrecy.

While the project was underway and safely under wraps, the General told me his commanding officer tasked him to determine how many people were involved with the project. He also wanted to know exactly who they were and precisely what they knew, in case the secret project sprung a leak. After completing his assigned task, General McCloud's commanding officer was astounded to know that 36,000 individuals were involved with the project; in one capacity or another. I asked the General how they succeeded in keeping that many people quiet. He said, in a word, "Compartmentalization."

He gave me what he referred to as a series of "simplified" examples. Here's a simplified condensed version of what he shared with me (paraphrased):

> "If someone was working on F-117 tire designs, that person knew little more about the aircraft beyond the size of the wheel it needed to fit, and some pressure specifications. The team working on the wheel attach points of the landing gear, knew nothing about the tires or the rest of the struts; and so forth. The design team working on the wheel might not know anything about either the tires or the attach points."

> ***An aside...***
> I understand General McCloud passed away when an aircraft he was piloting crashed. I'm sorry to know that. He was a kind man. He and his wife were a special couple. He was survived by his wife, Anna, and two children. What a tragedy. Cola's heart ached then, and

continues to ache, over his loss. David McCloud was a great American!

Back to The Wall...
General McCloud said compartmentalization was ultimately credited as the reason the project remained entirely secret. That, too, is a good reason Cola's Operations over decades were far more sturdy and reliable than other individuals and entities involved in Corporate Espionage. I know of one group that encouraged everyone in the espionage organization to know everything about each other and their Espionage Operations, because they wanted their organization to have a culture of trust. That group of spies lasted a couple of years before legal problems brought down their house of cards.

I often recommend that specific Clients compartmentalize their own organizations as part of their Corporate Counterintelligence strategy.

Many years ago I constructed Cola's Chinese Wall. I will continue to maintain that Wall. The Wall works and serves as an excellent tool in my business.

Facial Hair
Throughout history, mustaches and other facial hair configurations have provided the foundation for identity concealments. Mustaches and beards are commonplace and easy to replicate.

On one occasion I decided to construct a fake mustache for myself, made out of my own hair. It was easy to conceive but difficult to accomplish. At the time I had an excellent mustache trimmed to my liking. I decided to shave it slowly over a couple of days in a hotel room.

Using the right kind of materials, I reconstructed my mustache on a fiber base, one hair at a time. When completed, it looked reasonably close to my original mustache. Of course, it helped that the hair was mine.

The very first time I attempted to use a fake mustache in an Operation, I was nearly nailed. The store-bought mustache was part of a plan. I went three months without a mustache. I was clean-shaven. I scheduled a meeting with a Mark from Oklahoma who had never seen me before. His name was Ray. I wanted Ray to depart and tell others the man with whom he'd met had a mustache. Those who knew me, and had seen me many times over the previous three months, knew my cleanly shaven face.

I met The Mark in a dark bar, owned by him. Ray was seated on a bar stool to my left. As we began our conversation, I realized one side of my mustache was loose. The adhesive, a spirit gum, wasn't holding the mustache as expected. I slowly lifted my glass for a drink and pressed the fake mustache back into place. It didn't stick. I was sweating bullets and came up with an idea.

Removing the straw from my drink, I put it in my mouth. Holding onto the straw, I slowly chewed on it. All the while I pressed my index finger against the mustache as I masticated. It seemed like I chewed forever, but it was only about forty minutes. I ended up walking away chewing the decimated straw, with my finger holding the loose mustache in place. Fortunately, the Operation came off without a hitch. Although it was one of the longest hours I've ever spent when operational.

Pickpockets

A good pickpocket is excellent to have around. I have one on my Team who has unbelievable skills. We never used "Fingers" to steal money. His most common lifts were USBs, hotel room keys, and magnetic key cards.

Bugs

One of the most successful bugs I've ever used in a car was a product developed by a short time member of our OneSeven family. He installed it in the windshield mounted powered rear view mirror. The powered mirror provided constant power and sat a mere eighteen inches from our Subject's mouth. We picked up everything that he said in that car. It was wonderful.

Bugs are essential tools in the espionage trade.

Magnetic License Plates

Temporary magnetic license plates saved my bacon on more than one occasion. I would not say I liked using them but found them invaluable at times. We'd drive a popular car with standard colors and affix magnetic license plates to it while we were operational. Once away from the scene of the Op, or otherwise in the clear, we'd remove the plates. All of our magnetic plates used rare earth magnets to ensure they wouldn't become dislodged on rough roads.

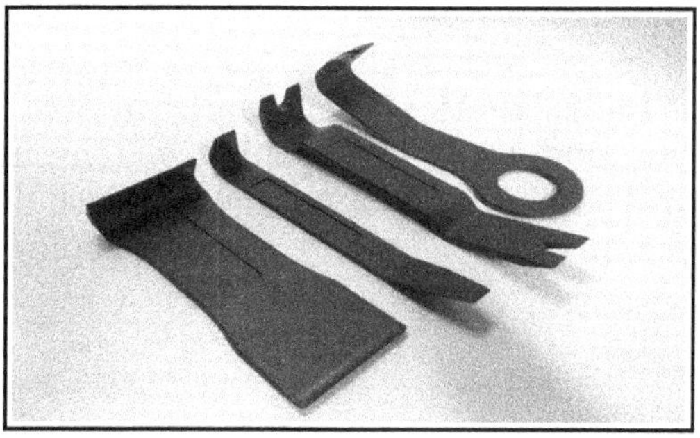

CAR "POPPING" TOOLS

Popping a Car

Body Shop tools would allow us the ability to pop off covers and door panels in cars so we could hide listening devices, documents, etc. We called it "Popping a Car."

Today those tools might be used to pop off a panel and install a GPS. Those tools help users avoid breaking the little plastic tabs designed to hold panels in place. We would also carry spare tabs that hold those covers secure, in the event we broke them while Popping a Car.

Watches

Inexpensive old analog wrist watches without bands or small pocket watches were always in my possession when operational. I'd pick up old timepieces at pawn shops for pennies and use them to know what time a Subject departed in his or her car. I'd position a watch on each side of a parked car's tire. If the vehicle were against a curb or some other immovable object, I'd only place one timepiece against the tire on the logical side. When the car pulled away, the tire would smash the watch and forever freeze the hands at the time of the departure.

We wouldn't place the watches directly on the ground. Someone might pick them up. We concealed them in smashed paper cups from nearby fast foot establishments, in dead flattened rodents, or in what appeared to be discarded candy wrappers.

Occasionally, it fails to work well because a watch might stop due to a winding need, dead battery, or a mechanical failure. Over time I learned to appreciate cheap quartz watches and learned how to change their batteries. Diamond Dave gave me a lead on watch batteries, and tools for opening watch cases. He also taught me how to open various watches, so I could install new batteries. Reliability and accuracy in timekeeping made them staples for Cola.

Taxi Drivers

Taxi drivers provide excellent opportunities to practice stories, accents, and to otherwise get into character; especially if you're trying to imitate their culture. They can be a helpful audience. If an audience, whatever a Spy shares with them needs to be mashed potatoes boring, so they'll forget about you in a day or two. Presenting oneself in a forgettable manner can be challenging. That's another way Cola spies are distinctly different from Wally. Everybody Wally encountered on his ill-fated espionage caper remembered him.

Water

Water has saved my bacon on more than one occasion during an Op. It's helped wash away evidence like footprints, create diversions, and caused damage for specific purposes.

I once crawled into the attic of an old Houston area office building to install a bug. While cautiously moving across the attic, I accidentally stepped off a beam and onto the insulation. No problem there, except the insulation was sitting atop a half inch of old sheetrock. I crashed through the sheetrock and landed on a desk below. I sprained my ankle in the process, but that was the least of my problems. There was no way to clean up the mess. Fortunately, the bug was already in place and very well hidden.

My activities up there needed to be covered up. I went back up into the ceiling and found a nearby waterline. I made it appear as if a connection on the waterline failed. That allowed water to come pouring out into the area where the hole was punched through the sheetrock. A casual onlooker would believe water weakened the waterlogged sheetrock directly above the desk and it eventually caused that area of the ceiling to collapse into the office, and onto the desk below. I also used a bucket to collect water and to saturate the area and the sheetrock that fell to the floor. Doing so made it look like accumulated water caused the ceiling's failure.

It covered up my activities, and the bugs worked out as expected. They were well-hidden and weren't discovered during cleanup or the repair process. You have to be so extremely careful when operational. One misstep (literally or figuratively) can throw everything into disarray, not to mention the risk of going to the hospital, jail, or morgue.

The Surrounding Environment

This might sound a little curious, but the environment can make or break an Op. I accepted a contract to make sure a particular suitor didn't purchase a small water utility My Client wanted. We made certain The Suitor received a recommendation to hire a consultant to review the transaction. He unknowingly hired Cola.

I tried to kill his interest in purchasing the utility by informing him I'd consulted on many utility transfers, and this one didn't smell right. I told The Suitor that the utility's infrastructure was old and problematic. Cola said well-casing corrosion was a red flag. I also informed him the relatively new well houses were nice, but the piping, wiring, and pumps were old and would require replacement in the near future. The water table had dropped precipitously in recent years, and he'd have to drill new wells in short order. I complained about the old transite asbestos cement piping used in the streets as main-lines. I also expressed concerns about the 3/4" galvanized piping servicing each property. I told The Suitor, the potential for electrolysis caused corrosion was high; and that piping might need replacement soon. None of that seemed to scare him off. I was beginning to run out of ideas. Darn!

One day, near the end of his due diligence, The Suitor and I walked one of the neighborhoods served by the utility. He wanted to check pressures and water quality. This was a little outside of my plans for the Op, but I went along with The Suitor.

Stopping in front of one residence, he reached into his briefcase and pulled out a glass jar. He asked me to get a sample of the water so he could have it tested. Remembering this guy didn't know anything about purchasing a water utility, I realized I had an additional opportunity to kill the sale.

I walked to the back of a nearby home that had a long black garden hose coiled haphazardly on the lawn. It had been pretty warm over the previous week, and I suspected the old hose still contained standing water. Knowing germs love warm dark wet locations, I believed a high bacterial count probably existed in the hose. I picked up one end of the hose and turned the faucet on slowly, allowing the jar to fill with water. That sample was primarily composed of old hose water. Capping the jar, I returned it to The Suitor.

A couple of days later The Suitor told me my services were no longer needed. When I asked why he was cutting me loose, he said the deal was off because of groundwater contamination. He said the bacterial count was off the charts and unacceptable to him. The Suitor said he wanted no part of that utility. I received final payment in the mail a few weeks later.

In the meantime, My Client swooped in and bought the utility for a song.

Changing situations and environmental possibilities can be helpful tools in the tool chest of a quick-thinking Spy.

Drones, GPS, Cell Phone Jammers , Miniature Cameras, Audio Bugs and other High Tech Devices

These tools are the basis for volumes of literary works. They are common in Corporate Espionage. I believe these high tech devices will provide exciting opportunities for spies. They'll unquestionably prove valuable with judicious use. There is a danger, however, if lazy, unqualified, and unprofessional spies rely on them too much. They'll squander opportunities and blow Ops with over reliance and overuse. Technology is a helpful ingredient in espionage, but it's not the end-all some believe it to be.

THE NUCLEAR OPERATION

RUSTY AT A TVA FACILITY

I chose to name this chapter, The Nuclear Operation, for three reasons. One, the Op involved mothballed partially constructed nuclear power plants. Two, I went nuclear when My Client double-crossed me. Three, I ended up nuking my Former Client's business because of his behaviors.

In the 1980's the Tennessee Valley Authority (TVA) canceled the completion of a dozen nuclear power plants either planned or under construction by the TVA. The vacated facilities were in various stages of development when the TVA Board voted to halt the projects. Among those impacted were the two reactor facilities at Phipps Bend near Tennessee's Tri-Cities area in 1981; followed by Bellefonte's two reactors in Hollywood, Alabama; the four reactors designated for Hartsville, Tennessee; as well as those in Yellow Creek near Corinth, Mississippi; and the Clinch River project in Oak Ridge, Tennessee.

My role in this Operation began at the Phipps Bend Nuclear Power Plant near Surgoinsville, Tennessee. An auction was underway, involving millions of dollars worth of construction materials. Bidders, like carrion-eating scavengers, were gathered together to take part in consuming the remains of the unfinished nuclear facility.

The auction included hundreds of miles of plumbing materials. Tens of thousands of valves and other valuable parts. There were miles of electrical conduit, spools containing many hundreds (if not thousands) of miles of electrical wire, and tons of packaged cement. The auction included air conditioners, gigantic ice makers the size of office buildings, boxes of telephones, shop tools, lumber, paint, and much much more. Acres and acres were devoted to storing miles of massive ductile iron piping, intended to cool an operating nuclear reactor. Thousands of pallets containing roofing materials, light fixtures, electronic detection equipment, and other items necessary for the facility were also up for auction.

My Client had interest in acquiring large piping from one of the TVA's facilities and was at that first auction to review the inventory there. He flew me to Phipps Bend to assist me in better understanding his goals for the Operation. I was amazed at what I witnessed on that TVA property. From Phipps Bend, we flew a light plane to the Hartsville nuclear facility. We made other related stops in several additional states after departing

Tennessee. He used our journeys to tell me how to handle the Op. I made it abundantly clear, he could define the goal, but planning and execution for the Op were in my wheelhouse; and mine alone.

I indicated I'd like to lean on him, from time to time, for information and advice. I also promised to report my progress upon reaching various milestones. He agreed to pay me the full amount, regardless of the Operation's length; even if the Op was cut short for any reason, other than a failure on my part. My Client agreed to a schedule of payments at predetermined milestones. On several occasions, and on a document he signed and conveyed to me, the Client conceded that I would be paid in full if he unilaterally pulled the plug on the Operation.

I'd done a few jobs for this Client previous to the TVA Op, so he wasn't surprised when I reminded him again that screwing Cola carried extremely negative consequences. He was sitting in front of me smoking a cigar, blathering that he'd never do such a thing. Then he intentionally blew a mouthful of cigar smoke directly into my face. He laughed, saying "Cola. Trust me. I'd never blow smoke up your ass. hahaha"

I granted him nothing in the way of a reaction, other than to stare at the idiot.

Once we arrived at a full understanding of the nature and scope of the Op, and he made his first of several scheduled payments, we got back to work. He redoubled his efforts to provide me with as much relevant information as possible.

I recall him telling me the pipe was 42" in diameter and 18' 2" in length, weighing in at a whopping 2 tons each. A little more than 6,000 sticks of this pipe were available at this auction alone. The other mothballed power plants also had thousands of sticks of similar piping available at their own auctions. My Client's needs were simple. He needed as much as possible at an extremely low price.

My Client thought he might not be the winning bidder at this auction, or one of the following TVA auctions. Regardless, his need remained to fill an order for that particular type of pipe. He had no interest in coughing up the funds necessary to purchase the same pipe from a manufacturer.

After one of the auctions, I received an urgent call from My Client. He believed the perfect scenario just landed in his lap when a young man outbid him at one of the auctions. He asked me to exploit "the kid" and said it should be a "piece of cake." He said the man was "a wet behind the ears momma's boy." My Client wanted me to make sure the kid sold his pipe to him for pennies on the dollar. I went to work.

RUSTY AND HIS INVENTORY

I discovered the young man, Rusty, had been bidding on behalf of his father, who wanted the pipe for a massive construction project in his area. The winning bid involved hundreds of thousands of dollars but was only a fraction of the cost if they purchased the same piping from a manufacturer. After learning more about the pipe, I discovered there were different classifications of the material, depending on the pressures involved. Further research revealed the pipe auctioned off at the nuclear facility was the same classification needed by Rusty. Rusty's father received information from a colleague relating to the upcoming project's piping needs; to include pipe classification requirements.

A little more sleuthing unearthed an excellent fact. The project engineer for Rusty's father's project hadn't publicly released specifications for bidding, since the bid opening wouldn't occur for three more months. That provided me with a solid foundation, upon which I could plan the Operation.

A generous bundle of hundred dollar bills in the right engineer's hands resulted in the local newspaper's classified posting of a preliminary public notice. The notice served to alert contractors of a pending public works project. The classified ad innocently informed interested parties to keep an eye out for soon-to-be-released public notices seeking the solicitation of bids for the project. It also contained a brief description of the project and the clever inclusion of minimum pressure specifications for the piping.

RUSTY'S PIPE FITTINGS

Manufacturers produce five different pressure classifications of 42" ductile iron pipe. I paid the engineer to have a classification posted reflecting higher pressure requirements than the pipe obtained by Rusty from the TVA. In other words, Rusty's pipe wouldn't qualify for the project, and his father would have to sell off the TVA inventory. The engineer could always claim a typo or some other mistake that underwent correction when he rolled out the official bidding materials.

My role would be to scuttle all attempts by Rusty or his father to sell the pipe to anyone other than My Client; thereby enabling My Client an opportunity to leverage a lower sales price. Rusty and his father began trying to peddle the pipe. At the same time, a crew busied themselves loading the pipe onto several hundred railroad cars; without any specific destination in mind. At that point I sat down with My Client and told him where we stood; and what I was prepared to do next.

My Client incorrectly believed he didn't need my services anymore and was no longer under any obligation to pay me the remainder of the funds he owed under our agreement. He thought he'd purchase the pipe for a song and sell it back to whoever won the bidding for the construction project Rusty's family wanted to win. Big mistake.

Cola doesn't take disloyalty lightly and reneging on a contract with Cola is a dangerous offense. The Client's rash greedy decision resulted in his reclassification. My Client quickly became my Former Client, as well as a future Target of Cola Fugelere. However, my first order of business was to help Rusty out of the mess I created for him; thereby making life a little more difficult for my Former Client.

You'll recall me telling you I'm a firm believer in poetic justice. Mr. Former wanted the pipe and laughed about it potentially sending Rusty's family into financial ruin. When my Former Client decided to cut me out of our agreement, I chose to heap a pile of manure onto Mr. Former's head similar to the economic crapfest he laughed about delivering to Rusty's father. A nasty turn of events for my Former Client and an apt definition of poetic justice.

The most straightforward fix for the project would be to have the engineer quickly rescind the falsified information advanced in the public notice, by replacing it with corrected classification information. However, our planned error in the already posted classified advertisement produced an unintended consequence. A young engineer, wanting to make a name for himself within the public works department, noticed the discrepancy between the actual engineering specifications and the faux pressure specifications I planted.

Rusty and His TVA Pipe

The young engineering professional reviewed all the data used to engineer the original mathematically driven requirements. He discovered a computational error. In fact, the correct piping needed for the project turned out to be precisely the same as those defined in the salted specifications I paid handsomely to have placed in the newspaper. Cola's planted seed inadvertently grew into new and validated pipe specifications for the project, throwing a monkey wrench to my planned easy fix.

A few days after Rusty's successful acquisition of the ductile iron pipe at the TVA auction, his long-scheduled wedding took place. Immediately upon his return from a ten-day honeymoon aboard a cruise liner in the Mediterranean, Rusty's father informed the newlywed the pipe didn't meet specifications and needed to be sold right away. Finances were critical for the family.

> ***An aside...***
> In one respect, I didn't feel too sorry for Rusty. I, also, traveled to Phipps Bend immediately after my own honeymoon. My Client reached out to me the day after

> Treena and I returned home with a load of salmon from a wonderful getaway to a place called Alexander Creek in Alaska. A fellow named Craig Ketchum set us up in a wonderful remote cabin owned by his company, Ketchum Air Service. It was an excellent getaway. We caught huge salmon from one of Craig's boats.

Back to The Pipe...
To make matters worse, they were facing a storage problem. The TVA was about to begin charging them for storing the pipe if not removed from TVA property. Rusty's Dad made arrangements with the railroad to have the pipe loaded onto flat cars and await delivery instructions. That, too, was a time sensitive and potentially costly move; but there weren't any other good options.

Rusty's father told him to get on a plane, sell the pipe, and not to return home until it sold. *Yikes! Poor kid!* That was more than a decade before the Internet assisted in selling unique items having few interested buyers.

My Former Client was one of those contacted by Rusty, but "Mr. Former" was no longer interested in the pipe. He, too, discovered the TVA pipe no longer met specifications necessary for the project. Rusty was flying from state to state, plant to plant, reviewing bid documents trying to identify other interested parties. I, too, was working to find Rusty a buyer.

To that end, I pulled in as many Team Members as possible. We set up a "War Room," in a Memphis, Tennessee Holiday Inn. As I recall, it was next to the corporate offices of that hotel chain. I had them work the phones and, once they located a prospect, Team Members hit the road. We used trains, buses, airplanes, and cars as we traveled to meet prospective buyers.

Eighteen days later a member of my Team found a potential buyer. The buyer needed that classification of pipe as soon as possible. We didn't want Rusty directly involved in the sale to that buyer, so we conjured up a straw man.

An aside...
A straw man or straw party is, in effect, a middleman. Either the transaction is off-color, or one or more involved parties need to remain shielded; therein lies the reason for a middleman. Such intermediaries typically keep the parties apart and unknown to one another, while earning a profit when a successful transaction occurs.

Back to The New Buyer...
It took three full weeks for Rusty to find an interested buyer. Me. Yes, me. Cola. I was the interested buyer.

RUSTY'S PIPE

What Rusty didn't know is I was merely acting as a middleman. He never knew I was working hard to help make he and his father whole. I had a profit margin built into the transaction and, at the end of the day, both Cola and Rusty made a tidy profit. The real buyer acquired the pipe at a healthy discount below the going price from pipe manufacturers. It was a win-win for everyone involved; except for Mr. Former.

My profits were necessary to fund efforts to find Rusty a buyer, and to utterly destroy my Former Client's business activities. I figured Rusty needed a reasonable margin to garner his father's kudos and give him a little extra so that he could do something special for his new wife, and he did. One of my Agent's planted that seed with him while sitting in an adjoining airline seat, as Rusty was on his way to meet me to finalize the purchase and transfer.

Once we finalized the deal, I presented Rusty with a Cashier's Check. He scurried home to reintroduce himself to his new wife. Rusty's father gained a newfound respect for his son and figuratively placed a well-earned feather in his son's cap. They ended up winning the contract on the pipeline project and made a fortune through a clause in the agreement relating to gravel.

They bid the project very low. Far below any amount expected to allow anyone to reap a profit. However, Rusty's father had been building roads in that area for decades and knew the soils well. He realized the job would require far more gravel than the engineers estimated. Therefore, his bid included a meager figure for the amount of gravel expected for the project. He also chose a ridiculously high cost for any gravel overruns required to meet requirements for the rebuilt roadbed.

The engineers blew it when they estimated how much gravel would be needed. Rather than investing the time and resources to drill and quantify the actual infill required using validated empirical data, they merely guessed; thereby creating a windfall for Rusty's father. The project became a publicized scandal when the engineer who took my bribe underwent a polygraph examination. During the examination, he panicked and confessed to accepting a bribe that originated from my Former Client. Mr. Former wasn't identifiable, because there were two Cutout's involved in the bribery scheme.

I was the Cutout between Mr. Former and another professional Cutout. I used that second Cutout to pass the bride to the engineer, the same man who tinkered with the advertised pressure specifications. That same Cutout paid the engineer under the table to publish those phony specs. From an investigatory perspective, I was in the clear, as was my Former Client. Rusty and his father were nowhere near that sordid matter.

However, Mr. Former wasn't out of the woods with me. It took about two years, but when I was through with my Former Client, he had neither money nor his formerly positive, albeit phony, reputation. He ended up bankrupt and, during the bankruptcy process, investigators determined he'd hidden several hundreds of thousands of dollars in assets from the bankruptcy court.

> ***An aside...***
> My Former Client's efforts to hide those assets was commendable. I'm confident the bankruptcy court would have never discovered the fraud. Unfortunately for Mr. Former, I found what he was up to and, as an upstanding citizen myself I reported Mr. Former's fraudulent asset hiding actions to the court. Yes, of course. I used two Cutouts to deliver an arm's length document detailing the fraud.

Back to Nuking Mr. Former...
Mr. Former's new address contained the word penitentiary. His business and reputation were nuked so severely by me in "The Nuclear Operation" my Former Client's post-prison efforts to resurrect his business utterly failed. Mr. Former never screwed anyone ever again.

Looking back, I'm glad my Former Client decided to abandon his contract with me. Rusty was a very nice young man. He certainly didn't deserve to play a role in his family's financial ruin, simply because Mr. Former saw him as an easy Mark.

THE BLIND PILOT

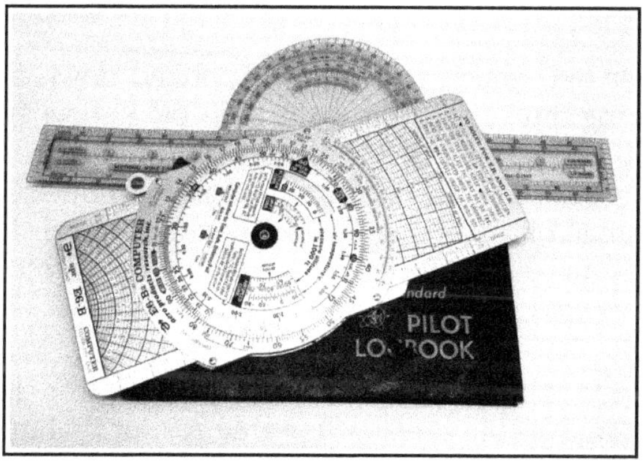

COLA'S NAVIGATION TOOLS FROM THAT SUICIDAL DAY

Aircraft have proven invaluable to me over the years. However, in today's world drones can do much of the heavy lifting once handled by airplanes and helicopters.

Once, when I was a young piloting Spy, I needed to do some aerial espionage. This Op would involve me and My Colleague, Rick Longo. We needed to capture photos from a remote facility. It was the dead of winter, and the facility was situated in a mountainous area. I rented a Cessna 172. Longo would be my spotter and photographer, while I was in charge of navigating and flying.

It was a beautiful, albeit cold, sunny morning when we lifted off with a full load of fuel. We'd taken off from a flat lowland area and needed to spiral up a few times to gain sufficient altitude before transitioning toward the nearby mountains. I screwed up and failed to check the weather. *But hey, it was clear and calm outside. No worries, right?*

We flew a long distance and arrived above the valley and the structures needing to be photographed. After circling a few times and burning through three or four rolls of quickly shot film, I looked at my fuel and noticed we had consumed almost half of the fuel. No worries. We wouldn't be climbing any longer, and there were no headwinds. We'd be fine. Again, no worries.

Shortly after our return trip began, I looked down and noticed smoke coming out of a cabin we passed by a short time before. On our first pass, smoke was rising lazily straight into the sky. As we approached the cabin on the way home, I noticed the smoke was now spread out in a long line drifting back toward the facility we'd just captured on film. *Uh oh! A headwind. Time to become a little concerned. A little worried.*

I ran through various scenarios in my mind and realized the closest airstrip was the one we departed earlier that morning; the same airstrip the spinning propeller was pulling us toward at that moment. Saying nothing to my young green Colleague, I tried to find an RPM that would conserve as much fuel as possible.

As we came to the edge of the mountain range, the valley we expected to drop into wasn't visible. All we could see were clouds. The mountains below and behind us were jagged and offered no opportunity for a safe landing. No roads, no flat spots. I could see peaks from another mountain range very far ahead and on the other side of the broad cloud-covered valley. Winds had picked up, and the storm threatened to ruin our day. We were close to the ocean, and I was fully aware such storms could arrive with little notice and sock-in area airports.

I radioed the airport and discovered the cloud ceiling was only a couple of hundred feet above ground level. Wind speeds were high and presented landing aircraft with a nasty crosswind. Fortunately, there were no aircraft anywhere nearby. The mountain range fell away behind the tail of the little Cessna 172. Nothing but clouds. The small airport had a single runway, but it was wide and extremely long. It was an emergency situation, and I needed plenty of asphalt, plus a measure of good fortune, if Longo and Cola were going to survive this flight; and save the Op's photos. I had no choice. I was forced to break all Visual Flight Rules (VFR) and fly into the clouds that covered the entire valley below. Fuel was low, the storm was picking up power. We were running out of time.

Saying nothing to Longo, I acted normal as we slowly dropped into the blinding aerial soup. My eyes were glued to the bouncing Cessna's instrument panel, as air turbulence tossed the plane like a child's toy. Managing my rate of descent, I crept downward, hoping the clouds didn't settle onto the ground below. I needed several hundred feet of ceiling, so I could safely maneuver the aircraft for landing. Until I broke through the clouds I saw absolutely nothing beyond the propeller.

We finally emerged from the clouds. I made a long flat 180° turn back toward the airport. Lining up with the runway, I felt like I was flying a bucking bronc. If I were a seasoned pilot, which I wasn't, I wouldn't have lowered the flaps. A rookie, I did just that. The Cessna's flaps were set to full as we crossed over the runway's threshold. A strong crosswind was threatening my ability to remain straight and level. The closer the plane got to the runway, the more difficulty I had getting it to go down further. Wind and ground effect repeatedly lifted the aircraft back into the air. My goal was to get closer to the ground, not go up again. *Yikes!*

Looking ahead, I realized I was about out of runway and needed to execute a go-around and a second landing attempt. We weren't going to land this time, so we had to go around and try it again. Pushing the throttle toward the firewall, I committed to executing a go-around. By now it was snowing hard. Visibility was getting worse. It was getting harder and harder to see.

Although outwardly calm, I was terrified. Adrenalin was coursing through my veins as I lined up for the second landing. Again, I couldn't get the single-engine aircraft to sit down on the runway.

As I began the second go-around, the radio squawked. A guy in the control tower suggested I raise the flaps. Sounded good to me. As we started the 360° turn necessary for a third landing attempt, Longo's voice came over my headset. He asked, "Is this normal?"

He'd never been in an aircraft before and had no expectations. Looking at Longo, I keyed my mike and said, "No, this isn't normal." Pointing to the fuel indicator, I said, "See this? We're out of fuel, and I can't get this bird on the ground."

All of a sudden, the unexpected happened. Longo grabbed the door handle and tried to push the door open. I grabbed the collar of his heavy coat and shouted over the din, telling Longo to calm down. I screamed at him asking, "What are you doing? What are you doing? Stop it!"

After a few tense moments he quieted down a little and told me, "Cola, I'm not going to die in a plane crash. There are ten feet of snow down there. I'm jumping out! I've seen it done safely on television. I'm O^2H!"

Safely done on television? *Yea right, you clown! On cartoons!*

Yikes! Spying was one thing, but being involved in Longo's death was an entirely different matter.

Longo's panic was helpful on one level. He had been so upset, he didn't realize he was still wearing his seatbelt. That, and the fact that the door wasn't happy about opening in the airstream, kept Longo inside and safe.

He finally settled down a little and listened to Cola's gentle words filling his headset. Lying to my young friend I said, "Longo, I'll let you jump out. There's enough fuel for one more landing attempt. If I can't get the plane on the ground, I'll turn into the wind, get low, and let you jump out. Sit there, keep quiet, and give me one more chance to land this bird."

He didn't move and stared straight ahead into the thick sideways snowfall. I relaxed a little and realized I'd lied to Longo in more than one way. Glancing down at the fuel indicators, I had no idea if I had enough fuel to get back to the runway. I couldn't do anything about fuel at that juncture, so I focused on what I could do, line up and prepare to land the plane.

> ***An aside...***
> Cola's a natural worry wart. My father continually reminds me of something his mother told him many times. She would say, "Gino, worrying is like rocking in a rocking chair. You can do it all day long, but it doesn't get you anywhere."

Back to Landing with a Suicidal Nut Onboard...
Approaching the runway's threshold in a no flap configuration, I moved in lower than on previous occasions. The crosswind continued to toss the little plane. As I crossed the numbers painted on the asphalt, I pushed the throttle to the firewall. A very determined Cola flew that Cessna down the runway at full throttle. At the last moment, I raised the nose slightly. I literally flew the plane onto the asphalt. When the rear wheels on the tricycle gear configuration touched the pavement, I chopped power and stood hard on the brakes. We made it. *No more worries!*

Longo never worked with me again, and that was okay with me. Nice guy, but I had no interest in conducting Espionage Operations with someone who might panic like Longo. Heck, what was he thinking? Ten feet of snow might protect his cartoon characters when jumping out of a plane, but not Longo. He would have died.

I remember coming in for that final landing attempt; thinking I had to get the plane on the ground no matter what. I feared if Longo jumped, my prison sentence could last many decades. I shouldn't have been flying that plane. I only had forty-eight hours of flight training and didn't have a pilot's license. I'd rented the aircraft with forged documents and a false ID. *Dummy Fugelere!*

Fiduciam Facit Hominem Tutum

One morning an old Lebanese diamond dealing Cola friend named Menag Nimari, whom I refer to as "Stones," received a credible tip that he was the target of a planned robbery. By coincidence, I'd just finished meeting him over coffee at LA's famous Langer's Delicatessen. Some people say Langer's serves the finest hot pastrami sandwich in the world. It's pretty doggone good.

Anyway, after Stones and I went our separate ways, Menag received news he was about to be robbed. He was an old friend of mine, and we had just been together. I was at the forefront of his mind when he received the tip. It made sense that I was the first person Stones reached out to for help.

> ***An aside...***
> Menag, called "Papa" by his family, passed away many years ago at his home in Lebanon. He was a good, hard-working, man with excellent family and business values. A real Tiger and tough negotiator. Unfortunately, so many of those values, and his generation, are disappearing.
>
> His extended family is now in a benign and much safer enterprise than the diamond business Stones worked for more than sixty years. His offspring Americanized their

> family name for several reasons. Regardless, exposing his family's former last name in this book is without risk to he and his family. Therefore, my ability to honor "Papa Stones" by using his family name.

Back to The Impending Robbery...
Stones asked me to meet him at his office right away and transport his valuables out of the building before the robbers arrived. We'd only departed the coffee shop about five minutes earlier. I was still in the area and made a beeline for his office.

After meeting him in his office and taking possession of his valuables, I escorted the old fellow to his Mercedes sports car. Stones personal parking space was located on the 2nd floor of a parking garage; situated at the base of a downtown Los Angeles diamond district office building. Delivering him safely to his car, I was now responsible for getting his valuables out of the building and to his bank.

I descended a stairway I'd used on a number of occasions previously. Stopping at the bottom, I failed to pay attention to my actions and went one way, when I should have turned the other. Each direction had exit doors. One was stenciled, "No Re-Entry."

Not paying attention, I exited the No Re-Entry door and stepped into an alley. I'd reconnoitered the building's ingress and egress options before that day and instantly knew I'd taken a wrong turn. I really didn't want to step out that door. Cola quickly turned to catch the door before it closed. I was too late. The door slammed shut, and I found myself staring at a blank door. No doorknob. Just a round rusty plate over the former door knob hole. I'd stepped into the gated alleyway behind the garage. There was no way to get back in from that location.

Turning left would take me about fifteen feet to a massive locked gate and no way out. Turning right would get me out of the alley, but I'd have to walk more than a hundred yards to reach an exit. Not exactly a good situation in the life of a Spy.

Looking up from the blank door and into the alley, I discovered the alleyway was blocked about thirty feet away by a dozen or so gangbangers. *Yikes!* They were, without question, a tough group of street thugs. Fortunately for me, adrenalin was already coursing through my body. With the world around me in slow motion and my brain working at Cola speed, I quickly assessed the situation and knew my only option would be to walk right toward and into the group of gangbangers.

Gang membership benefits included the innate gift of detecting fear in others. As predators, they thrive on fear. Persons showing fear brings out the animal in gangbangers. Cola knew better than to show concern. As my gaze fell on the clowns, I quickly assessed the danger and observed their body language. I was attempting to discover which clown was leading this little circus. If they challenged me, he'd be the first of their group to learn that Cola was not an easy target for street bullies. While in college I put on heavy boxing gloves, got in the ring, and boxed for a time. I was also a student of martial arts. Decking the leader might create temporary second-guessing by his troops, thereby allowing sufficient time for me to run away like a frightened schoolgirl.

Stepping off a small concrete stoop, I began a confident walk down the narrow alley, surrounded by old multi-story red brick buildings. As I approached the gauntlet, I saw expressions of surprise on their faces as the tall white guy approached them with obvious determination; neither showing fear nor concern. I briefly locked eyes with the apparent leader. I have him the hardest Cola look I could muster. Showing no fear, only confidence, I never modified my pace.

As they slowly parted like the Red Sea, I performed my Moses act and walked toward the promised land. After clearing the dirty dozen, I looked to my left and saw an emaciated unconscious woman lying on the curb with a needle sticking out of her arm. *Yikes!*

I really needed to get out of Egypt and onto downtown LA's feces encrusted sidewalk at the end of the alley; where I could enjoy the relative safety found in the sea of pedestrians. Maintaining my stride and relaxed, confident, body language I continued down the alley, feeling each of the twenty-four eyeballs piercing my back. I was waiting for the sound of a shuffle or scrape; ready to spring into action and pivot to face my adversaries or run. Cola was 100% prepared for either fight or flight. *Very scary.*

I am confident. If those punks knew what I was carrying, I would have received a beating, or worse. Under my jacket was a huge shoulder holster containing a bag of diamonds, two carats and larger; as well as three, ten thousand dollar banded bundles of one hundred dollar bills. My immediate goal was to get out of that alley without incident and meet Stones at his bank. Once there, he'd take possession of the goods and secure them in his family's safe deposit box.

I never looked back and turned onto the sidewalk without issue.

I studied Latin in high school and learned an important principle in the process. "Vestis Virum Reddit." Translated, it means "Clothes Make the Man." I wish my old Latin teacher were still around. If so, I'd ask her if "Fiduciam Facit Hominem Tutum" is the correct way to say, "Confidence Makes the Man Safe."

I fully believe, presenting a confident demeanor that day helped me avoid real trouble with the gangbangers.

COLA'S PARTING THOUGHTS

Getting Out of The Spy Game

I had been working for a Client, Rounder, off and on for a decade. At one point he asked me to catch a flight to Minnesota right away. He needed to discuss "a very important job." Flying to Minnesota to see him on short notice wasn't unusual. However, when he said the job was important, the tone of his voice caught my attention. It sounded strained, high pitched, and came out as a cracked whisper. That didn't fit his James Earl Jones kind of voice and, instead, reminded me of someone going through puberty.

I sent Ryan Shaughnessy to Minnesota one day before my scheduled arrival. His job was to reconnoiter the area, tail Rounder, and perform other duties to make sure I wasn't heading into a trap. My young protégé performed an SDR and thoroughly reconnoitered the area before entering Rounder's steel and glass building, and later tailing The Subject. Ryan's observations failed to conclude anything of real value, except he came away with the impression that Rounder's behavior and body language was far different than Ryan witnessed during previous surveillance runs. The Subject doesn't know My Colleague. Ryan's only involvement with Rounder was during several prior surveillance pre-Cola meeting screens he ran for me.

We decided to unilaterally change the venue from Rounder's offices to a motel. He was instructed to immediately travel to a motel about five miles away and pick up a key at the front desk. We conducted countersurvelliance operations as he traveled between the two points and determined he was alone. In the motel room he found the key to a vehicle we'd staged just outside his room, as well as a key to another hotel's room. Rounder was instructed to lock the cellphone in his personal car and drive the vehicle we provided to a large hotel complex ten miles away. A Cola Team followed him on the journey. No tails, followers, or watchers.

Rounder was accustomed to my cautious approach. We took great pains to insulate our Team from potential problems. A trusted Cutout had booked the rooms for Rounder and had a different Cutout deliver the other car's key to the motel.

My Client complied with our detailed instructions and traveled to his hotel as directed. He went directly to the room. The instructions he received at the motel told Rounder to take an elevator to the hotel's VIP Happy Hour Suite, two hours after his arrival. Located on an upper-level floor, it was a subdued setting where we'd met on a previous occasion. He expected us to meet there again, but that wasn't in the cards.

Immediately after he entered the hotel room, and two hours before Rounder expected to meet with me, I called the room and directed him to immediately step across the hall into another room using a key he'd find under the TV remote control in his current hotel room.

The room across the hall had an envelope sitting in the middle of the bed. The outside of the envelope instructed him to remove all of his clothes, shoes, and watch. The instructions commanded him to fold his clothes neatly, place into a stable pile, then set his bundle on the counter in the bathroom. Then close the bathroom door and return to the bedroom fully naked. No jewelry. No nothing, except for that room's key.

Earlier in the day, we planted a video camera in the bedroom. The final sentence written on the outside of the envelope said he could open the envelope once everything was in the bathroom and he was beside the bed totally naked, holding the room key. The note inside the envelope told him to put on the sweatpants, sweatshirt, socks, and tennis shoes quickly. The document told him he'd find those items in the top drawer of his dresser. He was to place the current room's key in his front right pocket. A large plain white envelope was laying on the bed. He was instructed to take that envelope with him, open it in the stairwell, remove the contents, set the envelope on the landing, place a big footprint in the middle of the envelope, leave it on the floor, and continue walking.

> ***An aside...***
> The activities involving the "footprint" and "front right pocket" served as mental distractions only, no other purpose. We wanted Rounder to be confused, with his mind racing and focused on trying to figure out what might be going on. Ryan had rubbed graphite into the soles of the tennis shoes to assist with making a visible mark on the big white envelope. In situations like this, one of our goals is to distract the thought processes of The Subject. Keep him off balance. Such distractions assist in confusing Subjects, by camouflaging what is important, with that which is not. It helps confuse The Subject, scatter thoughts, and screw with memory.

Back to The Second Hotel Room...
Rounder was instructed to exit the room and walk quickly down the hallway to the right, use the emergency exit, and descend the stairs two floors. The large white envelope activity took place in the stairwell. Inside the envelope was a folded paper with further instructions. Taped to those instructions was another room key. Those instructions said, "Walk down the hallway on the destination floor, and enter a hotel room number identified on the key affixed to this note."

I was in a nearby room and watched Rounder walk into the new room on a portable video monitor. Ryan was at a neighboring hotel, monitoring video feeds we'd set up. My Colleague was on the phone with me and gave the "all clear." I darted down the hall and stepped into Rounder's new room, startling him as I entered. He was certainly jumpy. I found the entire situation fishy.

Rounder was a tall man with mutton chops, a big belly, a gruff demeanor and a deep James Earl Jones voice. A man of few words, he often did a thing with his throat that sounded like a cross between a grunt and a growl. He barked at me and demanded to know, "Why all the games, Cola?"

I was wearing wired headphones and, unbeknownst to Rounder, had an open mike and an active call with Ryan. Rounder didn't know I was receiving surveillance information from Ryan. My young Colleague indicated everything was quiet. Cola was good to proceed.

Facing him directly, I said, "Rounder, I've been working with you for more than ten years. Something is different this time and, contrary to your question, I am not playing games. This is deadly serious business for Cola. What's so important that you needed me on short notice?"

Rounder looked straight into my eyes and said, " I want you to kill my wife."

Wow! I couldn't have known the prescience of the words "This is deadly serious business for Cola" when I uttered them five seconds earlier. *Murder for hire? NOT!*

I stood looking at Rounder for a long minute, as adrenaline coursed through my body. The world slowed, and my mind raced. How had it come to this? Kill his bride? Although I was reeling inside, I'm certain Rounder was witnessing my typical cool Cola demeanor.

Why did this jerk think I would do a job like this? I needed to shut him down hard and fast. What kind of animal was standing before me?

I calmly stepped into his personal space, nose to nose with that horse's ass, and said, "I have a partner who has observed and recorded everything said since I stepped into this room,

Rounder. The envelope and your clothes have been removed from the other room. I'll be keeping your belongings to solidify a case against you if it becomes necessary."

> ***An aside...***
> The quotes in this section are 'deadly' accurate. Ryan's audio equipment AND my iPhone were recording everything. I'm working off the actual audio recordings as I write these passages."

Back to The Murder For Hire Plot...
Turning, I pointed to Ryan in the other hotel. I said, "Partner, wave at our former Client, place your rifle's laser designator on his chest, then get on the radio and verify that Faron is finished collecting Rounder's clothes in the changing room. If Rounder gets violent, take the shot."

That last statement contained three messages.

1. Wave at Rounder

2. Aim his pen-sized green laser at Rounder and let the clown see a green dot on his chest.

3. "Faron" was meant as a coded message for Ryan to rush to the changing room and collect Rounder's clothes and the envelope. Faron was a Colleague from Adam City, Colorado who ran everywhere he went, but he wasn't with us on this trip. Faron's Fast Jumpers were always accelerating. Ryan caught on immediately.

Ryan parted the curtains slightly and waved. Then a green dot appeared on Rounder's chest. I said, "Good spot, but don't shoot too low. That blubber might stop a 30-06 round."

Rounder looked at the green laser light dancing around his breastbone and turned white. Rounder stood absolutely still, shaken and dumbfounded. Ad-Libbing I said, "Any violence and my partner takes the shot. After I'm gone, if anything happens to either Cola or your lovely bride, every action I've ever taken on your behalf will be released by my attorney to the appropriate authorities. I've always had reservations about you Rounder, so I've kept a detailed dossier on you, in case I get double-crossed.

"Rounder, you'd better not [*unintelligible*...] and I'm deadly serious. I have never engaged in any activity designed to bring harm to any innocent party. You've crossed a line pal. Burned a bridge. Divorce her or love her, I don't care. But if I discover you've harmed a single head on her head, I'll take you down. A crime against your wife is a crime against Cola. You're a schmuck, a pig, a coward, and a piece of s**t. I'd better never see you again, or you'll rue the day we met. Don't contact me ever. Ever. Capisce a**hole?"

Cola needed to keep Rounder in that room until Ryan could collect his clothes from the changing room. How could I buy about ten minutes for Ryan? I quickly decided to use the "naked dream" fear most of us occasionally have, to address my need to give Ryan the time he needed.

Lifting the wired headset microphone to my mouth, I uttered the following words, "Obi-Wan, keep the video rolling. If this creep doesn't do exactly as I'm about to instruct him to do, use your cell phone to call 9-1-1. Tell the 9-1-1-Operator Rounder is trying to kill his wife. Give them this hotel's name and room number, then hang up. Let them assume it's happening right now. Leave the equipment, but get those recordings out of there. If he complies with my instructions, close the Operation as we planned. Again, if he exhibits any violent behaviors, take the shot. Got it Obi-Wan?"

> ***An aside...***
> Everything I'd just said was fiction, and Ryan knew it. Obi-Wan Kenobi, the fictional Star Wars character played by British actor Alec Guinness, wasn't real. Prefacing my instructions to Ryan with, "Obi-Wan" informed him everything that followed, until I said "Obi-Wan" again, was pure fiction.

Back to Rounder...
Stepping within an inch of Rounder's face, I said, "Move a single muscle, and you'll spend the next ten years in jail, or you'll leave a large pool of sticky blood on this very spot."

I calmly turned my back on him and walked into the bathroom. As I entered the bathroom, I glanced over my shoulder. Rounder was ashen. Unmoving, he looked as though he'd turned into a pillar of salt.

I ripped the shower curtain from its supports and walked calmly out and placed in on the bed. Returning to the bathroom, I gathered all the towels and carried them out to the king size bed and placed them atop the shower curtain, followed by the pillows. Ignoring the drapes, I told Rounder to strip and set everything on the bed, including his shoes. He hesitated briefly; then I glanced out the window toward my Watcher's lair. Then the clown quickly stripped and tossed everything onto the bed. I reached into the pocket of the sweatpants and collected the key for the changing room. Pulling up the four corners of the bed linens, I made a gigantic ball of everything. I looked at Rounder for the last time and told him to stand there for at least a half hour; then I didn't care what he did. I said, "Obi-Wan, if he moves at all in the next thirty minutes, make the call, and meet me at the rendezvous point."

Cola picked up the bedsheet ball, exited the room, and walked to the stairwell. Leaving the linen ball on the landing, I darted downstairs. Ryan had just entered the room with an empty duffel bag. We filled the bag with everything Rounder and Ryan took into the room.

Ryan dashed down the hallway to gather the video equipment he'd left in the other hotel. We left the area and never heard from Rounder again. I check on his wife regularly, and she remains in good health.

The murder for hire plot is one of the best examples I can share regarding what went into my decision to get out of The Spy Game. Some people like Rounder become enthralled with the narcotic feeling of having power over everyone and everything.

Like naked Rounder, some of those people can become dangerous. I want nothing to do with evil people.

Rounder's murder for hire request turned out to be the final straw, resulting in my decision to get out of the The Spy Game.

The Mercenary

In the 1980's I completed an Op that required the use of a welding truck. I purchased a truck for the need. After completing the Operation, on a late Friday afternoon, I parked outside a greasy spoon filled with construction workers. I popped in and asked if anyone might be interested in purchasing my welding truck. The truck was sitting prominently outside the restaurant's large picture window. The price I mentioned was about 50% of its value.

A big fellow immediately stood and said he needed a truck to get home to Tennessee. He was a recently unemployed welder. We went outside, he looked it over and asked if I had an open title. When I showed it to him, he suggested we, "Mozy across the street to the Continental Bank." We did.

It was a busy payday, and the bank had a long line. The man was huge and hairy. The top of my head almost reached his chin. Built like a brick outhouse, he had a deep voice and a strong southern twang. He seemed like a friendly enough guy.

While waiting our turn, I looked up into his eyes and asked if he had a job back in Tennessee. He said, "No. It's just home. I'll be visiting my kinfolks until I head back to Africa.

I asked, "What's in Africa."

He told me he worked on a road construction job running heavy equipment the previous year and had a few months off. That's why he was working in this community. He told me his vacation was nearly over and it was time to get back to his African job.

About five minutes before we reached a bank teller, He said, "Hey, you're a nice fella, and my momma always told me to be straight with nice folks. Since you're a nice fella, I should oughta be tell'in you the truth. I lied. I ain't a construction worker when I'm in Africa."

In all innocence, I looked at him and asked, "So, if you don't build roads, what do you do?"

He looked me right in the eyes and said, "I shoot ni***rs. I'm paid to kill as many as I can." Then he chuckled.

Cola just about crapped his pants. I had no reason to doubt the soulless Killer for Hire standing before me. I stood there wondering, "What kind of an animal would do such a thing, and then almost brag about doing so; and chuckle about it?"

I've been in sewers and have crossed paths with societal bottom feeders on more than a few occasions, but I've never encountered the kind of evil I witnessed in that man. I finalized the deal a few minutes later, then went away with a sick feeling in my stomach. I kept an eye on my six until I was well away from that town and the Killer for Hire.

Mrs. Taylor

My conscience is another reason getting out of The Spy Game was relatively easy for Cola. I've recognized the enormity of my conscience for many years. I'm surprised I don't have an ulcer. I feel terrible when I hurt someone else, and I have a hard time letting go. I guess that's not such a bad thing. Here's an example that has eaten at me for many decades.

I was a 7th-grade student who, like my buddies, was always engaged in silly kid stuff. A small group of us especially enjoyed tormenting girls and our teachers. We had a new young teacher, Mrs. Taylor. A kind redheaded lady, Mrs. Taylor had my number. She was always pushing back at my games. She saw them for what they were. *Mrs. Taylor would have been a good Spy.*

One day I was not feeling well and approached Mrs. Taylor's desk at the front center of our classroom. I told her I felt ill and was afraid I was going to throw up. She didn't believe me and instructed young Mr. Fugelere to return to his desk. I complied. A few minutes later I dashed up to her desk and urgently repeated my request. Again, the answer was "No." Mrs. Taylor's cynicism was valid. She endured many previous experiences with Con Man Cola.

I stood above the seated Mrs. Taylor and continued pleading. All of a sudden, without any warning, I threw up; hitting my teacher full in the chest with explosive vomit. She screamed at me to get out. "Go to the nurse's office!"

Mrs. Taylor didn't return to school after that disastrous day. I heard she decided to leave the teaching profession. To this day I feel terrible. I'm so sorry for the role I played in ending her career. I hope she landed on her feet and lived out a good life.

Decked by My Mother

I respected my mother, showed her the respect she deserved, and honored both Mama and Papa with my conduct. However, I wasn't perfect. On one occasion I reacted without thinking and showed disrespect to Mama in front of others. *Not Smart!*

It was a Friday evening. Three of my fraternity brothers and I stopped by my parents home to raid her large Sub-Zero refrigerator. We were sitting at a four topper just off the kitchen. I stood up and walked over to the kitchen counter for a napkin. As I was doing so, my mother told me to do something I chose not to do. I told her, "No." *Big Mistake!*

I don't recall treating my mother like that, before or since. I knew better then, and still know better today. It's been more than forty years since I said "No" to my mother, and I recall her reaction as vividly today as I did the moment it happened.

In front of my buddies, Mama swung her left hand to slap me on the mouth for disrespecting her with my words. I was boxing in college at the time, as well as regularly practicing Karate. My reactions were fast, and I clasped my right hand around her left wrist, stopping her hand inches from my face. Mistake!

Embarrassed about her trying to slap my face in front of my college friends, I said, "Mom, I'm too old for you to slap my face."

Looking directly into my eyes, she said, "You'll never be old enough to talk back to me."

At that same moment, and unbeknownst to Cola, Mama was balling up her right hand into a fist. Her right jab landed squarely on my nose and flattened it against my brown skin. That sucker punch immediately sent blood running from my nostrils. *Ouch!*

I don't recall much more from that evening, except for the look of horror on the faces of my fraternity brothers. All three were wide-eyed and white as ghosts. They couldn't believe they witnessed a woman take out Cola Fugelere.

My mother and I still laugh about that incident to this day. On occasion, I pretend to show Mama my cocky side. When I do, she's quick to remind me about her right jab. *I really love that woman!*

My Work, My Career

I've done so many different types of jobs; I cannot remember them all. Many Operations concluded successfully, and are not worthy of elaboration in this book. Below are just a few I recall off the top of my head, and in no particular order.

- Purloining a Competitor's Chocolate Chip Cookie Recipe
- Obtaining Design Specifications for a Specialized Household Appliance
- Co-opting a Processing Facility's Proprietary Workflow Flowchart
- A Software Company's Hiring Algorithm
- Manufacturing Processes for a Specialized Adhesive
- The Unpublished Efficacies Involving Homeopathic Medications
- A Manufacturer's Internals Relating to Battery

Performance
- Internal Union Deliberations
- Political Opposition Research
- Tactical Planning for Trucking Company Contract Negotiations
- Marketing Strategies Involving Major Retailers
- Background Research Involving Candidates for Employment
- Mineral Exploration Reports
- Sporting Match Handicapping Using Non-Public Information
- Manufactured News
- Tourism Manipulation
- Projection Data for Farming, Fishery, and Oil Production

Dulled and Lulled?
Look Before You Leap?
Loss of Situational Awareness?
Any of those titles aptly describe a Cola lapse that has, unfortunately, occurred more than once. *Bad Cola.*

One night a Colleague, B.L., and I were traveling through Missouri in "The Silver Streak." That's a name we affectionately bestowed on a silver Monte Carlo we drove. Needing gas, B.L. pulled into a rural gas station. While he was filling The Silver Streak, I darted to the men's restroom on the backside of the old gas station. Unbeknownst to me, B.L. finished gassing the car and pulled forward and away from the lights.

Coincidentally, another silver Monte Carlo pulled up and stopped where The Silver Streak had been sitting when I exited the car. Dulled by the lateness of the day and lulled by the remoteness of the area. I returned from the restroom, jumped into the other silver Monte Carlo, put on my seatbelt, and looking straight ahead I said, "Let's rally!" The car didn't move.

I looked at B.L., but it wasn't B.L. I glanced to my left and nearly jumped through the roof. A total stranger was staring at me. I thought I was about to be a dead Spy. Who finally caught up with Cola?

The guy started laughing and said, " I think you should be in that car over there."

Pointing out the front window, he was directing my gaze to B.L. and The Silver Streak about thirty feet away. I breathed a sigh of relief, apologized to the laughing man, and exited the car. Awkward and embarrassing. Scary.

Then more than two decades later, I did the same thing in Wisconsin. After using the restroom at a rural gas station, I tried jumping into the back seat of a large white SUV. We were driving a large white SUV. *Uh oh! Mismo!*

On that occasion, the man driving the other big SUV was hopping mad. Understandable. When I opened the door, I saw a tiny baby strapped into a car seat inches from Cola. *Yikes!*

The man assumed I was trying to do something to his baby. Not good. The man was, understandably, protective of his child and came off very very unhappy. An apologetic Cola managed to get out of that awkward situation without having to physically defend himself.

As a follow-on to the above...

Is Brain Engaged?

When I was a young man, a Colleague and I snuck into Fort Knox (see below). We hadn't planned or given much thought to what we were doing. We dodged a bullet on that occasion, and it morphed into a lesson learned.

When I was in high school, my mother placed a black plaque in my bedroom. The sign's gold lettering said, "Be sure brain is engaged, before putting mouth into gear."

I've taken that one step further. "Be sure brain is engaged, when planning and running an Op."

Work the Problem
In the movie Apollo 13, engineers were told to "Work the problem."

Problems exist in all our lives and are, in most cases, solvable. Many are pesky irritants that merely annoy us and are readily addressable. There are, however, challenging problems that require intense investigation, thoughtful imagination, and dedicated focus in the quest for a solution. Such pursuits energize me, and the resulting passion drives me to develop reasoned solutions. That's me. Cola the Spy. A problem solver, I love to "Work the problem."

Peace In Your Career and Life
I was once on a ferry in the Baltic Sea. It was early in the morning. The sea was relatively calm, and a stiff breeze blew below the gray sky. While standing at an outside rail on the ferry, I watched a seagull surfing on the updraft caused by the boat's forward momentum. He seldom flapped his wings. He was gliding. Soaring. Hovering. Floating in the air. It went on for miles. He looked at peace. Relaxed. All the while he maintained a parallel course with the vessel.

I try to conduct my business affairs similarly. Peacefully, while continuing to move forward, parallel with Cola's goals. A Spy conducting his affairs quietly, rather than in a frantic, hectic manner, is less likely to be discovered. Less likely to err. More likely to enjoy a successful, pleasant life.

Sneaking into Fort Knox
When I was a young man, I was very impulsive. I sought opportunities to push barriers, read people, understand body languages, do what others thought impossible, and more. Those were self-training exercises.

Neophyte Spy, Cola Fugelere, and B.L. decided to see just how close we could get to the gold at Fort Knox. We successfully snuck onto the U.S. Army post at Fort Knox. The two dummies didn't realize it was an army facility until we arrived at the entrance. We assumed Fort Knox was strictly a government repository for billions of dollars in gold. No preplanning. No homework. No brains.

We were young and clean cut. As was often the case in the 1970's and 1980's, young men could simply drive onto military installations by saluting lazy guards. That's precisely what we did at Fort Knox. Looking back though, I'm surprised we pulled it off. Both of us wore mustaches. Mine was more substantial than allowable under army regulations. That should have alerted the sentry.

We drove The Silver Streak around the base and a few helpful soldiers we encountered walking down the streets within the facility directed B.L. and Cola toward the repository. We saw the facility from a distance, through a fence or two, and went away happy. We knew we'd gotten as close to the gold as we were going to get.

Later I became very disappointed with our conduct. Planning that adventure without engaging our brains was foolish. That silly trip taught me to know what I needed to know, even if I didn't know what I needed to know. I learned to understand more about what I was getting myself into, before leaping. Cola is now very deliberate and thoughtful. I do very little based on the spur of the moment decisions. I research everything ad nauseam, to make sure I know what I'm getting myself into; and look before I leap.

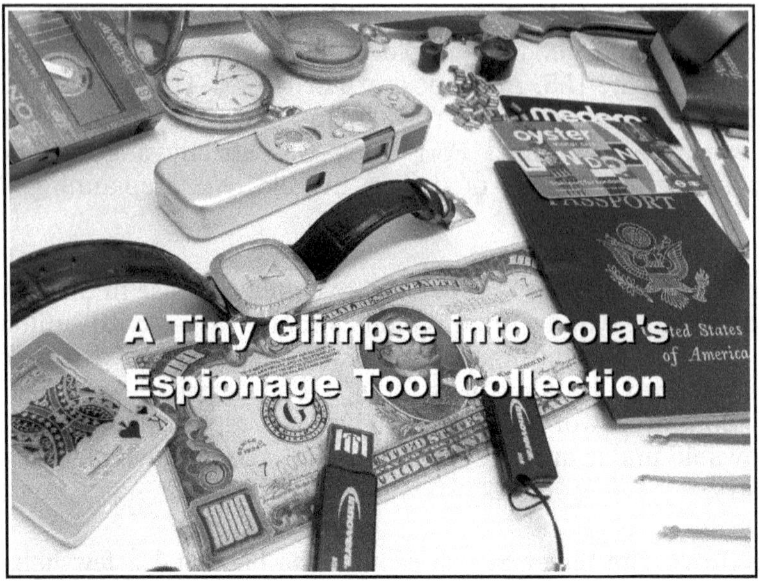

COLA'S $1000 BILL AND OTHER SPY TOOLS

Cola carried this in his wallet for more than three decades. It now resides in a safe deposit box.

$1000 Bill

A Client introduced me to a nice German man when I was conducting one of my first few jobs. I call him Mr. Geld. Geld was the grandson of a German industrialist. During Hitler's rise to power, Mr. Geld's grandfather recognized the dangers associated with the National Socialist German Workers' Party (Nationalsozialistische Deutsche Arbeiterpartei) aka Nazi Party. In fear, he sold all his holdings in Germany and converted them to American dollars. Geld told me his grandfather filled safe deposit boxes in Switzerland with $500 and $1000 bills.

When I met Geld, he was in America for an elaborate high-end big game hunting trip on the North American continent. He arrived on our shores with a pocket full of $500 and $1000 bills. He was shocked to discover merchants were afraid to accept those bills as payment for goods and services. It didn't help that the backside of the 1934 Series $1000 bill looks like something out of a comic book. Geld didn't realize few Americans ever lay their eyes on those denominations.

Cola was called in and successfully converted his bills into $100 bills. In exchange for the large transaction, Geld gave me three $1000 bills and a $500 bill. I gave two of the $1000 bills to a pair of loyal Colleagues and sold the $500 bill to someone else. I still have my $1000 bill. After carrying it in my wallet for more than thirty years, I now store it in a safe deposit box.

My $1000 bill has always been designated as a last resort asset to make certain my family will get fed. Perhaps silly, it remains symbolic of my need and desire to care for my loved ones down to the last bill in my pocket. It's old and tired. However, it remains worth every penny of the $1000 printed on its face.

The Senator

I'm about to introduce Readers to a man who taught me to have fun at every turn. Cola's education under that man's tutelage included learning the importance of stopping and smelling the roses, the "fun" associated with butchering the English language by substituting other words (e.g., he referred to 'shopping' as 'shoplifting'), and showing kindness at every turn. Those and other everyday activities were "fun" for him, and by extension, have become fun for the Fugelere family as well.

I became a close personal friend of a man considered a national treasure of a large collegiate fraternal organization. A member of his fraternity since shortly after World War II ended, he was a well-respected and loved a leader within his organization, and within the interfraternal universe. His fraternity brothers called him, Mr. *** ***, bestowing the name of the fraternity on him. His appearance and mannerisms were dignified, respectful, distinguished, and successful. He once shared with me a nickname one of his young protégés conferred upon him. The young man called him "Senator." After hearing that story, Cola called him Senator as well.

My association with The Senator began upon his retirement. I was in Tucson with Treena celebrating our wedding anniversary at a wonderful southern Arizona resort called The Arizona Inn. The property has been a beloved Tucson landmark for nearly 100 years.

One afternoon while my wife napped, I dropped into The Arizona Inn's comfortable library to peruse the books located there. A kind gentleman, who was already in the library, struck up a conversation with me. He explained the interesting history of the property and mentioned that John Kennedy, Franklin Roosevelt, and other politicians, as well as Hollywood notables like Clark Gable and Gary Cooper, were guests of The Arizona Inn's owner, Isabella Greenway. John D. Rockefeller and other well-known business leaders also vacationed at The Arizona Inn.

He showed me two volumes of his fraternity's history kept in the Inn's library. The man I'd eventually call, Senator, said he'd donated them to the library some years earlier. After chatting a while, he invited me into what he called, "The Saloon" for a glass of white wine. We enjoyed each other's company that afternoon and for decades thereafter.

That evening he invited Treena and me to join him for dinner at a Five Star restaurant called The Tack Room. We enjoyed a wonderful dinner and finished it off with three Grand Marnier Soufflés. Treena said her evening was "delightful." My bride grew to love that fine gentleman and always looked forward to our engagements with him.

Senator became a OneSeven Courier for the Cola organization. We shared fine food, hours-long meals, and excellent wine. We discussed interesting people, wonderful venues, and history. He was a pleasant, non-threatening gentleman who traveled often and kept my secrets. The Senator enjoyed his courier role because it afforded him opportunities to travel, stay at fine hotels, and enjoy excellent food and wine - all at my expense. Besides, Cola was a helpful piggy bank for the retired fellow. I enjoyed his company for more than thirty years. Our friendship lasted until the day he passed away, not too long ago.

The Senator liked a Latin phrase I often utter, "Vestis virum reddit." The Senator agreed that "Clothes make the man." In fact, he lived that maxim. The Senator seldom went anywhere without a coat and tie. He often said, "I can leave the house in a coat and tie, enjoy a spectacular lunch in a fine restaurant. Remove the tie for some afternoon shopping and a casual happy hour. Then abandon the jacket when I arrive at a friend's home for a barbecue. Upon leaving, I can put the tie and jacket back on and duck into a fine gentleman's saloon for a cigar and an after dinner drink. It's easy to dress down, but difficult to dress up when already out and about."

He wore a tiny round object on his lapel. I realized he wore it consistently over those thirty years we dined together. On one occasion, I asked what it was, and he said two words, "Edgewater Conference" and changed the subject. I didn't press. Curious.

AN OLD BAZIL'S SIGN

We'd speak for hours. He was Cola's confidant. I thoroughly trusted The Senator with my deepest secrets. We'd often sit in restaurants for so many hours, the staff would occasionally forget about us. One night we realized we'd overstayed our welcome at a restaurant called Bazil's, on Speedway Boulevard in Tucson, Arizona. As we were chatting, the lights went out. It went completely dark, and I heard a bolt secure a door somewhere in the far reaches of the restaurant. I jumped up and ran to the front door. It was locked. We were trapped. I dashed through the kitchen and began pounding on the bolted back door, yelling loudly. Before the staff departed the parking lot, someone heard the commotion and freed us from that wonderful prison. Embarrassing.

The Senator taught me a lot. He was both an excellent OneSeven and a special friend. I truly miss Mr. *** ***.

There Are No Coincidences?
I was introduced to a young South American transplant in Washington D.C. many years ago. It was a party of some kind, and the introduction was brief. Many years later I noticed "The Man" from Bolivia in a Dallas restaurant and thought he might have been looking at me. My Contact arrived at my table, and after greeting him I told him we needed to leave. Standing up, I looked toward The Man. He was gone. Small World or something else? *Coincidence?*

> ***An aside...***
> In my line of work, it is dangerous to chalk something up to coincidence. We have to approach such situations as potentially dangerous. That is why spies often adopt the adage, "There is no such thing as coincidence in The Spy Game."

Back to The Man...
Several years later I was in a Philz Coffee at Folsom and 24th in San Francisco's Mission District. While sitting on a couch watching a soccer match and drinking a tasty "Philz Handmade Coffee," I noticed The Man enter Philz with a young attractive blond woman. They ordered coffee and sat down at a table chatting about an Internet startup project. I didn't think he was following me, but... I didn't like the situation. This was the third time I'd seen him. Moreover, just like the second encounter, it was more than thirteen hundred miles from the previous sighting. *Not good.*

After a while, the woman departed. The Man opened a MacBook Air and began pounding away at the keyboard. I placed a call to Ryan, who was himself enjoying a Starbucks coffee inside San Francisco's Ferry Building. I told him I needed him to join me right away for a surveillance run. Ryan caught a cab and arrived less than a half hour later. I put him onto The Man and ducked out.

Over the following days, Ryan uncovered reams of information. The Man was a tech sector professional. His girlfriend was a marketing genius, coveted by Internet startup companies. They were engaged to be married. Ryan didn't discover anything that should concern me, but I don't like coincidences.

Ryan and I were scheduled to depart San Francisco shortly, for an overseas Operation. We'd been in SFO for R & R and well as some casual "Pre Game Planning." I'd have to continue checking out The Man when we completed the overseas Op.

Months later I returned to San Francisco, just in time for The Man's wedding. I rented a tuxedo and crashed the downtown San Francisco wedding. Then it happened. Another coincidence!

As I was mingling and tasting finger food, I saw Diamond Dave across the room with a woman and another couple. *Yikes!* How can this be? Not Good. I spent two hours dodging Dave while listening to people talk about The Man and his bride. At one point, during the reception dinner, guests were invited to give speeches.

A short bespeckled man in a dark suit lifted a microphone and spoke about working with The Man. He discussed their various meetings with venture capitalists and how impressed he was with The Man's candor, ethics, and honesty; even in the face of responding to hard questions with less than glowing answers.

As the short man was speaking, I thought about the intelligence Ryan gathered and what I'd heard that evening. The Man was an exceptional individual and certainly wasn't tailing Cola. I ended up deciding the Washington D.C., Dallas, and Mission District encounters were pure coincidence. Tough to accept. Cola doesn't believe in coincidences.

Twist the Lid

Little problems can create significant issues. Taking care of something now will prevent more work later. The early bird catches the worm. Procrastination is the thief of time.

My Team Members and Clients know those phrases well, but I doubt they've ever heard them from me. I have my own way of stating that immediate energies spent can save far more effort than putting things off until later. I consistently use coffee cup lids as an example. Cola people are very familiar with, "Twist the Lid."

I was drinking a cup of coffee just before a delicate undercover meeting with a substantial Silicon Valley venture capitalist. Another time I was about to meet a potential Client and share a well-polished presentation. Before both critical meetings, I purchased a cup of coffee at a well-known coffee house. Those two drinks ended up staining the front of my white monogrammed dress shirt..

The first time it happened I thought the cup had a defective lid. It was on all the way and appeared secure. My attention, however, was more squarely focused on walking into a meeting in five minutes, looking like a slob. It happened again a few months later. I investigated and figured it out.

If the seam of the cup is not entirely smooth and faces directly toward the person drinking the coffee, it'll likely drip onto the unsuspecting victim's chest; no matter how well one secures the lid. I've faithfully twisted the lid 100% of the time since that second mess. When the barista hands me my drink, I set it down, remove the lid, and turn the seam to the backside of the cup's lid. Why is the seam almost always on the front of the container near the placement of the little drink hole in the lid when the baristas hand me my coffee? *Do they know? Are they trying to soil my shirts?*

I'm surprised big coffee chains don't teach their people to turn the seam to the back before installing the lid. Undoubtedly others have experienced dripping coffee associated with the seam problem. Baristas and their bosses can do better by us.

"Twist the Lid" like "A Stitch in Time" is all about avoiding headaches and saving time; as well as protecting white monogrammed dress shirts.

Correct Synchronized Time

All operational times are Zulu based. Operations occasionally involved multiple time zones. Errors = Surprises = Failed Ops. Zulu assisted in avoiding mistakes. However, I've always insisted on repeated reviews for Zulu conversions when conducting an Op involving either single or multiple time zones. We more than double checked conversions. It wasn't unusual for me to insist on five or more reviews of time zone calculations. Cola believes the entire world should use a universal time system.

Counterintelligence Advice for Owners: Know All and Let Them Know You Know

It is important for business owners and managers to make staff members aware they know about their foibles. It is important NOT to put one's head into the figurative sand.

For example, if a staff member has a sensitive position at work, and is sneaking around with someone outside his or her marriage, it is crucial to make sure that individual is aware that others know. It reduces blackmail opportunities. However, coercion continues to be a potential concern if a spouse remains in the dark about the affair.

In short, adulterers are not to be trusted. Common sense suggests that someone who was unfaithful to his wife, if he should become divorced and remarries, he will probably be an untrustworthy mate for the new person. People don't often change their spots.

The same thing happens with Agents who spy on behalf of another company. For example, if a lab worker steals secrets from one company, and hopes to leverage that information so he can get hired by a second company, he cannot be trusted. Some business owners will dangle a job opportunity, in exchange for information about the Agent's current employer's business. If the turncoat does come through with useful information, know this: If you hire that person, nothing says he won't do the same thing to your company.

It Can Be As Simple As
Effective Corporate Espionage can be as simple as...

- The competition having someone parked near the entrance of your company headquarters, counting the number of vehicles traveling in and out of your parking lot on a daily basis. Garnering sufficient data like this, over time, will assist competitors in quantifying your company's business activities. Busy? Growing? Slowing? You get the idea.

- The competition having someone drive slowly through your parking lot, one or more times each day, to count the number of cars and/or empty parking spaces. Similar to the previous tactic, requiring less on-site time and more trips for the Spy.

- The competition having someone drive slowly through your visitor parking area to see how many visitors, vendors, clients, etc... may be visiting your company on a daily basis. Over time, this tactic will help them determine if sales are up or down; if business is up or down.

- The competition having someone drive slowly through your employees-only parking area to try and determine if your staff levels are rising, shrinking, or are remaining relatively static. As with the previous tactic, comparing this data over time may help competitors understand the health of your business.

Laymen can conduct the examples above. They are simple, effective, and relatively inexpensive espionage tools.

Is It Really J. Edgar Hoover on the Phone?
More than a few espionage professionals have placed telephone calls to co-workers, lovers, neighbors, and others to collect information necessary to conduct effective operations.

One approach they might use would be to call with the following introduction:

> "Hello, Mr. Smith? My name is Special Agent Jones with the Federal Bureau of Investigation. We're conducting telephone interviews with relatives, friends, neighbors, and associates of Mr. John Doe as part of a routine background investigations.
>
> "Information provided by you to me during this call will be held in the strictest confidence and your responses will not be revealed to Mr. Doe. However, I must inform you that any failure by you to fully disclose that information with honest and accurate responses is punishable by up to five years in prison."

Most recipients of such calls will roll over and answer every question asked by the Spy.

Of course, anyone impersonating and FBI Agent jeopardizes his or her own freedom. In fact, they might end up with that five year prison sentence. On the other hand, many corporate espionage professionals don't concern themselves with such matters. After all, espionage is a risky business.

No Training

The contemporary use of relatively new technologies is changing The Spy Game and, in many cases, making espionage easier for novices and seasoned professionals (notice I didn't say less dangerous?). Those technologies include drones, specific computer software tools, photographic advancements, audio trickery, video manipulations, and eavesdropping hardware.

There are certain subjects that I have faithfully avoided discussing in this book. Cola has no interest in educating people in some of the contemporary methods for obtaining information to further Corporate Espionage efforts. Everything I've shared in this book is already available in somewhere in the public domain; in published works of fiction and non-fiction, on the web, in newspapers, magazines, and other periodicals.

The Scary Evolution of Corporate Espionage Driven by Nation States

Nation States are driving the future of Corporate Espionage. It's already begun to unfold. AI (Artificial Intelligence), Drone Technology, Self-Driving Vehicles (Land, Water, and Air), Miniaturization Technologies (MT), and more. There will always be middlemen who want to wet their beaks with lucre generated by garnering valuable information and sharing it with their Clients. However, when Nation States conduct espionage activities, they are both the Spy and the Client. Nation States have deep pockets and commitment. They are driven and dangerous.

The most significant and concerning arena for this former Spy is in the artificial intelligence space. Fortunes will be made and lost in that arena. Merciless thugs increasingly target engineers in that field, and companies will have to throw tremendous resources as protecting their assets from competing entities. Most of those competing entities are turning out to be Nation States.

I was on the SpaceX campus earlier this week. My visit was unrelated to Corporate Espionage. However, while there I considered the many technology campuses I've visited, primarily in Silicon Valley. Those companies are, without question, targeted. More than a few Nation States and international hi-tech companies have painted huge bulls-eyes on those valuable repositories of proprietary information. Many dollars and lives are and will be squandered for their secrets.

State-sponsored espionage operators have heavily populated the Corporate Espionage arena; although they'll often contract with private espionage professionals. Smaller dangerously powerful actors like Pakistan and Iran present more than a few concerns in this arena. I believe the most dangerous Corporate Espionage operators are two Nation States. China and Russia, in that order. The Corporate Espionage arena is already dominated by China's MSS (Ministry of State Security), followed by Russia's SVR (Sluzhba Vneshney Razvedki). In fact, both organizations have a firm foothold within the European Union and the United States.

The Spy Game is going to become increasingly dangerous and more damaging for the U.S. and E.U.

In fact, Corporate Espionage is morphing into a high priority national security concern for the U.S. Government. We are at war, and most people have no appreciation for the dangerous environment in which we're living, because of the State Involved Evolution into The Spy Game. The Corporate Spy Game.

My Story

I hope your journey into Cola's life has been worthwhile. I tried to reveal my life's story in a manner designed to pique your interest, rather than boring My Readers. My next project is underway, and I believe you'll find it far more fun and exciting than the life of Cola the Spy. I'm having fun with The Adventures of Ryan Tate. I believe you'll enjoy Ryan's adventures as well.

Thank you for allowing me an opportunity to offer you a peek inside the mysterious, murky world of Corporate Espionage. A glimpse into Cola Fugelere's world. The story of his world is my world. My story.

GLOSSARY

THE LANGUAGE OF COLA

Practices, items, and idioms often used in my world

After Action Reporting
Cola and each of his Colleagues are required to issue After Action Reports, detailing each phase of an Operation. I'm a student of Solutions Development. We work hard to identify problems and find pathways to improvement. I believe my decades of success in the espionage space can be attributed to judiciously analyzing what occurred, what we could have done better, risks we took, exposure we faced or suffered, mistakes we made, and all other facets of an Operation. Doing so prevents future problems, mitigates risk, and increases our ability to assist Clients in the best manner possible.

Asset
A person, system, or item, generally associated with our Target that holds value to our Operation.

Agent
A person either associated with our Target or is an outsider working against our Target, which holds value to our Operation.

Audio Stud
An audio stud is a device meant to be inserted into the headphone jack of a computer, thereby telling the speakers to shut down.

BackStop
A Backstop is, for me, a Plan B (usually one of several backup plans). It can also be stories, props, actions, reactions, etc... that can provide reasonably valid reasons for my activities. Emergency moves, last resorts, precautionary steps, and reinforcement actions.

Brush Passes aka Pillar Passes
Agents generally use a standard espionage Brush Pass with their Handlers to covertly pass information and/or items from one person to another. It usually involves two individuals walking toward one another (sometimes in the same direction), passing very closely, exchanging items, then continuing forward without pause. When done correctly neither person appears to have done anything other than walking by the other person.

I've called Brush Passes something different. I refer to them as Pillar Pass. In fact, I prefer the opportunities for activity concealment by using line-of-sight obstacles like pillars, statutes, bushes and trees, people, vehicles, etc...

B.E. aka Butterfly Effect
The Butterfly Effect was a term coined by twentieth-century meteorologist and mathematician Edward Lorenz. Using a branch of mathematics called Chaos Theory, Lorenz postulated a tornado's formation could have been influenced by, and theoretically traced back to, the flapping of the wings of a tiny butterfly several weeks earlier. Small issues can result in significant changes.

In my cloak and dagger world, seemingly inconsequential outside influences can impact Espionage Operations in tremendous ways. I continually remind My Colleagues of the dangers associated with B.E.'s.

C2V aka Close to the Vest

Close to the Vest" conversations (aka C2V's) are exchanges in which the Target is purposefully attempting to conceal valuable information.

CCM

CCM is an acronym I use for a "Candid Cola Moment." In short, it means I surprised someone with my presence when they least expected it.

In my lexicon, a Candid Cola Moment reflected the culmination of a clandestine Surveillance Detection Run where I surprised The Subject of my surveillance when they'd least expect my presence. The purpose for the contact was to force impromptu meetings when The Subject could have no foreknowledge that I'd be making an appearance. Thereby creating an environment designed to insulate me from vulnerabilities. A self-preservation ritual, if you will, that I'd use to gain the safest access possible to Clients, Agents, and other actors in the theater of my working life.

Although I refer to the meetings as impromptu, they are neither improvised, nor conducted without preparation. The impromptu nature of my appearances were from the initial perspective of The Subject, believing contact occurred without any obvious preplanning. However, my efforts to prepare for such meetings were thorough and cautiously considered.

My favorite "attack point" for a CCM was when subjects were on vacation, especially overseas. My Subjects have been caught off guard 100% of the time and certainly didn't expect Cola to interrupt their detached bliss. Risk mitigation was the ultimate goal and serious purpose for the approach.

That said, however, overseas attack points did present entry and exit exposure when traveling to foreign countries. Cola's many

CCM adventures could fill volumes, but they were mundane. Reader interest would be minimal, and those exploits aren't worthy of your time. Government agencies have never detained me outside the United States. The few close calls were short-lived and inconsequential.

Chinese Wall Compartmentalization

"Chinese Wall" is a term used in business describing an information barrier. It's a figurative wall that acts as a communications barrier, designed to secure specific information and keep it under wraps. It's a valuable tool when working in the espionage arena.

Cola Color Alert Levels

Homeland Security, law enforcement agencies, and others have a system of color-coded alert levels. Spies do as well. In Cola's world, I use White, Yellow, Orange, and Red.

I'm only at condition White when sleeping in my own bed. You might think Cola is relaxed and in Condition White while inside secure facilities (e.g., on a White House tour or beyond TSA screeners in airline club lounges), but I'm not. In those situations, I'm usually relaxed but continue scanning for adversaries, unwelcome officials, and others. I call that, Condition Yellow.

Condition Orange is when I suspect a potential threat or am beyond relaxed, and without any specific identifiable threats. Condition Red is when a situation becomes threatening and Cola is in unmistakable jeopardy.

Cola Meow and the MCR

A Cola Meow heard during an Operation served as an alert to My Colleagues that the Op was either over or blown. If they heard a Cola Meow, the Op's pre-planned "Meow Contingency Response" was invoked. Everyone knew what to do.

Cookie Crumbs
Physical or digital footprints, indicating where someone has traveled.

Counterespionage
Espionage efforts designed to thwart ongoing espionage activities targeting a company, an individual, or a government.

Counterintelligence
Counterintelligence is an internal process or activity designed to prevent or thwart espionage efforts that may occur sometime in the future.

CryptoCola
A system for secure communications between Cola and Colleagues, before smartphones. CryptoCola was a collaborative approach to cryptic communications designed by Skookum Jim. A Printing OneSeven, Roy, manufactured customized cards for me (see the chapter "The Arch and The Needle" to learn more about Roy).

CryptoCola involved the use of a card jacket having rectangular cutouts with the ABC's on the face. Inside the jacket, a sliding card was used to change up the alphabet. I used a different set of sliding cards for each Colleague, and I had a duplicate set in my possession so we could enjoy relatively secure communications.

Using something called "Master Numbers" that appeared along the top of the card, we'd be able to decipher each other's coded messages. It was slow and cumbersome but worked well in maintaining a margin of security in our communications. Also, as an additional measure of security, no two Colleagues had the same sliding cards.

During a phone call, I might say something like, "Cola 48 CP 6-12." My Colleague would know to use the Cola 48 card set, then use one particular card identified as "CP" to decode a long string of numbers they'll soon receive from me by fax or some other method. Once received, the numeric string was decodable using Master Number 6 for letters A, C, E, G, I, K, M, O, Q, S, U, W, and Y. Master Number 12 would decode the remaining alpha characters. Yes, it was slow, but without our card system or a supercomputer, unlocking the cipher would be extremely unlikely.

Here's an example of the information a Colleague might receive in a fax:

"87571291588298180580598131091 5"

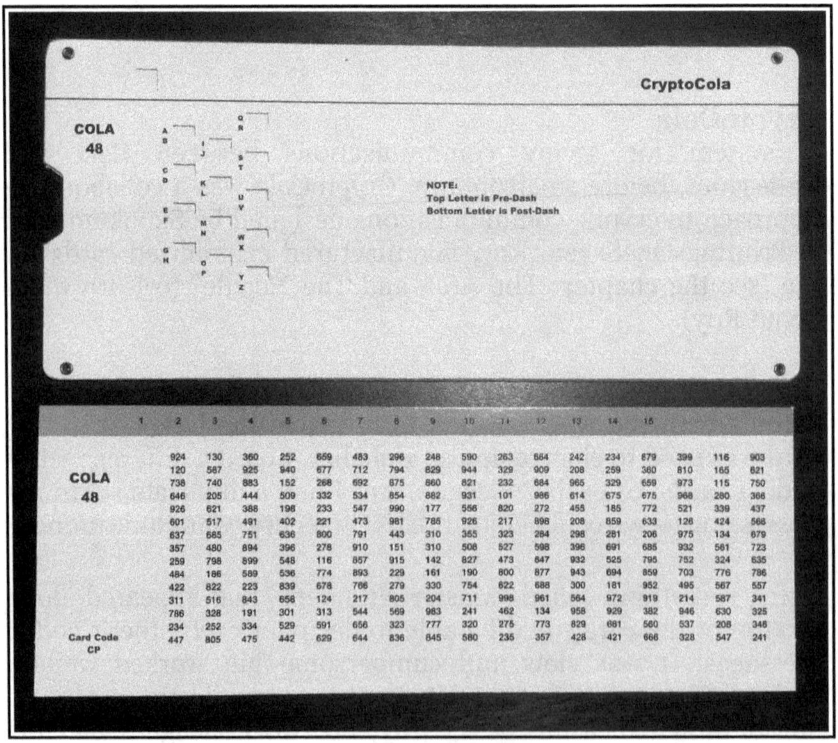

CRYPTOCOLA CARD SYSTEM

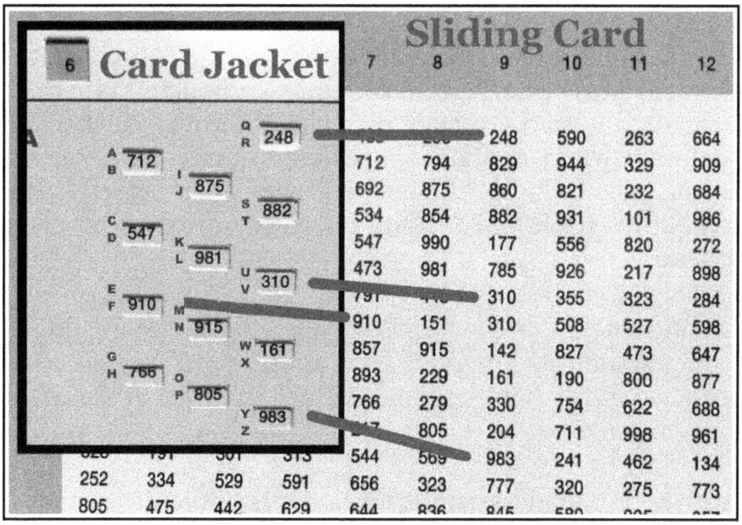

CRYPTOCOLA CODE CARD

You can decipher the following yourself.
Use the "Card Jacket" image shown above to the left.

First, split three numeral groups from the string:

875-712-915-882-981-805-805-981-310-915

Second, a letter is assigned to each three numeral group:

875 (I) + 712 (A) + 915 (M) + 882 (S) + 981 (K) + 805 (O) + 805 (O) + 981 (K) + 310 (U) + 915 (M)

Third, the letters are assembled, and the receiver adds in spacing:

IAMSKOOKUM = I AM SKOOKUM

875712915882981805805981310915 = I AM SKOOKUM

Spacing errors can result in garbled or problematic messages. When drafting and transcribing messages, we needed to be aware of words and word combinations that could become confusing.

For example:
Using the same three-letter codes, the word MANAGE might be interpreted MAN and AGE. Over time we updated our cards to include six additional rectangular cutouts on the jacket. Those six cutouts would contain six different three numeral codes. However, they all represented a space. That helped separate words better, while not making it overly obvious where spaces occurred.

A run-on sentence created an issue once, so we began adding the code 383 to indicate a period. Then another problem was created because we didn't have commas. After that issue arose, we used 838 for commas.

Here's the commaless sentence that was misinterpreted: "NO MEETING IS POSSIBLE."

The sender had earlier received a question in CryptoCola that read, "Is it going to be impossible for us to meet?" The sender meant it as, "No, meeting IS possible." He was answering "yes" to the meeting. The receiver read it as, "No meeting is possible." If the message included a period, that issue wouldn't have existed "NO. MEETING IS POSSIBLE." To be safe though, we added the 838 for commas. I cautioned each of My Colleagues to remember punctuation can make a huge difference in the meaning.

A devout man once informed me a particular verse in the Bible held a different meaning if a comma existed in the original text. He told me the original Aramaic in the New Testament didn't use commas (I've never looked into it his assertions). He said the verse, Luke 23:43 "I say to you today you shall be with me in Paradise" would hold an entirely different meaning if a comma were placed in front of "today" as opposed to behind it. In many post-Aramaic translations the comma precedes "today."

I agree. Notice the difference?

- I say to you, today you shall be with me in Paradise.

- I say to you today, you shall be with me in Paradise.

Was he saying, "I'm telling you today" or, was he saying, "Today you will be with me?"

I choose to avoid debating anyone on such matters. I once watched a bible college student, and a high school student argue about predestination. As with the "today" conundrum, I choose to focus on more practical matters of faith; rather than debate specific passages for which no answers are available in this life.

Regardless, punctuation is important and eventually worked its way into CryptoCola.

Cutout
A person or company in place to insulate parties involved in passing goods or information. Proper usage dictates multiple Cutouts and is generally structured to keep one of the parties from identifying the other party.

Cyber Alt
Cola's approach to going up against robust Cyber Security. Cyber Alt means Cola is going to the ground with On The Ground (OTG) espionage tactics such as HUMINT.

Drafting
It's not unusual for spies to use free email accounts for communicating with each other, as well as their Assets. They don't send any emails containing sensitive information. Both users have equal access to the account. One of the users creates a single draft email. It is never sent out, and they specifically make sure they don't accidentally do so, by keeping the TO, CC, and BCC fields intentionally blank. The Subject Line remains blank as well. Communication done using that single draft email is referred to by some of us in the espionage community as "Drafting."

The draft email is used to write a message from one person to the other. Saved as a draft, when that person logs off, and another logs on, the email is read, and the reader replaces the body of that email with a response; and so forth. It's a very helpful, hard to track and breach, and an excellent surreptitious communication system.

Escort
An Escort is usually assigned the responsibility of escorting a Subject, usually a meeting attendee, to a specific location to meet with Cola.

EWA's (Entitled With Attitudes)
These personality types are consumed with self and looking inward, and they don't often see the costs associated with their behaviors. Spies like to target them because they are considered weak, their self-assured arrogance notwithstanding.

Fast Jumpers
Tennis Shoes

Handler
This person will meet with Inside Men, Agents, and Assets, away from the Op site, to receive instructions and pass along purloined information.

Hide
A Hide is a hiding place where a Spy will position himself and/or his equipment, as needed, to surreptitiously collect information and/or items necessary to successfully prosecute the Operation. When constructing a Hide outdoors, camouflage is generally integral to the design. When indoors, a Hide might be as simple as a closet or bathroom stall.

HUMINT
Human Intelligence (HUMINT) is the bread and butter of my business. HUMINT involves personal relationships, face-to-face encounters, trust, mouth to ear information sharing, etc...

An example of HUMINT would be a Spy, sitting in a Starbucks with a Tall Flat White or Iced Green Tea, engaged in the act of recruiting or debriefing an Asset.

Hummingbird Effect
Cola neither runs, nor does he stall, stammer, or blather when something unexpected occurs. His adrenaline kicks in, without any apparent external changes. What happens to me is weird, but helpful. I get tunnel vision, and everything slows down. I continue thinking at my pace, while everything else in the world turns to thick honey and scarcely moves. I feel like I'm inside myself looking out. It's probably akin to Hummingbird experiences, due to their ultrahigh metabolic rate. It can happen to soldiers when engaged in battle.

Again, weird, but helpful. In effect, I can quickly work out issues, without the delays expected by others. My ability to recall those moments is amazing. Unreal.

During adrenaline dumps, I not only remember the tiniest details from my five senses, but my recall is unbelievably vivid; allowing me to remember exactly what I was thinking and other thought processes. My Colleagues find it fascinating. I merely consider it an opportunistic gift.

On the other hand, I get what I call an Adrenaline Hangover when my blood chemistry returns to normal. I get the shakes for a few minutes, then am entirely drained afterward. I'm spent. No energy.

IMINT
Imagery Intelligence

Inside Man
A person, male or female, closely associated with, and trusted by, the Target.

An Inside Man is simultaneously valuable and a potential threat to an OP. An Inside Man is often seen as a potential Double Agent and is usually on the payroll of both the Target and the Client.

LeapFrog Surveillance
A surveillance option often used when tailing individuals to help avoid discovery by The Subject of the surveillance. LeapFrogging works best in vehicle surveillance scenarios.

See Picket Surveillance

Lorem Ipsum Text
Spies will use multiple iterations of Lorem Ipsum Text, or other text copied from the net, to obfuscate earlier versions of information used by them and their confederates in espionage communications. More commonly, Lorem Ipsum Text, aka Greeking, is often used as placeholder text for graphical design, printing, and website design. As placeholder text, it serves Readers by showing how text might appear in a document or online. Here's an example of Lorem Ipsum Text:

Lorem ipsum dolor sit amet, consectetur adipiscing elit, sed do eiusmod tempor incididunt ut labore et dolore magna aliqua. Ut enim ad minim veniam, quis nostrud exercitation ullamco laboris nisi ut aliquip ex ea commodo consequat. Duis aute irure dolor in reprehenderit in voluptate velit esse cillum dolore eu fugiat nulla pariatur. Excepteur sint occaecat cupidatat non proident, sunt in culpa qui officia deserunt mollit anim id est laborum.

Mark
Mark, like Subject and Target, is a word that describes the focal point of our espionage efforts. The person, place, or thing we target for espionage activities; to misappropriate information and/or items necessary for our mission.

OneSeven
I've always enjoyed great movies involving stings, scams, and espionage. My favorites include "Three Days of the Condor," the Danny Ocean movies, Jason Bourne, and the James Bond franchise. Most Readers know grumbling "Q" of the 007 movies. Although his total career screen time was minimal, his impact was considerable. He provided Bond with a wide variety of high tech devices and tools that 007 would eventually need to save the day.

I, too, required tools, technical skills, and inventiveness far beyond my ability to personally manage or create. Unlike Bond and his single Q, over the years I've had dozens of Q's assist me with Cola needs. Electronic technicians, forgers, audio and video experts, pickpockets, carpenters, plumbers, electricians, chemists, microbiologists, fingerprint analysts, linguists, firearms experts, metallurgists, and others.

I've always used the generic "OneSeven" when discussing my technical suppliers. OneSeven is a play on Q, given Q's position as the 17th letter of the English alphabet. Time has revealed that my practice of referring to all of my various technical support people as OneSeven has kept them all safe.

OP
An Operation. An espionage action.

OTG aka On The Ground Espionage
A good example of an On The Ground (OTG) espionage tactic is HUMINT.

O^2H aka Out Of Here
In Cola's world we say "O^2H" when we want or need to get "Out Of Here."

Package
A Package is usually a person being escorted by a Cola Escort, to a meeting with me. Cola Escorts are adept at delivering my "Packages" safely; using oft-practiced evasion techniques and SDR tactics.

Picket Surveillance
A surveillance option often used when tailing individuals to help avoid discovery by The Subject of the surveillance. Pickets are helpful in many situations (e.g., vehicle tails and pedestrian tails), but generally require large teams.

See LeapFrog Surveillance

Pillar Passes
See Brush Passes

PMS (Pinhole Marking System)
The PMS device drills a pinhole through a wall from the inside. The PMS then shoots a gas carrying fine green powder through the tiny hole. That permits installers to drill from inside to the outside; without worrying about splintering the finished side of the wall. Then installers transition around the wall and locate the green powdery residue, deposited by the PMS, in and around the pinhole. The pinhole becomes the intended location for drilling inward, so installers can avoid splintering surfaces.

On occasion when both sides of the wall are finished, a short full-sized hole is drilled, followed by a PMS perforation. When drilled again from the opposite side, we can accurately hit the full-sized hole without worrying about splintering or otherwise damaging the opposite side. We use this method when both sides of a wall are finished and maintaining a pristine condition on both surfaces is important.

Pocket Litter
Pocket Litter is usually an assortment of innocuous items such as business cards, claim checks, documents, receipts, and other seemingly inconsequential items kept on or about a Spy; designed to support the pre-planned backstop and cover stories of an Espionage Agent.

Popping Tools aka Car Popping Tools
"Popping a Car," using body shop tools, would allow us the ability to pop covers and door panels off cars so we could hide listening devices, documents, etc...

Sanitize
To remove all traces of espionage activity.

SDR
Surveillance Detection Runs are tactics used to ensure a Spy isn't under observation. SDR's are critical to maintaining anonymity and in preserving the integrity of a Spy's identity; and the sanctuary of his residence, hotel room, operational and non-operational relationships, travels, etc...

SIGINT
Signals Intelligence

Small World/Chance Encounters
The girth of the globe upon which we live is large, sporting a nearly 25,000-mile circumference. Earth is, nevertheless, a relatively small satellite. Populated by more than seven billion human beings. It's amazing just how easy it is to literally bump into people we know, thousands of miles from where we'd expect to see them.

Chance encounters with someone we know, far from home and in unexpected locations, can be simultaneously surprising, amazing, and disconcerting. In espionage is can be downright dangerous.

Solutions Development
See "After Action Reporting"

Straw Party Transaction
A straw man or straw party is, in effect, a middleman. Either the transaction is off-color, or one or more involved parties need to remain shielded; therein lies the reason for a middleman. Such intermediaries typically keep the parties apart and unknown to one another, while earning a profit when a successful transaction occurs.

Subject
A Subject is an individual garnering our focus at the time. Sometimes we are tailing a Subject, on other occasions we might be meeting with a Subject. At times a person who is the focus of our due diligence is considered a Subject. You get the idea.

Subject, like Mark and Target, is a word that describes the focal point of our espionage efforts. The person, place, or thing we either need or target for espionage activities; to misappropriate information and/or items necessary for our mission.

Target
Target, like Subject and Mark, is a word that describes the focal point of our espionage efforts. The person, place, or thing we target for espionage activities; to misappropriate information and/or items necessary for our mission.

TECHINT
Technology Driven Intelligence (TECHINT) is all about devices and equipment that garner much-needed information; often unavailable through HUMINT. TECHINT includes Signals Intelligence (SIGINT), Imagery Intelligence (IMINT), and other technology-driven methods of gathering intelligence. Spy cameras, listening devices, drones, hacks, and GPS trackers are examples of devices and tools used by professional Espionage Agents.

Tradecraft aka SpyCraft

First, Cola doesn't like the term "SpyCraft" because it doesn't reflect reality well. People spy on one another all the time. They listen to gossip, try to deduce whose car is at the neighbor's house, peek into medicine cabinets at parties, and check out the prices at competing businesses. People are often snoopy. They are spying, but aren't engaging in the trade of spying.

On the other hand, Cola engages in espionage activities for a living. It is my trade. I employ certain skills, techniques, tools, systems, technologies, and protocols in the process of carrying out my activities. This is true for any craft. In the espionage world, we carry out our activities using what we call "Tradecraft."

Trap Door

A Trap Door in my world is an Operational Escape and Evasion Plan. A trap door in a building might lead to a tunnel, further leading to an adjacent building; thereby providing a secret way out. Sometimes Cola needs a way out. If Backstopping doesn't work, Cola always has a few Trap Doors up his sleeve. I'll leave an Op behind if necessary. I don't like it when it happens, but sometimes Forrest just needs to run. *Run Forrest! Run!*

TwoStep

TwoStep is a code system I devised that was easy to teach and use, but also simplistic and easy to crack by rookie cryptologists. I came up with it as I prepared for note keeping during my college-era Espionage Operation. One of the service bay guys in a quick lube store I was studying asked about the code. I told him it was "reporter shorthand." Later, on that same Op while reviewing a Target's accounting information, a Cop asked me what I was doing. I was comforted in knowing my legal pad contained notes that would likely have been undecipherable by the Police Officer. I was prepared to tell him they were engineering notes.

On other occasions, I've told people I was writing computer code for a vendor who wanted projections on hot dog and soft drink sales during different types of weather at football games. I actually wrote programming for those projections while in college, except the language was Fortran, not TwoStep. That was okay in the old days when few individuals could recognize computer code. Code is so ubiquitous today any Spy using that story would crash and burn far too often.

TwoStep Coding Revealed

Since I'm no longer an active Spy and my notes from those days have all been destroyed, showing Readers the TwoStep system is doable without revealing anything that would compromise me or others. Here you go:

NUMBERS

When writing numbers, I use the letters "OILCHANGES" to correspond with "1234567890." For example, 5,280 translates to "HIGS" and 3.14159 appears as "L.OCOHE."

Numbers are converted to the "OILCHANGES" lettering and bookended by ZZ and YZ.

LETTERS

Letters are straightforward. Using all caps, I substitute the actual character with the next letter in the alphabet. "A Dog" would read "B EPH" or "BEPH." I often left out spaces to throw off junior detectives who might attempt to break my code. I also threw in fillers, to make the uninitiated think I was writing Cyrillic or similar. Those fillers were backward versions of "R" "K" and "E." Here's how they appear: Я, ꓘ, and Ǝ.

Since double E's, O's, L's, and others are commonplace, I wrote them as follows. "EE" = the next letter (F), followed by Z1 to indicate there were two E's. "Feel" for example, would be written, "GFZ1M." Here's my table for double letters:

The code for doubled vowels is Z1.

The code for doubled consonants is X9.

E = F

EE = FZ1

L = M
LL = MX9

O = P
OO = PZ1

S = T
SS = TX9

I = J
II = JZ1

T = U
TT = UX9

EXAMPLE
“President Franklin D. Roosevelt: Yesterday, December 7, 1941—a date which will live in infamy...”

“QSFTJEFOUꓘGSBOLMJOEƐSPZ1TFWFMU:Я
ZFTUFSEBZEFDFNCFSZZNYZ ZZOECƎOYZ

BEBUF XIJDIXJMMЯMJWFJO ƎJOGBNZ...”

Watchers
Surveillance teams are often referred to by me as Watchers. I seldom use a single Watcher. A single Watcher provides too many opportunities for detection and/or the visual loss of The Subject.

Two Loons Press

www.ingramcontent.com/pod-product-compliance
Lightning Source LLC
Chambersburg PA
CBHW060350190426
43201CB00044B/1913
* 9 7 8 1 7 3 2 4 7 3 7 3 7 *